W9-BGF-866

Of Bears and Man

Dr. Lynn Rogers photographing a black bear at a garbage dump—part of the research on bears that Dr. Rogers directs from the U.S. Department of Agriculture Forestry Station in Ely, Minnesota.

Of Bears and Man

By Mike Cramond

Illustrated by Lissa Calvert

UNIVERSITY OF OKLAHOMA PRESS: NORMAN AND LONDON

BY MIKE CRAMOND

Hunting and Fishing in North America (Norman, 1953)
Game Fishing in the West (Vancouver, B.C., 1964)
Big Game Hunting in the West (Vancouver, B.C., 1965)
Game Bird Shooting in the West (Vancouver, B.C., 1967)
Fishing Holes of the West, vol. 1, *Salt Water* (Vancouver, B.C., 1972)
A Bear Behind (Vancouver, B.C., 1973)
Killer Bears (New York, 1981)
Vancouver Island Fishin' Holes (Victoria, B.C., 1982)
Of Bears and Man (Norman, 1986)

Library of Congress Cataloging-in-Publication Data

Cramond, Mike, 1913–
  Of bears and man.

  Includes index.
  1. Bears.   2. Bear attacks.   3. Bear hunting.
I. Title.
QL737.C27C734   1986   599.74′446   85-40472
ISBN 0-8061-1948-9 (alk. paper)

The news stories on page 244 and pages 310 through 312 are reprinted with permission of The Associated Press and The Canadian Press, respectively.
  Drawings © 1986 by Lissa Calvert.
  Copyright 1986 © by the University of Oklahoma Press, Norman, Publishing Division of the University of Oklahoma. Manufactured in the U.S.A. First edition.

Contents

Preface   ix

Acknowledgments   xi

Book 1. MEN AMONG BEARS

Introduction to Book 1   3

1. The Black-Bear Man   15
   The Redhead I   26

2. They Almost Never Come to Blows   28
   The Redhead II   41

3. What Is It Like in a Bear Den?   44
   The Redhead III   61

4. He Has Tapped a Grizzly on the Nose   64
   The Redhead IV   86

5. Look a Grizzly in the Eye   88
   The Redhead V   100

6. "Yeah, I've Killed a Couple . . ."   103
   The Redhead VI   118

7. Polar Bears Are Pussycats?   121
   The Redhead VIII   129

8. How to Live with Polar Bears   133
   The Redhead VIII   147

9. What Is in the Future for Polar Bears?   151

Book 2. MAULINGS AND KILLINGS

Introduction to Book 2   169

1. So It Couldn't Happen to You!   171
   The Runt I   184

2. "We Are the Luckiest People We Know"   186
   The Runt II   194

3. The Mother Instinct   196
   The Runt III   203

  4. He Was Chasing Dragonflies   206
        The Runt IV   216

  5. They Were Competing for a Livelihood   218
        The Runt V   222

  6. Another Idyllic Place of Death   225
        The Runt VI   240

  7. He Was Warned   244
        The Runt VII   254

  8. How to Stop a Bear   257
        The Runt VIII   262

  9. The Kokanees Were Running   266
        The Runt IX   271

 10. The Unguarded Moment   274
        The Runt X   287

 11. "I Am not an Aggressive Type—the Bear Was!"   290
        The Runt XI   301

 12. The Downtown Banff Killings   304

Book 3. IN PURSUIT OF BEARS

Introduction to Book 3   317

  1. The Skid-Road Bear   319
        The Cannibal I   325

  2. The Flume Bears   329
        The Cannibal II   334

  3. Brownie   336
        The Cannibal III   344

  4. Without Warning   347
        The Cannibal IV   353

  5. Want a Grizzly?   355
        The Cannibal V   366

  6. A Home Visit   371
        The Cannibal VI   379

  7. The Bowman and the Grizzly   382
        The Cannibal VII   399

8. The Stunted Grizzly   402
        The Cannibal VIII   416

9. This One Came in Person   419
        The Cannibal IX   424

Epilogue   427
Index   431

Illustrations

Dr. Lynn Rogers Photographing a Bear   *Frontispiece*
Dr. Lynn Rogers with His Research Crew   52
Dr. Lynn Rogers Collaring a Black Bear   54
Stan Price's Pack Creek Compound   74
Stan and Esther Price   78
Vern Beier Tranquilizing a Grizzly   92
Susan Warner Measuring a Grizzly   94
Artist Brian Ladoon of Churchill, Manitoba   134
Dr. Ian Stirling of the Canadian Federal Wildlife Service   163
Sheila Bliesath and Her Family   201
A Sketch Map of George Doerksen's Campsite and Remains   208
Squamish Valley Black Bear   320
Squamish Valley Black Bear   337
Mike Cramond and One Grizzly He Killed   363
Bob Kuhn and the Grizzly Hide   364
The Cramond Family and the Black Bear That Invaded Their Yard   377
Ed Wiseman Shows His Scars   392

(*All photographs are by Mike Cramond.*)

Preface

The many humanlike qualities, both good and bad, that bears exhibit have always impressed me. Similarity to humankind may be considered by some to be an odious trait rather than an appealing one, but in any event, the bear family shows a high degree of intelligence and dexterity (witness circus bears).

Bears display at least as many variations of temperament as humans do, from extreme belligerence and territorialism to passivity, playfulness, and extreme solicitude for their young. The sows (females) cuddle, cherish, defend, teach, and discipline their cubs. Grizzlies, like people, sometimes allow their freshly killed meat to "mature." Grizzlies do so by covering it with earth and debris (a habit that has enabled some victims to survive after a mauling). Black bears love the taste of wild honey and bee pupae and will suffer untold numbers of stings to steal both delicacies from the hives. Polar bears, like Eskimos, use great cunning to hunt seals.

Members of the bear family occasionally become tractable enough to be trained. This has inspired producers of films and television shows to give fascinating portrayals of bears relating like faithful dogs to their owners, though bears do not, by nature, have the canine quality of ready submission. The famous bear man George Capen ("Grizzly") Adams actually used a heavy club on his animals before beginning training. The impression of fidelity began with physical discipline to instill in the animal the fear of corporal punishment. That may seem to be a cynical statement, but it is simple candor. Most trainers of performing wild animals first subject the animal to some degree of pain in order to achieve human dominance and gain response to training. Trainers later add reward for performance. Even mild-mannered hunting dogs are trained with punishment-and-reward methods. Bears, like lions, tigers, elephants, and sharks, are totally unpredictable. That fact should never be disregarded, despite any romantic or "authoritative" opinions to the contrary.

Because of their quite massive proportions bears are usually accorded by other animals the status of "boss of the woods." They have little to fear, even from the equally massive bull moose, which is belligerent and well fortified with great strength, huge antlers, and sharp cloven hooves. Grizzly bears do attack moose and will fight them to the death.

It is the bears' complexity that causes their unpredictability and encourages human folly in response to them. My own experience and extensive research tell me that bears themselves sometimes seem unsure how to act.

The anthropomorphising of bears has a long tradition. Even the deification of bears has been common in northern civilizations, from Cro-Magnon men to modern Homo Sapiens, who have given ritual attention to bears, honoring them, before or after they are eaten, sometimes as a projection of human afterlife or as the originals from which a tribe is descended. Latter-day literature has continued to create anthropomorphic legends, such as "Goldilocks and the Three Bears," the story of Smokey the Bear, and television programs portraying bears as human beings' friends and allies.

Possibly because of these fictional portrayals, humans are sometimes mauled and killed, even eaten, and bears are destroyed. Impressions early in life, reinforced by unrealistic media presentations, have led people to believe that bears are not particularly dangerous, that humans can enter the domain of a bear with impunity. Some so-called experts and self-styled "naturalists" still lead people to believe that contact with bears is not highly perilous. Nonetheless, since 1950 (the initial year for the studies in this book), bears have mauled or killed well over three hundred humans, and, unfortunately, there have been at least that number of retaliatory bear deaths.

Bears and humans will continue to kill each other, but our acceptance of facts regarding the lives of bears could prevent many of these tragedies.

My chronicling of bear-human encounters inadvertently began some sixty years ago, when at the age of eight or nine, I received a grizzly bear cub as my first "very own" pet. That early association led to a more-than-ordinary interest and curiosity concerning the species, which was further heightened by nearly fifty years of media-related exposure. Capping my own studies is my investigative research in association with bear scientists both in the field and in their laboratories.

Some sixty thousand miles of air, land, and sea travel, studying polar bears in the sub-Arctic, brown grizzlies in the northern Alaskan islands, black bears in the American West and midwest, and silvertip grizzlies in the West, Northwest, and Southwest, have taught me that popular beliefs, which frequently are contrary to the evidence, today create one of the main stumbling blocks to the prevention of these continuing tragedies.

Using my experience as a hunter of game, an observer of wildlife, and a writer on conservation who has accumulated ten awards and citations, I have attempted to maintain a balanced point of view. The facts, of course, are incontrovertible. My purpose has been to dispel the fictions handed down from generation to generation, to discount unreliable conclusions (found even in some modern scientific studies), and to call attention to the newer knowledge and conclusions about the North American bear family—facts that are available but not as widely known as they might be.

In the following pages are some statements that no informed reader would accept today. These statements reflect my early opinions, of which only a few were accepted. Since then, of course, my fund of knowledge has grown in quantity and quality. Even so, I expect that my more recent insights will be challenged and some of them rejected or modified. The facts must continue to be assessed objectively.

MIKE CRAMOND

West Vancouver, British Columbia

Acknowledgments

During the writing of a documentary manuscript the materials have to be exposed, explained, examined and exhibited; the truths and untruths revealed. Then that abundance of research material has to be sorted, salvaged, and set in type. The assistance of many is required to accomplish it all. Without the aid of my wife, Thelma, this book just could not have come about. Many others unselfishly cooperated, among them Dr. Lynn Rogers, Dr. Charles Jonkel, Cliff Martinka, Jim Schoen, Vern Beier, Susan Warner, Wayne Lankinen, Sheila Bliesath, Karen Austrom, Harry Rowed, Stan Price, Rob Powell, Pat Rakowski, Wilfred Lulu, Doug Robertson, Jack Shaw, Ed Wiseman, Robert McKelvie, Jim McKeachy, Lee Miller, Bill Shaber, Bob Switzer, and others, who are also a host of friends; the R.C.M.P.; the B.C. Provincial Parks branch; and the reporters and executives of the various media who allowed the use of published materials, in particular from the *Lethbridge Herald*, the *Vancouver Sun*, and the *Vancouver Province*. My extreme gratitude for cooperation must be expressed herewith. Thank you very much.

BOOK ONE

Men Among Bears

For my brother, Pat

Introduction to Book One

There are three distinct species of the bear family in North America. They are the black, which includes the cinnamon, Kermodei, and blue; the grizzly, which includes the silvertip and the brown-bear grizzly; and the Arctic polar bear.

Although the grizzly bear is the most feared of North American wild animals, the black bear is almost equally dangerous. In 1980 my compiled statistics gave black bears the edge as killers and maulers of human beings; in 1981 and 1982 the grizzlies proved more dangerous. Both bears are omnivorous, but most of their foods are vegetable. Their chief danger to man lies in their unpredictability.

There seems to be little or no interbreeding among the species of the bear family. The following story was related to me by a trapper during a wildlife conference at which I was a speaker, in response to my observation of the species' disinclination to interbreed. The trapper's story, though it does not address directly the question of interbreeding, does underscore the hostility that may occur between bear species.

The trapper was making a summer check along his trapline. His trail led along the side of a lightly forested valley the bottom of which was filled with quite heavy undergrowth. This natural trough carried a small stream which had its source in the hillside, where a spring welled from quite open terrain. About three hundred yards from where he stopped to rest on the steep bank, the trapper was amazed to see a grizzly bear skulking along the slanting terrain of the valley directly opposite to him. The animal would hide, run ahead a few paces, then again duck behind some bushes. At first, the observer thought that he himself might be the grizzly's quarry. He was in full view of it. He remained very still, watching. The grizzly ignored him and continued its deliberate hide-and-seek.

The bear kept glancing down into the thick scrub growth at the bottom of the valley. Eventually, the trapper saw something else moving in the shadows of the scrub poplar and taller conifers. Slowly but surely, the grizzly's quarry was also moving up the valley. Although the other animal was almost completely obscured, it appeared to be very large. The trapper thought it might be a moose. Fascinated by the developing wildlife drama, he quietly sat down to observe the outcome. He considered trying to scare off the grizzly by firing his rifle near it, but curiosity made him wait.

In the meantime, the grizzly was keeping pace with the other animal's slow progress through the thinning growth of the valley bottom. The determined skulker seemed to know that whatever was down below would have to emerge from its cover at the end of the greenery and then make its way up the mountain across the fairly open and unprotected slope. The big silver-grey bear actually appeared to be enjoyed its stalk.

When the quarry below moved noisily, or when it was totally obscured, the grizzly would move silently on again, then crouch behind a large bush, stump, or rock, over which it would peer expectantly and apparently eagerly.

The trapper was amazed and enthralled. Eventually, near the upper end of the thicker growth in the ravine, the stalked animal came into view, moving along the trapper's side of the valley. To his amazement it was a very large black bear.

He thought that the grizzly was in for a surprise. He was sure that it had not yet seen its quarry. With both bears in view from his own side, he realized that there were not many pounds difference in the bulk of the two animals. In fact, that weight difference might have favored the very large black bear. The trapper stared intently at the grizzly. There was no doubt about it now: the grizzly could clearly see the animal that it was stalking. The grizzly, far from being surprised, pressed itself to the earth behind a small bush, almost as a cat does while stalking a bird. For no apparent reason the black bear turned its head toward where the trapper sat quietly on the hillside, then put its snout down to browse from some ground cover. In that instant, obscured by low brush, the grizzly sped across the hillside. It stopped on an ambush point at the top of a ten-foot-high outcropping of rock overhanging the ravine, just where the black bear would have to move out into the open. That animal, moving unconcerned on the valley floor, did not seem to see or hear the other's movements. The grizzly flattened itself down on the exposed top of the rock with only its muzzle protruding above that ambush.

So obvious was the planning and cunning of the grizzly that the trapper said he could not believe his eyes.

The black bear began to ascend the path, which led directly beneath the rocky outcropping. The grizzly lifted its head to peer down the ravine, and at that same instant the black bear moved its head as if scenting or listening. Soon, however, it resumed its climb up the open slope. The grizzly immediately pulled its head back, in the manner of a man fearful of being caught spying, and from then on it remained on the rock top in silent, alert readiness. Unsuspecting, the black bear walked right into the trap.

The bear was fewer than fifteen feet from the grizzly's perch when the big grey animal sprang downward in a headlong plunge. The force of its impact bowled the black bear over twice. The last thing the trapper saw clearly, just as the two animals disappeared in a tangle into the low brush, was that the grizzly had a firm death bite on the black bear's neck, its jaws placed just behind the head. The roaring sounds of the scuffle were unbelievable, he said. He moved up the hillside to improve his view of the fight, which was now obscured behind the rock outcropping. By the time he gained a view into the area of the struggle, the grizzly was standing over the bleeding prostrate form of the other bear, which obviously was dead. The trapper said the ambush had been contrived and achieved with such cunning that it nauseated him.

Later in the week, while on his way back from the far reaches of his trapline, he purposely made a detour to observe the ambush area more closely. The substantially devoured carcass of the black bear had been dragged down into the ravine and partially covered. Obviously, the grizzly was saving the balance for further provender. That was a meal the trapper did not wish to contest. He left the area quickly.

The trapper's story gives some measure of evidence that the twain do not meet. From the many years of my own research and study of bears, coupled with the findings of knowledgeable and experienced laymen and scientists, I am now virtually certain that in their very nature, the different species of bear differ so greatly that interbreeding would be unlikely even where their territories overlap. And because the bears differ both physically and in character traits, they are treated separately in the following pages.

BLACK BEARS

Black bears, the most abundant species of the bear family, are thought to be descended from the Asiatic, or Himalayan, black bears. They are not always black; they can be brown, henna, almost blond, or very nearly white. There is a "blue" variety (the glacial, or blue, bear), and there is a classification that is "white," the Kermodei bear.

Usually, however, the common black bear is, indeed, coal black, although in the Midwest the brown or cinnamon phase and the tawny phase are common enough to create confusion. In Yellowstone Park I have photographed a black bear sow with three cubs, two of which were actually the rich color of naturally red human hair, while the third was as black as obsidian. Not far away in the same park, a cinnamon-hued beauty fondled and played with her single jet-black cub. In the same few miles of highway where these "road bums" exhibited their adaptive skill, my companion and I counted, almost alternately, at least five pure black and five cinnamon boars (male bears). On the other hand, in British Columbia, where I have seen hundreds of black bears, and have photographed many, not one was in the "brown" phase.

Although there are records of black bears weighing more than 800 pounds, they more commonly range between 150 and 300 pounds—not a very large animal. Most females I have seen would not break the 200-pound mark, and black boars seldom weigh more than 300 pounds, about the same as the true mountain grizzly. Yet remarkably strong animals of both species have been known to lift a whole steer (weighing at least 500 pounds) over a corral fence and then lug it half a mile. Their speed is almost fantastic; they have been clocked at thirty miles per hour (and when they come at you it seems more like a hundred miles per hour!).

Black bears eat mainly vegetation and fruit. They regularly feed on alfalfa, wild berries, nuts, coniferous tree bark, grasses, lily roots, apples, and honey, although they will readily eat grubs, ants, carrion, fish, and, on impulse, other available animals. This varied diet is almost like that of humans, and bears' teeth, like humans' teeth, develop cavities. Perhaps this accounts for the colloquial description of a man in an evil temper as "sore as a bear with a toothache."

Watching a family of black bears, one soon observes their humanlike qualities. The females of the species usually give birth to one or more cubs during the winter dormant period. For the next year and a half the sows fondle, feed, lick, spank, and teach their rambunctious cubs. (Unless you have seen the unbridled mischief of bear cubs, you haven't really seen mischief.) The next winter, when they are yearlings weighing up to one hundred pounds, she takes them into winter "hibernation" with her. After the second summer season they are on their own, though siblings often travel together for a short time. Then the sow is free to go looking for a boar.

I know only one man who ever photographed bears copulating. He was a fellow member of the British Columbia Provincial Police force while I was on the roster. He was an amateur photographer, and a brave one. One day while walking in the forest, he heard a noise in a grassy glade nearby. Peering through timber he was surprised and a little nervous to find two bears circling. The smaller one, the sow, was prancing around in the skittish manner of a mating bitch. She would coquettishly mince up to the rather large, fat old boar and rub herself against him where he sat panting in the sunny, grassy glade. He would make a purposeful pass at her, and she would skitter away. My friend said that the boar seemed to respond to her antics with a patient and sly waiting game. He would lick at whatever portion was presented to his waiting tongue and occasionally attempt to get her in the well-known bear hug. Finally, all in one quick movement, the boar took her on, and she cooperated fully.

My fascinated friend took this opportunity to click a photograph and such was the preoccupation of the bruins that at first they did not even notice him. Emboldened, he approached the entangled twain to within a distance of about twenty-five feet. He took a couple of more frames. Noticing him, the big boar flicked an uninterested glance at him and continued copulating.

The photographer walked around the two grunting, snorting animals to find other vantage points that would be in the interest of science. He said that the old boar's face wore a look of complete absorption, and the female also seemed to be in a trance. The man moved in to obtain a close-up of the boar's satisfied and preoccupied face. When he was less than ten feet away, the boar turned to him with a slightly annoyed look which seemed to say, "Look, fella! You've got your photos! Why the hell don't you just beat it!"

Suddenly regaining his common sense, my friend returned to the path through the woods. He said the muted sounds of orgy went on for at least another twenty minutes. I remember his remark in conclusion: "They were almost *human* in nature! I actually felt embarrassed."

Bears are also humanlike in the way they teach and discipline their young. I remember one mother black bear very well. She was lying down in a little circular, grassy meadow between two rolling hills in the Cascades. The sun shone on her belly, as if she meant to expose the greyish patches surrounding her teats to the relaxing, therapeutic warmth. Nearby two cubs of that spring, about the size of cocker spaniels, were rolling and tumbling in a free-for-all, wrestling and boxing with antics as amusing as they were dexterous.

Occasionally, as I watched them from nearby cover, one of them would break away from the playful tumult. It would then run and actually nip the old sow on the rump. This action would bring the mother's head up from its pillow of grass with a quick snap of her teeth and a warning woof. After each nip the cub would scuttle out of reach before she was completely up from her somnolent position.

The repeated act was just as intentionally mischievous as that of a child sneaking in and pinching the backside of another youngster, then getting quickly out of range. The cub too, like a naughty boy, was full of the glee accompanying such pernicious play. Lifting her head after each sortie, the old sow, grumbling, would again drop her head to the turf. The catch-as-catch-can fight between the two cubs would resume. They would roll over each other, run, drop flat and trip the oncoming pursuer, stand off and box and spar, until one of them, out of breath, would slump sacklike to the earth. The more militant cub would worry and nip at the other until the fallen cub's teeth were exposed in a needle-point snap. The harrier would then take a run at a bush or a branch, or just roll on its side or back until the other was ready to resume the rumpus.

The one alternative to this play was the rush up to the old sow's posterior, then the quick nip at her unprotected behind.

Lying flat on the hillock top, watching this comedy, I remember thinking, "That little guy is sucking for his lumps about as hard as anyone I ever saw. And that old lady is the most patient mother I ever did see!"

My position was fewer than thirty-five yards above them. The slope of the hillock left only my forehead within full view downwind. I was actually so close that I could see the sow's face and expressions. I watched as at least four times she endured the annoying nip of her backside. The cub continued hassling its littermate. Eventually the cub that tired more easily rolled on its side and again quit battling. The sounds of scuffling stopped.

The sow's eye opened on the side of her head clearly visible to me. There seemed to be tension in her body. I half expected her to lift her head and stare directly at me. She was quite noticeably wide awake, but she did not raise her head. The cub made a sudden rush for her backside for another nip.

He didn't make it! The old sow, using the swiftest motion I have witnessed in a bear, lifted herself into a sitting position, swinging her front paw in an unerring arc. Her paw hit the cub amidships, knocking it a full ten feet. It rolled another five feet to a squalling stop.

The cub then struggled groggily to its feet, squealing with the unmistakable, hoarse cry of an injured, frightened, or angered child. For a moment it stood on shaky legs, crying pitifully. The old lady still squatting, watched the cub with what appeared to be compassion. Then she uttered a gentle, throaty sound somewhat like the cooing of a patient mother over an injured child. The cub then ran to her, burying its nose in her belly fur. Immediately forgiving, she put her paw over it, just like a human mother holding a child to her waist. She then began licking it affectionately, and a couple of minutes later the cub was again wrangling with its littermate.

Bears are tough. A man receiving such a blow would have had half the bones in his body broken.

A sow also teaches her cubs to climb trees. This is often accomplished with a couple of warning woofs and a swat to the recalcitrant cub. The result is that the cubs become amazing tree climbers. They actually appear to *walk* up the wall of tree bark as if they had glue on their feet. A closer examination of the tree trunks will show that these "baby" animals can drive their claws deep into the wood, even the hard, bare wood of a dead tree, as if it were blotting paper. They come down the trunk with much the same ease, using their nonretractable claws.

North American bears do not "hibernate" in the strict sense of the word. Black bears choose a sheltered spot out of the weather. They usually take great pains to construct a nest of twigs and branches under some cover, occasionally in a natural fissure or tunnel, and then lie down in it curled up in a ball. Usually snow drifts in to cover them. They do go into a deep sleep; they can be awakened readily. True hibernators drop into a comatose slumber accompanied by a noticeable drop in body temperature and a slowing of respiration and pulse; bears maintain a moderate heartbeat and body temperature. The fat accumulated during a spring, summer, and fall of gorging is absorbed back into their systems to maintain body heat. During the sow's dormancy its cubs are born and suckled. At birth they are hairless and about eight or ten inches long; they look more like rats than little bears.

Bears normally lose 15 to 25 percent of their weight during their winter sleep. The sleeping bear's coat continues to grow slightly, the claws lengthen somewhat, and some of the hard footpads peel off and renew. Among the indigenous peoples of northern climates there are legends that bears suck sustenance from their paws during this winter denning, a notion probably drawn from seeing bears lick their paw pads at this time of peeling and renewing.

The presence of water or vermin in a den will make a bear rub patches of fur from its hide. Professional hunters and trappers have told me that bears tend to den up on a northern slope, where a warm winter sun will not cause melted snow to flood their chosen hideaway. If for some reason they find the bed unwisely chosen, they will wander about until they find another hospitable spot, dig in under the snow, and go back to sleep. This probably accounts for occasional sightings of bears during the depths of winter.

The bear's long sleep shows a marvelous natural coordination. It coincides with the end of the season for berries and spawning fish, and it continues until the warm weather brings forth the new spring growth. Bears need this vegetation to satisfy their gluttonous appetites (they eat up to sixty pounds a day). The pattern is somewhat different in a milder climate, for example, in central Mexico.

The American Black Bear. The common black bear, *Ursus americanus*, is almost immediately recognizable to the trained eye. These bears tend to be of moderately large stature. Their skull structure is slightly more elongated than that of the grizzly bear, with a "dish" between nose bridge and forehead that is less pronounced. They also have a much less pronounced shoulder hump than the grizzly. The head of a black bear, however, even when viewed from a short distance, cannot yield a fully reliable identification.

Many generations of experienced outdoorsmen have been misled, as I was for years, by the obvious differences in the body structure of individual black bears. There seemed to be different varieties of the animal, particularly the black bear with a long-nosed, almost wolflike head and a lean, bony structure, as opposed to the more round-headed and full-bodied bear. To certify the age of a bear, until recently there were no criteria except the degree of wear on the teeth and the animal's size: usually a large bear was considered to be older. Recent studies, however, by Dr. Lynn Rogers of Minnesota, who may be the foremost authority on black bears, indicate that these notions are wrong.

Dr. Rogers pointed out that age is readily and accurately ascertained by counting the rings in a premolar tooth, like rings in a tree. Also Dr. Rogers says that black bears continue to grow *all their life*. When the animal is immature, it is inclined to be elongate, or lean, in both head and body. Depending on the availability of good food, an individual bear may be either larger or smaller than the average bear at a given age. Thus the lean black is probably a young bear, while the roundheaded, full-bodied black is generally older.

Perhaps the most visible characteristic of the black bear (not always discernible at a distance) is the fawn to reddish shade of the muzzle and the reddish or red-blond eyebrows. These hues shade down the length of the snout to the nostrils. In addition, below the head, at the juncture of throat and chest, a white patch of varying size (usually palm size) usually is visible. This chest patch occurs in both the cinnamon, or brown, and the black phases.

The Glacier (Blue) Bear. A black coat, or pelage, shot with white or light greyish overtones is the main distinguishing trait of the little-known glacier or blue bear. *Ursus americanus emmonii.* It is the smallest of the black bears. Actually, the coat resembles that of the silver fox, the underfur having grey-blue tones that, combined with the black and white guard hair, give the subtle blue color for which it is named. Apparently, nature has provided this animal a measure of adaptation to its habitat, which is primarily adjacent to the "blue" ices formed by snow pressure in a glaciated area.

Like the silvertip grizzly, the blue bear is predominantly a mountainside bear. It is known to range over an area roughly limited to the northern portions of British Columbia and the sub-Artic regions of southern Alaska. Its life cycle and habits, though little known, are currently under study. Because it is scarce, it is protected.

Although I have hunted several times where blue bears are known to range, I have not seen one or heard of any sightings by local guides or Indians. However, on a wall of the hunting lodge in the Cassiar district of British Columbia I did see small "blue" pelt unlike any other I have seen. When I asked about the unusual pelage color I was told that it was a small "black grizzly" shot somewhere in the vicinity of Dease Lake. Quite frankly I had never seen any grizzly colored anything resembling the same hues. Black coats with white or silvertip guard hairs, yes, but not that color covering the entire bear hide, nor with such contrasting tones. The owner didn't know the exact origin of the pelt and was surprised when I suggested that it might be a blue bear pelt.

The Kermodei Bear. Also protected because of its extremely limited range and finite numbers is the Kermodei bear, *Ursus americanus Kermodei*. This subspecies is known as the "white" member of the black bear species, but it is not a true white. Those I have seen are the hue of crystalized honey with a tendency to creamy yellow undertones, much like the shades of a caged polar bear's underparts. When the animal is fully exposed in the sun, its color looks somewhat like that of unbleached silk.

One of these bears was for many years a captive on display in the zoo at Beaconhill Park, Victoria, British Columbia. When I lived in that city, the animal was so fascinating to me that I made many visits to watch it. Most often the lovely Kermodei reposed in the sun almost as if it knew it was a "star," perched on a small, raised concrete dais in the enclosure. It was always quiet during my observations, with a disposition to match the mild, sunny days. It was hard to believe that the animal was a predator, that in the wild it could be dangerous to humans.

The subspecies was discovered in the Princess Royal and Gribbell Islands area of British Columbia's coastline, where Kermodei bears have long been known and revered by the Indians as "spirit bears."

GRIZZLY BEARS

When the clear sunlight of its mountain habitat shines off the near-white guard hairs of its coat, the silvertip grizzly seems almost to be illuminated in a spotlight of its own. Also magnificent, and set apart by the muscular power of its very deliberate movements, the brown-bear grizzly of the coastal rivers grips the eye and knots the belly of the viewer. Both bears are quite readily distinguishable as grizzlies, yet the two are quite different from each other in appearance. The "Great Plains grizzly" was believed by viewers to be a third subspecies, but judging from early descriptions in historical records, one would say it was a silvertip of enormous proportions that lived on the western North American plains, surviving there mainly as a buffalo predator.

The familiar grizzly of the western-interior mountains is often designated in lay speech as a "silvertip," and it is classified in early categories as *Ursus arctos horribilis* along with its variant, the coastal (Pacific) grizzly, more usually called a "brown-bear grizzly." The other subspecies, the "Alaskan brown" or "Kodiak," is classified as *Ursus arctos middendorffi*. Patterns of birth and longevity appear to be similar in all the grizzly species. Like the polar bear, the grizzlies are believed to be descended from the Siberian and European brown bears.

The Silvertip Grizzly. There remains some doubt as to the original root of the name "grizzly." Some favor the derivation from the English word *grizzle*, which, as Webster's dictionary defines it, comes from the French word *gris* meaning "gray": "a gray color, a mixture of white and black, which is not a precise description of the bear's coat. Others favor derivation from the other English word of the same pronunciation, *grisly*, which in turn derives from the Anglo-Saxon *grislic*, *grisan*, or *agrisan*, meaning "to dread, to fear greatly," emotions that must have been inspired by the great bear. It must be noted, however, that an alternate meaning for *grisly* is gray: "of a mixed color, grizzled." Thus the name *grizzly bear* is actually a description of the animal.

The grizzly bear's pelage has a very wide variance in color, from black to almost white. This variation has led to tragic mistakes in identification after attacks and killings. The melanistic, or black, phase is not common; under close examination it usually reveals a large proportion of light-hued guard hairs. The "white" phases that I have seen had more "caping" at the shoulders and along the back, with predominantly dark-hued limbs and underparts, the lighter hues caused in part by a preponderance of whitish guard hairs.

The contour of the grizzly provides another means of visual identification; indeed, the hump at the shoulders is the species' most pronounced feature. The hump is related to the muscle structure of the grizzly. Probably it developed from persistent daily digging for roots and rodents, or moving of logs and boulders to get at insects, much as a man who "pumps iron" is identifiable by his upper body structure. When a grizzly is skinned out, this muscle structure appears quite different from that of a black bear, as the shoulders of a laborer or boxer differ from those of a woman. Adding to the exterior bulk is the thicker and longer hairy growth, which tends to stand up on the arch over the shoulder structure.

The heads of bears are difficult to differentiate. They vary widely, in both full-face view and profile. The grizzly is more likely to have a "dishing" between the nose and the top of the forehead, but it is not pronounced to the untrained eye. The face is slightly wider than that of the black bear, although at certain stages of their growth and body condition, all bears have a pronounced canine look.

It is mainly the squareness of the grizzly's body structure that gives it a unique appearance. Its bulk, generally much greater in the brown-bear grizzly, distinguishes it from any other variety. The simplest identification, where doubt exists, is the presence of extremely long, rakelike claws on the forefeet. Their sharp marks stand out clearly in soft soil and snow.

Determining precisely where silvertips range is difficult, but my own field experience suggests that they confine themselves to the eastern slopes of mountains in the Pacific Coast Ranges between California (earlier, Mexico) and Alaska. The brown grizzly bears range along the base of the western slopes of the same coastal range, beginning in the middle British Columbia and extending southward, principally near river mouths. I have seen silvertips all the way from the top of the coastal ranges to the prairies of Alberta and Montana, and slightly eastward, but never on the salt water environs common to brown-bear grizzlies. The Alaskan brown is confined to Alaskan islands.

The weight of silvertips, well established in the field studies of Frank C. and John Craighead, ranges from 140 pounds (as yearlings) to between 250 and 600 pounds in maturity. Sows weigh about one-third less. Not mentioned in the Craighead data is the fact that a few animals have been weighed in at more than 1,000 pounds. Those that I have killed or viewed in the wild would average approximately 300 pounds (about 100 pounds heavier than an average black bear).

The Brown-Bear Grizzly. The brown-bear grizzly has a characteristic contour very similar to that of the silvertip. The brown-bear often is much more imposing, but even more notable is its color: light brown to dark brown and, at times, almost black (particularly when in shade, or when wet). That color is not as often characterized by the clearly silver or light-tipped guard hairs of the silvertip. Light-hued guard hairs do exist, however; they are quite apparent in most pelts, and noticeable when a dry animal is seen at close range. The sun catches this almost-transparent hair, making the coat "grizzled," with less of the contrasting black undercoat or other hair. I have seen perhaps thirty brown-bear grizzlies, and those I have actually seen or handled were predominantly brown. Perhaps "nut brown" is the best description. The hue is not seen in the pelage of black bears in either the cinnamon or the henna phase.

The size of the largest known strain of grizzlies, the mature kodiak, is on record as more than 1,200 pounds, with a body length of ten feet, outweighing the average silvertip by 300 to 500 pounds. Grizzlies have longer legs than black bears, and this trait is very pronounced in the kodiak.

The body shape of the brown-bear grizzly is more angular than that of the silvertip. At times the brown-bear grizzly looks almost doglike, particularly when slenderized by daily consumption of large amounts of salmon protein.

It is difficult to be specific about the actual temperament of the brown grizzly. When they are salmon fishing they seem less easily provoked than silvertips by the proximity of a human, but that trait (if it is a trait) could be related to the abundance of readily available food. Even a sow with cubs may be less "territorial" about the distances between another adult bear, or a human, and her cubs. On the other hand, because the annual records of the Alaska Fish and Wildlife Service show that recently many bears have been killed because they "endanger life and/or property," it is best to revere and fear the brown grizzly, as did the Indians.

CHAPTER I

The Black-Bear Man

Lynn Rogers is a tall, red-haired man with wide shoulders jutting over narrow, blue-jeaned hips. Most of the time he wears a patient half-smile, belied by unswerving blue eyes that reflect the intensity of his interest. His broad, capable hands are calloused, and on his right arm a long white scar runs from wrist to elbow. Just above the bronzed knuckles of his right hand are perforations filled with scar tissue, the single real evidence that once a bear got the best of him. That is not bad, considering the twelve hundred or more times he has manhandled large black bears, over five hundred individual animals (several of them more than twice during the eleven years he has spent with them). The good doctor (Ph.D., biology) would not pass in a crowd for an academic; he's too robust, too strong, too obviously an outdoorsman. He usually dresses like a logger and often smells of sweat and bear dung. The latter, which he calls "scat" (its technical name), interests him greatly. Its contents—blueberries, grass, leaves, garbage from dumps, carrion—speak volumes to him.

The life of the North American black bear is the subject of Lynn Rogers's broad and intensive studies—so much so that it is also his life. The quality of his work has made him the best-informed "black-bear scientist" in North America. Really none of these things fit together, bear crap, blue eyes, broad shoulders, scars, and expertise. Like any interesting and worthwhile puzzle, however, this one rewards close attention. I know because I have been a long time fitting the pieces together. Just after the publication of my book *Killer Bears*, my editor, Neil Soderstrom, wrote to me of "a biologist who, during the winter, goes into bear dens and examines the animals, takes their temperatures, and so on." Now, *that* interested me! Anyone who will go into a bear den while the occupant is resting, let alone shove a cold thermometer up its rectum, knowing full well the consequences, has to be at least interesting, if not downright unique. I called him long distance.

"Hello. May I speak to Dr. Lynn Rogers?"

There was a pause, as if to digest that request.

"Lynn Rogers speaking. Who is this?"

"Mike Cramond, in West Vancouver. I'm a writer."

"Oh, yes. I've heard from Neil Soderstrom about you! How are you? You have done a good book. I've read much of it with interest."

"Oh, that's nice! Thank you! Neil tells me that you go into black bear dens during their winter dormancy." (I avoided the word *hibernation*.) "I was wondering if it would be possible to visit with you this winter during your examinations?"

"Most certainly you can! I usually do the examinations during March. Would you like to come into a den or two?"

This time the hesitation was mine.

"Yeah. *If you go first!*"

He laughed.

"Oh, I tranquilize the bear before I go right in. It's quite safe."

"Well! I'll enjoy—no, perhaps not enjoy—I'll be very interested in, do-ing just that, visiting a bear den or two." I was hedging somewhat. If he noticed though, he did not let me know.

"Well, Mike, you'd be most welcome."

I thought about that. "Welcome in a bear den. Hell!"

Yes! I thought about that considerably, after we had had a good conversa-tion and hung up. We had agreed on an exchange of gathered data. I had files of several hundred bear incidents, and he said that after perusing the appen-dix list in *Killer Bears*, he might add several from other sources.

During the following March my commitments to another trip and his ar-rangements with a television crew to film his den examinations prevented our joint study. However, during July 1982, when my own research required that I travel across the United States and Canada interviewing people whose experiences and studies involved bears, Lynn Rogers was at the top of the list.

Late one afternoon, after several days of driving hundreds of miles in hot, sticky weather, I arrived at the door of his cottage in downtown Ely, Min-nesota. His wife, Donna, pretty, pleasant young mother of two small daugh-ters, said, "Oh, Mr. Cramond, Lynn has been expecting you! But he's out at the dump photographing bears. He probably won't be back until about eleven."

"That late?" was my surprised reply.

"Well, he doesn't quit until the daylight fails," she stated apologetically. "He does it after work."

"Oh. No problem! I can wait. I'll go take a swim in the lake. I need a bath."

"Won't you come in and have something to eat! You could bathe here," she suggested.

I smiled at her earnest hospitality.

"Well, I've been looking forward to a good swim in the lake ever since leaving Colorado—over a thousand miles of hot highways. I'll see you and Lynn later in the evening."

I found an almost abandoned spot at the lake, went skinny-dipping, and soaped myself all over. It was a relief, and after a steak dinner prepared in the camper, I drove over to Rogers's home. Lynn came in minutes after I got there, in the near darkness, tired from the seventy-mile drive, but satisfied with his efforts at getting photographs. He was immediately hospitable.

"Bring your stuff in, Mike! Stay in the house!"

"Thanks, Lynn. I'm comfortable in the camper, but thank you. Many bears at the dump?"

"Oh, off and on, perhaps a dozen!"

"*That* many?"

"We'll show you tomorrow. There are a couple of big males worth seeing. But we'll have to get on with whatever results there are in the traps we set out. We're expecting some friends to do some circulatory system tests related to the bears' cardiology—if we have any in the traps."

"That should be interesting! Are these tests comparable to tests made on man?"

"Exactly."

Donna had brought him a bowl of hot soup and a sandwich, pointing out that he had missed dinner again. Interested in answering my questions about bears, he barely heard the remonstrance and ate without noticing his food, obviously habitual practice. We talked for a few minutes before he grinned and got up.

"Mike, we'll have lots of things to do tomorrow and lots to discuss. We'd better get some sleep."

Early the next morning we were out at the forestry station near Ely, a complex with offices, bunkhouses, kitchens, and traps and cages. Centrally placed was a long, low individual complex composed of Lynn's broad, windowed laboratory, a kitchen cum aid station with refrigeration, a large sleeping room, and a bathroom. The central room, with several desks and an abundance of technical and photographic equipment, was Lynn's laboratory. It was strewn and almost filled with documents, maps with pins in them, screens, field equipment made up of the highest-quality instruments, and one easy chair, which Rogers never used. He was busy between desk telephones and the screening of his latest photographs, all of which were of bears and other animals and flora related to his work.

He answered my questions without the reserve common to many biological scientists. His responses were not even qualified with "to the best of our knowledge"; he simply gave me the facts of the field as he had accumulated them. One of the first things he explained had to do with the apparent variety of bears in the same species.

"Well, Mike, the long-nosed, almost wolflike, slender type of bear you describe is usually a young subadult, or developing, black bear. The heavy, round-faced, thick-shouldered, more heavily proportioned bear is an adult, or older, bear. Bears grow throughout their lives. The longer they live with abundance, the larger their proportions during good health, and the rounder their appearance."

That statement surprised me.

"Then we're not talking about types but simply growth characteristics."

"I'm afraid so. It is often misleading to the public, who don't have any reason to calculate the bears' ages but simply go by their outward appearance. When we do examine for age, we go mainly by the rings in a particular tooth, just the way we count tree rings for age and weather conditions."

"But how about the live bears?"

"We remove a premolar—a tooth that is small and of little importance to their feeding or mouth structure—while they are under anesthesia, and keep it for laboratory examination. Under a microscope the rings tell us the history and age of the bear. If the bear has been through a couple of bad years, the rings are less well defined. At first this indefiniteness led to the belief that rings do not reflect actual age. However, closer microscopic examination revealed a barely discernible change in the opaque quality of the ring structure. Now we're quite confident about their ages."

For me this was extremely interesting new knowledge.

"Then this aging study is confirmed in your own continuing examinations of bears in this area?"

"Not much doubt in any case! But yes, it is confirmed here."

"Damn it, Lynn, I didn't know I was so ignorant of the facts. Those of us laymen who've shot or examined bears over these many long years have completely missed the point that long-nosed black bears are essentially young bears, and that round-faced or round-headed bears, whatever size, are more mature.

"That's right. Our studies show that bears that have access to an abundance of food show extremely high percentages of growth and good health in comparison to those that have little access to food or garbage."

It was new ground (I had not yet read his doctoral dissertation). I suggested, "I suppose there's the gene structure or hereditary factor to be considered. For example, a small, slight man may grow in middle age into a squat, broad, fat man, a replica of his parentage to some extent. Or a man from a strain having larger bone structure might also grow into a corpulent, big man, although he may have been a tall, slender youth."

Lynn grinned, nodding his head.

"The genes in any life form affect its general structure and capabilities. In black bears the genetic factor is less noticeable, perhaps because they all live in essentially the same climatic zone, but the factor of continuing growth contributes to their large size in advanced age."

I sought for parallels with mankind.

"No pituitary glandular control, as in humans, to cut off growth at a particular age?"

He shook his head.

"We have no evidence to support anything but continued growth, Mike. Sorry!"

He grinned while I expostulated.

"Hell! How can one live to be so old and know so little! I'm sure this will be a surprise to many people. I don't know how I could have been so stupid so long."

Lynn was smiling, shaking his head.

"We have laboratories where we can prove our thesis. You're not stupid; you simply lack facilities for continuous examination. What you have believed is commonly accepted."

The phone rang, and he picked it up.

"Oh, there is! Great! Where? What number? Okay, we'll be right out!"

He was jotting down notes on a slip of paper. He looked up with a broad smile.

"Let's go! We've got a good bear in trap number sixteen. This will be great for Steve Durst's efforts when he arrives here tomorrow. It's a big one."

Within moments we were driving at breakneck speed deep into a network of logging roads. We passed hundreds of acres of small, slow-growing coniferous trees and faster-gaining deciduous competitors. The windshield shed snapping branches as Rogers maneuvered his rather well-worn pickup over bumps and around potholes, stopping at last where another pickup was parked by the edge of the narrow road. My belly was tingling with some strange excitement. It was my first actual experience with an entrapped bear. Surprisingly, at least to my inner self, I was apprehensive. For five years I had been continuously researching the effects of human confrontations with bears, often seeing tragic and sometimes fatal results of bear damage to human flesh. Now, here I was! In effect, to put myself on the line.

Lynn was out of the truck and with the members of his crew almost before the vehicle stopped. Among the crew I noted a long-legged young woman in a mackinaw shirt and dirty jeans—not really what I had expected as part of a bear-trapping expedition. I was to learn more about this woman and her extraordinary bear management capabilities during the next couple of days. She was a graduate student in biology, working in wildlife management studies. What particularly attracted my interest at that time was her evident delight at the robust nature and large size of the trapped animal. It was, she exalted, a prize specimen!

I followed her, manfully, to the side of the trap, which was a homemade contraption—two steel oil barrels welded end to end—wedged between two trees growing just that far apart. I took one look at the rusty, weather-beaten, battered object and carefully peered back along the bushed-in "trail" to the road as a line of retreat. I had been expecting the game department "culvert" trap, which is a formidable prison for any wild animal. Not this primitive setup! I looked at the center welding from a safe distance, while the others discussed the removal of the trap, obviously unconcerned.

So why should I be?

One of the crew moved his hand past a breather hole in the end near me. A resounding thump shook the whole trap as the bear swatted at the movement. The young man merely drew his hand back. I looked for a crack in the welding and then, once more, back down the trail.

Lynn had been around the trap, end to end. "Well! He's facing this way.

He looks like a big one." He bent over the end of the closest barrel. "Why look at this! He's torn a piece of metal loose on the end here. I hope he hasn't damaged his teeth."

Another loud thump. Again I looked at the center welds, expecting to see the metal separate. Again I glanced back down the trail.

One of the young men said, "He's heavy, and it's hot. We should get him out of this as soon as possible!"

"Yes," Lynn agreed. "How long has he been in? Overnight?"

"No," said the young woman. "He wasn't in late last evening when we made our rounds. Early this morning, I'd say. But he could do with cooling off. Did you bring any water?"

No one had. There was a murmur of consternation. Then Lynn went into action. Following an examination of the bear to calculate its weight, he placed a "one shot" disposable hypodermic needle on the end of a newly cut stick. Into the needle he had drawn the tranquilizing dosage required to settle the bear down. He moved nearer to one of the smaller slits, putting a slender stick into it. Almost instantaneously the stick was snapped off, so quickly that human movement could not have withdrawn it. Rogers grinned.

"He's in good shape! Give him a stick to chew on!"

One of the young men handed him a stick about two inches thick. When it went into the end of the barrel, it was smashed and pulled inward so quickly I could hardly believe the speed of the bear's reaction. Rogers pointed to a two-by-four lying nearby, then indicated the large hole torn by the bear in the solid end of the barrel.

"He's very strong. Try him with that one!"

As it entered the narrow hole the two-by-four of pine was bitten and pulled in lengthwise so quickly that the young man handling it almost had his fist drawn smack into the metal. Inside, wood smashed as if it was being both hit by an axe and severed by a wood chipper. While the bear was thus occupied, Lynn went to the opposite end and, finding the most effective entrance, slipped the stick holding the hypo into the interior and he then jabbed quickly. Almost in the same instant the stick was smashed from within.

Once again I looked at the welds.

"What do you think he weighs?" I asked, trying not to show my apprehension.

Lynn looked quizzically at the crew. One of them ventured a guess: "I'd say nearly three hundred pounds."

There was rending of wood inside the barrels. Again a glance down the back trail. Shortly thereafter I noted a sound of slavering inside the barrel. One of the crew knelt down, peering into the dark interior through a slit. There was a half-hearted thump from within. The youth pulled back and stood up.

"He's swallowing, sticking his tongue out. Looks like you got a good shot into him. Won't be long now."

Lynn looked at his watch, calculating the time since he had administered the hypodermic. "He should be calmer now. Let's get him into the truck and down to some water to cool him off. Let's go!"

My last few minutes had been spent taking photographs. When they began, all six of the crew, struggling to take the trap from between the two trees, it was apparent that the weight of the bear was wedging it down. This was no place for an old man. If the rig came apart, I would get trampled underfoot in the rush—or so I imagined. I was still unaware of the fearlessness, the effectiveness, and the knowledge of bear trapping and marking crews. There was a creaking and swaying of the joined barrels as the crew tilted the trap to get it out of the V between the trees. Thumps came from inside the barrel. I got out to the roadway to photograph from nearer the pickup—where I had thoughtfully left the door open on my side.

The crew, with Lynn carrying much of the forward weight, came out of the thick bush, sliding the trap quickly into the back of the other truck. I heard few objections from the bear, just an ominous deep breathing. Lynn spoke to the crew for a moment, then jumped into our vehicle and began his fast-paced passage through the maze of narrow roads. I was quiet.

After a while I broke into Lynn's thoughts.

"*That* scared the hell out of me!"

Lynn's face registered denial.

"You didn't show it." He paused. "Anyway, there wasn't any reason for worry. It was just a routine capture, and a very nice bear—a fine specimen."

I shook my head.

"You smell like bear shit," I accused.

He laughed.

"Yes, Donna sometimes accuses me of that—before I take a bath."

During the next hour I was to see more evidence of Lynn Rogers's intrepidity, both as leader and as teacher. When we arrived at the compound, the first order of work was to cool off the overheated animal, which in its cramped quarters was rapidly recovering from the tranquilizer. Then the crew had to get it into the link-fence and steel-pipe cage. The cage was mounted on deep concrete footings right at the edge of the surrounding forest, where trees shaded it throughout the day.

The barrel trap was pulled from the truck to the ground. Another young woman, a student of natural resources management, joined the group. Six persons picked up the unwieldy object containing the slowly responding bear. They lugged the clumsy unit between two cabins to the entrance of the open cage. I looked at the cage speculatively. A wire wall divided it into two equal compartments with "den" quarters in each section. A door in the wall could be shut in order to separate the occupants. The floor of the cage was earth, raised and with "lies" where an animal could rest above the damp earth. Straw was piled on the higher ground. The entire circumference was made of the link-fence, heavy-duty wire commonly used to surround high-voltage installations. Accustomed to seeing half- to three-quarter-inch steel bars around enclosures for large animals, I gazed at the almost fragile-looking wire with doubt. My common sense, however, told me that its safety in use had been proven many times over the years.

Even so, I had some mental reservations, because everybody kept saying, "This is one *big* bear!"

Rogers worked with the crew to get the barrel trap's sheet-iron sliding door facing into the large cage. He was making sure that the now hard-breathing and wide-awake animal would have an unimpeded exit into the larger enclosures. Anything obstructing the bear's passage would be dangerous. He peered into the trap's interior, searching it. He had the remains of the still-protruding pine two-by-four removed. The timber had been shorn, as if with an axe, sections of it torn apart. I was amazed at Lynn Rogers's next move.

Quickly he lifted the trap door, reached inside, and pulled out a section of broken timber slamming the door before the bear could grasp his arm.

Standing near one of the young women, I expressed my amazement.

"He's got a lot of guts to do *that!*"

The feminine voice also expressed surprise. "Yes, he has! I've never seen him do anything like that before!"

Shaking my head I moved to the side of the cage and away from the present endeavors, taking a look around to see just where a clear escape path might lie. There was only one way to get that big, unhappy bear into the open cage: place the end of the barrel trap directly over the sill of the concrete wall entrance, with the cage's main gate open, and thereafter dump the animal from the narrow cell into the enclosure—*while the steel gate was still wide open*!

There was a real struggle to get a foot or two of the elongated contraption across the concrete sill and into the main cage. I stood well back, preoccupied with "taking photos." Even as the trap was slid into the doorway, it hung up twice on its cross members. It might just do that again as the crew attempted to withdraw it in order to *close that main door*.

Perhaps, I thought, they will shove the trap in all the way, then pull the trap door up by remote control, later to remove the barrel.

It was not to be so.

Lynn was standing beside the half-intruded trap.

"Okay, who's going to go in and lift the door?"

There was a moment of silence. I shook my head thoughtfully. Lynn's voice came pseudoresignedly, half humorously.

"Then I guess it'll be me!"

He slipped into the main cage and peered briefly into the darkness of the trap through two of the breather slits. Then he heaved the metal container to a better position, pulled the lock of the sliding door on one end, and hopped up beside the barrel.

"Get ready!" he ordered briskly. With a quick motion he lifted the end door of the trap and jumped back from inside the cage doorway. The crew tilted the trap, and one of the largest back bears I have seen shot backwards through the opening, to land upright on the dirt floor of its new enclosure. The gang heaved the door against the side of the trap and turned the end of the contraption upward. The resounding clatter of steel on concrete, iron on iron, and steel wire against the drum was thunderous enough to turn the bear from the group of surrounding people and toward the opening of the door in the second compartment, beyond which the forest was visible through the not-too-apparent mesh of the wire screen.

The bear's lightninglike turn was that of a fast welterweight dodging a blow. In a split second it had sized up the knot of human captors, their yells and clanging steel, noted the intervening open door to the second compartment, and the open forest beyond. The bear shot through the inner door like a steel spring, hitting the wire wall on the far side with such a shock that the whole twenty-foot cage shuddered. Knocked back from its own impact, in the same movement it sprang in two straight jumps from that end of the cage to the other, striking that wall of steel wire with another earth-shaking wallop. Stunned at the impenetrability of this strange, apparently fragile but unbreakable barrier, it stood momentarily looking at the corner nearest the overhanging trees.

Shouted orders to hurry and get the trap out of the entrance were accompanied by the clanging and scrape of metal on concrete and of steel pipe on sheet metal. The continuous noise of the next two seconds impelled the huge animal animal to hurl itself against the metal screen in the far corner. A quick shift of direction at the other end brought it smashing into the mesh twice, the quick bite from its jaws against bending steel mesh producing the sickening sound of tooth enamel rending itself on steel.

I heard Lynn's voice.

"Oh hell! He'll break his teeth." And I saw a piece of white material fly away from the spring of the returning steel.

The door was now closed at the main entrance, the steel trap lying crosswise outside, where it had been flung.

I breathed a sigh of relief, but none of the crew expressed a similar release of tension. They were too interested in the size and condition of the bear. One of them noted that he thought the animal's bite at the netting had broken a tooth, and I added that I had seen a chip fly away at the time. Lynn's face showed deep concern, and he said he hoped it was not so. But when he blamed himself for the incident, I shook my head in amazement.

"You did everything you could to avoid it. That animal is just frantic to get away. Hell, you just went into the cage to free him from the heat of that trap! You could have waited and lifted the door from the outside. What more could you have done?"

Rogers just looked at me, listening as if he had not heard. He nodded thoughtfully.

"He's an excellent specimen," he stated absently.

The animal took another run at the far wire fencing and bulged it outward, shaking the cage to its foundations. The bear then jumped straight at the side of the fence, both back feet striking the cross bracing with the precision of a gymnast mounting a balance beam, and in the same movement it smashed its head upward against the top netting with such force that the upper mesh billowed like canvas—but held. Twice more the animal made this striking jump before recognizing that it could not loosen the material that had seemed so light and fragile but was so strong. It sat back on its haunches momentarily, breathing very deeply.

Ignoring the dozen people gathered around the cage, the bear stared at the sides facing the forest. With a quick move it lunged straight at the wire in front of two young members of the crew who had come up close for a better look. The wire bulged momentarily but threw the bear back. Next the animal sought the door into the first compartment, into which it had been so recently dumped. Its short rushes at the fence wire were not nearly so ferocious as the first charges. Only a couple of minutes had passed since the bear had been caged in the pen, but already it was recognizing the impenetrability of steel fiber, accepting that the barrier would not give way even to the enormous strength of a large animal that previously had smashed wooden two-by-fours at will.

Members of the crew had gone to bring the fire hose. Moments later they found that the water supply had been cut off. It had not been turned back on after winter snows, and there was no available hydrant wrench. The crew formed a bucket brigade to bring water. Some was tossed over the steaming bear, some dumped into the trough in the cage. As the contents of one bucket splashed over it, the bear made a rush at the wire and, as the bucket wielder jumped back, slapped the netting with a resounding thump, as if to say, "Don't get smart with that stuff!"

As it shook the water from its coat, its pelage turned a nut brown, almost the color of a coastal grizzly, a brown bear. Highlights of filtered sunlight glistened in the upper guard hairs. And when it turned to face in my direction, the roundness of face, the high-set tufts of ears, the thickness of neck and shoulders—about which I had asked Rogers earlier in the day—were all there. In fact, if I had seen this bear at a distance of fifty yards, I would have sworn that I had seen a grizzly, even to the erect guard hairs over the shoulders, which actually produced a noticeable "hump."

So! This probably explains why so many reports of many bear-man confrontations contained inaccurate identifications.

As I stared at the bear in front of me, the shiny, jet-black coats of a hundred or more Pacific Coast bears passed by in memory. Not once while in those woods west of the Cascades had I ever seen a black bear that was not obsidian black. In the Rockies of Yellowstone Park, there were henna-hued black bears. Even in the Canadian Rockies, where I had seen several black bears, all had been jet black. This one, as the sun struck the hair and the water shook free, definitely had a coastal brown-bear hue, not of the mutant henna pigment. As I went over to stand beside Lynn, I nodded at the animal.

"A large bear. What do you figure he weighs?"

Turning wordlessly from me, he stared calculatingly at the animal, which was pacing about the cage.

"What is your guess, Mike?"

I noted the small grin, then the attentiveness of the surrounding crew. I shook my head and also grinned.

"Well, I'd say about 275. It could go 300. But allowing for weight loss in capture—about 275. Okay, what is yours?"

There was a ripple of laughter from the crew.

"I'd say 268—and a half," Lynn ventured, responding to the humor.

"Playing TV games!" I accused.

"Just on the safe side," he laughed. Other guesses bandied about by the crew were closer to 300 pounds. None guessed lower than Rogers or me. The bear was settling down, somewhat. The crew was melting away to other duties.

I went back with Lynn to his laboratory and asked him if I might read his dissertation. He had shown the discourse to me earlier, and as I had leafed through it, the lucidity of it had struck me as unique. It was presented almost in the vernacular, very readable, understandable even to a layman. He handed the bound volume to me just before he was called out on other duties. His friends Steve Durst and Carrole Houliston were flying in by private plane the following morning, and he had to pick them up at the airport. He asked me if I would like to accompany him.

"No, Lynn. I want to read your paper now. I mightn't get a chance later."

"Hope you don't find it boring. Anyway, we'll go out to the dump tonight and photograph some bears!"

That was, indeed, to be a memorable experience.

The Redhead I

The rock formations of the Appalachian Shield, scoured by glaciers and thinly covered with humus, were soaking up the rays of the July sun. During the night the heat would be released gradually through the thin layer of topsoil, creating a greenhouse effect that would promote the fast summer growth of flora. Strawberries were ripening, and blueberries were gradually changing color from ivory to pink-green, then to the powdered blue of the ripe, sweet fruit.

With her short claws barely penetrating the rich soil on which she stood, the five-year-old female black bear, who had a distinctive coat of henna red, was sensing a change in the daily stream of her consciousness. Her daylong harvests of berries, roots, ants, and leaves had filled the growing paunch slung beneath her short, thick back. Fatty tissues were filling in the areas between her skin and muscle. For more than two years now, ever since her mother's death, the unmarked borders of the territory had been established as hers alone. Her mother had dominated that territory for twelve years, but now only a fading patch of blood and guts marked the spot where the old sow had lost her territory forever. Two bright, acrid-smelling brass cartridge casings lay a few yards from the spot. Ever since the old she-bear's death, the Redhead (as she was called by people who caught glimpses of her through the brush) had associated the man-smell with a distinct memory of ugliness. Even clumsy noises of humans in her territory moved her quickly away from their intrusions.

Her inherited territory was bountiful: skunk lilies during the spring; many kinds of succulent grasses, each sprouting in its own time; later on; the ripening berries and ants swarming under the abundant rotting timber left on the ground from twenty-five years of logging operations. Because she had been large enough to thwart other female bears' attempts to intrude, she had enjoyed her two good summers of plenty.

Her prehensile lips swiftly pulled the small, ripe blueberries from the foot-high bushes. Her rotating bicuspids crushed the fruit slightly before flowing saliva eased the masses down her nearly full gullet. Suddenly, she stopped eating and lifted her head. From a great distance she caught the vague scent of the large old black male whose territory cut through hers. Ordinarily she would have "blown," made a gasp of air rush through her half-opened lips and nostrils, signaling her displeasure.

Twice that same old boar had chased her while he was passing through her territory. Once he had silently come close while she was preoccupied and upwind of him, and he had piled his bulk over her in a split second. Alarmed and uninitiated, she had bitten his belly. He had swatted her rear angrily, out of surprise and pain. Her sudden, fast, squealing retreat into the safety of the nearby bushes had left him swinging his head and woofing in mild reproach. Later that day, when she had returned to the place, the track of his scent had been strong enough for her to follow it, out of curiosity, to her own territorial line. There it led straight into an older female's domain. For two more years his sudden and overbearing "call" had left her reluctant to stay close to any area bearing his scent or spoor.

This July day, however, was different. For five days now the odor of her urine had taken on an unusual and disturbing scent: the smell of blood, ordinarily associated with injury but now strangely different. Associated with it was a swelling of the entrance to her womb. Some vague, new urge, a powerful, instinctive longing was entering her virginal life. She moved restlessly over her domain, neglecting sources of food, urinating near the edge of her territory. She stared up at the rocky ridges from which the big male had occasionally passed through her domain. She waved her narrow head in small circles, scenting the air. Then she moved toward the high ground of the ridges, occasionally urinating in her path. When she caught the scent of the big male bear, carried on the downdraft from the hill, she was not apprehensive. In fact, occasionally she raised her head to inhale more deeply the scent of the old male.

CHAPTER 2

They Almost Never Come to Blows

My four hours of immersion in Rogers's doctoral dissertation proved to be one of the most educational experiences of my life. Rogers had amassed an incredible amount of detail on the specific habits and habitat of the most abundant of all bears, North America's black bear. His dissertation is a study of the black bear's adaptation to and impact on its habitat.

Accompanied by one of his crew, Lynn came into the laboratory late in the afternoon. After some consultation about the traps that were out and the latest reports, he nodded toward the door, saying to me, "Okay, let's go." He had a couple of lunches lying on the truck seat, individually wrapped in a large paper bag. As we climbed in, he motioned toward the bag casually.

"Donna put something up for us to eat. We'll go directly from here to the dump. It should be a good evening for photographing."

Mentally I observed, the Rogers pace: "If he ever stopped for one moment during a day, no one trying to keep pace would have time to notice it."

Lynn lifted out a thick meat sandwich with one hand, the other hand occupied at the steering wheel.

"There might be some bears worth observing, Mike. Some differing age groups."

"Yeah. I'm learning. How old would you say the big one in the cage is?"

"Oh, between ten and fourteen years of age."

"You took a risk, reaching into that cage this morning. And going into the big enclosure to open the trap. Had you considered the danger?"

He thought back for a moment, then grinned.

"It might have *looked* risky, as you define it. But in both instances it was a calculated risk. The bear was facing in the opposite direction when I reached in. It was too large an animal to turn around in that confinement."

I nodded, "I figured you on that one. But, what about going into the big cage?"

Evincing a half-smile, he said, "Well. Black bears are inclined always to avoid trouble. If I was well out of its line of exit, I was safe enough. And I was. Not much risk there."

"Some?"

He shrugged. "There is an element of risk in almost anything. Handling bears is no different."

I laughed. "You're beginning to convince me."

He grinned reassuringly. "Then I'll keep trying."

So interesting was Rogers's perspective on black bear behavior that the thirty-five miles to the dump passed in what seemed like moments. I wondered if my persistent questioning might seem boring. He shook his head.

"We're both learning."

And I was to learn much more at the dump site.

He parked the truck at the far end from our approach. As we had passed by the near end, a rather slender young bear was just crossing the road. The sight aroused some new apprehensions, most of which had been instilled by my long-time investigations of bear attacks. Lynn got out of the truck to set up his cameras (he had two) and boxes of gear, along with cardboard cartons of spoiled meat (fats) nearby. I watched him during his quick arrangement of the photographic setup. He turned to me with a beckoning hand. "Come on! We'll see what's doing."

I walked beside him to the midsection of the dump, which had been built up by tons of local municipal waste materials. A cliff of debris obscured the activities at its jumbled-junk bottom. As we approached the face of the cliff, the rattle of rolling cans became audible.

I noted this. "Sounds like that young bear is down there."

Preoccupied with his thoughts, Lynn nodded. "Oh, I hope more than just him."

We reached the thirty-foot drop from the edge of the dump fill, where it blocked the small, densely forested valley. Right in plain sight three bears were working over the odious mess. One of them was the small one we'd seen earlier. It was staying well to the far side. A large, fatter bear was in the center, and a third was closer to our parked truck. None of them was more than fifty feet away. I felt I had to express my appreciation in order to conceal my nervousness.

Lynn, staring into the valley, seemed not to hear me.

"I need that elderberry bush down there for a prop."

I shook my head derisively. "That might be difficult to get—with *them* down there!"

He looked at me as if not quite comprehending what I had said, then smiled half-heartedly. He had brought a small hatchet with him. Without saying anything more, he stepped over the piled junk at the edge of the fill and moved down through the disarray of garbage. The largest bear, a 250-pounder, looked at him, then moved off toward the bushes. The other two bears just as casually moved out of sight. I stood on top thinking, "My God, he's not going into the bushes to cut that elderberry—not with three bears around!"

But he did. It was all I could do to remain courageously at the top of the spill, contemplating how I could get to the truck if one of the animals happened to come in my direction. A couple of minutes later Rogers mounted the dump edge carrying a quite large elderberry bush that he had cut off near its root stem, almost the entire shrub. I went with him as he carried it over beyond the truck to the leveled far end. Out of the corner of my eye I saw the two larger bears returning to the dump bottom. I nodded back at them. "Don't you consider that type of foray dangerous?"

Lynn shook his head. "No, Mike. Black bears usually avoid any type of confrontation."

"Usually?"

"They almost never come to blows. You watch them for a while, and you'll notice that."

"They also *kill* people!"

He shook his head at that statement. "They have," he acknowledged. "Your works have established that." He hesitated. "But if you keep a careful eye on them, you can see what they are going to do."

I could not understand how one could "keep a careful eye on them" during an almost blind approach to a bush growing deep in the tangled forest floor near the place where three of these animals had just been feeding, then putting one's whole attention to cutting out the large bush, which had obscured all vision both near and far. My thoughts returned to a time earlier in the day, when this "bear scientist" had shown me close-ups of bears' heads at differing angles, explaining the facial expressions of the individual animals. To one of these slides he had paid particular attention, saying, "Mike, you see that forward extension of the upper lip. That is the sign of a disturbed bear that may become aggressive." I had stared at the bear's mouth with some diligence, unable to see much "expression." Rogers had continued with half a dozen other photographs, coming back each time to the one with the extended lips. Each time he returned to it, more of the minute details of the expression registered with me. I had brought up other presumed danger signs, asking, for example, "What about the 'wuffing' or 'whooshing' when they expel that rush of air?" He had replied, "That is really a sign that they are distressed—and uncertain." And I had argued, "How about the 'popping' or snapping of their teeth?" His answer was just as firm. "It is impressive, Mike, but it is more in the form of a cautionary threat than an expression of their intent to attack. It is a defense mechanism. As you know, they don't snarl like a canine." To that I had said simply, "Oh," while trying to recall if I had ever seen the lips of any bear actually curl upward to show its canine teeth. And the memory bank came up blank. Damned if I could revisualize *any* tooth-baring snarl! Damned if I could! Teeth? Yes! Snarl? Hmmm? And Rogers had filled the void with, "The 'snarl' is usually the product of the taxidermist's art. It makes the head mount more dramatic. But I've never seen one snarl!"

Down the drain went another prop for the dramatic writer. My eyes had gone again and again to the particular photograph of the extended lip of the bear head in close-up. Slowly it had registered. And my one infallible conclusion was that anyone who recognized that lip extension in the field would have to be so close that he was within reach of the bear. I had said, "What happened when you took *that* photograph? Of course, it was a telephoto lens." His head shake was emphatic. "No, I stayed still, and he backed up."

As I watched Lynn placing the elderberry shrub between two large boulders in order to keep it erect, I saw a black bear on the road beyond, about a hundred feet away, downwind from us and the stench of meat.

"There is a bear moving in this way."

Lynn looked up eagerly. "Oh good! That is another one." Obviously he could tell them apart.

I was staying close to the truck door, which was open on my side. A station wagon swung into the dump grounds, drove directly up to the center area, and two men and a small boy got out.

The larger man lifted a load of tangled debris out of the vehicle. The other one carried some garbage to the top, and there was a clatter of cans and metal refuse as they tossed their loads over the brink. The little boy had accompanied them—and they were not more than fifty feet from where the three bears had just been, the ones I had seen returning. Their voices came faintly on the evening air, that of the driver more clearly than the others. He was obviously a resident, used to the area.

"Just a couple of them down there. Nothing big. A couple of real big bastards do come around, though."

It was difficult to catch the words of the youngster, but not his excitement. I turned back to watch Rogers. He had the elderberry bush propped erect and looked very much as though it had grown where he put it. He was hanging tiny pieces of sliced fat on the branches.

As I watched him he turned around apologetically. "You'll think I'm a phony, setting up like this to get photographs. But this brings them right up into the light, where you can get a clear shot of them when the sun goes down."

I laughed. "A good photograph justifies any maneuver you use to get the effect. I'm only against jerking fish out of the water to get action shots. But, aren't your cameras a little close to the action?"

There was less than twenty feet between the elderberry prop and the log with the cameras lying on it. And right beside the log was a cardboard box filled to the brim with stinking meat cuttings. That, at least, I had expected him to remove. He came back to the truck and retrieved another box of "goodies," more meat cuttings from the local butcher shops. He began to bait the area in such a manner that the cuttings would lead the bears directly toward his camera setup, and that arrangement was right in the open, fifty feet from the safety of the truck cab.

The sun was now on an evident curve toward evening. My glance was drawn across the road to a spot about three hundred yards distant where a tall bluff gently slanted from its forested top to the dirt highway. There was a bear walking unconcernedly down the edge of the steep cliff and along the lip of a bluff above a gravel pit. Occasionally, the animal turned its head toward the humans gathered on the fill. It viewed the two trucks and three cars that within minutes had gathered at the edge of the dump. The bear's path took it into a small clump of trees about fifty feet from the dirt road. With my binoculars I watched the area. Moments later the bear crossed the road a few feet from the entrance to the fill. It had trotted quickly across the road, then disappeared from sight. It was a larger bear than most, heavier in the belly section. I said so to Lynn as he set about checking his cameras.

"Good, good," he replied absently. "There'll probably be more as the sun goes down."

He went on depositing small slices of bait, this time leading toward the cameras and elderberry bush from the other end of the dump. When the elderberry bush, blown by a vagrant puff of air, tipped over to one side, I walked over to assist him. For some reason I looked up. There was a large, brownish-hued bear about thirty feet away, down in the niche between the dumped fill and the natural forest cover. I pointed to it. Lynn nodded.

"That's an old female. She's around most nights. A good-sized one. She may come in."

He quietly moved back to the log upon which his cameras were placed at the ready. I moved back to the side of the truck, making sure the door was still open. Frankly, I was questioning my courage. Lynn was not in the least perturbed. What would I do if the bear came after him? After all, there was lots of meat around to attract the bears. While I was thinking this, the head of a smaller bear, perhaps not more than two full years old, judging from his slender silhouette, poked up from behind some elderberry bushes. It was about forty feet away from me, thirty from Lynn, whose full attention was directed to setting a focus on the she-bear. And she was now hesitating behind a loosely dumped shield of discarded building timbers and excavated roots. I spoke quietly.

"There's a small one coming on your left."

He nodded without answering, awaiting the diffident actions of the big female. Though reluctant to leave the roots and timbers, she had come out into the open, moving toward Lynn. Her nose was working, her head swaying in response to the enticement of the stinking meat cuttings. Finally, moving completely out of the tangle and into full view, she spied and picked up a piece of the white fat on the ground. Lynn was picking up his cameras alternately, and the lens shutters were clicking. In the meantime, the smaller bear was plucking tiny pieces of cut fats off the elderberry bush, not more than twenty feet from Rogers. He quickly swung his camera toward it, clicking twice.

Suddenly both bears became disturbed. They moved back. Then the larger head of a big male black bear was thrust abruptly over the top of the broken timbers.

"Jeez! That's a *big* one, Lynn!"

I moved closer to the truck. Lynn was cocking his second camera as the animal's head ducked away. I was surprised. There were now five trucks and cars at the dump site. One of the cars had been driven unnoticed right up to ours, and its owner was standing right behind me. When he spoke, I jumped a foot, but he didn't seem to notice it. He was affable.

"You guys news people? Photographers?"

"No. That guy with the cameras is Lynn Rogers, the bear biologist. I'm just along with him."

While I was speaking, all three black bears came up around the elderberry bush. Each was intent upon picking up meat scraps. Lynn was methodically taking photographs. Suddenly the old she-bear moved in a line toward the large male. I expected to see a short charge and melee, wondering if Lynn was aware. He was intently occupied, cutting slices of fat from the chunks laid out on the log top. The big male animal waved his head back and forth, then slowly backed up. The female continued to push him, using a slow, aggressive gait, until eventually she had backed him into the surrounding growth. Then, as if satisfied, she turned and came back toward the meat source. The smaller bear had moved to the side of the bushes nearest her, and I expected her to charge right at him. Instead, she moved slowly up to him, brushed against him, then turned back toward the man with the meat. The smaller animal, as if warned by the close brush, stayed where it was.

Lynn was actually photographing her as she moved toward him, enticing her closer by tossing bits of fat to within three or four feet of where he sat on the log. I was flabbergasted. The bear was moving in. At ten feet, when he moved to pick up another camera, she wavered. For a moment she paced back and forth in a line about six feet in front of him. The other two bears had come into the clear behind her, fifteen or twenty feet away.

Fascination overcame my apprehension. I advanced the film in both of my own cameras, then moved slowly into line between the truck and Lynn. This I had to get! A man sitting down in front of three adult black bears, with two boxes of meat in front of him, objectively photographing the antics and even the expressions of the bears. *Three bears, two boxes of meat, one man with a camera.*

I walked cautiously in behind him. When I could photograph over his shoulder and get the full shot, I was less than ten feet from the she-bear. She was trying to pick pieces of meat off the end of the log where Lynn had stretched out to place them. The other two bears filled the rear of my viewfinder.

Suddenly the she-bear backed off. I moved silently backward toward the truck. Lynn was changing the film in one of his cameras. One of the bears had pulled a piece of meat from the branches of the prop elderberry bush and had knocked the shrub to the ground. I pointed it out to Lynn. For some reason the bears had all moved over into the obscuring growth, well beyond the edge of the dump.

Rogers and I reset the bush into its nest of rocks. He walked around, distributing more meat. As we moved back, I looked up at the hill on the opposite side of the road. What appeared to be a very large black bear of the rounder-built kind was sitting complacently on its haunches at the edge of the cliff, where it overlooked the entire dump. Quite obviously the animal was observing the activity on the dumpsite. I pointed it out to Lynn.

"That one looks very large, Lynn."

I offered him my 10-power Bausch and Lomb binoculars. After he had squinted thoughtfully at the bear, he took the magnifiers and studied the animal.

"Yes! That is a good-sized male. He's been around here for some time. I think I recognize him. He's a large one. I'd like to get a shot of him."

"Did you notice any ear tags?" I asked. I had looked but was unable to see the glint of any such items.

"No, he's not marked. I looked carefully. Let's go and see what those other visitors are looking at. Sounds like there are a few bears over there."

He turned to look at the elderberry bush and changed his mind. The young bear was back, and the old female was moving into the open spot near the cache of meat. Quietly Lynn again took his place with the cameras on the log.

This time the female was bolder. She moved right up to the source of the meat, within five feet of Rogers while he photographed her. She was reaching for the meat, which was about arm's length away, when Lynn tried to shoo her away with his hand. She refused to retreat. My heart jumped.

Rogers's hand made one quick movement toward his shirt pocket. I saw the flash of metal. With his other hand he put down the camera, waving at the defiant bear. He said, "Shoo! Beat it!" authoritatively. "Beat it! Now!"

She remained doubtful, her eyes fixed upon him from less than five feet away, refusing to back up. Suddenly a fine squirt of clear liquid shot from the nozzle of the canister in Lynn's hand. The spray caught the animal on the forehead, and as she moved to avoid it, another squirt hit the side of one cheek. She shook her head, but turned quickly away. Suddenly she was in a fast trot directly away from Rogers and the bait, heading toward the safety of the root and brush background. She had not grunted, squealed, or sneezed. She had simply raised one paw once to her face in a brushing motion and disappeared.

I stared at Lynn, who had turned to face me.

"Damn!" He announced. "I didn't want to do that. But I guess it had to be tested."

"What was that stuff—tear gas? Mace?" I asked incredulously.

"The stuff postmen use to discourage dogs. It's the first time I ever used it. I didn't get any of it in her eyes—I don't think. But she didn't like it. What time is it?" He looked at his watch. "We'll see if she comes back."

He was jotting a note on some record. He looked up at me. "How long would you say it took to react?"

"Oh, instantaneously—less than seconds."

"Hmmm," he nodded, writing something down.

I looked over at the rising edge of the cliff along the opposite side of the road. The very large bear was gone, but a medium-sized one was pacing down the same slanted approach to a crossing of the road. When I turned around and looked down the road in the other direction, the form of our she-bear, which only a minute ago had been squirted with the repellent, was already fifty yards away, headed purposefully along the edge of the road in the opposite direction from her entrance. She was not shaking her head, or brushing at her face, or sneezing, grunting, or coughing; she was simply going away, at a determined walk, from the source of her noxious encounter. I watched her until she disappeared into the roadside brush about a hundred yards away. It seemed very convincing evidence of the effectiveness of the deterrent spray on a wild animal, even one as large as a bear.

Lynn was again preoccupied with photographing a fourth and even larger male, which had come in toward the baited elderberry bush. I spoke quietly.

"That old lady is now over a hundred yards down the road—heading away. She doesn't seem to be in any distress—not rubbing or making any sign of being injured."

He nodded, not looking back. "That's interesting. It really drove her off— about two minutes since she got it."

"Yeah. Just about." I motioned to the large male. "He seems wary, doesn't want to come in for a bait."

At that moment the bear turned and disappeared. Two more cars had come into the dump area, one carrying two noisy young men accompanied by a youngster about ten years old. They had glanced over the embankment and now were heading for us. Lynn got up and came over to the truck for some more bait. The leader of the newcomers, a rather handsome fellow, the "village flirt" type, came up to us.

"Hey, what're you guys doin'? Taking photos? You from some magazine or sumpin'?"

I nodded my head and muttered "Yeah. 'Or *sumpin'*."

He was the type who would not listen for an answer to his own questions. Rogers was quietly digging out a roll of new film from the litter on the truck seat. Curious, the young man watched him.

"Say! You can get some good pictures here sometimes! 'Specially when they go into their mating act. The big bear, the male, makes a sort of cooing sound before he goes after the female."

Lynn was listening, seemingly intently, as he always does to anyone who is talking. Regardless of what they are saying, he is polite, deferential, nodding his head and saying, "Hmmm. Well, well." He doesn't argue or cut anyone off. But I do. This brash, talkative young man was overstepping himself.

I interrupted the swaggering statement, which was obviously designed to show off the young man's knowledge: "This is Lynn Rogers—bear biologist—he knows a bit. . . ." I never finished the sentence. The young guy was in full fettle.

"There's some big ones around here. Really big ones. They get into fights sometimes—over the females. You see some real goings on. There's one great big one! You sure see a lot of stuff you wouldn't believe. I come here lots. I've been thinkin' of doin' a magazine story about it."

"Yeah, you should do that," I got out quickly and then turned to the small boy with him. "Are you seeing lots of bears, son?"

"Yeah, we just seen a couple down there." He pointed to the middle of the dump where they had first stopped. That broke up the monologue. People usually stop to listen when children speak up.

Lynn was facing the middle of the dump, where a knot of seven people from two cars were gathered. Without saying anything, he was expressing himself. I strode past the noisy one with a "Pardon me, son." As I caught up to Lynn, I said, "Boy, what a know-it-all."

Lynn shrugged. "He's quite right about the little cooing sound the male makes when he is after an estrous female."

The words stopped mine. At the edge of the center of the dump we stopped. Two cars moved off, carrying the noisy ones, who, from their rather foolish discussions, appeared to be drinking. About a hundred feet from us, two rather hesitant older people, a man and woman, stayed close to their car. A dozen yards beyond them were two men dumping material from a pickup. It left a clear space of a hundred yards between us and our car, where one other visitor was talking to the three we had just left. Effectively, the entire perimeter of the dump was occupied by the groups. It left an open field only through the center, similar in extent to the area beyond the second baseman in a baseball diamond when fielders close in. For some reason I noted that. The distance to the truck was about 150 feet.

Lynn was at the edge of the dump, looking downward. I went over and stood beside him. Within seventy-five feet of us were seven bears, three of them within thirty feet, two of them quite large. They were unconcernedly grubbing in the garbage just tossed over by occupants from three of the departed vehicles. I pointed to the larger, more rounded bear of the bunch.

"Looks like the big one from the hillside?"

Lynn had been studying it. "There's a larger one, just in the bushes down in the middle. Either of them could be that one. I'd like to get one of them over to the baits." He stopped, turning his cheek to the almost motionless evening air. "The wind has changed, I think, coming from the direction of the truck. Maybe they'll smell the baits."

"The *big* one?" I laughed.

Actually, my nervousness was somewhat more controlled since I had seen the unconcerned entrance of the dozen visitors, two of them little children, plus three women, into the theater of bear activities. I was watching a large bear pull apart a plastic sack, then delve into its contents. The bears, paying not the slightest heed to any of the humans, were intent only upon discovering morsels of food in the offal. As my glance moved across the face of the dump, I was abruptly taken aback.

The severed, flyblown head of a large black bear was lying within twelve feet of me. It was not more than fifteen feet from the larger bear feeding in the plastic sack. I pointed to the grisly object.

"Jeez, Lynn! There's a bear's head right down there! That's what I heard those noisy people discussing."

He nodded reflectively. "It's been there for several days. Someone killed it somewhere—not here, took the hide and dumped the rest here."

Obviously concerned about such an act, he was nevertheless acknowledging that such acts are committed. He did not say any more. I could not help but stare at the macabre head and think, "The bears haven't touched it. Aren't affected by its presence. They are eating within feet of it. Yet, despite their known reputation for cannibalism, eating the carcasses of their own kind, they aren't interested in eating that head. Their only interest here is human garbage." I remembered the statement in Rogers's doctoral thesis that bears with access to garbage from human dumpsites were recognizably healthier and larger, endured the winters and bad years better, and progressively produced healthier litters.

But my attention was drawn back by sudden movements on the dump. The larger bear that Rogers had mentioned had come out of the bushes at the center of the dump, and its appearance had interrupted three other bears. One of the animals moved eastward along the dump in search of another source of food; two of them came at a forty-five-degree angle right up the slope of the dump in our direction. The action caught me off guard. Lynn was about fifteen feet from me, out of the line of their movement, while I was within ten feet of where both the animals would come up the face. Seeing Lynn and me, the hindmost bear changed its course to one more directly along the face of the dump. But the larger of the two continued on his oblique angle, which would take him very close to me. I stepped back two more silent paces, my every nerve jangling. The animal's eyes had come full upon me, the one on my side seeming to show a cautious, even belligerent watchfulness. The bear showed no sign of deference, only the desire to be out of the way of the larger bear, which now was eating from the green plastic bag the bear near me had opened.

I saw Lynn watching me and thought, "He's got that tear gas squirter. He'd come back this way if necessary." I stood my ground, facing the animal. It reached the top of the dump, mounting the level dirt surface about twenty feet from me. Its head was down. It stopped and surveyed the acre-wide top of the fill, noted the two cars to the northwest, which were right in line with that exit, and stared at the other three cars parked with our truck nearly in the middle of the circumference. All exits were blocked except the space open in the middle, a large opening. I thought "Dammit! Wild animals don't like to get into the open for any long distance. The ends are blocked by people. He has to go past me to get back around Lynn and over the dump. He won't face that open spot. And he doesn't want to go back down the dump where the bigger bear is."

His head swung toward me, and I turned my silhouette toward him, head down, a quasisubmissive gesture.

Boy! At that moment it wasn't difficult to evince nonaggression.

Then I saw the *peculiar tiny outward thrust of the upper lip*! Standing stock still, I raised my head and stared directly at him.

The big animal balanced himself uncertainly back and forth on his front paws, his head slowly turning to peer away and toward the people on the other side, who were seventy-five feet away. Then, with a direct look at me, he turned and moved at an angle that would take him past the other people, not too close but back in the direction that would carry him away from the face of the dump he had just left. He lumbered slowly, purposefully, off and over the edge.

I looked over at Lynn for the first time. He had not moved, but was nodding his head in recognition of the event. I was, strangely enough, not shaking, and I had thought I would be. My voice sounded steady.

"I saw that forelip movement, Lynn. It shook me up!"

"Yes. I saw it. He was uncertain."

"Hell! *He* was uncertain!"

He grinned and turned toward the area of the baiting. Three of the bears on the face of the dump had headed in that direction. So did he. And I followed. Within the next twenty minutes there were four bears back around the camera emplacement. Two of them were feeding off the knocked-down elderberry bush. Lynn and I reset it in between the boulders. I looked up toward the camera site. The old sow that had been sprayed was on her way toward the closest box to us.

"*She's* back, Lynn! After your bait."

"So she is," he replied with some exasperation.

There was a space of less than twenty feet between us and her, and about ten feet between her and the box full of fatty meat cuttings. Her nose was working with obvious anticipation. Lynn moved directly toward the box. In his left hand he held the long slender-bladed carving knife with which he had been slicing pieces of bait to put back on the bush. He moved very purposely toward the meat box, saying very patiently but authoritively, "Shoo! You! Shoo!"

But the old lady was not having any of that. Her nostrils were obviously filled only with the strong scent of the meat in the box beside the camera log. Lynn's approach was in a slight curve, to face her directly as she reached out her nose to eat from the box. His tall, spare frame was six feet from her and advancing. The knife blade in his left hand flashed in the evening sunlight. The bear halted in her dive for the box. She pushed forward to grasp a hunk of meat hanging over its edge. Lynn stepped to within arm's length of her, saying strongly, "Shoo! Get away, you! Shoo! Shoo!"

The knife was pointed at her head, not in aggression, but simply because it still happened to be in his hand, just as he would have gestured with a stick against a dog. She stopped, snatched the piece of meat, and backed up, all in the same motion. Slowly she retreated, gulping the meat section into her throat, backing farther away uncertainly. She was sure, though, that she did not want any part of the overbearing redheaded man who was telling her to beat it.

I was so fascinated that I just stood there, not even attempting to take a photograph. For the first time I had witnessed a man bluff a bear away from an open box of meat as one would wave off a dog. The knife in his hand would not be recognizable to the bear. His attitude of possession and dominance—fearlessness, that is—had to be the deciding factor. I shook my head.

"At least you had a knife, Lynn." I acknowledged.

He looked down at his hand as if it was a discovery to him.

"My, yes! I did, didn't I!" And he put it down on the log.

"You bluffed her—like a dog."

He shrugged and, saying nothing, began to cut up more slices of meat and toss them out around the area. Eventually he looked up at the sky.

"We're losing our light fast. It's almost too late for good exposures."

Two more bears came into the camera area, and we both took slides of them. The sun was down. The tourist who had come up earlier had gotten out of his car. He came over to where I was standing.

"That guy is something else!"

"Yeah. He's the bear biologist for this area. . . ."

"I know. I've seen him on TV. He knows his bears. Say, I'm sorry. My camera flash scared a couple of those bears away when you guys were photographing. I hope it didn't mess it up for you."

Lynn had come over. "It didn't mess anything up for us," he stated. "But, you don't get any flash reaction on your film from thirty feet. It won't help you to take photos."

They were in conversation about photographs while I looked up at the hillside, where the largest bear had been. A smaller one was up there, right where the big one had sat staring at the dumpsite. Then the massive shoulders of the large bear emerged abruptly from bushes, not ten feet from the smaller bear. I expected to see a sudden retreat. But, as the smaller bear sat still, the big one walked up to it, nuzzled, then went over and sat beside a fifteen-foot poplar tree. In fact, it sat with the tree in front of it, as if taking advantage of the leafy shade from a top cluster of branches. Obviously that was its usual point of observation: it was within inches of where I had first noticed it. I pointed to the big bear. My companions looked up, admiring its size, then turned away.

Then the bear did a strange thing. It stood on its hind legs. With a push of its paw downward it broke off a large branch on one side; then, using the other paw, it stripped another branch off the other side. It stopped momentarily, and I said aloud, "That bear just stripped a couple of branches off that poplar sapling!" As I said the words, it reached higher and knocked another branch from the first side. The height would be about seven feet up the trunk. It sat down just as the smaller bear came over to it. Then the large one got up once more, stood tall on its hind legs, and stripped two more branches off the small sapling, one either side, just as a man would prune a tree. I was fascinated and said so.

"He's just stripped four more branches from that poplar!"

Neither man looked up. They were talking about something of more immediate interest. I continued watching the bear. It sat down and stared out over the dump for a long moment. Again it stood to its full height, leaning against the small tree. This time it put a paw around the sapling, reared up to its full height, and turned its head at an angle. It bit the top of the sapling off like a piece of spaghetti! The full six feet of the top, with branches jutting out that distance all around it, tumbled to the foot of the tree. The big animal then turned away as if it had enjoyed its amusement and began to walk slowly up the incline toward the timbered top of the high bluff.

"Did you guys see that?" I asked.

I was so amazed at what the bear had been doing that I had been speechless. The sapling was two inches thick where the bear had neatly topped it right after "pruning" it. It was the same type of wilful act that I had done to trees with a hatchet during my youth.

Just why the animal did it I have no idea, unless it was a form of play, a conquering act of sorts, a self-gratification. A "bear tree"?

When the act was completed, the animal had simply walked away, leaving the seven-foot-high stump of a totally stripped poplar sapling.

The Redhead II

She paused as the acrid scent of ants came from nearby. Working her nostrils, she felt the slight drool of moisture from the nasal membranes wetting the edges of the black, rubbery flesh of her nose. The faint odor was coming from a rotting log with one end partially covered by undergrowth. The exposed section of the timber lay where the granite of the Appalachian Shield still thrust its glacially smoothed surface above the sparse loam. She could hear sounds of ants moving, both under the log and in the minute channels the colony had carved in its dry interior.

She stared at the timber and noted the scurrying passage of ants from under the dry, exposed end. Casually her long tongue flicked out, drawing back with it three ants that had just left the cover of the rotting wood. She swallowed them with the fresh saliva activated by the expectation of her favorite food. A deft paw hooked over the exposed log end, and like ice tongs the claws deeply penetrated the rotting wood. Almost effortlessly, using one forepaw braced on the granite for leverage, she tore a two-foot section of wood from the rotting side of the timber. A flurry of disturbed ants scurried among the sundered channels, and white eggs and grubs fell to the ground, where her pink tongue quickly licked them up. Her attention was drawn to the sudden, frantic ant activity in the exposed log interior, as the shiny, black, adult insects tried to protect the exposed eggs, grasping them in their pincers as they rushed for the newly exposed channels leading back into the torn wood. With quick, deft movements of her tongue, she licked the milling ants and their pupa into her mouth. When the insects were cleaned from the fresh surface, her claws once more hooked into the timber, and the main claws went deeper under the round of the log. With a rending sound the log tore free from the earth and undergrowth, revealing a trough of rotted bark filled with ant channels and swarming with its denizens. She licked avidly, the flavor of formic acid tickling her taste buds, a tingling sensation to which she had become almost addicted. Whenever ants were readily available, she would neglect berries, roots, grasses, even carrion.

Once more her paw was tearing at the rotting wood. The demolition and pursuit had been noisy, her preoccupation intense as she licked up the bonanza.

Without warning the hot animal scent came abruptly to her. It was another bear, in her territory, very close by. Instinctively her head flicked over her shoulder, in the direction of the source of the odor.

Barely obscured by the shadow of the nearby undergrowth, the glistening obsidian coat of a male bear revealed his presence. He too was preoccupied, his nose buried deeply in the loam where she had urinated earlier, on her way toward the ant log. The other animal was so engrossed in the scent that he did not see her, and she stayed completely still. Something primal was opening within her, a strange feeling of welcoming stronger than her accustomed defensiveness and territorialism.

Slowly she raised her head, scenting the air. Her movement was immediately caught by the male, who was less than thirty feet away. He was quite large, an animal she had never seen in or near her territory.

The male's advance was deferential, almost mincing, as he walked pigeon-toed to within ten feet. From his throat came an almost melodic gurgle, and the way he extended his head was not aggressive. His nose was working energetically in an effort to ascertain the estrous quality of her scent. A slight, almost involuntary woof escaped from her throat, but she did not flee or raise her hackles. Encouraged, the male sidled slowly up to her, moving to the area of her rump. Quickly she spun around and away from him.

He stood still momentarily, then gently extended his snout toward hers with a downward thrust of his large head. She responded by touching her snout to his. He moved along her side, brushing her gently until his head was even with her rear. She braced herself to jump away, but something held her back. The warmth of his breath and tongue aroused her, and she pressed back against his shoulder with her rump.

Suddenly, both bears were startled by a loud whoosh of air suddenly expelled from another bear's tightly vented mouth. Then came a bellowing sound, quickly

punctuated by the sharp snapping of canine teeth against the teeth of the lower jaw. The noise shattered the silent moments of the budding love affair. Then, without further warning, the hurtling bulk of the enormous black bear of the ridge-tops struck the smaller male's shoulder. The power of the strike bowled him over twice, throwing him into the short undergrowth.

Almost immediately he was on his feet, head down, facing the larger bear, which had stopped short and was eyeing the female speculatively.

In that instant, the urge for battle burst forth in the younger bear. His retaliatory charge almost caught the large bear in the midsection, but the instantaneous reaction of the older animal showed his experience. The younger bear's bite missed the older one's front shoulder as his fangs slid harmlessly through the thick fur, and the larger bear responded by sinking his teeth deeply into the young adversary's exposed front shoulder. Pained, the younger one wrenched quickly away from the fangs, leaving a rush of blood from the torn hide.

In an instant, both bears were up on their hind legs. Like two heavyweight boxers, but twice as fast in the delivery of their swipes, they sparred. The larger bear was many pounds heavier and four inches higher at the standing shoulder. He feinted with his head as if to bite. When the smaller animal lunged, mouth open, the larger bear struck viciously with his heavy forepaw into his opponent's extended neck, knocking him off his feet. Immediately the weight of the larger animal was smashing heavily down upon his adversary's kicking body, pinning him down as he attempted vainly to rise. The sudden pain of fangs sinking into the back of his neck made him panic. This was the death hold!

All the strength of his six healthy years exploded. Pressing desperately upward, he threw the larger bear off its planted back feet and twisted away. The killing hold was broken. Freed, he plunged wildly off into the tangle of growth, while the larger bear merely lunged half-heartedly after him.

The reddish hue of the female had caught the sunlight, and her warm scent was surging into his nostrils. During the brief battle she had moved only when the two warring animals' efforts had ranged in her direction. She had simply watched the struggle with the apparent impartiality of a referee.

The new, pleasant gurgling sound now came from the throat of the victor. His scent, known to her and disliked for many years, seemed now to hold no threat. He approached her in a possessive, pigeon-toed walk, head turned slightly aside, as if to show her his lack of aggression. Their noses touched briefly. He moved purposefully along her side, the brushing of his fur against hers no longer disconcerting.

CHAPTER 3

What Is It Like in a Bear Den?

Warmth from the previous hot July evening had left a heavy dew on the metal tailgate of my camper. The surrounding grasses of the forestry department compound were as if doused by sprinkler. Through the spaces between the surrounding trees, I saw the brightness of late dawn sparking from the calm surface of the adjacent lake. When I had arrived the evening before, it had been too late to look at "Big Brownie," the name that I had attached to the animal captured and handled earlier that day. He had seemed to suffer from the unaccustomed heat of the narrow tunnel of steel that had entrapped him. The drugs had worn off, but there were still the effects of his thunderous charges at the unyielding wire cage and the bruises from his leaps at the top meshes, which, like springs, had shot him heavily back to earth. It must have been a shock to an animal that had known nothing but unchallenged freedom, always the master, to be incarcerated. I wondered about the thought processes of animals, why we credit them with neither emotions nor wisdom, denying them the ability to "figure things out." Perhaps it is our own vanity that makes us want to "tame" them, or subdue them to our own whims, and that denies other animals a soul. I do not believe the popular view. We wonder at their "instincts," challenge their reasoning power, accept them as dumb; then they show us marvelous abilities, such as the power to home (yes, bears do it also) over hundreds, even thousands, of miles, to the places of their origins. We interpret their feats as some strange power involved with the earth's magnetism, but never to memory or to reasoning ability.

Why does a salmon remember that substance in the water of its own home stream and return through thousands of blind underwater miles to the gravels from which it was hatched? How did my springer spaniel Trudy learn to climb a ladder and follow me up onto my roof after she had seen me working there for several days? Did she watch from the ground and "figure out" that act of climbing? I don't know.

After I carried her to the ground, and she reclimbed the ladder, I said: "Trudy, you figured out how to get *up* there. Now you can damn well figure out how to get *down*! You've seen me come down backwards, carrying you. Maybe you've got that figured out too!" And I stayed on the ground, leaving her whining expectantly at the top of the ladder. She actually tried to back down but could not seem to figure out where to put her hind feet next. I watched her feeling blindly for the ladder rungs, prodding into empty space. She did that several times, meanwhile beseeching me with her eloquent spaniel eyes, at which I shook my head firmly, a gesture she knew was final. She sat down for a moment, actually staring at the ladder. Then, without any further hesitation, she faced downward through the nearest rungs and, placing first one front foot and then the other on the next downward aluminum rung, she came down the ladder *head first*. Sometime, you might just try that! Thereafter she repeatedly followed me up and down. I cannot get it through my head that she did not "figure" that out, using definite reasoning power. I would never question the emotional attachment of Trudy, or any alley cat or pedigreed dog, or Anna's hummingbird (which actually sings to us and stays all winter). Why does the cat with its belly full snuggle into a lap or seek a caressing hand while brushing at your leg? Why does my dog bring in the morning paper from the gate a hundred feet away when simply told, "Paper"? Why does the hummingbird, when its feeder is well filled, sit on the wire and actually sing for our attention, or "buzz" us when we are preoccupied and working in the garden? It will not go to any nearby flower. And why does it choose to sit out the cold winter snows, when it could, like all the rest of its kind, simply fly south for the winter?

Oh, did you say it has been "imprinted"? They have all been *imprinted*! Well, how about the ladder incident? How about the female hummingbird which, when chased by our protective male, flew right behind my head as I sat in the kitchen having breakfast. With her wings fanning my hair noticeably, she stayed there until I chased the male away from the window. How was she aware that I would defend her? I, a big hulk of slow-moving flesh that could crush her with an inadvertent swing of a clumsy fist. Okay! Those *are* morning thoughts. All the feelings that go with them had occasionally bothered me since the capture of the brown-hued bear.

Was he all right? Had he settled down? Figured things out?

Quietly, hoping not to disturb him, I walked to a place where I could look past the corner of the building and see him sitting on the high point in the entrance cage. His mien was one of dejection, front legs stiff, head hanging down from the shoulders at an angle, with his nose pointed toward the ground. Covertly, I watched him until I saw his head lift ever so slightly and swing in my direction, nostrils working. The slight draft of an early breeze had drifted my scent to him. I walked quietly to within ten feet of the cage wire. As I did so, his head came up to a more alert angle. My voice did not seem to have any effect upon him, not even the soothing tones I employed.

"Hi, ol' guy. You okay?" The words meant no more to him than a rustle of brush, but it was a relief to express my feelings for him. He turned his head away from me to stare at the wire fencing that prevented his escape into the timber beyond. When he did not look back at me again, I turned silently and walked away, somehow feeling justifiably rejected. There seemed to be dignity in his knowledge that the human who approached him so close in captivity would have run from him in fear in the wild. In the bush his own senses would at least have protected him from conflict with the interloper. Here, caged, there was nothing to be done. He simply had to accept the situation.

Back at the camper, I ate my breakfast thoughtfully. Well! "Big Brownie" was apparently settled down, obviously not much the worse for wear. Lynn Rogers was pleased with him as a specimen. The medical examination would be another trauma, but once more he would be unconscious of the inquisitive human need-for-knowledge exploration.

Rogers had said, "He will be a good specimen for Steve Durst's examination."

My own curiosity about Durst's examination had brought out the fact that his laboratories had developed a method of inserting lengths of plastic tubing into the circulatory system of humans, running the tube right through the aorta into the left vertricle of the heart. There an expanding bubble head on the tube closed off the circulation while instruments and graphs attached to the intricate system used for the operation recorded the resulting pressures. This information had led to better understanding and treatment of human cardiac problems. Big Brownie might well be entered into medical annals for reference in the treatment of future problems. His examination was set for this day.

Since the previous evening with Rogers among garbage-dump black bears, my apprehension had been steadily alleviated, and I was looking forward to assisting with, and photographing, the cardiac operation. Rogers has a way of inspiring confidence by imparting his own experiences and findings. His words of the day before, spoken while driving home, came back to me.

"Oh sure, Mike, I've had incidents with bears which, in retrospect, may have been more dangerous than I actually realized at the time. One big, very big, black did give me some cause for concern."

I looked over at him, where his eyes remained intent upon the road passing fast beneath his steering wheel. "Oh, what happened with that one, Lynn?"

He smiled and half looked at me. Then he looked quickly back to the road. "Well, it was during photography on the dump again. I was right down at the foot of the dump face, almost among the bears. I had taken the precaution of clearing a bit of debris away from me, in a circle, and was practically bedded down in the stuff so I could get close-up photographs of the bears as they fed nearby. I had been trying for several minutes to get a good shot of one of the larger ones. I think I had seen the other really big one come into the end of the dump, but its size didn't particularly register with me. My whole attention was fixed on getting the other two bears into proper focus. I didn't pay the new bear much heed."

He paused and looked into my steadily curious gaze. "Well. Perhaps, I first heard him breathe close by. He was standing on the edge of the area I had cleared out, a couple of feet away. And he seemed as big as a house. His presence had driven all the other bears off that area of the dump, and he was making the bears I was trying to get shots of nervous. I was startled by his closeness. I said, 'Go away! Go away!'"

Rogers was half smiling at the memory. I interjected a hurried question. "And, *did* he go away?"

Lynn shook his head emphatically. "No. He didn't. He took a couple of steps right up to where I was sitting, now almost rigid, knowing I couldn't react fast enough to do anything at all. I stared at him saying 'No! No!' His big head was right at my shoulder. All of a sudden he stuck out his big pink tongue and licked my bare arm right at the elbow.

"He licked your arm!" incredulously from me.

"Yes. He licked it twice, while I prayed and said in as firm a voice as I could muster, 'No! No!' Then he put his big paw on my shoulder, just as you would do to a man when you wanted to impress him with what you meant. I thought, 'Well, I'll just lie still. Try not to arouse him. Just lie *still*!' He pushed forward with his paw and shoved me right down onto the ground. No threat. No chomping of teeth. No whoosh. Just a silent push right onto my back. His strength was irresistible, just resolutely pushing me down. I stayed down, wondering just what was coming. I guess I was thinking my time was up. Then he just turned away and walked along the dump to see what goodies he had been able to drive the rest of the bears away from. All of them simply left as he moved along."

The story was one of the strangest that I have ever heard from any man. From some, I would have doubted it. Not from Lynn Rogers. I simply shook my head in wonderment.

"He just *left*—like that? No show or threat?"

"No. Simply accepted that I was no threat to him and walked off. Black bears will do almost anything to avoid trouble. When you watch them, you see that factor in their make-up. If another animal exhibits a dominant attitude and there is no good reason to dispute it, they don't."

I was still wondering about the incident. "And, if you had disputed the animal? What would he have done?"

"Who knows that. Now it's only hypothetical."

Earlier that day I had asked Lynn about his handling of more than five hundred bears in at least twelve hundred trappings and markings. Had he been injured? He had pulled up his sleeve and exposed his right arm, wrist to elbow. A long white scar ran up the inside of the forearm to the elbow. It wasn't that of a knife cut or an operation scar. At the bottom end of the long scar and on the hand there were also light-hued marks filled in with scar tissue. To me, now, they were obviously the bites of a bear. "You aren't unscathed then, Lynn."

"No. Those are the only major ones. They were my own fault. I was demonstrating bear handling and marking to a bunch of students with a bear under anaesthesia. I must have used a lesser dose than was necessary. The bear came out of it more quickly than I had expected, and I tried to hold the animal down for another administration of anaesthetic. The bear scratched and bit me before I got it under control. It wasn't much—a bit painful at the time. My main worry was whether it might become septic. Bites often do."

I nodded emphatically. "It is a very bad factor. Doctors and physicians worry more about infection than anything else—common bacterial infection."

He nodded and named the bacteria.

"Any other incidents, Lynn?"

"Oh, a couple. Four of us were trying to handle a small black bear, a young adult we had just released from a snare. It gave us a bad time, trying to get away. Each of us moved into positions to stop it from running off."

"Was it fully free of the snare?"

"Yes, but, we didn't want to lose it, so we surrounded it, preventing it from moving out of the circle. It would rush at an opening. We would close up, and it would pull back. It was near the road, and a car with a tourist in it stopped. The man, who had seen what was going on, offered to help."

"He wanted to *help* you with a bear at large?"

Lynn laughed good-humoredly at my disbelief. "That's what *we* thought. But he said he was used to handling animals, was a rancher from out west. With his help we managed to subdue the bear under our combined weight, and we got him sedated and marked."

"You must be nuts at times, Lynn!"

"There are times, when you look back, that you wonder at just what got into you!" he admitted.

The vision of Lynn going into the bear cage ahead of the trap containing the big black bear the previous day was still clear in my mnd. It was obvious that Dr. Lynn Rogers was aware of the risks, the calculated risks of his profession. I had to say something.

"You could have become a dentist with less study!"

We both laughed.

At eight-thirty next morning Lynn was again busy in his laboratory. He told me that the crew was bringing in another, smaller, black bear that had just been trapped. He had earlier examined the big male bear and decided it wasn't in top shape. They had elected to use the newly trapped animal. Steve Durst and his fiancée, Carrole Houliston, came into the office and were introduced. I asked Durst if he minded my taking photographs of the medical procedure. He was fully agreeable. Photographs, he pointed out, were always useful in after-procedure examinations. Durst was a big, bearded, capable, easy-natured fellow. Carrole Houliston was small and blond, pretty and robust, fitting her jeans well, suntanned. And she proved to be very efficient. She was Durst's assistant, like him a qualified lab technician. He had developed the cardiology apparatus widely used in hospitals and had made it portable, so that it could be taken to the patient. It would be the first time the equipment had been used on a bear.

About an hour later, the young crew of the previous day were all on hand. Added to the spectators were Lynn's former associate, biologist Jeff Marioni, and the local staff. The trapping crew, assisted by Lynn, carried the dual-barrel trap between the buildings and to the lawn in front of Lynn's office.

A clean tarpaulin had been laid out on the grass, and on another cover beside it was the medical paraphernalia.

As soon as the trap was at rest, Lynn administered the required dose of tranquilizer by hypodermic syringe, enough to bolster the dose that had quieted the bear for transport. A few minutes later, Durst looked into the end of the trap.

"She's licking. Nearly under, Lynn."

"Give her a couple of minutes, yet. Are you ready, Steve? Okay, we'll try her."

Lynn prodded a small stick through the holes in the steel container. There was no reaction. He went to the other end of the barrel and examined the head, touching the mouth area with the stick. The animal was inert. They lifted the door, and Rogers leaned in and grabbed a hind leg. Eager hands took hold as the bear slid out. She was lifted into a rope sling, where she was weighed. She was a small bear, weighing not more than 165 pounds. When she was laid out on her back, legs extended, Durst shaved the area near her crotch, just as attendants would have prepared a hairy human. He marked the area for insertion of the tube.

Rogers's crew were busy measuring head size, claw length, pad spread, dental conditions, in fact, some measurements I wasn't aware would have the slightest scientific use. Books and printed pads for the required data were in the hands of the recorder, while another person did the measurements and checked the calipered figures to be sure they were correct. One young man took a pair of dental pliers from the set of gear and inserted the pincers behind the lower incisor tooth. He pushed the tool down into the gum and very carefully closed it on the small premolar tooth, then began to work it free. It was a tiny, nonutilitarian-looking tooth, one that the bear would not miss but that would be very useful in reading the age and past health of the bear. Once freed of the lower jaw, it was carefully deposited in a bag that would be attached to the other vital statistics. Meanwhile, Durst made incisions with medical scalpels he had removed from sealed hygienic bags. He carefully stanched the blood from the incisions and sterilized the wounds with alcohol. At the same time, Houliston was readying the equipment, checking dials.

Moments later, Durst had the tube, which had been inserted at an incision in the crotch area, in the aorta. As carefully as if the animal had been a human on a high-priced hospital operating table, the vital signs of the bear had been monitored. Pulse and respiration had been checked, nostrils cleaned, throat examined for possible blockage of breathing, temperature recorded, and—of utmost interest—blood pressures recorded. It was difficult not to believe one was actually watching a surgical operation on a human heart patient, given the care and the detail, the satisfaction at the results. I saw Durst's face becoming more relaxed as the operation went along. I couldn't help remarking, "Is the patient going to survive, Doctor?"

"She certainly is! A very healthy bear! And the data are all very similar to human records. Amazingly so!" he answered happily.

Soon all the dials had been checked long enough, the lengthy tube removed, and the insertion point taped up and sterilized. The bear was still inert, her breathing as if in deep, regular sleep. Blood samples required by both Durst and Rogers had been taken in their vials to the nearby refrigerator. I heard Lynn's questioning voice.

"May we keep the paraphernalia, Steve?" he asked.

"Sure, Lynn. It isn't of any further use to us. It would just be discarded. All we keep are the recording instruments and the data." He nodded toward the bear. "She looks like she is coming out of it."

Rogers looked at the animal's head, examined her eyes carefully. He touched her head almost affectionately. "She gave us a lot of data." Then he turned to his crew. "She will probably stay down until you get her away."

"Are you going to do the same operation on the large male?" I asked.

Durst shook his head. "No need to. We got all the information we need from this one."

Rogers nodded his head in agreement. "No, Mike. All we have to do with him is record his measurements and general data and put a radio collar on him. He is new to us, and I'd like to get some data on him."

I had been busy taking pictures of the bear being loaded into the station wagon. Lynn came over and motioned toward his truck.

"Let's go, Mike! You can see her on her way!"

The Minnesota forest lands were an interesting contrast with the logged-off and regrowing forest areas of my province of British Columbia. While Pacific coastal forests were logged down to the underbrush, then slash-burned, leaving oven-brick bare earth hummocked only with charcoaled stumps, the Minnesota method seemed to be a clear-cut, leaving the slashed forest to regenerate from among its fallen debris. Because much of the forest there is deciduous, mixed with only medium-sized coniferous trees, the regeneration appeared to be quite different. There was a heavy ground cover, of low brush, with deciduous tree growth almost equal to the regrowing conifers, giving the impression that, like most northerly lands, it would be tough going for animal and man. It would provide the abundant bear population with plenty of cover and endless berry and nut bushes.

The logging roads, however, were equally rugged. They were narrow, their surfaces pitted and potholed. The curves and twists were comparable to those of coastal mountain roads but had none of the breathtaking cliff drop-offs common to that terrain. It was an uncomfortable ride, through an indescribable maze. Lynn's eleven years there had prepared him well to locate this or that fork in the road, something that amazed me as he picked out those twists and turns. Within half an hour of the major operation and examination of her cardiology, the small female bear was gently carried (it is al-

Lynn Rogers with his research crew in Ely, Minnesota, 1981.

ways a surprise to me to witness the gentleness and clinical care with which these animal-marking crews handle their precious charges) up a little spur road and deposited in mid-path, where she could recover with ample room and have an open road ahead of her on which to escape her observers.

The recovery symptoms, the movements of the tongue that could be described as a licking motion, had been going on for some time. The front legs had shown more voluntary movement, and some muscle reaction was beginning in the rear quarters, which usually are the last section of the animal to revive. As she became more mobile, we watched the bear intermittently. Carrole Houliston and I picked blueberries from low bushes, and I found a profusion of wild strawberries giving off their ripe, pungent aroma. There was no doubt that these ridges had sufficient bear food of that kind. Carrole brought me a handful of blueberries from a patch she had found. Their aroma was almost equal to that of the strawberries. I munched them, watching the small female bear become more and more active. After about five minutes of increasing movement, she tried to arise, only to tumble drunkenly. This effort occurred several times, until finally she coordinated her hind and front legs. After falling several more times, she got irresolutely to her feet and headed in the direction in which she had been pointed when deposited on the spur road. She was feeling the aftereffects of the drugging, but her recovery time was good, and her movements and instincts to remove herself from human company were normal. The marking and tagging and the cardiac information that she had provided would be of utmost value to further studies of the relations between bears and man.

Reluctantly I got into the truck with the others for the drive back. Shortly afterward we all had gathered by the wire cages at the station. Rogers had decided that, following the heat and trauma of the previous day, cardiology tests might be detrimental to the big brown-hued bear. Now, however, in view of its impending release he prepared the tranquilizer syringe for injection. While two of the crew attracted the bear's attention, Lynn poked a hypodermic needle quickly and deeply into its rear quarters. We all watched quietly as the large animal lost control of his locomotive abilities. Eventually he settled down quietly to his resting place at midcage. When two tests with a long pole evoked little or no response, Rogers and his crew entered the enclosure, lifted the bear out of the cage, carried it over to the space between the two buildings, and there weighed it in a sling. Lack of appetite for the food earlier offered, dehydration from the heat in the trap, and his own mighty efforts to smash his way out of the cage, had taken their toll on the bear. Despite his huge bulk and outsize height, the bear weighed only 258½ pounds, perhaps the regulation size for a football linebacker. My guess had been off nearly twenty pounds, and Lynn's half of that. We were both mildly surprised.

Once the bear was laid out on the tarpaulin, the young crew swarmed over him. They made plaster casts of front and rear feet; they measured the skull, from nose to vertebrae; and they performed dental checks, removing a premolar. They tattooed a number on the inside of his lip, measured the individual teeth and recorded their condition, noted body girth and overall length, and took blood samples in small vials. One of the young women (I could scarcely believe it!) was delicately calipering the testicles and measuring the penis. It was difficult for me to conceal a smile. She was experiencing some difficulty in taking the penis measurement. Rogers watched the measurements and written notations, then leaned over the bear at its stern.

"I'll check those measurements," he said quietly.

His hand went deftly to the end of the penis near the testicles and pushed quickly forward. The penis bone was thrust well forward, beyond its sheath, and following one quick measurement with the steel tape he gave the length in centimeters to the recording crew. There were ripples of laughter, but none of the crew, including the young woman, seemed to be embarrassed. Rogers picked up one of the clipboard sheets and glanced at it quickly. "Have we forgotten anything?" he asked. Nothing had been neglected. "Okay. Let's get the collar on him."

The collar itself is like a tough plastic dog collar and has a transistorized

Dr. Rogers collaring a black bear.

radio transmitter in a miniature box securely attached to the belting. The transmitters are equipped with batteries that last up to a year, all the while sending out a beep signal strong enough to be received ten miles off. Turning the receiving antenna until the signal is most audible reveals the location of the bear. Continuous travel in line with the loudest reception will bring the observer into contact with the animal. If it moves continuously, the searcher can change directions in pursuit. The later models also indicate whether the animal is at rest or moving about. Even the semidormant movements of a bear in its den cause variations of the signal. The latest units are so powerful that their signals have been recorded even through the earthen layers of a den.

Thus a collar provides information previously obtained only by person-to-animal contact or, at best, by close visual observations, such as Lynn Rogers's winter visits to the dens. Obviously, visits to dens will still be required for physical examinations, but an Alaskan scientist informed me that, with the establishment of more satellite stations, it is possible that channels will be available to relay signals from bears (especially those in the Arctic and Alaska) as they meander over the wild country. As a bear moves, the radio signal will establish its position each time the satellite crosses its path in continuous orbit, thereby recording miles traveled, hours taken, periods of rest. Thus we will have a full account of the collared bears' activities and their hour-to-hour positions in their habitats. Such data will reveal, even in an uncharted habitat, the areas used by bears, the time spent seal or salmon hunting, the time in pasturelands or areas of berry growth, and the periods of dormancy. Such valuable data are the raw material from which scientists are hoping to determine the territorial and habitat needs of such species, and thus protect the animals' futures. The collar is essential in furthering human understanding of bears.

Watching Rogers and his crew prepare that collar, taping the waterproofing and other protective materials carefully into place, was a lesson in how scientific research sometimes depends upon electronic engineering. Rogers fitted the collar carefully on the neck. Marking the proper length for the plastic belting, he used a heavy punch tool to pierce buckle-pin holes in the plastic belting. He then cut off the excess length and began to fit the unit. The collar was adjusted until it was loose enough to move with moderate pressure, but could not be pushed easily over the ears and the larger, rounded back of the skull. The collar could not be readily torn off by the bear's paws, or by some object accidentally thrust under it while the animal was freely moving through bushes and trees.

When the fitting was correct, and the final tape binding and locking in place were done, the signal was tested on a nearby monitor. All this time Big Brownie had been totally unconscious. Now, however, occasional licking movements of the tongue were becoming evident—the initial signs that the powerful drugs were wearing off.

The operation was complete at last. The metal ear tags, a different color in each ear, glistened in the sunlight; and the wounds of punch, plier, and needle had all been sterilized and dressed with astringent ointments to prevent infection. Big Brownie was showing some slight movement in the legs, and the pulsing of his large, pink dangling tongue was more evident.

Rogers was talking with his crew. "We'll take him in the jeep back to the spot where he was captured. Okay. You follow in my truck. Fine, let's get him into the center seat."

Six of the crew, assisted by Steve Durst, lifted the bear into the center seat of the station wagon, a four-wheel-drive vehicle, leaving the back space empty. Rogers was eager to get going.

"Hop in, Mike!"

"With that damn bear coming out of anaesthetic?"

He laughed, as did Steve and Carrole, who had said they wanted to accompany the bear to the release point to watch it recover. I turned to Carrole and pointed to the seat beside Lynn who was impatiently waiting at the wheel.

"You get in with Lynn—take the front seat!"

She smiled appreciatively. "Steve and I are going to get in the back space! *You* take the front seat, Mike!"

"I insist! I don't even *need* to go!"

I was watching the fairly regular tongue movements as Big Brownie lay relaxed on the double seat. His eyes were open, but unrecognizing in their stare. Carrole's mind was made up.

"No! Steve and I will ride in the back!"

And she followed him into the flat, load-carrying space behind the middle seat. I did not want to sit with my back to a large bear that was rapidly recovering from its injection. But Hell! If a small young woman was carefree enough to sit behind the bear, just where were my guts—er, lack of apprehension—that I would not sit in front. I got in, carefully turning to a position from which I could watch the bear. A few minutes earlier Lynn had said, "Oh, it's about fifteen miles from here. We should make it." *Should* make it? Lynn was turning the wheel for takeoff.

About the fifth mile out, just after passing two cars near a bend and beginning to pull uphill on a steep little slope, Rogers depressed the clutch and tried to shift gears. There was a slight grating sound, and the vehicle lost speed. Again he tried, but there was no movement in the gearshift. The jeep was slowing to a few miles per hour.

"Damn! She won't shift gears!" Lynn muttered.

"Stop her," I suggested, "and try shifting into gear with the motor stopped."

I turned to look at the bear. Its mouth movements were now regular. Rogers stopped the vehicle and attempted to shift the gears. Nothing worked. We were now in a vehicle with a recovering black bear—needless to say a good big one—miles from anywhere out on a highway. Attempting to sound casual, I said, "I guess you can give him another shot of tranquilizer?"

He nodded, but something told me that he didn't have any tranquilizer with him. He peered thoughtfully up and down the road.

"I don't want to release him here. He could get hurt on the road—or hurt someone who might be curious."

A car, with another one closely following it, shot by along the paved surface. The next vehicle, about a minute later, was a pickup truck. It stopped, and the driver leaned out the window.

"You folks in trouble? Can I help you?"

The sound of another vehicle approaching from the direction of home base could be heard over his voice. It was the follow-up truck, which had been delayed for a few minutes at the forestry installation. Lynn thanked the pickup truck driver for stopping, then strode back to the forestry truck, which had stopped behind us. In a minute he was back, saying, "We'll pick up my truck and transfer the bear to this one. We'll be back right away!"

I looked into the disabled jeep, where the bear was still inert but showing more signs of recuperation. Steve and Carrole were looking at me, unworried. They had been party to bear-tagging procedures with Rogers before. They were both familiar with the recovery symptoms of bears, too, which I was not.

"Doesn't look like it will be *too long* before he is up. I hope Lynn isn't too long."

Steve grinned in response.

"Yeah, Mike, we all do! Have you chosen your spot to be when he comes to?"

"Yeah, right on top of the jeep," I nodded emphatically.

"Ladies first, Mike!" said Carrole.

"Ladies first, Hell! Don't get in my way, that's all!"

She smiled in agreement at the humor of the situation.

Now who would expect the vehicle, formerly dependable on all types of terrain over thousands of miles, to become suddenly inert—even more so than the bear that was in it—on a highway remote (believe me, five miles felt remote) from all aid and habitation. Yeah, who would? And the minutes ticked away. Carrole and I went searching for blueberries. Cars passed. One or two of them offered aid in getting to a repair or towing service. How could we say casually, "Oh thanks! It's okay, we've already sent for help," and mean it? But we all did it. In the back of my mind was the thought, "Should I let *this one* get away," or should I just get in and casually explain that there was a bear in that vehicle, recovering from anaesthetic, and that I would just as soon be a couple of miles down the road from it when it did. I even thought of the time the motor of one of the planes in which I had been doing wartime reconnaissance work was suddenly on fire right beside my window. And I preferred *that*! A bear in the back seat is a hell of a lot more formidable to the uninitiated, believe me. Then came the sounds of the returning truck carrying Lynn. Quickly the bear was lifted from one vehicle to the other, and once again we piled in with it. In adamant support of their cause, Steve and Carrole rode with the slightly moving animal in the back of the pickup. Lynn was navigating the backroads now, adeptly swinging the wheel in order to keep passing branches from stinging those in back of the truck.

I asked Rogers, only once, if he thought the bear would stay under, and he nodded speculatively, shrugged. He seemed to be unworried.

At last, near a ridgetop, the truck came to a stop where at one edge of the road there was a slight drop-off into fairly thick alder brush and fern growth. This looked like a good spot for the bear to recover. The evening light was beginning to yellow. I got out and cleared a space in the entangling scrub alder, then trampled down some growth under an overhanging spread of hazelnut branches. Lynn and the crew, with Steve assisting, carried the bear down the slope. They lined it up with its feet slanted downward, its head over a slight hummock to keep it from swallowing its tongue. It was now moving all quarters with some mild spasmodic efforts. Its eyes were almost fully open and less glazed. I stared up at Lynn, who was watching the signs, and voiced my uppermost thought. "Will he be out soon?"

"He should be on his way in an hour. I gave him some tranquilizer to avoid any spasms during his withdrawal. They can convulse under the heavier drug and harm themselves. With the added tranquilizer they come around more slowly, but they are less likely to be harmed by their efforts to get up."

A last look back at Big Brownie revealed him lying as snug as an awakening cub in the little cleared depression beneath the hazelnut bushes.

A short distance along the road, Rogers spoke casually.

"Mike, do you remember that large bear I was telling you about—the nonaggressive big one that I called Big Mac that we tracked for ten years?"

"Yes, I do! Very well! The one that eventually disappeared. The one you used to check in his den during the winter."

"Yes. That's the one. Would you like to see his den while we are out this way?"

"I sure as hell would! I think we all would."

Steve and Carrole and the crew member who was with us all nodded in willing agreement. Rogers drove a short distance farther on, identified the road he was searching for, then drove on it for about a mile. He hesitated at a couple of branch roads, neither of which seemed different from any others in that Minnesota bush country. He took a fork to the west. At a spot of rising land with old forest timber still upon it, he stopped. We all piled out, following him into the forest. In three minutes of occasionally changing directions I was as lost as I would have been two days into a tropical jungle. Rogers seemed unconcerned, but was searching for identifiable terrain. We crossed a couple of swalelike valleys, proceeded along a ridge, over the top, and down. Lynn was changing direction more often. We were about quarter-way down the slope, an excellent location in which to discover deer, bears, and grouse: ideal forest cover with visible expanses below and an easy exit over the ridge. Rogers began to move along the slope and slightly upward to where it curved back into an adjoining ridge. He stopped about thirty feet away.

"There it is!" He pointed downward.

When we arrived in a bunch beside him, the opening into the ridge face was barely apparent. Beside a channel of indigenous rock, a fissure about thirty inches high, and nearly the same width at its bottom, was disclosed only by its dark shadows against the other terrain. Fern and brush grew close to it, and a person not knowing the location could have searched for months and not found it. I nodded toward it.

"Anything in there now, Lynn?"

"I don't think so," he laughed.

Wishing to get surrounding views of the den's location and a photograph that might show it, I climbed down the slope and to one side, thence upward and around it in a broad circle. I was also looking for some indication that a regular path led to it. There was no such evidence. I went back to the knot of people.

"Is *this* one of the dens we might have visited last spring if I had been able to get here?"

"It could have been. It's been regularly inhabited during winters. Would you like to look into it now?"

"Is there anything in there?"

Lynn shook his head. His assistant grinned, and said, "No, Mr. Cramond, there *isn't* anything in there! I checked it out."

"Today?" I grinned back.

"Just *now*!" he laughed, as did the others.

Even at that I didn't want to go in face first. It was a strange, inexplicable feeling, entering a known bear den just after releasing a bear within a short distance. Hell, a couple of miles! I put my feet into the narrow approach crevice, turned around to insert my buttocks first, then quite slowly backed into the hole. As the dusk of the interior began to surround me it was eerier than I had expected. The den went inward at a slight slope for the first two feet, then it leveled off into a dry dirt floor, with no odor, no mustiness or dampness, the chamber's breadth widening out sufficiently to accommodate man or beast in comfort. Without a light to examine it, I felt around for walls, abruptly deciding that I did not want to back right up to the end of it, regardless of the fact that it was otherwise unoccupied. Perhaps that temerity had kept me alive for sixty-nine years. Whatever the instinct, I had it to get out of there. And I am not claustrophobic! So this was a bear's denning spot. Given sufficient food and clothing, even a man could have lived in it during a winter and survived. I began to move out.

The click of cameras was audible as I poked my face from the aperture. I handed one of the smiling group my own camera, for photographs to be kept in my own files. All of them had had such experiences. They were as amused by my reactions as I was, even more so.

So! I had now been into a bear den!

On the way back to the road our party split up. Two of them got lost in one direction, and the third in another. I stayed on Lynn Rogers' trail, and that was the only reason I came directly out. The two of us whistled and honked the truck horn for ten minutes to give the others their direction. And, somewhat embarrassed, they admitted that they had needed the help. I felt tolerably better about that.

The Redhead III

Still uncertain about the large male, yet newly willing to endure the closeness of one of her kind, the reddish bear moved hesitantly away from the brush of the large male's shoulder on her haunches. The warmth of his breath close to her vent was disturbing. Suddenly the large bear's huge paw pulled her towards him, but she bolted away from that intimate pose. The boar gurgled a discernibly pleasant and reassuring sound, and it stopped her. Still faced away from him, however, she was ready for flight. His attention was directed to her hind end once more. She stood quietly, irresolute.

During the warm, sunlit hour which followed, she and the male continued to flirt. The male's pink tongue was panting, but his patience earned her growing trust, wearing down her urge to flee. Abruptly, it became a strong urge to be receptive to him.

As she stood once more for the caress at her rear, his powerful forepaws suddenly clasped her well down in front of her haunches. A heavy weight bore suddenly down upon her. She felt a sharp pain, followed by a feeling of complete receptivity.

The boar roamed idly with her for three days of intermittent mating. Twice he chased away the young boar he had earlier wounded. Then on the morning of the fourth day the large male became restless.

In the air, noticeable even to herself, was the vague estrous scent of the neighboring she-bear. Late in the afternoon, when the newly initiated female awakened from a deep sleep in the sun-warmed grasses, she was conscious that the big animal was no longer close by. Instead, more strongly, she smelled the distinct scent of the younger male bear, and none too distant.

Still attracted to the large male, she arose and nosed about, searching for his trail. It led away, in the direction of the other she-bear's territory. The scent was faint, telling her that he had moved away quite some time ago.

The gurgle of the younger male bear, a signal which she had grown accustomed to from the departed boar, sounded nearby. The sound did not alarm her. Instead, she watched the bushes from which they had come.

Hesitantly the smaller male poked his nose from the deep cover of bushes, and the gurgle sounded again.

She remained in her position in the open, alert but not alarmed. The younger bear emerged timidly from the cover of the brush. He raised his nose warily, scenting the air. Fully in view, he picked up the scent of the recently departed big boar. Its quality reassured him: it was not fresh.

Tentatively she watched his body movements and easily read their language. Washed by the late afternoon sun, the other animal's coal black coat glistened. He turned resolutely toward her. Caked blood showed clearly on his shoulder, and she was aware that he was the male who had first approached her, before the battle. The mating urges within her were still strong.

She accepted the advances of the young bear and even encouraged him. Once more she was fulfilling an instinct stronger than that of territorialism. Fully involved, they roamed about together through one afternoon and the next morning.

Abruptly, about midafternoon of the second day, she turned on the male, swatting his sniffing head aside. Momentarily stunned, he backed off. She charged him. He swiveled quickly and plunged into the surrounding bushes. Only twice more did he attempt to approach her.

The last time he did so, she bit him in the previously bloodied shoulder, and he immediately retreated from sight and hearing. She made a determined trek to the far reaches of the southern end of her territory. There an amber stream trickled endlessly over dark boulders. The brush was thick and nearly impenetrable; no visitor could approach silently. For much of the balance of the week she slept, occasionally stripping berries and buds from the thick surrounding bushes.

Twice during her retreat she heard the approach of other bears whose scent told her they were males. Each time she departed quickly, putting at least a mile between herself and the visitor. One of the animals had been the large boar, who was returning through her territory to his haunts on the long, high ridges.

Within her reproductive organs, two of her ova had accepted the spermattozoa from her first encounter. For the next five months the embryos would remain almost dormant, remote from the placenta which would later nurture them to growth.

During the rest of the hot summer and into the fall, she frequented the most fertile areas of her territory, constantly feeding on berries, nuts, roots, and ants. Later the first fallen acorns and hazelnuts dropped to the earth, which was still warmed daily by the sun. She gathered the mast and even climbing into the oaks to bite and shake the acorns loose. She stripped filbert bushes as far up as she could reach, or broke off the higher branches to a level where she could glean their bounty. Each kind of food in the wild became bulk in her growing belly. The inner fats covering her kidneys and abdomen bulged her paunch. Layers of fatty tissue were gathering around her ribs and muscles and eventually over her back. Her weight almost doubled from the previous spring, but it was a burden she carried gracefully. The exercise of her constant foraging had also built larger muscles and sinews. The first frosts of October found her rotund and well prepared for the snows that were soon to come. Still she foraged daily. A second hunger from her interior, of which she was unaware, was directing her.

After a longer than usual Indian summer, in late October she found herself eating more of the mature grasses. Only a light flurry of snow had come, and it now lay only in the shadiest spots. There it partially covered the steadily browning layer of leaves that once had been a brilliant yellow, red, or orange.

Almost reluctantly, she moved to the higher ground of her territory, where the more exposed rock formations provided overhanging ledges and contours. Finding that her previous winter den was inadequate, she sought a less vulnerable hideaway. As if she knew that this winter was going to be a special one, she searched until she found a vacant crevice under a big tree root. She began to tear aside the brush and fallen leaves. Beyond the roots she reached the black opening of a small tunnel. She sniffed into that chamber.

The scent of squirrel or other rodent dung was distinct, but very old. She pushed in farther and discovered a chamber somewhat deeper than her own shoulder height and as wide as half her length. She backed out and stood uncertainly for some time, staring into the newly uncovered denning area, then felt suddenly hungry for grasses.

Without a backward look at her accomplishment, she headed for one of the small, grassy meadows at the foot of the ridge. There she licked and bit the dried, frostbitten remnants of grass until their bulk appeased the hunger. Her appetite had been gradually diminishing for two weeks, ever since the first major snowfalls had spilled from an atmosphere that was growing colder by the day.

One evening the falling snow curtained the open meadow. Shaking the gathering flakes from her heavy fur, she trotted back toward the den. After the snow abruptly gave way to bright sunlight, she lazed around the outside of the den for two days. On the third day she began to gather branches and leaves, carrying them into the den chamber in her mouth or in one crooked paw. As they accumulated, she pushed the materials deeper into the den. Inside she gathered the materials into the corner farthest from the den mouth. Several more times she left the tunnel to gather branches and leaves. Twice she forayed to the meadows, looking for dry grasses to eat.

Following a short, bitterly cold spell, the air temperature heightened. New snow began to pelt heavily into the mouth of the small cavern. Eyeing the thick snowfall, she turned and retreated to the collection of branches and leaves and lay down comfortably. Sleep came easily. She stayed there for two whole days, and the mouth of the den became blocked with fresh snow.

Arising only once, almost reluctantly, she pushed her head tentatively through the entrance and peered outside. All down the slopes the foot-deep blanket of new snow had drifted and filled in the small gullies. Its weight had pushed the light berry bushes flat to the ground and had bent the taller, nut-bearing ones into arches, their ends tied down in the frozen drifts. A rain was drizzling lightly through the mist. Vaguely the she-bear recognized the seasonal condition that would bring a crust of ice with a knifelike edge onto the fallen snows, ice that would cut heavy paws. Nowhere was there any sign of food. The lately consumed grasses in her belly had completely alleviated the intestinal grumblings that commonly had followed a meal of mast or berries. Unknown to her, the grasses were forming an anal plug, and the flow of digestive juices had completely ceased. Lethargy was overtaking her.

She backed toward the newly contoured mass of branches and leaves and sat down. The glare of light from the hole which she had just poked through the entrance curtain was causing her to blink. Turning her head to one side, she circled several times and lay down in a foetal position, paws curled inward toward her face.

Within minutes she slept. Three times, when the light of the tunnel entrance brightened during minor thaws, she turned somnolently, before easing her body into a newly comfortable position. Opening her eyes brought her no comprehension of her surroundings. A continuous heavy sleep came upon her.

Several days after the onset of denning, and after a series of restless turnings in her bed, something within her body responded and changed without her volition. The previously dormant ova, earlier fertilized by the spermatozoa, attached themselves individually to the uterus. Within hours they were deeply implanted, and the warm blood of the mother began to supply the nutrients demanded for continuing growth. The tiny foetuses of the two cubs, a male and a female, began to grow within her womb, drawing from her their sustenance.

CHAPTER 4

He Has Tapped a Grizzly on the Nose

I was thinking about Stan Price, the "man who taps grizzly bears on the nose with a long stick when they get too close," when the pilot on the Alaska flight, scheduled to land in Juneau at 9:15 A.M., announced that there was fog and rain over the landing strip—near zero visibility. I recall he said over the intercom, "We'll have a look at it."

I could feel the tilt of the aircraft downward. The plane broke through the layer of cloud, and a second layer of even frothier cloud appeared beneath. Abruptly we were into the mist. Even the wing tips were invisible. I know. I looked.

The plane came down, down, down. There was a shuffle of wing flaps, a change in the pitch of the motor, and we were level. Abruptly, the motors roared, the nose tilted upward, and we were headed for the skies again.

Landing aborted. That is what the stewardess said. "Aborted." She walked forward against the angle of the climbing plane. I leaned over and said, "Where do we land now, miss?"

She smiled, "Oh, he was just taking a look. He's going to try again, sir. We may get in yet."

"Oh, thank you," I said and looked at the buckle of my safety belt.

About ten minutes later I once again felt the slight tilt downward in the big airplane. "Oh no, not again!" I cannot help looking out of plane windows. I hope to see what happens. Suddenly there was water below the shredded fog that covered most of the barely visible land. And right alongside us, well *above* the height of the aircraft, was a mountainside covered with green timber. Then fog blotted it out. A vaguely familiar landfall seemed to be right alongside. The flaps went down, we were leveling out, and it *had to be* a landing. At this point, he could not abort. Buildings shot by at a terrific speed, still well below. Then a roar of the motors and the bump of wheels.

I smiled. "Alaska, bring on your grizzly bears!" I thought.

Behind me the passengers had been thumping their feet and cheering. They are a rugged lot, those Alaskans. I said to the stewardess, who had stopped to open the luggage rack above me, "I've never before heard a cheer like that upon landing." She smiled. "Oh, they do that almost every time we put down in Juneau."

The last time I had been in Juneau was as a thirteen-year-old runaway working as a porter aboard the old Canadian Pacific steamship *Princess Charlotte*, in the year 1926. Now a built-up coastal port, the city lies some distance from the airport. A phone call to the main hotel told me that virtually all accommodations in town were booked up, but the typical Alaskan hospitality began. The clerk arranged a small room in their "heritage" hostelry. A Juneau lawyer I had met at the luggage area offered me a ride into town and squeezed my stuff into his small Japanese-made pickup. A lawyer driving a pickup? In Alaska they do! *Successful* lawyers. He told me he had been out to Admiralty Island where I was headed, had camped there regularly each year. He also said he was frightened of grizzlies.

I asked him why he went to a place that was known to have a lot of large coastal grizzlies. He laughed and said, "When you get out there, you'll see why we would brave grizzly bears. It is simply—so remotely beautiful."

My grin was spontaneous.

"And some beautiful *brown bears*?"

"Yes, that too!"

"Have you seen many grizzlies during your visits?"

"No, only a couple. We camp well away from the streams that they are working for salmon."

"Do you know Stan Price at Pack Creek, the grizzly man?"

"No, I don't know him, but I've read about him. We usually go to another part of the islands." Then he said appreciatively, "I sure wouldn't bang a grizzly bear on the nose and expect to get away with it—like he is supposed to do."

Stan Price of Pack Creek, Admiralty Island, had answered my letter by way of his remote two-way radio telephone just four days before. When my wife had handed me the telephone, the operator had asked if I would accept the charges from Admiralty Island. Upon my acceptance, I had first heard Stan's weathered old voice in greeting.

"If that's Mr. Cramond"—crackle, crackle on the wire—"you can come up anytime." Cracklings, then silence and more cracklings in my ear. "I'm on radio-phone, I don't hear you!"

"Mr. Price, I am a writer. I want to come up and do an interview for a book."

The static was loud and continuous, but I did hear a distinct pronouncement: "You'd better come soon! The grizzly bears are on the beach. They're taking salmon. They'll leave soon."

I shouted into the phone, "I'll try to get out there Tuesday or Wednesday."

Static interference was even louder, followed by a lengthy silence. Then, faintly, I heard, "Fine. You come soon. We'll see you"—more crackling, then what sounded like "Channel Five," and a final click.

I had not the vaguest idea how to get out to Pack Creek on Alaska's Admiralty Island, but a call to Alaska Airlines at least set up a Tuesday reservation for the flight from Seattle to Juneau. Someone in Juneau would know how to get out there.

I tried a Monday morning call to the Alaska Department of Fish and Game, where research biologist John Schoen confirmed that he knew of Stan Price and how to get out there, and he invited me to come on up.

My night in the "heritage hotel" with its single overhead light bulb and down-the-hall toilet brought back vivid fifty-six-year-old memories of evenings ashore, the mines and their workers, the "good-time gals," and the "one-horse street" that in 1926 had been recently hewn from the mountain forest. I looked through the wet window pane with awe at the new bustling city and taller buildings, now barely visible in the rain-fog, thinking that in half a century many things had changed.

The next morning was still wet, fogged in, drizzly, but I *had* made it "by Tuesday!" A short, water-soaked walk took me to the Department of Fish and Game, which was housed in a modern ten-story building near downtown Juneau. On the second floor a passing wildlife man in denims and windbreaker said, "Sure, I'll take you to John's office. Follow me!" And after threading through the network of typical game-department offices, past curing hides, animal skulls, outdoors gear, piles of files, and papers, we came to a small cubicle with a desk, two chairs, and other office materials—a workplace with barely room to put a coffee cup down. Over the desk papers John Schoen extended his hand and smile.

"You were inquiring about Stan Price, Mr. Cramond?"

"Yes. Please call me Mike. Yes, I'd like to get out to see him and do a definitive article about him and his place at . . ." I had forgotten the name. Schoen supplied "Pack Creek," and I continued, "Yes, Pack Creek. And try to get a proper perspective on him and his interaction with grizzly bears. Does he actually tap them on the nose if they come too close?"

Schoen looked straight at me, knowing my words were meant to be exactly as they sounded—provocative.

"Well, Mike, he has a very long-time association with brown bears—lives among them, so to speak. His float house is right on the beach, and the bears are around him. And he hasn't had any trouble with them."

"You didn't say *yet*," I responded. He smiled and shrugged his shoulders. "I don't have any reason to say that," he replied.

"But John, *I* do! I fear for him! He might tap a brown bear that has just migrated from some other territory."

"We both know that is possible—anywhere."

It was a good answer, what I had expected.

"Well, my feeling is that he is unique." I stopped, trying to find a more suitable description, but Schoen intervened.

"He's unique, all right. He has been there nearly thirty years. His bear population appears to remain constant. He and his wife get along there alone, and with brown bears around them."

The story *was* authentic, not exaggerated. That was a relief.

"Do you ever go out there to visit?"

Schoen looked down at a large map on his desk. "Oh, we drop in if there is something to check up on," he responded easily. "We are marking brown bears on Admiralty Island in connection with our studies on 'old growth forests' versus 'clear-cut logging.'"

This was new to me.

"What is *that* study about?"

Schoen picked up a corner of the map.

"Our data suggest that old-growth forest may be the optimal habitat for many wildlife species. Up here in Alaska it takes 250 to 300 years to return to old-growth forest. Here, I'll show you."

He handed me some illustrated material that showed color photographs of the stages of forest: the clear-cut after logging, brown and barren; the early second growth, green and tightly woven with brush and tree regeneration; a tract of up to seventy years of tree-logged second growth; then illustrations of the original forest cover. It was quite obvious, just from the photographs, that old-growth forests offered wider spacing of the large coniferous trees commonly used for lumber and, between those giants, open space that supported many kinds of vegetation, with room for sunlight to get to the floor of the forest.

Schoen pointed out that a variety of vegetation supplies a variety of foods for more kinds of animals. Thus there are more animals per square mile in old-growth forests, and the species are in better health throughout the year. Schoen's studies had produced charts showing that deer are more numerous in old areas, and that their numbers are depleted in regrowth areas. In contradiction, I pointed out that newly cut areas in the southern coastal regions showed highly upgraded populations of deer, grouse, and bears because of the new, early cover of berries, bracken ferns, and grasses. I explained that years ago I had done a study of it and had written what was then a very controversial article that proved to be right, stating that when an area was logged, even the trout in the lakes and streams were more abundant, because of the ant and other insect structures in the downed and rotted trees on the ground.

Schoen listened intently before he spoke. "Mike, in southern British Columbia, Washington, and Oregon you may have a point to make. There snow is not a problem in recent clear-cuts, the clear-cuts are productive for a longer period, and second growth becomes productive earlier than in northern British Columbia and, particularly, southeastern Alaska. That is why we are studying the brown bears. Our studies deal with the effects of both mining and logging. Out in southeast Alaska they are putting in a big mine—a Canadian company, the Noranda group. We want to know what effect they will have upon the numbers of bear."

He picked up the map and showed me the area, with lines delineating the territory of the bear program. I asked him how far it was from Stan Price's bears.

"About twenty miles away. If you look at the larger map on the wall, you'll see where we last located our bears, the radio-collared ones. We've had nearly 100 percent success in locating them, even in hibernation."

The map showed three water drainage systems running to the opposite side of Admiralty Island. The mine-site area was almost dead center. There were pins indicating the game department's last contact, by radio from aircraft, with the marked, collared bears. They did look quite close to Stan Price's Pack Creek. It is accepted that grizzly bears, particularly males, roam forty to fifty miles. I said so. Schoen agreed, but noted also that during the past two years none of their marked bears had turned up among the animals in the Pack Creek meadows. I wondered about Price's reaction.

"How does Stan Price feel about your program?"

"He has expressed his opposition. We would expect him to. There is no ill feeling. He just doesn't believe in it."

I filled in the momentary silence. "There are a lot of people who don't believe we should mark or handle bears. He isn't alone. I myself have doubts—from what I've seen and heard. On the other hand, the gathered information is of untold use. And among all the cases I've studied and discussed, I have yet to find among marked bears that have attacked or killed a person a single example of one that hadn't already been classified as a 'nuisance bear' before it was tagged or collared. People have been attacked and killed by marked bears. In one case, however, no proof of human consumption was in the bear after it was killed, even though it was near the remains of the corpse. A second opinion expressed by a competent disinterested obsever was that the bear killed after the human fatality was not the bear that had killed the human, that an even larger male had been quite close to the corpse, a bear that was not killed. Who knows?"

Schoen was listening thoughtfully. "We don't have any records that show that any of the bears in our studies, or more broadly, in our department's other studies, have at any time attacked humans. If we felt that the programs posed a threat to humans, we would not proceed. However, our data are certainly improving our knowledge of bears and our hopes to keep them in the future."

My feelings were with him. Over the years I had fought for conservation measures and won ten awards for putting those themes in print. I had been closely associated with natural-resource people and wildlife managers and had aided and even taken part in their works, and they had been open and trusting of me as a newsman. Only a couple of them had been overambitious and prone to self-promotion. The greater number were conscientiously looking for ways to protect our natural resources and the species that were endangered. Schoen was typical of the best.

We talked more about the bear marking program. Schoen outlined some of the details of the survey, in which they had a record of fifty-five brown bears, of which twenty-four were tagged, and eighteen collared with radio equipment. This was in an area of 100,000 acres, which included the Hawk, Green, and Fowler rivers. During the operations they had lost only one bear, that to an overdose of drugs earlier in the program. They had found some interesting similarities in individual bears' lives. Five of the bears had not left their alpine habitat at any time during the year, though the general habit was to migrate to the mouth of a creek or river during the salmon runs. Of the entire group 65 percent were sows. One sow had a cub large enough to accept a radio collar, which was marked, producing excellent data on the life cycle of the pair.

Most of Schoen's work had been done with a former guide and trapper, Vern Beier, who had much experience in guiding hunters to grizzlies and was now employed by the game department. In fact, Vern was at that moment helping build a culvert trap to take out to Admiralty Island. He was going to work with Susan Warner, who was heading a project of trapping and marking. Would I like to meet them and discuss their project? I jumped at the chance.

"You say they are going out to Admiralty Island, John?"

"Yes. They are planning on it tomorrow—if the fog lifts enough to fly out there."

I had a sudden hopeful thought. "Is it possible that I could go along with them on the same charter plane? I would be quite willing to pay my share of the charter."

"Why don't you discuss it with them. They are chartering a large plane because of the abundance of equipment, and they have a helicopter chartered to take the new trap out. It would be up to Susan Warner to okay the extra passenger."

"Where are they going? Near Stan Price's area?"

"Yes. *To* Stan Price's area. They'll be working there."

It was an excellent happenstance. *If* Miss Warner could find room! I said so, and Schoen gave me the address of the place where Vern was working on the culvert trap. Susan Warner would be there too, supervising the details of the venture. Schoen phoned to tell someone I would be on my way there in a few minutes.

Blame the fog, I did! In some manner I got the directions wrong, and by the time I got the waterfront site I had missed Susan Warner. Vern Beier came out to meet me, a surprisingly small man with a heavy reddish beard, which was combed into a surrounding mass of black curly hair. Vern, in denims and a rain jacket, took me out to see the new trap. A man was welding quarter-inch steel mesh to the galvanized edges of an ordinary steel stream culvert. The metal mesh, originally a screen from a gravel crusher, had been cut to fit the circle of the culvert. The trap door was unlike any I had seen. Triggered by a mechanism that held the bait, it was operated by coil springs that slammed it shut like a swinging door. I noted that this trap was different from most I had seen, which generally were the guillotine type, a sliding metal drop door that cuts off retreat. Vern took pains to show me the spring door.

"It is pretty positive. Whatever gets into it has to be at the opposite end. There is no fear of the guillotine-type door coming down on the animal, or someone else." That statement was unusual.

"In the middle of *someone* else?"

"Oh yes. It happens. Even kids have been caught in traps near outlying dwellings. They could be hurt if the door fell on them—or on a person setting the trap. The spring-loaded door swings shut and automatically locks."

He set the trap mechanism, then triggered it from the outside. Indeed, the door did snap shut very quickly and effectively locked on spring catches. I told him about the two welded steel oil drums that Lynn Rogers had used effectively to catch at least five hundred black bears. He shook his head.

"I don't think you'd have too much success with brown bears in that size trap. I doubt if they would go into it."

My memory of the large grizzly-type black that had been trapped and tagged while I was with Rogers came to my mind. Beier was talking about an animal that commonly went over 600 pounds. The black that I recalled had looked very large, but was only 258 pounds. I examined the trap. It appeared rugged, efficiently designed and structured, and I asked him who had planned it. He patted it thoughtfully.

"We did it here from scratch, with available materials."

"You've done a good job. The last one I saw anything like it was one designed by Dale Nuss, chief ranger at Yellowstone Park. It was to be carried by helicopter and was designed so that it would not spin during transport, and it had an electrically operated release on the door so that it could be operated from within the cab of the truck. More than once with other traps, when the truck was moving, the door had been opened accidentally by a man standing in the pickup box."

Vern Beier was impressed.

"That design, for carrying by helicopter, would be good to know," he observed. "We have to move this one that way."

We talked about the grizzly project. He was a bit worried about the reaction Stan Price would have to the trapping and marking near Pack Creek. He liked Stan and had always been on good terms with him while he was guiding hunters on Admiralty Island. To my question about the possibility of getting out with them to Pack Creek, he said simply that Susan Warner was in charge. She knew that I wanted to do, and when all the gear for trapping and marking and weighing was accumulated, she would know if there was room. She would get in touch with me. I walked back to my hotel to see if she had phoned there. She had not. It was after five o'clock. On Juneau's main street I found a spot where I could get a "Deluxe Hamburger, with Chips," for six bucks, and settled for that. No messages when I got back to the room. I telephoned the charter services known as Channel Flying. (This was the "Channel 'Five'" I thought Stan Price had mentioned.) The outfit regularly flew to Pack Creek and outposts surrounding it. The dispatcher said, "We don't know if we will be flying tomorrow or not. We haven't been today. It is closed in everywhere. We may be able to fly tomorrow. Yes, we'll book you for a charter out. If you phone in the morning, you will get up-to-date information on scheduling. We have a backup of flights to handle. Thank you. I have your name. You are on the list."

The evening was well spent reading the scientific papers John Schoen had given me and sorting out my gear for Admiralty Island. A lightweight down Yukon Junior sleeping bag was the first item. A set of quilted Tyrelene underwear, two wool shirts, and wool pants, a set of rain gear, an insulated Floater Coat, three pairs of woolen sox, a change of shorts, a razor, and two cameras (black-and-white and color). That was it. I would wear the insulated gear and Grebb Kodiak hunting boots, which meant carrying only the cameras and the sleeping bag sack loaded with sox and razor. But how about eating? Well, that would come! When it was all separated and packed, I got the hotel clerk to store the suitcases, tape recorder, and other things until I returned. Then I went to sleep, still awaiting word from Susan Warner, whose home address I had neglected to get.

At first light the fog was still heavy in the hills, down to the building tops. I got up, shaved, and went downtown for a reasonably good breakfast. When I got back to the hotel, there had been no calls. From the lobby I phoned Channel Flying Services. A dispatcher said, "We may fly around noon. We have you marked down."

I went back to my room. A note was sticking on the door frame. The clerk who had left it had not seen me on the lobby phone, and he had written, I quote: "Mike Cramond. Somebody called that you can go to the plane of Patrick of fish and game." Nothing else! Well, John Schoen would have the answer. He did. Would I like to come into the office and meet with Susan Warner.

Ten minutes later Schoen introduced me to the most unlikely Alaskan brown-bear trapper and marker that I would have been able to imagine. Susan Warner, it turned out, was young, slightly built, fairly tall, with sun-bleached Nordic blonde hair, blue eyes, and startlingly white, even teeth—pretty in any sense of the word. When she put out her hand in response to mine, it was a definite shock. Small though it was, her hand was both firm and calloused. She was not demure but was very feminine, and she was reassuringly composed about the nature of her work.

"You don't look like a girl who would be expected to be in the handling of grizzly bears. How did you get into it?"

She gave a half-smile.

"My university studies, which were in geology, had some wildlife-management programs, and I began working for the fisheries department during the summer, counting salmon in the Alaska streams. That put me in contact with brown bears on streams and led to this work."

The matter-of-fact stance aroused my interest.

"Have you ever been chased by a brown bear?"

"No, Mr. Cramond, I've found it better to get out of their way when I know they are on a stream. Once or twice I've thought of climbing a tree, when one came my way. But none have chased me."

"They don't show very good sense then," I noted.

She smiled at the compliment.

"John Schoen says you'd like to go out to Pack Creek with us. There will be enough room on the plane if you would like to share the charter costs. It will help our budget. Our charter is for 1:30 P.M., and it looks as though it's going to clear up. Do you have much gear?"

"A sleeping bag and rain gear."

"That shouldn't be any trouble. We do have a large load. How does $50 as your share of the plane charter seem?"

I jumped at the opportunity. The price for a single-person charter to Pack Creek quoted by the Channel Flying line had been from $90 to $130, one way. That had been, I presumed, based on the possibility that someone else might share the flight. It would prove to be typically Alaskan, this sharing accommodations, grub, cost, effort, and companionship, sudden friendship and shared laughter, and afterward the sadness of knowing that probably you would never see that warm, friendly person again.

As I walked back to the hotel, the sky cleared in one small blue patch, right in front of the sun. The opening lasted about three minutes, the surrounding rain clouds sprinkling diamond drops before the white glare. Then, the sun was gone, for days to follow.

An hour later than scheduled, nearer 3:00 o'clock, in an afternoon shrouded by intermittent fog banks and rain, Susan Warner and Vern Beier, in well-weathered denims and woolen mackinaw clothing, waited on Channel Flying's float for the pilot to climb into the front seat. I motioned Susan into the front seat beside him. She shook her head.

"I don't like flying in the front seat, thanks!"

Vern also shook his head. I climbed in, and soon they were ensconced behind the pilot and me, their heads almost touching the pile of gear crammed into the stern of the aircraft. I had wondered, as I watched the loading, if it all could possibly go into the small Cessna 180 and still allow for takeoff.

The pilot, a well-seasoned man of forty-odd, ran the plane a short distance along the still waters of the harbor, then shot it into the sky like a mallard jumping from a pothole. He leveled off almost due west. Ahead was a very low ceiling, with big patches of fog even at water level. In southern British Columbia it would have been difficult to convince a bush pilot to take off under such conditions. In the Juneau area of Alaska it is commonplace. The airmen of that northern state know their weather, and they are not foolhardy. They are resourceful enough to put down wherever they are and hole up for the hours or days necessary before getting airborne again. They fly in closed-in conditions all their lives.

We had leveled off over the water about fifteen hundred feet up. As the great wide sound between the mainland and Admiralty Island showed below, I saw a school of orcas, or killer whales, leaving white blows of exhaled air as they swam in a northerly direction. When I pointed to them, the pilot just nodded, listening to the almost constant air conversations from headquarters and other pilots on the radio's flying frequencies. He brought the aircraft even higher above the beginning of the land, Admiralty Island's shores, and navigated just beneath the low cloud cover. Ahead there was a pass between the higher surrounding mountains. The sides of the peaks were shrouded in thick cloud layers, and the timber seemed only a few feet below us. My eyes sought the open patches among timber stands, searching for any sign of game in clearings. John Schoen had said there were both deer and brown bears in good quantities, no moose. The cover below was typical rain forest, large areas of dense coniferous timber of old forest, with occasional mountain valleys of low brush; the very small swamps showed little water but were carpeted with green growth right to the timber surrounding them. There was no sign of trails or roads; the terrain was as the glaciers had left it aeons ago.

The plane was through the pass and out over waters again. On the calm, misted water below, rafts of surf scoters or scaup ducks were plying the surface. On one set of reefs a mass of sea lions or seals was resting. Then we were over our destination, Pack Creek. Below us a small unit of weathered wooden squares appeared against the ragged edge of the forest, barely in the water—Stan Price's float house and buildings. I searched the flats of the sea marshes split by the old and new stream channels. There were a couple of grizzly bears, brown blobs—I was sure they were grizzlies—in the green-yellow meadow of marsh grass.

The plane circled a quarter of a mile away from the calm little bay. Then, in the curve of a pebble-strewn beach spit that had been revealed by the very low tide, it was set down as gracefully as a gull. We would have a long pack up the acres of sands to the edge of the dry pebble beach and a much longer one to the environs of Pack Creek.

Vern Beier, noting my short, eleven-inch boots, walked up to the plane float and swung his back to me.

"I'll pack you ashore, Mike!" he said.

For the first time in my adult life I was carried piggyback by someone else. Usually I did that kind of duty. It was a strangely humbling experience. As he set me down he looked up at me. "You aren't as heavy as you look!"

The three of us began a bucket-brigade line of gear from the plane to a spot on the wet tidal shingle.

Were those really grizzlies that I had seen near Price's? Had they already

The border of Stan Price's compound at Pack Creek on Alaska's Admiralty Island.

left the beach area? With my first load of gear packed to the upper beach, the questions were answered. I saw three great piles of fresh dung, a couple of cuplike bedding areas scooped out of fresh gravel and sand, and great paw prints over a foot in length on the upper, drier sands. The dung was no more than a day old.

Who would know about beds or tracks in beach sands above the tide level? Stan Price would!

After we had packed the gear up the beach and out of the reach of the incoming tide, I stood with Susan and Vern a moment, unaware of where they were planning to stay. Just above the beach a slightly higher promontory lay at the foot of a fast-rising land shelf. Much of it was fenced with wire strung on beach-timber and split posts. A glance at the enameled insulators told me that it was an electrically charged fence, a surprise until I peered beyond the weed-grown outside of the fence to see a very healthy vegetable garden within. But electricity? Up here? Price must be a very ingenious pioneer. That was soon to be proven. I nodded toward the encirclement.

"He seems to do well with his garden."

Vern grinned. "Yeah, that is only one of them. He shares them with the grizzlies and deer."

"You mean the electric fence doesn't always work?"

"He'll probably tell you about that when you get to talk to him."

That brought to mind the whereabouts of their planned stay at Pack Creek and, incidentally, my own. I stared down at the duffle bag containing my sleeping robe and cameras. The only provisions in it were six chocolate bars I had purchased hastily in Juneau, presuming that Stan Price might not have provisions for visitors and that I could subsist (it was something I had done in the woods) on two or three candy bars a day and, for at least two days, keep up my bodily heat. That presumed a maximum stay of forty-eight hours, time enough for a good interview and charter trip out again—weather permitting. Neither at the airport dock nor during the plane ride out had there been any opportunity to discuss the problem of lodging and board.

"Where are you going to set up camp—here?" I asked.

Vern's answer was a quietly announced surprise.

"No. We're hoping to stay in the smaller cabin at Stan's."

"Oh, he's expecting you, then?"

"Well—he knows we are coming."

Somehow, I had accepted the idea that the Department of Fish and Game and Price were at loggerheads over the marking of grizzly bears. It seemed that Price had a permit from the Department of Mines that allowed him to remain in the Pack Creek area because of past and existing mineral claims he had, for years, worked in the vicinity. His residence in the beach area of Pack Creek had been accepted by that governmental agency, while his resistance to grizzly counting and marking in that specific area had been stoutly proclaimed to the department in charge of game management. My conclusions in this regard seemed to negate any extension of hospitality by either party. It shows how wrong a suburban's concept of the state of things as they are worked out in Alaska may be. Since I was there primarily to visit Price for his viewpoint on grizzlies and I was entering his domain in company with the game department, it had frequently occurred to me that with such an entrance I too might be persona non grata—something I would have to work a way around. But, not so! I stared along the beach thoughtfully.

"Well! I guess I'd better get along to see him."

"We'll come with you, Mike," said Susan, who had heard our short discussion. She reached down and picked up my duffle bag and slung it over one shoulder. The action surprised me, and I said quickly, "I'll take *that*, Susan!"

"Well, we can share it!" she said, dropping the bag to one hand where there were two carrying handles. I took the rope handle on my side and we started toward the Price establishment, which lay about a quarter-mile away along the beach, out of sight around a promontory. Within the first fifty yards we saw the tracks of grizzly bears deeply embedded in the loose sands. The beach strand between the water and the trees averaged about thirty feet wide most of the way, a sheer embankment of glacial moraine rising abruptly from the high-tide line. If any bear, or several of the large animals, had wanted to share the path, as they obviously did sometimes, the person on the beach had the alternative of rushing out into the salt water or attempting to clamber up the precipitous mossy and timber-covered slope. There were no trees that could be climbed without pole-climbing spurs: they were old timber with branches beginning about thirty feet up. (Oh yes, I looked very carefully!) With the tide out, it was some three hundred yards across sandy tidal flats to the water. A grizzly's rush could catch the fastest human in about fifty of those yards. This then was the normal daily exposure to bears of Esther and Stan Price in their idyllic northern home. The three of us walked in quiet conversation along the narrow strand. At the promontory, which still shielded from view the float house and beach installations, it was a surprise to see another well-kept and electrically fenced garden. This one, quite recently used, had cabbages and cauliflowers that looked to be two feet wide across their down-turned leaves. Late blossoming dahlias and cosmo daisies mingled colorfully, their pink and flamingo-orange hues a hedge of beauty around the food plants. The garden gate on the beach path was open beside the printed yellow sign warning that the fence was charged with electricity. It seemed an almost incongruous appendage attached to a post fully an hour's wilderness flight from the urban outpost of Juneau. But all summer long the Prices were subjected to tourists who made the long journey out there to photograph the "tame" Alaskan grizzlies. And nearby there was a mute reminder of the need for the jolt in the wires. Just as we left the beach, I saw the hard, round, brown scats of one bear that had been eating salmon and, nearby, the pancake splat from consumption of items from the garden.

Grizzly tracks had been constantly in view along the beach, and near the garden there were comfortably rounded excavations in the sand that, judging by their size, could contain the resting body of a thousand-pound bear.

Susan and Vern, if they noticed them, took them as evidence that their stay at Pack Creek was to be a success. My own thoughts? Well, I was disconcerted! We were moments away now from the float house, which nestled in plain view in the cozy little bay behind the garden promontory. In minutes I would meet with the couple who had provoked my journey. Vern had stepped ahead and entered the open door of the massive shed housing the Prices' logging, mining, and fishing equipment. The shake-covered walls of the shelter were weathered gray. It measured about fifteen feet to the gable's peak and the same in width. Past the darkened entrance another fifty feet of building extended in two parts. One side was filled with freshly cut and sweet-smelling "inside" fir wood, cut to stove length. Its walls were hung with mechanical equipment for past and present uses: axes, saws, engines and machinery below them. In the seaside wing of the shop the benches and walls held motors, engine parts, and mechanic's tools strewn where their owner had last worked them. This building housed that part of the path used in common by the grizzlies and the Prices. There were no doors blocking either entrance; it was simply a thoroughfare for both animal and man. The shake doors could be pulled shut if Price wished to work without having to defer to one of the grizzlies.

At each door, resting with the heavier end against the rough siding, were wooden staffs about shoulder high, tapering from one inch to one and a half inches in thickness, of the type commonly depicted supporting biblical characters. There were one or two of these staffs side by side at each of several vantage points, which would make them fairly accessible almost anywhere in the building. The thought went through my head, vaguely I must admit, "Well! Either he needs them regularly—or else they're good stage props for the tourists!" (Within twenty-four hours I would have my answer.)

The path through this workshed joined a wooden bridge that led across mud flats to the slat-boarded walkway at the Prices' house, about fifty feet away. At ebb tide now, the house rested solidly on the exposed sedimental muds from Pack Creek. Vern and Susan were in the lead, and shortly Susan's loud rapping on the outer doorway brought an elderly woman's face hesitantly to the opened crack. She looked up almost shyly, certainly expectantly. She pointed, in slight agitation, to the recumbent old form visible from the doorway, sleeping, open-mouthed on the bed in the inner room.

"He's just gone to sleep! He'll be up soon. I'll awaken him."

Susan shook her head.

"No, Esther! Don't wake him now. We'll come back. We'd like to use the small cabin if we can."

The old lady was agreeable, it seemed, to almost anything that would not disturb her husband's nap.

"He's got the keys. You can go to the shack. It's all right."

Stan and Esther Price, Pack Creek, Admiralty Island.

Susan pressed further as the woman turned slightly away from the half-opened door.

"Esther, this is Mr. Cramond—from Vancouver, Canada."

"Oh, yes! The man who phoned about doing an article about us—er, him."

I was watching her somewhat care-lined face, sensing a growing weariness with the rigors of outpost living, meanwhile remembering from the news item I had read, that she had been the childhood sweetheart of the grizzly thumper, who had come at his bidding after his first wife and her own late husband had gone. She looked frail for a life among grizzlies on a remote float house. I extended my hand.

"Mrs. Price, Stan—Mr. Price—telephoned me three days ago to come up while the grizzlies were still in view on the beach."

"I know! He's expecting you. I'll waken him. You come on in!"

"No, I'll just go over to the cabin with Susan and Vern."

"You can come in now. I'll waken him."

The old man on the bed stirred but did not open an eye. I remembered he was reportedly deaf and would not hear the conversation. I insisted that she close the door and that I would come back later. She acquiesced reluctantly.

Within half an hour I was sitting with Stan Price beside the living room table, taking notes about some of his colorful life. Esther was fussing over tea for the three of us. Stan, when he had greeted me, had been a surprise. His venerable frame was surprisingly slight. His manner was definite; clearly he was accustomed to respect. But he was not overbearing. In fact, the mid-Victorian upbringing termed "mannerly" was most evident in him. He was a quiet, thoughtful person who listened to what was being said or asked and replied with clarity of purpose. We related well immediately.

He looked at me with some amusement as I asked his age.

"I'm a bit older than you are, Mr. Cramond. I was born in 1899 in Billings, Missouri. Esther and I went to a country school together."

Esther nodded, and said, "When his wife died, he wrote me and asked me if we could meet."

He didn't hear her. I asked how he happened to come to Alaska.

"Well, I was twenty-three. I was an electrical plant engineer with Edison Company. I came up here to Alaska in the winter of 1924, then went back to Aberdeen, Washington, to rewind a motor. I stayed there and built a house in 1929."

He was gazing out the window, which opened out on the spit where it recurved to make a bay of near-perfect anchorage. On the inside of that promontory was the large wooden hulk of a very capable-looking vessel. While waiting for Stan to awaken, I had admired the lines of the old craft, the deep water curves flowing from stem to stern. Although she was grey in her timbers from northern coastal weather, and green on the shady side with mosses and mold, the flowing lines of her original lofting showed that behind the well-fitted planking the ribs still adhered perfectly to the strong, straight keel. The beaching and weathering had not broken her back, simply mellowed her, brought her closer to the earth from which her wooden structure had first been hewn. Now I was impressed by something in the man who was staring at her, perhaps with only subconscious recognition. I looked past Stan at the old ship.

"Is that the boat you came up in, Stan?"

"Yes. I built her in Washington, a forty-two-foot ketch-rigged schooner. It took eleven months to complete her hull. I put a good engine in her and came up here. For a while I did a little coastal freighting with her, towing some of the float houses for canneries and loggers and making regular calls. For a while we had a fur farm, and we owned Fox Island. That was when everybody was going into fox and mink breeding. Then I got more interested in mining."

"How did that come about?" I asked.

He looked at me reflectively, and I thought perhaps his earphone had not been turned up sufficiently. I repeated the question. He nodded pensively.

"One winter, when I was a young man, a geologist left his book on geology with me, and I read it cover to cover. It aroused my interest in mining.

When the fur business turned out poorly, I began to do some serious prospecting. I've got some properties partially proven up near here. There's one across the bay that a partner and I put a lot of time on. One of the large mining companies was interested in it, but mining in this area is not too feasible. The cost of power and milling with modern fuels makes it impossible to operate what would be a paying mine on the mainland. We had some pretty fair assays."

"What were they, Stan?"

"Base metals, mostly copper, lead, silver, zinc—a low gold content."

"Is that what brought you to Pack Creek—eventually?"

"Yes, it was. I came in here with two house floats to work a prospect in 1952. There is good copper-bearing ore across the bay."

"And you stayed."

"Yes. Most of the time, I wintered in here for twenty-five years."

"When did you first have contact with the grizzlies here?"

He thought for a moment, looking out the window.

"Susie was born that spring, about twenty-eight years ago. She was the first one we got to know. She had cubs at four years old. Belinda came the second year. She's about twenty-seven years old."

"You mean that these two grizzly sows are still alive!"

"Yes. Susie is about twenty-eight years old."

"She's been around all that time?"

"Yes. You'll probably see her today. She has her cub with her—only one cub. The big males kill the cubs, you know."

Stan's face was a well-lined map of age and experience, his speech that of an intelligent and thoughtful person. Anyone who had lived daily among grizzly bears and survived must also have courage and initiative. He was saying that one of the bears that currently occupied his gardens, paths, and meadows, and even the walkway through his work shed, was at least twenty-eight years old, and *with cub*. My own conversations with bushmen, wardens, trappers, scientists, biologists, and rangers, together with the reading of thousands of pages of authenticated testimony from field studies, did show that bears in zoos had attained the age of thirty-five years; there were tentative accounts of bears twenty-five years old in the wilds. Only two accounts, one from Dale Nuss, my ranger friend at Yellowstone National Park, had given evidence of a grizzly bearing young after twenty years of age. One sow with two cubs had rushed him several times while he was bicycling to a departmental outpost cabin, and was deemed a possible threat to life. After she was killed, the laboratory tests showed her to be twenty-one years of age, and that she weighed only 126 pounds. In his excellent book, *The Track of the Grizzly*, author-biologist Frank C. Craighead, Jr., states that the tooth cementum layers verified one female with cubs at twenty-six years of age, also in Yellowstone Park.

For an Alaskan grizzly bear sow to be alive and bearing cubs at twenty-eight years of age seemed phenomenal. Too, I knew that men with years of practice in marking, tagging, and following bears often had difficulty identifying regularly observed but unmarked animals at different seasons of the year because body contours are changed by weight gains and losses, coloration is bleached by sunlight, and pelages change in response to changing atmospheric and chemical conditions throughout the year. An animal that is dark and thin in the spring could appear browner and even taller and fatter by late fall. Apart from tagged bears, only those that have distinctive body features—a limp from a healed injury, a scarring of the body, particularly about the head, that has left bare skin, torn ears, or light-hued hair covering deep scar tissue—are easily identifiable. Although some constant feature such as a distinctive collaring or hooding in the neck or shoulders is often quite noticeable in younger bears, it has a tendency to be less noticeable as the years pass. One means of identification cited among all types of bear observers is the actual nature or habits of the animal, most commonly either the docility or the aggressiveness of the bear, displayed in its approach to other animals (including man) or to food sources. These things were passing through my mind as I listened to Stan Price reminiscing.

"Susan and her cub are around yet. I saw them yesterday. They come right around the floats. Edna, my first wife, would shoo them off when they got too pushy. She would go out and hammer on a frying pan."

"When do they usually come around, Stan? What time of the year?"

"Usually you see more of them when the salmon begin to run up the river, about July 1 to 15. There is a run of big cohos about September 15, and the dog and pink runs. But the bears do come out on the grass at the river mouth sometimes in April. We saw our first bear about the fifteenth of May this year. Sometimes there are as many as a dozen of them at a time."

The thought of the electrically fenced gardens came to mind. I said so.

Stan half smiled. "Oh, we share the garden with them after we get most of the crops out. I put those electrical fences up to deter them. They'd plow right through any other fence, wire or wood. The shock from the electric wire will make them back off. They don't like it, and avoid it. They make a mess of a garden in a hurry, once they get it. I watched a young cub start at one end of a parsnip row and pull out and eat every parsnip from one end to the other!"

"Did you ever have one dispute your right to be in the gardens?"

He nodded quite calmly. "Oh yes. I was digging potatoes in the garden there, the one near the house." He pointed out the window. "And a sow with two cubs plowed right through the fence and rushed at me. She charged right up and raised her paw as if she was going to bat at me. I guess I had a nervous reflex: I hit her in the face with the shovel. After I hit her, she ran out the gate."

These statements could have been left as they were. However, knowing the speed of any bear's reaction, I just could not visualize how any man, let alone a man as slight and elderly as Price, could slap a militant grizzly in the face with a clumsy shovel.

"Stan, you say you *hit* her in the face with the shovel. Do you mind describing just what happened, again."

He eyed me thoughtfully.

"When she ran up and raised her foot, I had heard her and turned to face her. I jabbed the shovel blade right into her face—just a reflex action."

"You jabbed directly into her face?"

"Yes. Why?"

He was eyeing me deliberately, assessing. I grinned my relief.

"Stan, we both know that a grizzly, or any bear, is so quick, that a man wouldn't get time to *swing* a shovel unless the bear was facing away or turning. If it was facing a person, the only reaction you could probably get away with would be a direct jab. Am I right?"

He smiled and nodded his head in agreement.

"You're quite right, Mike. I wouldn't have had time to swing a shovel. But she didn't like the metal in her face. I think she just heard me working in the garden when she was about fifteen or twenty feet away, outside the fence with her cubs. That was too close for her, and she just charged right through the fence to get at me—to drive me away. She had no way of knowing that I wouldn't hurt her. I was just too close to her and her cubs."

Watching Stan Price's face during this explanation gave full witness to his empathy with Alaskan brown bears, the reason why he has had a quiet association with what is considered to be the most formidable and ferociously protective mother of any kind. What made him tick and survive is not in most of us. I was beginning to admire him.

"Stan, you show a lot of guts—without any desire to retaliate. Most of us would have gone and got a gun and shot the bear."

He was judging my words as they were uttered, silent for a moment.

"The bear was defending her cubs. That is no reason to kill her. She didn't harm me."

"Did you ever hunt, Stan?"

"Oh yes. I once hunted deer and partridge or grouse. But I gave up hunting a long time ago. I'd rather feed them. The deer come in here in the winter too. Sometimes they are a nuisance. Even the game department brought a young brown cub out in a gunnysack one summer. Susie had her cub with her, and we thought she might adopt it. I kept it away from her for three or four days, then let it go up on the bank. When Susie would come by with her cub, she would chase it. It would go up in a tree just a short distance from the shed when she would come around, and stay there, shivering with fear. We fed it, but it wasn't getting much other natural food. It was losing weight instead of gaining."

Compassion for the small animal was revealed in the old man's eyes, but not emotionality. He was glancing out the window, watching the sand spit. When he spoke his voice was low with finality.

"I guess Susie finally killed it. Gary found its hide and the partially eaten carcass up in the bushes above here."

"Sows commonly adopt cubs," I offered lamely.

"Yes, I know that, although I've never seen it. That is what the department hoped. Bears are all different. Some might. There was one big male around here this year that was a bad one. He killed Sam."

Esther, who had been quiet except for casual noddings of her head and almost whispered qualifications, spoke out clearly.

"At least we thought *she* was Sam—until she was dead!"

Price acknowledged the sally without rancor, smiling noncommittally.

"I guess Samantha should have been her name. The big male came in this spring. He saw her out on the spit there." He pointed to the sandy land in front of the cabin window, where it formed the elevation that shielded his home from the outer bay. He spoke again. "Well, the big male caught Sam in the open. He was less than a thousand feet from him—her. The big one just came on the run and took her before she could get away. He had no trouble at all overtaking her. He took hold of her by the back of the neck. She didn't even struggle, just slumped down and lay still. He let go of her and walked around her for about five minutes, then sauntered away up into the marsh. She was dead. That was last June, the sixteenth."

I wanted to ask him if the big boar had fed on the carcass, but the question seemed indelicate in light of the obvious affection that Price had shown for "Sam". Instead, I asked him if he had experienced other confrontations.

"Oh yes. There have been a couple. I was proving up a mining claim near here. I was tracing the vein in bedrock, blasting some of the stuff away. I was down in the hole, knee deep, when this rascal came up to the edge of it. I just tapped him quickly in the face with the shovel, and he took off. They don't like to get hit on the nose."

I was grinning, because this was the sort of story that was of paramount news interest—the story line, so to speak. The quote "He just taps them on the nose if they get too close!" would lead the reader to think it was an almost daily routine. Misleading? Yes! Untruthful? No! I asked him if he had had many such encounters.

"Not too many. But one of them was funny. There was a friend of mine who came up several years in a row. He wanted to test out his new fly line and rod down on the river there. There were bears around, so I went out there after him and sat on a high riverbank near him. I was on the opposite side of the river. I saw the bear coming upstream toward him, but he was so busy using the fly line that he didn't see it. When it got about sixty feet from me, I hollered to the bear—it was done on the spur of the moment. It was a big bear, and it came right at me. Gary was about seventy-five feet away and didn't know what was going on. The bear was on *his* side of the river, but it jumped in and came right across, charging at me. I had my stick with me, and when he put on the brakes—he really skidded to a stop—I was ready. I reached out with the stick and swatted him right on the tender end of the nose. He backed up and shook his head. I poked him in the face again with the stick. He backed up again and turned away. He just didn't want any more stick!"

Intrepid Stan Price was half smiling with the remembrance.

No question about it! He *did* actually smack them on the nose when they were preparing to attack. Be it a shovel end in the teeth or face, or a solid whack on the tender nose with a cudgel, the grizzly bear, even the famed and ferocious man-eater of Alaska's Admiralty Island, backs down before an adversary of unquestioned courage. Stan's life with bears had shown him that they recognized dominant authority, and where there was nothing for them to prove or lose by attack, the best route for them was to retreat.

Price was standing with his hands warming against the graying wood-burned metal of the living-room heater. "Would you like to go for a walk out on the spit, Mike?"

"Yes, certainly."

"We may see a couple of bears."

Those last words had a strangely cooling effect that I could neither show nor express. Stan was accepted by his bears. If I walked out on the spit, which was to be reached by way of the garden walk, and a bear, or bears, approached, *would* my fear determine the outcome? Oh yes! Fear may have something to do with triggering attacks. It is quite commonly known that people who are afraid of dogs are often the ones who get bitten by them. All my life I have been accepted or avoided by dogs, even vicious ones, because I don't fear them. I am wary of them. I approach a snarling or barking dog straight on, talking to them both reassuringly and demandingly if necessary. My body language may also tell them that I'd kick them under the jaw too, if necessary. Or I carry a stick, or make the grimace of picking up a stone from the ground. Dogs know all those movements from experience with other men. You don't even need to pick up the stick or stone. They know the maneuver, and they expect the stick or stone to come up in the hand. The gesture usually cows them, makes them circle—often they leave at a dead run. Too, as I do not really fear them, they detect none of the adrenaline that is released into the bloodstream and immediately transmitted through the skin of a fearful human.

The "smell of fear" that is spoken of occasionally is a very real thing. More than once I have had to handle people in great terror, and their odor is best described as skunklike. I have smelled the same odor in frightened dogs and cats, so I am inclined to believe that this smell may also trigger an attack from an animal.

Would the odor of my adrenaline discharge trigger a bear, if perchance one did approach Stan and me on the spit? Well, I was going to find out.

As we passed through the shed toward the entrance that led to the garden on the spit, Stan picked up one of his "sticks." As his hand grasped the staff, mine went out for one, but I thought better of it. Don't ask me why. I do not know. I followed him past the open garden gate and remarked on the wonderful size of the vegetables and beautiful blooms of the flowers. He acknowledged that the Alaskan climate produced excellent summer growth in some things, such as cabbage and cauliflower, taking no credit for his methods of gardening. We walked along the beach to the point of the promontory. There he sat down on a sun- and salt-bleached log to rest. His eyes searched the far beaches and down into the meadow. Thankfully, I noted that there were no brown bears in sight. We talked awhile.

Price gazed over the tranquil surrounding deltas and seascape. All was natural peace and beauty there. He nodded toward the river mouth, where the stream was split into two channels of fast-running water. Even in the distance the shiny black flash of the odd salmon breaking the surface in its run up the gravels was evident to him.

"Still lots of salmon coming up," he noted. "The bears will stay for a while, as long as they can feed on them. It's been a good run this year, they tell me."

"Do you put any salmon up for the winter—can any?"

"No, I'm not too fond of canned salmon."

The statement verified what Esther had said. She had told me that Stan would not eat canned salmon, that she had tried putting it up, but he would not eat it. We sat quietly for a few minutes.

The sound of the chopper came first as a drumming, then as constant rhythmic beats of the rotors. I saw it about a quarter-mile off, and the pendant load hanging beneath it. That was the game department's culvert trap! I looked at Stan's face as he watched the big bird maneuver directly into the river mouth, then across it and up the meadows to the edge of the trees, where the stream left the forest. His mien showed no animosity, nor did his voice when I pointed out that the load was a bear trap.

"Well, Mike, they believe that they know what they are doing. They say it is necessary to learn."

"I'm not sure myself, Stan, what bad results may have come from tagging. My files show marked animals have attacked people, but they were troublesome bears before tagging. I don't know. The information gathered is certainly valuable in studying their life needs."

He didn't reply, simply watched, as I did, the release of the helicopter's load and listened to the thumping sounds of its rotor as it left the bay.

The drizzle of foggy rain began to show on the sleeve of my jacket. Stan also noticed the precipitation. He got up stiffly, not much more or less so than I, from the log. We walked back up the spit and along the path to the sheds. To be honest, I was relieved no bears had yet appeared.

The Redhead IV

Temperatures on the Appalachian Shield dropped below zero night after night in mid-December, while the she-bear slumbered deeply. The air in the darkened chamber of her winter sleep interchanged with the outside air only through an ice-edged two-inch split in the rockbound entrance. Thus the temperature inside the den often remained twenty degrees above the external weather, well insulated from the changeable wind-chill factors. Shielded within her heavy, almost feltlike pelage, and curled atop the gathered insulation of six to eight inches of compressed twigs, leaves, and conifer needles, she also had up to two inches of layers of body fat directly beneath her skin. With her respiration and body temperature lowered, the freezing rigors of the outside weather barely affected her. Occasionally she responded to some body chemistry by changing her position on the warm underpad. She would then resume her prenatal posture in deep sleep.

In her slowly circulating bloodstream, the nutrients so bountifully garnered from her summer foraging were being channeled to the placentas and thence by tiny umbilical cords into the growing circulatory systems of the two foetuses. With many pounds of excess fat and flesh layers from which to draw sustenance, the foetuses were developing rapidly.

By the colder days of January the small animals had the bone and muscular structures of their kind, down to the most minute of paws, to which were appended tiny claws. The new mother slumbered, unaware of the profound changes occurring within her, which would also change her life patterns.

During early March contractions and expansions of the muscles surrounding her womb aroused her from the deep sleep. She moved restlessly on her bed until fully awake. Almost placidly, she accepted the new stresses within her body as it prepared to give birth. Her only reactions were her restless changes of position. When the contractions became irresistibly painful, she strained with her muscles to eject the small beings from the birth canal.

By the time the firstborn was down the passage from the womb and at the entrance, she was fully awake. Her own body temperature had been rising, and her teats had swollen with the nourishment required for her expected brood. She began to lick regularly at her vagina, both to ease the unfamiliar pains and to absorb the secretions. Following a strong involuntary contraction, she strained desperately. The first cub emerged.

Her pink tongue touched the strange result of her pains and found the new creature moving weakly in response. Some primal instinct assured her that the scent of the new cub was the smell of her own. The strand of the umbilical cord interfered with her lickings, and she bit through it, thus releasing the tiny being. Gently, she continued to lick the newborn, ignoring the continuing contractions within her body. When the pains became once more urgent, she transferred her licking to the vaginal entrance. Again, an involuntary contraction and her own muscular effort combined to eject another new living being. She began licking the uterine fluids from the second cub, and the small new life responded jerkily. Once more she bit through the umbilical cord and gave it freedom.

The irritation from her swelling nipples had brought unaccustomed warmth to her outer belly. She pulled the squirrel-sized new arrivals up to the warmth of that fur, licking each in turn. The stridency of the cubs' first wails in the otherwise completely silent tomb of her hibernation was startling. She pulled them closer, using gentle manipulations of her paws. One bobbing little head found the bare warm skin surrounding a nipple. The involuntary movements of its tiny mouth and tongue won a slight dribble of milk, emitted in answer to pressure on the teat.

The tiny cub licked some of the fluid and swallowed when the milk slid into its throat. Immediately the new sensation—hunger—instigated licking and sucking motions. The cub's first direct contact with the nipple drew a trickle of warm milk, which incited the small being to greater sucking efforts. The cub's extreme eagerness to feed made it pull away from the source, in the hope of finding something even better. When it found only damp hairs nearby, it struggled to get its mouth back to the flow of milk which had been assuaging its hunger pangs. Once more the pink mouth closed desperately over the mound of the nipple, and the welcomed fluid trickled down the cub's throat. Soon both small beings were attached to the newly flowing life sources. When the efforts to gain sustenance caused fatigue, the sucking instinct gave way quite naturally to slumber.

The new mother, rid of her internal pains and nipple irritants, slept, but less soundly than she had during her winter dormancy. Even the slightest movements of the cubs or the sounds of their hunger aroused her. When the cubs' stomachs became distended with unreleased urine and fecal materials, she licked at the anal and genital areas to initiate the release of the fluid and solids. She ingested them, thus keeping the den clean of bacteria that could endanger the cubs.

Within a week the cubs had doubled their weight, to more than a pound each. The mother's weight had been reduced by the sum of both, plus a little more for the energy required to keep herself and the cubs warm. Their hairless, pink skins attracted the licking of her tongue. The motherly attachment to that which was no longer part of her, yet was as familiar as her own flesh and scent, was growing strong.

By the end of March she was able to sleep more soundly, and if the cubs' bellies happened to be filled at the same time, she would occasionally drop off into the comfort of near dormancy.

Look a Grizzly in the Eye

During much of the first hour I spent with Stan and Esther Price, Vern Beier and Susan Warner had worked in relays, packing their stacks of gear to the workshed. As I returned with Price, I noted the accumulation near the garden entrance at the beach and began to carry some of it along through the shed. The material was both heavy and cumbersome, and when I realized that Susan and Vern had carried it for a quarter-mile, I felt guilty. Having been invited to dinner with the Prices, and knowing now that Susan and Vern were actually on good terms with them and were staying in the shack, I said I would bunk there too. The young people had agreed to that arrangement, but Esther had insisted that Susan stay in the main house.

When I visited the outlying cabin, I was surprised. The whole, small building was about seven feet wide and ten feet long, and inside were a table and two chairs, a round, barrel-like, flat-topped stove on a wooden pedestal, several assorted cans of gas and oil, some outboard motors, and some saws in pieces, while hanging from the ceiling were three large chainsaw blades. There was a window opposite the doorway, and the end facing the sea had two rough-hewn bunks, each with two thin mattresses. It was a crowded room even without people. I was glad that Susan had accepted the hospitality of the float house. She and Vern had agreed that I could share meals with them, but they steadfastly refused any donation toward the cost. My explanation about having made no provision for food, because I did not know what was out at Pack Creek or readily available, met with their protests that they were aware of the situation and that I was very welcome. And they said they had lots of food.

It was a good thing. Esther Price had informed me earlier that they had not been in Juneau for two months and were "out of food." It was as I had thought it might be in an outpost. Anyone on the trail was expected to have his own provisions.

So far I had seen one grizzly sow with her cub!

Later in the evening, after a flavorful meal of fresh liver brought out to Pack Creek by Susan Warner for Esther and Stan, with pan-fried buns, or "fried bread," as Esther called it, Stan asked us if we would like to see a reel of color film on grizzlies. Having heard of his excellent Super-eight showings while in Juneau I was eager, and Susan and Vern were willing. Stan set up a folding screen. The projector was powered by a generator that had been started in the workshed. Its thrumming was only slightly audible as the old man explained the shots. As he ran the film which sometimes was excellent and only occasionally was out of focus, it was apparent that some close-ups had been taken without telescopic lenses. The photographer would have had to be within ten feet of the brown bears. This was particularly noticeable in a series showing how a cub played clumsily on the drum of a logging winch while the mother, seemingly unperturbed, peered into the camera lens.

Somewhere around this point Stan mentioned a "German woman with lots of money" who had come out for several successive summers in order to take films of "her" grizzlies, which she showed in her native land. Housed in the cabin in which we were now billeted, she had fed the grizzlies, Susie and her cubs of the year, from the window. Stan had very much discouraged the practice, and the lady promised that she would not do so again. When Stan saw the she-bear and cub going regularly to the window side of the cabin, though, he was almost sure that she had not kept her word. The lady soon ceased, however, when Susie or some other grizzly began tearing off the wall boards under the window in order to enter the cabin. The smell of food inside the shack had so enlivened the bear's appetite that it tore away the flimsy, one-inch board siding like tissue paper. The German lady, having had a great scare, was then quite willing to share the main house on the float with Esther and Stan. She no longer wanted to feed free-roaming bears.

As I walked (with a flashlight Stan had loaned me) gingerly back to the cabin that evening, the realization came to me that *this was the path the grizzlies walked*. And they are often nocturnal in their habits! Once happily inside the cabin, sparsely built as it was, I looked beneath the window and saw that three boards had been flimsily nailed back over the two-foot hole made by the lady's enterprising grizzly. The patch was simply a closure to prevent easy access, not a structural repair.

It occurred to me that we had food in the building and that there were several containers of food and "bait" right outside the door. It is a well-established fact that grizzlies have almost a phenomenal memory of where they have found a food source and regularly return to it, and I noted that the cabin door was simply latched inside to a small nail with a bent clothes hanger. Vern came in a few minutes later, and the fact that he was a thoroughly experienced grizzly bear guide and was now marking and collaring those animals probably took the edge off my apprehensions. About twenty minutes later we were both asleep.

Morning light came on a bit slowly, it seemed—possibly because I had awakened about 5:00 A.M. and, not wanting to arouse Vern, dozed fitfully until the fog and rain outside allowed the light through. Vern got up and immediately looked out the window toward the river. Then he went outside and looked through a spotting scope to affirm what he had seen. He came back in and matter of factly announced, "We've got something in the trap."

I was surprised at his casual attitude, but should not have been. Later in the day I would learn why. My question was an eager one. "Is it a grizzly, or can you tell?"

He nodded, frowning. "It probably is a grizzly; the whole trap is moved around from the direction in which we baited it. And the way it's facing, there seems to be something large in it."

A few minutes later Susan appeared. She too was aware that the trap had been moved. There were obviously no prospects of breakfast. Indeed, they began immediately sorting out the gear that had to be packed across the meadows to accommodate their work. When I asked if I could accompany them during the marking, they said "Of course" and promptly gave me a substantial load in a packsack. Susan was carrying on her back a load that reached high over her head, and Vern was carrying a similar load and, in his hand, a large canvas duffle bag. The weight of all his gear would have bowed the legs of most six-footers. I was not surprised that crossing the muddy sections of the tidal flats his shoes sank six inches into the soil where mine sank only three.

On a sling over one shoulder, Vern was packing a .45–70 rifle, tailored to his requirements in both stock and short barrel. Over my shoulder was the sling of a standard Stevens 12-gauge pump-action shotgun, very similar to my own back-of-the-truck-ready model. I tested the injection mechanism as I loaded it and found it very sticky, a bit unreliable in a sudden emergency. The shell that I was handed, and which I loaded it with, was No. 8 birdshot. When I had questioned Vern about the light load shells, his answer had been that there would probably not be any reason to use them, and that it was, in effect, only to discharge in an effort to scare off a bear.

When we had crossed the open delta dotted with grizzly tracks, I was relieved to get out from under the pack. We dumped all the gear next to a lean-ing alder. Vern had positioned the bear trap to require only a short haul to bring the heavy animal to the spring scale. The scale would be attached to the alder with a block and tackle (which he had carried, with pack, on his back). Once rid of the heavy gear, Vern and Susan immediately went to the side of the trap, both speaking in calm, low voices that would alert the grizzly to their presence yet not incite it to bang helplessly at its steel caging. I followed them, going to the door end of the trap.

At the bait end, behind the mesh, an Alaskan brown bear sat quietly, wait-ing. When I ventured that her weight was around 280 pounds, Vern shook his head, saying he thought she would go well over 300.

With Susan distracting the bear at one end of the trap, Vern slipped in a metal prod carrying the prescribed dosage of the drug, Sernalyn. The grizzly spun around and batted at the area of the injection. Watching, I re-called Ted Watchuk's statement about when he was battling a grizzly hand-to-hand: "Mike, by the time you think of what actions to take, the bear has already reached for your move." Ursine quickness, indeed. This bear was no exception.

We all stood back to watch and await the results. I nodded at the quiet brown form sitting in the end of the cage.

"She seems to have accepted the trap."

Vern replied very simply, "Some are like that. She's a quiet one."

Susan had been slowly circling the cage, looking in from different positions, and she came over.

"She is dropping her head a bit."

The two of them conferred on the readiness of their gear, then began to lay out several types of paraphernalia on the ground beside a well-used tarpaulin: a pack full of drugs and surgical instruments, another with a full complement of gear for skin tatooing, stacks of printed forms, a tooth extractor, cameras for recording the experiment, and miscellaneous items. As Susan set out the items, I photographed her preparations.

"Have you marked many brown bears, Susan?"

"This is my first," she said candidly.

That meant *two* of us. Vern had trapped and handled at least fifty black and brown bears. His experience was considerable, and he had yet to lose a bear from drugging. Earlier he had told me that during his hunting and trapping experiences, which included most of his twenty-nine years, he had three times been forced to kill charging Alaskan browns. His solicitous and cautious attentions to the grizzly in the cage were similar to Dr. Lynn Rogers's handling of the black bears. First, the prodding of the slumped form through the steel mesh cage, then a prod or two gently in the mouth area. It took about fifteen to twenty minutes for the bear to become completely dormant. When it had slumped prone on the floor of the dung-spattered cage, Vern opened the door and moved inside, very cautiously. After a pat or two with his bare hand on the bear's shoulder he was convinced. He beckoned to Susan, who went in quite calmly.

With some difficulty the two of them then hauled the slack-muscled animal from the trap. I photographed their joint efforts. The big brown form, lying prone on the tarp to which they hauled it, looked much larger than it had in the cage. I watched them with interest as they took paw measurements; measured body girth, head size, and length; examined the teeth; and recorded the results. Engrossed in their operation, I had not looked about any farther than the half-acre surrounding the trap. Then for some reason I happened to glance downstream, where a quarter-mile of flat marsh, unmasked by either bush or tree, stretched to the low tidewater.

A big brown bear was, even at that moment, standing up in the inimitable boxer's stance, bowed hind legs set, front legs at the ready angles of a barroom brawler's, his head alert. The head was pointed in our direction, identifiably so, even at five hundred yards. I turned, as coolly as possible, to where Vern and Susan worked intently over the downed female.

"There is a bear looking at us downstream," I noted.

By the time Vern looked up from his tattooing of the bear's inner lip, the bear on the marshland had gone down on all fours and was biting at salmon in the waters of the branch stream in which it had been working.

Vern Beier jabs a tranquilizer into a brown grizzly bear at Pack Creek, Admiralty Island.

"It may not come," he commented, and went on with the marking.

The presence of a free, roving grizzly that close was, to me, a reason to take care. I watched it carefully, between taking photographs of the various operations being performed on the inert grizzly. The bear on the flats had moved upstream at least three hundred yards during the ten minutes since I had first seen it. It was fishing actively for salmon in the stream, and I saw it carry one carcass up to the marsh grasses to feed. On four or five occasions I had seen the bear go up on its hind legs and peer for several seconds right at us. No doubt it knew we were there; it was working, perhaps even surreptitiously, toward us. It was purposeful movement, such as I have seen in many bears while hunting. Usually, when the wind carries the scent, or some movement is made that will identify the intruder as a man, the bear acts quite uncertainly, perhaps shuffling and swinging its fore end side to side, and then makes a short run for the nearest cover, there to reverse direction and peer intently at the intruder.

Because of the angle covered by this bear's advance, I knew that it was interested in us. It was approaching, just as it might move toward another bear of which it was uncertain or a game animal it intended to down. Forget all the aspersions cast on bears' eyes. They pick up the movements of man or horse easily at a considerable distance (six hundred yards is the farthest I can verify). As they approach an object, they rely upon three highly developed senses: first, eyesight, to ascertain its position, second, hearing, to adjudge sounds and movements, and third, smell, which further refines their perception of the object. These three keen senses record the position, shape, movements, sounds, and odor. The bear knows exactly what is there and makes its moves, not tentatively but decisively.

This bear had made all his calculations. First, he had seen three perhaps unidentified objects moving about at the head of a familiar meadow; second, he had heard sounds of conversation and movement; third, he had smelled the scent of both the humans and a downed bear. Despite his fishing guise, he was moving in quite purposefully. Sometimes he was distracted by a salmon spurting away upstream, but after the first salmon I saw the bear take, he did not leave the river or take another salmon. The animal's progress was steadily in our direction even though there was at least half a mile open on each side of him.

I leaned over to where Vern was extracting a premolar tooth for the ageing certification procedures.

"The bear is coming right toward us, Vern!"

He looked up and studied the approaching animal.

"Yes. There is no doubt he's curious. He probably smells this female." He turned to Susan. "Let's get her weighed!"

Just like that! He continued with his work. It was now time to lift the female and weigh her. A couple of times the big bear in the meadow had risen to his hind legs to survey us, and still he was moving quite deliberately in our direction. I pointed this out to Vern.

"Yes, he's coming all right. Maybe I can get him with the dart gun."

I was flabbergasted. One grizzly down and soon to recover, the other a free-roving animal targeted for capture using a gun usually shot only from a helicopter! I was learning fast! The reaction to the drug takes five to ten minutes, and in that length of time a grizzly could make short work of three people, cripple an automobile, even demolish a cabin interior.

I stared at Vern. He had put down his end of the weighing net and picked up the dart gun. He then walked purposefully toward the meadow and the approaching bear. Glancing at Susan, I asked, "You okay?"

"Oh, I'll climb a tree, or go into the trap—if I have to."

The grizzly was now within fifty yards. It had identified Vern moving forward, but it showed no fear (which is more than I could say for myself). Because I have an arthritic shoulder, I cannot get up a tree without a ladder. I would have liked to take Susan's alternative and enter the bear trap. Grizzly dung and all, it would have smelled sweetly of safety. Even so I found myself walking behind Vern with the shotgun slung across my forearm. At least if

Susan Warner measures the brown grizzly at Pack Creek, Admiralty Island.

the bear charged either of us, I could get in one shot, even with the gun's faulty injection mechanism. At close quarters a 12-gauge shotgun, even with No. 8 bird shot, is a formidable weapon.

Near where the stream bank formed a V at the confluence of two branches of the river, Vern stopped moving forward. The bear, which now seemed enormous, was within a hundred feet of the prone bear and the trap, seventy-five feet from Vern, and a little more from my position. The grizzly went up on its hind legs for the last time, studied us and the trap very deliberately, kept his beady eyes on Vern, then moved to one side about fifteen or twenty feet. He then came back at an angle that put him closer to Vern, at about fifty feet. Vern put up the dart gun and aimed it. Even a native spearsman could have thrown his missile right into the animal's vitals at that range. Vern waited, edged closer. The grizzly studied him. I do not think the bear even looked at me, where I stood about ten feet behind Vern.

After a good scrutiny the grizzly did that "old bear act" I had often experienced. He turned aside from the direct approach and moved about thirty feet to the left in a circling maneuver that kept him constantly at the same distance from us. He then crossed the main stream of water as if it was not even there, jumped to the top of the other bank, and moved upstream where he could approach much closer under the cover of trees and bushes, thus to avoid being in the open. The bear showed respect for the situation but no fear at all of the three humans before him. Vern moved to within thirty feet of the bear now on the other bank. Right behind him, I watched his approach studiously. The dart gun went up tentatively on three occasions, but the bear did not present the part of his anatomy that Vern wanted. Vern waited quite patiently and resolutely for the opportunity. Twice I thought he would take it, but he lowered his arm. Still the grizzly persisted. Finally, about ten minutes after the bear had come in close, he moved slowly up the creek into the area of bushes and forest behind us. When the animal had traveled about seventy-five yards up the creek, Vern turned and came back.

"I couldn't get a good spot to place the dart. He wouldn't turn around when he was close. It was too far away when he moved off. Oh well! We'll get this one finished. It would have been nice to have two to work with, a real bonus."

I said simply, "Yeah! "

To say that I was relieved was the understatement of a decade. Throughout the rest of the procedures I kept a very close eye on any area from which a grizzly could approach unseen through the bushes. About an hour and a half after we had arrived, the downed, weighed, and telemetrically collared sow was showing increasing signs of early recovery. Vern and Susan gathered their gear and records and piled them under a tarpaulin beneath the hanging scales. We headed back down to the flats.

After a late breakfast Susan and Vern conferred on the details of trapping the next bears. They spent the most of that day working in the meadows around the trap. Several other visitors had appeared in the deltas, braving the now continuous rains, hoping for brown-bear photographs. They were the members of a canoeing expedition. I walked over to Stan's float house, where he was operating his shortwave radio transmitter, talking to Channel Flying, arranging for a charter flight for the canoe voyagers. When he was finished we talked.

What did he think about the future of grizzlies?

"Well, here, I don't know. When I came out here, there were seventy-five brown bears, at least. The eye count I made last year was twenty-five. It's hard to say what happens. One of the sows is a fighter. We call her Brownie. She is eleven years old, had three litters, and only one cub survived. Once, when she had twins, she first lost one cub and then, three days later, was all alone."

He went over to a wall cabinet and retrieved an ancient file filled with clippings and memorabilia. For a few moments he sorted silently until he picked out a yellowed magazine article. It was by a favorite author of my youth, Stewart Edward White, and was from the *Saturday Evening Post*, 1910. He pointed to the underlined sections.

"White thought that they would be exterminated by now, from what he wrote then," he noted, handing the crumbling clipping to me.

He leaned back thoughtfully, as I read some of the underlined items. We talked awhile, then I went back to the cabin, where Susan and Vern were sorting gear and their notes. We talked and then had dinner. Afterwards we visited with the Prices, but returned early for the convenience of early rising, Susan with us. I tried to insist that she take the lower bunk, saying that we could split up the four mattresses, and I would bunk on the floor. She shook her head.

"No, Mike, you stay in the bunk! *I'll* take the floor. I'm used to it. It's not uncomfortable."

And I let this capable young woman talk me out of it, though I felt a vague sense of guilt. Within minutes the hissing Coleman gasoline lantern was silent, and sleep was soon upon all of us.

Once during the night I had to get up and go down the wet trail, barefoot. Not that the dampness mattered. I just hoped that grizzly bears could be blinded by the rays of such a small pocket flashlight. Despite the smelly beaver-castor bait lying right outside the door, *that night* the Price grizzlies were not nocturnal.

It was 8:00 A.M. before any of us showed any inclination to get out of our sleeping bags. Susan was up first. She and Vern both had first looks at the trap through the window, then ascertained by spotting scope that the trap door was still open. There was no captured bear to handle, yet. They cooperated on cooking breakfast, insisting that I stay out of their way. Immediately after we had eaten the meal, they began to don the bulky rain gear and rubber boots necessary for crossing the marshes and stream channels. They noted that there were two bears out on the flats, but none near the trap. Moments later, packing substantial loads of gear, they left. I had insisted that they leave the breakfast dishes, and I would stay in camp and do them. They did not need me to pack a load, and I was still stiff from the activities of the previous day.

While the kettle was boiling on the two-burner Coleman, I wiped the plates off with a piece of paper toweling and put them in the small dishpan; thereafter pouring boiling water upon them. I looked out the window, which Susan had slid open earlier because the glass was murky. There were five other visitors on the meadow, members of the canoe party, all hopeful of close-up photography. Vern and Susan had disappeared around the bend. I looked down. The boiling water had taken the breakfast residue off the plates. I swilled out the cups, laying them upside down on the table to drain. The window was open in front of me just across the 20-inch table. I turned to pick up a paper towel, then lifted the first cup to dry it.

As I looked up, a grizzly was staring me *right in the face*! Its face was in the window sill, two feet away! In view over her shoulder was an eager cub up on its hind feet.

My first yell must have come from a fear-strangled larynx, because I do not remember any sound at all.

But the grizzly, as surprised by our closeness as I was, moved back a pace.

"Get ouuuuut! You old bitch!" was what my mind said. I do not have the slightest idea if I voiced it, but I roared blue-bloody murder. "Geeeet!"

She didn't *get*, just backed up two more paces on her hind legs. My hand shot to the sliding window and slammed it shut. Jeez! A pane of thin glass between the grizzly and her cub and me! She was not, even now, more than three feet away! Then, for some reason, I looked around. Behind me the wooden door to the shack was wide open!

In one quick jump, I grabbed the edge of the door and looked for the bolt. That was the first time I really noticed that the only latch was a piece of thin coat-hanger wire, simply bent to hook over a small nail. Panic leaves me quickly, sometimes. I stared intently around to see if there was a gun in the shack. There was not. I heard the grizzly sow "whuff-whuff." *That* is a sound designed to dislodge constipation!

I looked for some sort of weapon. An axe, a crowbar! Anything! Hanging from the ceiling joists over the table was a three-foot steel blade, a spare from a chain saw. I grabbed it, pulling the nail loose while yanking it down. I was now facing the window through which the grizzly had poked her head seconds previously. And she was still right outside it, now sitting back on her hunkers almost expectantly, waving her head. The cub, sitting beside her, also was staring up at me.

"Get away you old bitch!" I roared.

She sat there undeterred.

I looked down at the steel blade in my hands. If you ever have to get a grip on a chainsaw blade to use it as a weapon, you will know what I found. It is a heavy, very awkward two-edged tapered piece of steel with a machined slot at the motor end; and it has two knifelike edges on either side, channels where the chain circles it under power. The grip in the engine slot will not let your fingers in. I found that out. But I got my hand, desperately, around the narrow end. All reaction from me, from there on, was strictly impulsive. I slammed the edge of the blade against the wall of the shack with a resounding thud.

The female reacted just as would a person that close. She winced and threw her head aside. Seeing her draw back, I thumped the wall again. She winced again, and so did the cub. In fact, it climbed up on the logging winch beside her and faced me. After the fourth thump and corresponding recoils from the bear, she backed up a step. The cub jumped down from the winch drum beside her, and she turned away. She began to move toward the slope on the edge of which the cabin stood. I thought, "You old bitch, you can get through that door without any effort. But, I'll get at least one good swipe at you with the saw blade *before you get in.*"

But she fooled me completely. There was a rending sound of wood being torn at by her nails.

"Holy Creeist! She's trying to get in here through the patch!"

That is exactly what she was doing. I jumped across the room, away from the door. I smashed the chain-saw blade against the inside of the patch. If she would jump at the sound of the blade smacking wood, the impact of it on her nails might make her wince even more. After the thump there was silence. Then came another tentative scratch of her nails. This time I thumped the wall so hard that the saw blade almost knocked the patch outward into her.

I looked out the window. She was now six feet back, looking resentfully up at my face in the window. But she was getting the idea she was not welcome!

For about two minutes we glowered at each other, and needless to say, my expression was pure bluff. The look on her face showed hers was not. She woofed at the cub, bringing it to the other side of her; then, looking back twice at me, she angled down the slope past the cabin, on a route that would take her easily, in twenty strides, *right around to the front door*! By which time I was wondering if Stan—oh no, he was deaf—or anyone, would know my predicament.

I walked over to the blind side of the door, standing against the side of the stove, holding the saw blade overhead. If she moved, as I sensed she would, pulled the door open or nosed the thin wire off the nail with a slight push inward, the steel saw blade would come down right on the back of whatever portion of her entered first, preferably her head.

I heard her nails on the path outside.

Silence!

Bears move, even in noisy bush, soundlessly.

I waited—and waited.

Then I moved, ever so quietly, to peek through the crack between door and jamb. She was on the path, fifteen feet away, staring irresolutely back at the cabin. The cub was beside her. She looked down at it, then nudged it behind her. I smacked the saw blade hard against the thin wooden door. Twice more, I thumped it hard. She was not wincing at the sound at fifteen feet, but she did not like it.

Slowly, she bent her head and nuzzled the cub, turning it away. She then took two steps away along the path toward Stan's workshop. Once more she turned around, as if to change her mind and come back. Her nostrils were working and picking up the smell of beaver castor bait on the landing in front of the door. Finally, as if it was not worth it, she nudged her cub in the rear and climbed slowly up the steep bank as easily as if she had been walking on the level.

Twice she halted and looked back, as if to make sure that I was not following. In seconds she was gone into the deep brush covering of the slope.

My hand was actually frozen around the saw blade from the fear and strength of my grip. It was difficult to let go of the metal. She was gone, and so was I, almost.

The Redhead V

The sound of movements in the snow outside the den first aroused her. There had been outside sounds continuously since she had first entered her winter retreat: the whistle of high winds, the popping of tree trunks fractured by the extreme cold. None of these, not even the nearby call of the cruising timber wolf, aroused by her scent emanating from the vent of the den, had created in her any note of apprehension. These new sounds, however, were not those of wolf nor wind, nor splitting deciduous woods. Then the snow was being quietly removed from the den mouth, increasing the light in the chamber. Only vaguely in her drowsiness did she recognize the sounds as the feared voices of mankind.

"Dave, I think she's in here. This is the area in which I saw her last fall. The redhead sow. I'd like to get some data on her. This is the den that old Baldy used for six years, until he was killed three years ago. I hope it's her!"

The words had no meaning to her, yet something in the quiet tones reassured her. Regardless, she moved instinctively and with unexpected quickness. Her shift of position dislodged the nursing cubs, and they emitted tiny, panicky wails. Their pink skins were now sparsely covered with fast-growing fur. Their eyes were open, blinking from the unaccustomed light beginning to enter. Increasingly disturbed, they again bawled in unison. Her shifted position had brought her into a curl about them, shoving them to the back of the nest. Her broad stern now provided a bulwark against an invader. Suddenly the temperature at the top of the chamber decreased, and the soft winter daylight dispelled the customary gloom. She was aroused but reluctant to believe that intruders had entered her sanctuary. A sudden, brilliant light crossed the top of her head and struck the back wall of the cave, reflecting on the cubs. The shadowy movement at the den mouth, seen in the corner of her eye, distracted her from the single brilliant light. She blinked. The human sounds were now very close at hand.

"I can get a poke at her rear end, Dave. Hand me the needle. She's looking right at me, awake."

She turned her head across her shoulder to face the light source once more. Her bulk was still providing the protection between the cubs and the wall. She turned her eyes from the strong light.

"She's turned away! Here goes!"

The jab at the top side of her rump hurt little more than would a hawthorn barb sticking her while she gathered succulent berries. It carried no association with aggression as would the slam of a nailed paw or the incision of a tooth. Still not wide awake, she endured it, and then a dullness set in. The main thought left in her consciousness was to keep a buttress between the invader and her young. Instinctively she curled more tightly about them, dreamily experiencing the comfort of their nursing. Then, involuntarily, she drifted off into deepest slumber, even deeper than that of her winter dormancy.

While she was unconscious, the man, now right inside the closely confined chamber, examined her cubs. He reported their condition to his assistants, then replaced the cubs against protruding nipples. He checked her temperature by inserting a rectal thermometer and noted her respiration by the hands of his watch. He pierced her ears and fitted them with numbered steel tags. Finally, he fitted a plastic collar tightly about her short neck, riveting it securely into place. The collar's radio signals, transmitted to data-receiving centers, would thenceforth continuously divulge her location, thus revealing the pattern of her life within her wild habitat.

Their mission completed, the invaders closed the den entrance and departed. When consciousness finally returned to the bear, it was with a deeper reluctance to awaken than she had ever known. At first she moved with spasmodic effort, then with growing concern. The chamber was now in total darkness and was warm again, but the new smell of mankind still permeated it. She was still suspended in a realm of sedation when the high-pitched squall of her male cub seemed to split her eardrums.

Reacting to the agonized bleat, she struggled to rise to her feet, but the unsteadiness of her legs caused her to fall off the slightly raised platform of her nest. The move was fortuitous. In her earlier catatonic state she had accidentally rolled upon both the cubs. Their frightened squalling now came plaintively from the bed. She moved slowly, with extreme deliberation. These new charges had become her most important concern. To warm and suckle the litter was her strongest drive. She wavered on her unsteady legs, but managed to drop her belly to the floor of the nest. In order to prevent her weight from coming down upon her cubs, she rolled away from them, exposing her teats, which they found quickly. Their nursing period was very short. They had absorbed the residual drugs now in her milk, and they slept. She also lay inert, barely conscious.

When she fully regained consciousness, the cubs' strangely quiet dispositions set her to licking them almost continuously. Finally they began to respond and automatically sought again the solace of her teats. The painful metal irritations in her ears and the annoying binding collar were being slowly assimilated and accepted as an inevitable part of her existence. Within hours she was once again engaged in the routines of suckling, licking, and cleansing her fast-growing infants.

CHAPTER 6

"Yeah, I've Killed a Couple."

After the tumult of apparently thwarting the sow grizzly's entrance into the cabin, a settling calmness filled me. In the torpor that followed the surge of adrenaline through my veins, my mind was strangely clear in recollection. Earlier I had asked Vern Beier and Susan Warner if they had ever experienced the attack of a grizzly. Susan shook her head and said that she had climbed a tree on a couple of occasions and waited until the bear had departed. Vern nodded his head affirmatively, but did not go any further. At that point I recalled that when John Schoen was describing the marking program for grizzly bears, he had told me of a partner who recently had been forced to shoot a grizzly that had come after him. And if my recollection was right, Vern Beier had been John's partner during the markings of grizzlies near the proposed Admiralty Island mine site.

"Vern, when I was talking to John Schoen, he said his partner had been forced to kill a couple of grizzlies—one of them over the other side of the island. Was that you?"

Vern nodded in agreement, saying, "Yeah, I've had to kill a couple," but still offered no comment.

At that time I had not known Vern beyond a few moments of conversation, and I felt he was still sizing me up as a newsman—showing a bushman's reluctance to talk openly to strangers. I let it go.

Now something else was coming through the haze of recollections, something vaguely familiar: The filmed picture of the grizzly cub sitting on the winch drum! I stared outside the cabin window. There was the winch! Its drum was facing directly into the window. About six feet distant.

It was the exact setting in which Stan's Super-eight film had been shot. The cub on the winch! That scene had been run at length, an appealing sight as the cub settled its little bum on the sun-heated metal, then moved restlessly about while the grizzly sow sat staring into the lens. This window was where Stan's footage had come from! Right out that window! No place else. This was the site from which the German lady had fed "her" grizzlies and had taken her film segments. It had not occurred to me that Price also might have taken advantage of the appealing subject from the relative safety of the cabin.

"Hell! The old bitch was just wanting to be fed!"

The statement was expelled from my half-closed lips. It would have been comforting at the time to know that *that* was Susie and her cub. Or *were* they Susie and cub? Perhaps not. I pursed my lips wryly on that one. Shortly afterward I cautiously made my way along the woodsy path to the workshed, thence down the ramp to Price's float house. A tap on the door brought

Esther. The opened crack showed Stan ensconced on the bed having his daily nap. I refused Esther's invitation to come in, for which I think she was thankful, then walked back along the path to the cabin. She had said nothing, so I supposed neither she nor Stan, had witnessed the grizzly's visit at my window. There were no windows in that side of the rooms that they used during the day, so they would not have seen anything, unless drawn by extraordinary noise. My yells and banging must have gone unheard, except by the sow and cub.

Damn! If I ever referred to the incident later, I could easily be branded a liar.

In the continuing drizzle I arrived back at our cabin, still carefully watching for nearby movements. Once at the doorway, I peered through the spotting scope out across the meadow. In the foreground, between four hundred and six hundred yards distant, were seven people hooded in varying types of rain gear, from brilliant fluorescent orange to camouflage. Some of them had tripods with them. Almost every person carried a camera or gear bag. Ahead of them, between the trap and the meadow, a grizzly was working the stream for salmon. Even as I watched, "Susie and cub," my recent friends, sauntered from the other side of the spit that sheltered the Price house from the sea. Coming from that direction, they would have had to pass Stan's succulent garden before reaching the stream. Because the photographers on her left were attempting to get shots of the other brown bear in the creek, they provided quite a wide area of approach upstream for Susie and her cub. The photographers were crowding the grizzly bear in the river. They were close enough to take a pro photographer's "prestige" shot rather than accept the foreshortened telephoto perspective. Their proximity to the bear was dictated by vanity, not by their recognition of the animal's defensive or territorial zone. For a grizzly with cubs, that distance can be four hundred yards. The photographers were within 70 to 120 *feet*.

I decided to go down and see Stan and Esther once more. When I arrived a young woman and a man were talking to Stan while he was trying to transmit a message from them over shortwave. These were the outfitters belonging to the canoe expedition. They were attempting to arrange a charter flight for the pickup of their luggage and a couple of passengers.

I asked the young woman if her party might want to share a charter, since it would be convenient to me, also, to get out the following day, weather permitting. Nothing was flying at the present. A little had been done the day before, and the weather-bureau prognostication was slightly optimistic for some small break the next day. Her attitude was a bit standoffish. Then she seemed to relent, and said, "We have a very heavy load, and people. How much gear do you have?" I replied that I had only myself and a sleeping bag. Well, that seemed okay. She would think about it.

Stan shut off the radio transmitter, and we talked. I asked if he had seen Susie and her cub go by, and he had. She had gone by about an hour ago.

I was going to tell him that she had stopped by the way, but thought, "What the hell. He'd see nothing unusual about that." So I kept quiet. About that time the young man interjected a statement. "Stan showed me your book on bears, Mr. Cramond."

"Yes. I'm out here to learn some more about them. People don't realize the danger of going close to bears."

He looked straight at me for a moment before speaking.

"Well! What do you think about our people out there?"

It was my turn to look him straight in the eyes.

"I think they are goddam fools! And they are taking advantage of the thirty years of discipline or acceptance that Stan has built up in the local population." I don't think he expected it that straight, but I must say he took it well.

"You apparently don't approve of our photographing the bears up that close."

"No. I'm sorry to be so frank about it, but you *asked* me!"

"Yes, I did! I'm not too happy about some of them."

"Just in case you don't know it, they are out there approaching two sets of grizzlies. The bear on the closest branch of the stream is being boxed in by three different camera groups, all approaching it from different angles. That doesn't leave the animal the alternative of moving away from them. One guy is so close that he is a challenge to so territorial an animal as an Alaskan brown bear. Again, I say your group is relying upon Stan's treatment having conditioned these animals to his nearness, as a nonaggressor. They might interpret that hemming in, by five men in three groups, as aggression.— Hell, you asked me, and that is the way I feel about it."

My eyes caught Stan's, wondering if he had his hearing aid turned on. His face showed no animosity or even silent disapproval, but he nodded his head. He did not say anything. The young outfitter spoke again.

"I've been out here several times. I think you are right. We do take advantage of Stan's years of association."

"Yes, you *do*! It might be a good idea to use telephoto lenses a bit more. I'm sorry to be blunt, but I've been around bears all my life and I wouldn't try what they are doing with a grizzly, even carrying a shotgun or magnum rifle. And *that* would be a shame to use particularly in this conditioned bear area."

He nodded a bit sheepishly. "You've made your point—but I *asked* for it."

The conversation once more became general. I left shortly afterward, returning to the cabin. It was growing dusk, an early darkness made deeper by rain clouds. When I looked out at the meadow through the scope, it was difficult to get any but a very dim view of what was going on. I could see what appeared to be four figures moving about, close to the trees where we had marked and weighed the grizzly. Two of them must have been Susan and Vern, because they had not returned to the cabin.

I wondered what I could get them for dinner, but decided not to start anything since I had no idea what they wished to eat. A few moments after dark, their voices came faintly through the rain and mist outside. They were elated when I asked what had gone on, Vern particularly.

"We were marking bears."

"They weren't in the trap! I watched to see if it was sprung. What did you get?"

"A sow and her cub."

"Stan's Susie and her cub! Jeez! They came over here just after you left, and scared the hell out of me! You left that window open, Susan, and she shoved her head right in."

Both of them broke into wide grins, and Vern's laugh was self-conscious.

"Yeah. We know! We saw them coming and saw her going up to the window."

I was surprised by the remark.

"You can laugh," I protested, "but she sure pushed my panic button! You didn't do a hell of a lot to dissuade her!"

"What could we do? We were over at the meadow. We couldn't have got back here—even if you were in trouble," laughed Vern.

"Well, I grabbed the chain saw blade and banged it against the wall a few times. You might have left me a rifle or shotgun!"

Vern nodded toward the doorway.

"There is a rifle out there! On the porch!"

"There *was*? *Now*, you tell me! That's comforting!"

Susan was listening, a quiet smile on her sun-tanned face.

"Anyhow, she went away, Mike. Vern tranquilized her and her cub, making the day a success."

I was grinning, feeling much better for the discussion. "Was it old Susie? Stan's old she-bear?"

Vern shook his head. "It may be one he calls Susie; but *that* bear was less than twelve to fourteen years old. She was a young bear. I think he might be mistaken in her identification. She definitely isn't any twenty-eight years old. Her teeth were perfect, and her condition great. We took a premolar that will give us her age."

Well, myths and beliefs die hard, particularly those apparently founded in truth. I wondered how Stan would take the news that the two bears he had known and trusted as Susie and cub were young bears. It was not going to be me who told him. But what the facts did affirm to me is that scientific observation and the marking of particular animals do produce exact knowledge. Bears of all species do look alike. A black grizzly does resemble a black bear; a blonde black bear looks like a grizzly. At a hundred yards, even the best eyes could have difficulty distinguishing two members of the same species unless there were very different markings or apparent physical distortions or scarring. When a bear has been marked—that is, has been tattooed with a number, or has its ears pierced by tags, or has been collared with a radio transmitter—there is no doubt about its identity.

We had a late meal, and Susan went down to talk with Esther, probably recognizing her need for feminine company. I noted that she took along an armload of fresh victuals from the camp supplies. Vern and I talked about bears and bear pursuits.

He informed me that he had been born in Wilton, Wisconsin, in 1952, and had moved to Alaska twelve years ago at the age of seventeen. He had lost his parents when he was nineteen and had been on his own since then. After high school, formal education had not interested him as much as the outdoors did.

At age eighteen he had teamed up with Bruce Johnston, a descendant of the renowned mountain man Jeremiah Johnson. Vern and Johnston had worked traplines on the Unuk River near its junction with Dream River. That was where he had encountered the first of three Alaskan brown bears he had been forced to kill in self-defense. I had asked him what he thought about the probability of such attacks—which I had recognized all too clearly during his attempts to tranquilize an approaching grizzly the day before, though it had not seemed to bother him.

He had answered a bit solemnly: "Grizzlies don't usually want to have anything to do with you. They are a little different from black bears. But you can't rely on that. Some *do* come."

He had a calmness about him that pertinent questions did not ruffle. When I had asked him if he was about five feet nine inches tall—a bit of diplomatic overstatement—he answered without hesitation: "No, I'm five foot six and a half. And I weigh 160 pounds." He was looking up at me with full knowledge that my estimate had been flattering, knowing why I had done it. That put us on even ground. I admired his frankness and was later to envy him his cool courage.

"You mentioned a grizzly that you had to kill when you were trapping. Was that your first? And did it come after you?"

"Yeah, it was my first. It came after me all right!"

"When and where, Vern?"

"Well, to be exact, it was May 9, 1973, at 7:30 P.M. Bruce Johnston and I were out on the trapline on the Unuk River, about fourteen miles up from its mouth. We had a cabin on Lake Creek. I was just twenty years old then. Bruce was eighty-four years old, born in 1889. That first year Bruce was on crutches. He had had a ball-and-socket operation on his hip, about a year and a half before, and was still recovering. It was near the end of the beaver season, with just a few days left to trap, when he became ill. I decided I'd go out to a beaver area a short way downstream, and I took the canoe and some traps. It was about half a mile downstream where I pulled the canoe on shore and walked down one of those dry river channels left where the streams have changed course. I came to this beaver pond. Because I'd left my traps in the canoe, I went back to get them. On the way, I looked at some grizzly tracks that I had seen coming down. They were big ones, and I thought 'Gee, *that* must be some grizzly!'"

He paused thoughtfully, and I interjected, "Did you ever hunt grizzly while you were trapping?"

He shook his head.

"No, they are big game, not fur. If they didn't bother us—and they didn't—we left them alone. I just examined the tracks and realized that they were pretty fresh, but there was no water drying out in them. I went back to the canoe and got the traps and made two sets for beaver. That was about one o'clock, so I went back to the cabin, figuring to get Bruce and myself something to eat. There is always something to do around a trapping cabin, and I was busy until about 5:30 or 6:00 in the evening. Then I told Bruce I was going back to get a look at the beaver sets. I took a Springfield .338 magnum and a .22 rifle with me. The latter was to shoot small game or trapped animals, but the .338 was because of the grizzly tracks. I hiked to the beaver pond and approached it from the treeless side. I wanted to see what was going on with the beavers. I hid behind a small log that was sticking out of the sands of the dry river channel, waiting for them to come out and go about their work. Two beavers came out and I watched one of them as it chewed on a tree. The other one got into one of the sets. Its partner then came over to it and swam around and around it. It was only the second time I'd seen this, and I was waiting to get a shot at it with the .22 rifle. It hadn't been too good a season, and it would help to have another pelt. They were worth about $40 that year, so I was pretty anxious to get this other one. Then I heard a heavy branch crack. I didn't want to look away, but I knew that it was something big, perhaps a moose. I kept watching the swimming beaver, waiting to get a shot in the head, in order not to spoil the skin. The sound of the brush breaking was quite loud, and I thought, 'You'd better turn around and take a look.' And I did.

"It was a big grizzly! Probably the one whose tracks I'd seen. He was walking toward me near the trees. It was also the first bear we had seen that year. I was between it and the pond. I realized the bear was stalking me. His head was down, sniffing and following my tracks where I had walked earlier. He hadn't seen me yet, and was about fifty yards away. I hoped he would turn around. I really didn't want to kill a bear, but he kept coming my way, tracking me down."

Vern was shaking his head as the picture came clearly back to him, and I thought, "Jeez, he's like most of the trappers and many hunters I know. They have a deeper empathy with wildlife than most people. Unless their livelihood, or part of it, is at stake, they don't kill. There's no sport in it for a trapper. It is a living, hard gained, amid elements most of us never see, let alone face day and night." I waited for Vern to continue. He did:

"I figured I'd better show myself to him. I stood up so he could see me.

I was clearly visible to him, and it was funny. He stopped and looked at me just one moment, then seemed to almost give a big smile with a look that said, 'There's dinner!' I remembered Bruce had said, 'They most often make a false charge when they see you.' I waited and he was coming right at me, fast. I looked at a spot where a small creek was between us and thought, 'If you cross that line, that's it!' The distance was about twenty feet to my line. Then he really started to haul ass toward me. When he hit the water in the small creek, I remember thinking, 'Oh, my God! It's really happening.' I just lifted the rifle up and shot at close range. He didn't go down, but reared up on his hind legs and started to bat at his eye with his paw. He was shaking his head too. My second shot hit him in the wrist, and he was spinning around in circles batting at it like a boxer. I shot again and then he was on the ground, biting at the earth. So I finished him off. I don't know why, I started crying. Then I haul-assed back for the canoe.

"When I got there, Bruce was already coming downriver, rowing our riverboat with skinning gear and a flashlight and lantern. I remember how glad I was to see him. He was grinning and said, 'When I heard the four shots I thought, that's gotta be four wolves, or one bear!' He was all ready to go, sick or not. We skinned it out. The skull measured twenty-five and seven-eighths inches. From what I now know, I guess the bear was older than I was, maybe twenty-five to twenty-eight years. His teeth were badly worn and broken, and abscessed deep into the skull."

Vern was looking at me rather gravely. It was the longest continuous speech I had heard from him during three days of association. I was curious about his trapping years.

"How long did you trap, Vern?"

"Oh, about nine years. I did other work besides. I like to consider myself a professional trapper, trapping for myself—ermine, mink, marten, musk-rat, otter, beaver, wolverine, and wolf. For the state of Alaska I've trapped black-tailed deer, wolf, black bears, and brown bears. I've been a fishing guide—worked for the fisheries department in Alaska and Canada—been a camp cook, an assistant hunting guide, and a game technician for a division of Fish and Game."

"Wasn't trapping fairly lucrative?"

He shook his head.

"Not really. Bruce and I split about $1,800 to a top of $2,500 a year, but I liked the life. The fondest memories I have are the three years I trapped with Bruce."

The imprint of that experience was evident in his eyes. I could think back on a few such years of my own. I broke in:

"You know, when you were talking about the grizzly batting around like a boxer, it brought back some vivid memories to me. I have seen both black bears and grizzlies do that. A couple of them not killed with my first shot acted just like that. They stood up on their hind legs and batted at the air around them, like a shadow boxer. I have it figured that they feel the shock of the bullet and think it is a thump from an adversary right beside them, and they swipe just anywhere around them, twisting, trying to find the other animal that hit them, striking out instinctively. But, as soon as they see you nearby, they usually come."

Vern nodded in agreement.

"Yeah. Unless your next bullet gets into a vital spot, you can be in trouble. They are awfully fast. You've killed a couple, Mike?"

It was my turn to nod assent.

"Yeh, I've killed a couple—both black and grizzly bears. They sure as hell *are* fast! But what about the others you've had to kill? Were they while you were trapping, too?"

"Yes. Two were while snaring brown bears for the state. One of them was out at Pile Driver. We were up there on a brown-bear research project. I was designated as the 'brown bear expert,' probably as a result of my big-game guiding experience, and maybe because I had been forced to kill one some years before. I had also accumulated some experience snaring black bears, using the Aldrich foot snare, which was the proposed method of capturing brown bears along the salmon streams in Hawk Inlet.

"Four of us worked in two-man teams, Loyal Johnson, the game area biologist for A.B.C. Islands, and his partner, game technician Scott Brainard, were on this expedition. I was teamed up with Dick Orchard, a forestry-sciences lab technician from Oregon. The fisheries division had given us key salmon stream information for Hawk Inlet, which told us which streams had salmon and which didn't, and the peak escapement periods for them.

"I remember it was August 12, a beautiful southeaster type of day. Loyal and Scott went to scout out streams for fish and bear sign at the head of the inlet. Dick and I ran our skiff to Wheeler Creek, at the mouth of Hawk Inlet. We went ashore and hiked maybe three-quarters of a mile upstream before deciding that there really didn't seem to be much fish or bear activity there, mostly because the stream was too deep and slow running. There were no good places for bears to fish, even if there were fish.

"We were going to go back to the main boat, since Wheeler Creek had been the big stream we were counting on, as suggested by the fisheries people. Previously, I had spent some weeks in Hawk Inlet during the winter, trapping deer for the department, but it looked much different in the summer. However, we cruised up the inlet and came around a point at Pile Driver Cove. Looking up that inlet, I saw several eagles and a couple of hundred seagulls. They seemed to be busy on a tiny stream that was around a point, out of sight. To me, that meant there must be salmon. And if there were salmon, that meant bears.

"So we took the boat in closer and into the small creek mouth. Sure enough, several hundred pink salmon and a few dogs [Keta, or dog salmon] were schooled up at the mouth. There was also a long meadow bordering the stream, and working on it were lots of eagles and seagulls. But what was more important, we saw lots of bear sign. They had padded down good trails through the tall meadow grasses, forming a maze of bear paths."

He stopped for a moment, as if vividly recalling the dramatic moments to come. I was curious about the setting.

"Was it similar to Pack Creek—here? It sounds like it."

"Yes. A meadow like the grassy one here. Anyway, Dick and I grabbed our snaring equipment and rifles from the boat and headed out. Dick was carrying a .375 H & H magnum Weatherby, right off the shelf, a .44 magnum handgun in a shoulder holster, and six trigger devices for the snares. Since I was usually the point man, I went lighter and carried items that wouldn't interfere with my maneuverability in case we ran into bear trouble. I had six cables for the bear snares and my own personal Model 70 Winchester .338 magnum.

"Dick was new to Alaska. He hadn't seen too many brown bears on the ground level, so I filled him in as we went along. We were getting beyond the grassy meadow and entering into the forested riverbanks, traveling pretty continually among bear tracks and salmon carcasses. At this point we started setting out snares, because the stream was filled with humpies [pink, or humpback, salmon]. We could wade the stream almost anywhere with 'Southeast Sneakers' [sixteen-inch rubber boots]. The gill plates from dead humpies littered the stream on the beach, in the pool bottoms, and on some of the logs crossing the stream. Most of the dead fish we saw seemed to have been freshly caught, and when I pointed this out, Dick disagreed with me."

Vern paused reflectively before continuing.

"In fact, it was looking bearier all the time. The fisheries people had never surveyed this stream, so they didn't know about the bears. But I had good reason to believe we had hit the action on the stream right during the feeding frenzy, on what I'd call a high-success bear fishin' stream: small shallow waters, plenty of fish. In fact, in a couple of days I figured the stream would be holding only a handful of the lucky survivors. It seemed to be a much more important bear stream than the other deep creeks we'd visited.

"Looking at things as I went upstream, I figured there were about eight different bears working the stream. But, Dick, expecting more excitement in the way of encountering bears, disagreed with my estimate. I went on selecting what I thought were the best places for setting snares, and I guess we had traveled about forty-five minutes from our skiff, not counting the time spent making our sets."

He paused again, lost in thought, before continuing.

"We went on upstream, me in the lead, and we busted through a thick patch of devil's club and blueberry growth. We were following a well-used bear trail that closely paralleled the stream. The trail came out on a narrow piece of ground between the river cutbank and the deep brush. On my left was a spruce tree four feet thick. Just as I was stepping over its roots to get around it, right there, about four steps away, was a sow and her yearling cub! They were right in heavy devil's club growth, hunched up over a pink salmon.''

Vern drew a deep breath, remembering.

"This was a real total surprise, and I knew we were in a bad situation.''

He paused, and I interjected a question.

"You said about *four* steps away—about ten feet?''

"Not any more. I don't know if Dick saw the bears, and I really didn't care. It sure wasn't any time for sightseeing! I immediately hissed back to him, 'We gotta get out of here!' As I shoved Dick back down the trail I kept looking over my shoulder, expecting the old lady to appear, charging after us. When I wasn't looking over my shoulder, I had visions of, and could practically feel, her grabbing me from behind. I just couldn't imagine their not having seen us! I sure wasn't prepared to fight, as I felt confined by the thick brush. We ran about thirty or forty yards, to a small opening between the brush and the trees, and I felt more comfortable with that much visibility. Dick was standing on the bear trail about four feet to my right and six feet behind me.''

Vern looked up at me as he related the story.

"When you're in a situation like that, Mike, what is the right thing to do? Shoot and waste a shot? I've had many bears ignore rifle shots. Should we holler and make a lot of noise? Or should we keep running down the trail? We had made it that far without being noticed. We could probably escape their attention.''

Vern shrugged disconsolately before continuing remorsefully.

"That is where we screwed up.''

"How?'' I asked.

"Well, we stood there for several moments. I couldn't stand the suspense, hemmed in like that, not knowing where the sow had gone and knowing that she must have heard us. I shouted 'Hey,' just like that. What had happened was that the old lady had sent her cub across the stream. She too had started across, following the cub. They were still behind the big spruce tree at this time. Then the old lady stopped on a gravel bar and stood on her hind legs. Boy! Of all the damn places for her to stand up! It was one of the few places where she could have seen us, and she spotted us immediately. Dick was wearing very light-colored clothes—a pinstripe hickory shirt, light-blue jeans, white sox—and he had a white beard, something that a bear could pick up even if it had poor eyesight. I was wearing my camouflage jump suit, and with my black beard I wasn't too visible.''

He was shaking his head thoughtfully.

"The sow dropped down on all fours and just disappeared from view. For a moment I thought, 'What a relief! She took off!' Then in a couple of seconds she scared the crap out of me. She appeared suddenly from behind the big spruce tree, charging down the trail we had been on, hell bent for election. I was caught totally off guard, still holding two cables in my left hand, with my rifle sling still on my shoulder.

"Her eyes were glued right on Dick, and I hollered 'Shoot! Shoot!' He did, right over my shoulder when the sow was about eighteen feet away. She didn't even hesitate. The muzzle blast from Dick's .375 magnum was right behind my ear as I slipped off my own rifle. There was a log about ten feet in front of me, and she jumped it with all her adrenaline up, headed right at Dick. She was in the air from the momentum of the jump, and I think she saw my gun come off my shoulder, and her right front leg stretched out with claws as long as my fingers, reaching for me as I leaned back to get out of the way. I could look right down her throat as I got my .338 up at my hip and pulled the trigger."

Vern was looking at the floor as he spoke.

"The power from the big rifle completely changed her direction in midair. It blew her off the trail, over the bank, and into the stream. At that same instant the cub started bawling and climbed into a tree, just about where the sow had stood up. I jumped down the riverbank and into the stream, to make sure that the sow was out of commission. I felt terrible, because we had provoked her attack. We should have kept on running."

He was genuinely affected by the death, even yet. I thought of a grizzly I had been filming that had reacted by attacking and that I'd had to kill. I knew just how he felt.

"Vern, these things happen. We know before we go into such a situation it is a calculated risk. Your job requires that you be in their territory, in an effort to learn something that might help them. You take the risk."

"Yeah. You tell yourself that, Mike, but you still don't like what happens. Anyway, we pulled her out of the stream, and the cub saw her and came down that tree like one of those tree toppers sliding down with climbing spikes, falling about ten to fifteen feet at a time. We grabbed up our rifles, but he took right off into the bush. We examined the sow and found that Dick's bullet had just caused a flesh wound about the size of two hands on the left side of her breast. No broken bones. He had been wondering how she could keep coming with a .375 magnum slug in her, and I told him, 'You have to *hit* 'em to stop 'em!' But he was still convinced his .44 magnum would have finished her in close. My own bullet went right into her mouth and blew out the back left side of her skull. There were powder burns on her muzzle."

I was shaking my head.

"That was mighty close!"

"Yeah. It was," he said with a wry look.

"What gun were you using—that had that impact? Your cutoff .45-70 rifle?"

"Yeah. That one." He nodded toward the stubby rifle hanging on a nail on the cabin wall.

When I had first seen him carrying it, the gun had interested me. First of all, it was a .45-70-caliber, a caliber I had not even seen previously. It looked like an extremely expensive gun—at least before the amputation of the stock. Vern got up, stepped over, and took it off the wall to hand it to me. It was a real surprise. Most cut-down guns are made from cheaper standard makes and of common, standard bore or caliber rifles or shotguns. This rifle was a prize, custom-made gun with an exquisitely carved pistol grip, and the stock was made of Circassian burl walnut of a higher grade than even the best of American burl black walnut. The original stock alone would have cost between $200 and $500. The once highly polished, blued barrel was cut down to about eighteen inches, making the full length of the arm about twenty-eight inches instead of the almost standard forty-six inches common in most big-game rifles. It was, in effect, a very high-powered magnum pistol, which could be carried slung under one arm with little of the unwieldiness of a full-length big-game rifle. It was a gun entirely designed for its purpose: last-minute, close-up, emergency self-defense.

I patted the finely finished remnant butt, which was simply the end of the pistol grip on a normal stock, noting that it was a professionally finished modification.

"Did you do the modification, Vern?"

"No. I had a gunsmith do the barrel and modified sights. I did the stock myself. I'm an avid archer, and had read articles about archers who were packing sawed-off rifles and shotguns for protection. Once when I was in a compact mass of bushes where there was a brown bear that I couldn't see, I decided that my job description required a customized, precision instrument of defense." He grimaced a bit ruefully. "And that's how this sawed-off .45-70 Siamese Mauser came about."

"It's a beautiful Circassian walnut stock. A hell of an expensive gun to cut down," I noted.

"Yeh. The guy who did it for me thought I was nuts. It was a specially made rifle for a big-game hunter who wanted the best. But this is the way I wanted it."

I thought about that for a moment.

"Is it the one that you used on the last grizzly that came after you?"

He nodded and got up to hang the gun back on the wall. The details of that experience would be worth knowing.

"What happened that time?"

"It was a similar incident, Mike," he said. "We were snagging and marking bears again in these Admiralty Islands, this time at Greens Creek, in Hawk Inlet. There were two field men, two former Malaysian Peace Corps wildlife biologists. Rod Flynn was a rhino expert, and Paul Conry, a gaur expert, whatever that is! And me, a 'grunt' game technician, Class 3. During our several days there we had bumped into bears every day, the most being seven in one day. And a few days before, we had snared three bears.

We had traplines on Pile Driver and Zinc and Greens creeks, and it was around the first of August, in a good salmon-escapement time.

"When we got to the beach we checked our equipment for replacing snares, then lifted on our packs. Paul and I carried frame packs. Both these guys were inexperienced with brown bears. Rod had been around bears a little in Glacier National Park, where they aren't allowed to carry guns, and Paul had even less association with bears, so I tried to encourage both of them to keep their guns loaded and handy when we were snaring the animals. You never know when someone may save your ass! I was carrying that .45-70 Mauser. We were working right along the bear trails, and sometimes it was fogged in. I was always the point man, out front. If it got 'beary,' I would flick off the safety, because I always kept a round in the chamber. It depended upon whether the bear looked threatening."

He stopped as if expecting criticism about his "round in the breach." I laughed.

"Vern, people who don't know guns and hunting conditions need to have a safety on! There is more crap written about that—like dragging a shotgun after you through a fence, leaning the gun against a tree—hell! If you don't know enough to lay down a gun so that it won't fall over, you don't deserve to be allowed to have it. And if you are stupid enough to pull one through the fence with the muzzle in your direction, eliminating you might be beneficial to others. Having an empty chamber while you are hunting, that's pure crap. Half the game that gets away does so because some guy is trying to figure out how to get his safety off and get a shell into the chamber. Good conservation measure, yes, but if you learn to handle a gun properly, you learn that, theoretically, there is *always* one in the chamber and the gun has a hair trigger. If you were on bear trails and didn't have a shell in the chamber, you would be jeopardizing the lives of novice companions and your own life. I don't know a really experienced woodsman, trapper, or hunter who doesn't keep a gun on ready. The only people I've met who militated against it didn't know their ass from bear crap. They were the so-called gun-safety experts, who have spent about as much time in the wilds as my three-year-old granddaughter!"

Vern smiled at my tirade and nodded his head a couple of times.

"Well, as I was saying. I had a shell in the chamber, as I usually did. We never knew when a sow might come chasing out at us if by chance one of the cubs got into a snare. We did have cub governors on the cables to prevent catching them, but you never know when clamps, swivels, and cables will react improperly, or whether the bear is well caught. So always be prepared, I impressed on these guys.

"It was a sunny day as we tramped up Greens Creek. A few pink salmon spurted upstream. We reached a place where a big skunk cabbage patch lay in front of the forest. It was along Zinc Creek, where there is a grassy flat. There were no signs of fish in Zinc Creek, but it was where our trapline began. We checked several bear snares set in well-worn bear trails parallel-ing the banks of the creek. It was where we had snared two bears before, one of them Number 67, a female too small for a radio collar."

He paused, recalling the details.

"From there we got onto our main-line game trail, which follows the bank of Zinc Creek. Our snares were well spaced out on the bear trails, and we had orange tape marking them and also the tributary trails leading off. It was nearly two and a half hours from the time we had left the skiff at the river mouth before we got to what we call Greens–Zinc Creek cutoff. The two creeks divide and are about a stone's throw apart."

He paused to think for a moment.

"I remember commenting on how dull things had been during the last couple of days. We hadn't seen any bears, and we had a couple of snares sprung. Since we were near Greens Creek, it was necessary to get on the best, or easiest, bear trail along it, and this took us downriver. We always took a shortcut, about a thirty-yard detour through thick brush and blow-downs, to locate one really fine bear trail along Greens Creek. Good bear trails don't always lead in the direction in which you are headed.

"I had just reached the last blowdown that we had to crawl over, about fifteen feet from our main trail leading downriver and about twenty more from the water. I could get a good look at Greens Creek, and I was just step-ping off the blowdown when I caught a glimpse just of the hair on the backs of what appeared to be a couple of brown bears, of different sizes, wading in the water downstream. They disappeared around a good big spruce tree that was lying between them and me.

"As soon as I saw them, I yelled, 'Bears!' to alert Rod and Paul. I couldn't see them behind me and didn't look back, because my whole attention was where the bears had disappeared. It was just as if I had called the big sow brown bear when I shouted, 'Bears!' She jumped up on the bank and came right from behind the big spruce tree. She made a couple of steps forward, swinging her head from side to side for a couple of moments as if taking inventory and sizing things up. She was less than twenty feet from me, with her front feet on the main trail."

Vern heaved in a deep breath.

"While she was there, eyeing us, I yelled, 'Spread out!'—not knowing where the other two guys were but thinking that, if she saw she was out-numbered, maybe she wouldn't want to get any closer.

"She then turned right around and disappeared behind the big spruce. Then, she went back down into the stream, out of sight. But just like that, in a couple of seconds she came bolting out from behind the same spruce tree. It was as if she had hesitated, then all of a sudden she was charging right at me. I hollered to the guys behind me, 'Shoot!'"

Vern's voice was lowered as he spoke.

"She got to about fifteen feet in her rush when I heard a shot ring out from my left. The bullet didn't have any effect on her, and she was almost on me when I just held my 45-70 out in front of my waist and pulled the trigger. She folded up within eight feet of me, and was thrashin' around. I jumped in and put a final shot in the back of her neck. Just as I did so, a big grizzly cub came flying by my right side at about ten feet and snapped at me."

Vern was nodding his head unhappily.

"I put my rifle up on him and nearly dumped him too, because Paul was yelling, 'Vern! There's another big one!' Looking across the river, I saw there were two more yearling cubs standing in the alders, bawling. The cub that passed me climbed a tree about twenty feet away, then dropped down and followed the other two across the stream. I looked back, and there were Rod and Paul, standing on the blowdown about ten and twenty feet behind me. It was Paul who shot. I was actually unable to back up, being pinned against another blowdown. I was wearing a nearly white shirt, and Paul and Rod both had on dark blue and were up on the blowdown, so I guess I appeared to be a threat to her cubs. When we examined the sow, we found that my first bullet had gone in at the base of her lower left jaw and come out on top of the right shoulder. She was about seven years old and weighed about four hundred pounds. I felt bad about that bear. She was just defending her cubs."

Vern was looking down at the planks of the cabin floor. I understood.

"At that distance from a charging bear, Vern, you don't have any alternative. It's your hide or *its* hide! Some of my friends, knowing the experiences I've had, have asked, 'What the hell are you going up to Alaska for, Mike? Getting yourself mixed up with grizzly bears.' If they don't know, I can't tell them. Anyway, I never expect anything to happen, and I hope what we both do will help the bears."

"Yeah," Vern said. "I hope the information we get helps to preserve them."

Some months later, Vern Beier sent me his own written accounts of the latter two bear killing incidents, along with a nice letter and several color photographs of the different bears his crews had been tagging and collaring. Verne had penciled in a note at the bottom:

> Everyone has their own philosophy. I believe it's a person's privilege to roam freely in brown-bear country. People are trespassers. Because of this, and because of my great admiration and respect for the brown bear, the bears I have had close brushes with, I have a personal policy: to let them charge to right up to my invisible threshhold, giving the bear the very maximum opportunity to bluff or have a change of heart.
>
> Some day it may catch up to me, but if I am packing a big rifle, and I know and trust its capabilities and awesome power, there's no reason in my book of ethics to shoot a charging bear at more than twenty feet."

Yeah, Vern, that's the way it is!

The Redhead VI

Water trickled slowly from a crack in the den roof—an occasional few drops following the unseasonal mid-March rain. She barely felt them on the guard hairs of her dry winter coat; they did not seep through her underfur. As the periods of light filtering through the snow-blocked entrance lengthened, so did the cries and the nursing times of the she-bear's two new companions. As the intense frigidity of the outside air waned steadily, the small cavern warmed. She felt an occasional itch and a general awakening. Periods of actual slumber were shorter. She became more conscious of the nails and milk teeth of the cubs pressing sharply against her mammary glands.

A birdsong eventually aroused her.

The trickle of water from the roof was now annoying. Occasionally it soaked down to her skin, where it remained in her matted underfur. To avoid the leak, she pushed the twig and leaf bedding closer to the entrance. But there the water collected even more moistly. Restlessly she moved again, but dampness was daily increasing in the den.

The cubs, increasingly more agile, had begun to feed more aggressively. Now conscious of their individual identities, they demanded more regular feedings. Their eyes had been open long enough only to allow them an unfocused gaze. They could see movement but were unable to identify objects clearly. They still found her wet teats by nuzzling through her belly hair. Afterward, they would roll about each other, and occasionally within the confines of their home, their bawling and whining became quite noisy—disconcertingly so to the she-bear.

After one noisier-than-usual session, when the light from the den entrance was quite strong, she got up restlessly from the bed. Abandoning the sleeping cubs to the pile of branches and leaves, she pawed at the snow in the entrance. The rigid ices were gone from it, and the mush parted readily. The calm, fresh, warm air alerted her to the April spring outside. She sniffed casually, then listened intently for outside sounds. No strange sounds or scents came with the freshening air. Only a distant birdsong came from the valley below.

Abruptly, she pushed her shoulders against the bank of snow and thrust her head fully out into the open air. The snow blocking the entrance was still fairly heavy, yet from her vantage point it seemed that the only snowbanks that remained were under trees or beneath the deep foliage of newly budding bushes. The scent of the yellow alder catkins and pollens came recognizably to her nostrils. They told her that new grasses would be growing in the valley below. Perhaps even the yellow spikes of the skunk-cabbage shoots were bursting from the mud of the nearby swamplands.

For a long time she stared irresolutely, tempted by the new life-forces. Then ignoring the plaintive wails of her cubs, she pushed herself clear of the entrance. On the tender pads newly forming on her feet, the coldness of the snow was a chilly surprise. She lifted a front paw to lick the ice granules from between her toes, then sat back on her buttocks and, one after the other, licked at all four paws.

From inside the cavern came a loud, insistent bawling. Aware that such noises could bring curious, perhaps predatory visitors, the she-bear woofed sharply. As if in total surprise at the unusual sound, the cubs' protests ceased, but seconds later they began anew.

She was reluctant to leave the balmy outside air, but she returned slowly to the darkness of the den. She moved directly to the nest, where she reclined with her back to the cave wall. In that position her eyes would now face the opened entrance. Immediately the cubs began to nurse, and moments later they drifted off into slumber, she with them. Darkness was returning outside.

The next ray of light that came to her in the semidarkness was not sunlight. It came from a five-celled flashlight, and the frightening human voices were nearby.

"She's in there, Dave. But look, she was out yesterday! See here! Her tracks show she didn't move away from the entrance, though. Better not to disturb her. We're getting a good signal, so we'll just follow her and the cubs for awhile."

The footsteps retreated, quietly into the distance. When she was certain that the intruders had left, she pushed herself cautiously out the entrance. The air was warm with the brightening sunlight. On the very slight breeze the acrid scent of the newly bursting poplar buds was heavy. Just below the den mouth, between the trees, the lush, verdant new grasses were visible. The skunk cabbages would now be flowering.

An awakening appetite was niggling at her. Where the snow had almost completely melted into the ground, she licked the moisture several minutes. She moved about fifteen feet from the den entrance and found a few tufts of newly growing grasses. She nipped them off delicately with her front teeth, grinding them slowly on her molars. The sounds of bawling cubs made her turn her head toward the den mouth. The smaller cub, which was now the more active one, the female, had her tiny head out in the open. Her milky eyes were blinking. Fully bewildered by the intensity of the sunshine, the cub let out an agonized cry that became a squeal.

The mother ambled quietly over to her cub and began to lick its head solicitously. The second cub was now beside his littermate with a sleepy, dazed expression on his face. Abruptly conscious that he was in a new element, he too squealed with sudden alarm. His mother's soft, throaty noises calmed him, and her pink tongue slid comfortingly across his face.

Seconds later she backed off from them, sat on her haunches, and there uttered a series of deep, gurgling sounds. Startled at her retreat, the cubs remained immobile at the cave entrance. First they tentatively uttered little cries. Then, hesitantly, each in turn wobbled on unsteady legs toward their mother's belly nipples, now exposed. A moment later they were nursing in the full sunshine, aware only of her sheltering presence. Shortly afterward, when she reclined, they curled up and slept next to her belly. Minutes later, she picked them up, holding them tenderly in her jaws, and carried them, each in turn, back into the den.

Aware that they would sleep only for a short time, she left the den. Moving slowly and scenting the air, she listened constantly, alert to other life. The long slope to a patch of green grasses was familiar. Once on the small meadows, she began to graze sparingly with the contented calmness of a bovine. Her appetite was increasing.

Satisfied, she moved toward the den, but the effort of climbing uphill brought cramps to her belly. Still well away from her den, she moved quietly off into the bushes. There, after much straining and changing of position, she evacuated the large anal plug that had restrained her digestive processes throughout the long winter. She also urinated away some of the water from the snow that she had consumed.

Relieved by the sortie, she continued uphill to the den and lay down on the slope outside the cave soaking up the rays of the sun, which was near the pink western horizon. Minutes later, she was abruptly conscious of the two strident voices coming from within the dark cavern.

She went inside.

CHAPTER 7

Polar Bears Are Pussycats?

In the Arctic wind wispy lines of granular white snow drifted off the pads of the polar bear crossing downwind of us. It was the kind of unforgettable sight that, when caught on film, repays the photographer the money spent and the months or years of waiting. It was the culmination of fifty years of waiting for me.

It was the embodiment of excitement to study the bear's every movement as we saw it walking overland from the southeast toward the tidal waters seventeen miles east of Churchill, Manitoba. Creamy-coated against the blue green of newly formed pond ice, outlined against the yellowed hedges of sub-Arctic growths, or highlighted in front of the blue-black glaciated boulders—no matter what the setting—the majesty of the animal was almost shocking. After three minutes of staring, I had to express my feelings.

"My God, what a magnificent sight!"

The laconic reply from one of my companions was, "Yeah. That's a small one, maybe 350 pounds. Wait until you see a *big* one!"

It was a wait that the subzero cold and wind-chill factor of the next few days in Churchill could only enhance. The day before, when I had boarded the Canadian Pacific airliner in Vancouver, fifteen hundred air miles south and westward, I really did not expect that within twenty-four hours I would see and photograph even one polar bear, let alone several.

Yet, here I was, learning visually the meaning of *tundra*. To say that Arctic tundra is barren is an understatement, as it would be to use the word *desert* to illuminate the intolerably bleak treelessness of hot, dry Saharan sands in the reader's mind. Neither of those labels actually alert the mind to the real vistas, to the actuality. The tundra surrounding the meagerly snow-swept lands upon which we watched the polar bear was a composite of small ice-hardened ponds, blue-green with recent freeze-up when seen from afar. Yet peering into them was like looking down through clear or murky glass panes, depending upon the surface powderings of ice crystals present. Below were the brown depths, in which frozen aquatic growths appeared pendant, gracefully draped over the black mud bottoms. On the surrounding plains the yellow grassy pond edges were a brilliant remnant, coloured very recently by the late Indian summer. Short, stiff brush mixtures of alder and willow trees reached only to waist height, but filling the sheltered pockets around ponds and scattered sparsely elsewhere were six- to sixteen-foot pines shadowed at their bases by dark low-growth junipers. All these flora were dwarfed by the short summer growth season, annually hammered, stunted, and shredded by the rigors of frigid air and perma-frost.

And because humans stand taller than most Arctic flora, their vision extends across and beyond out to the straight-line horizon. The stillness of the clear air intensifies the effect of barrenness.

But this landscape is not barren!

Only three miles beyond Churchill's bleak streets an Arctic fox, brilliant white in its new pelage, had scurried across the strip of tundra between the gravel road and the bordering frozen ponds, seeming bereft of the "wildness" that we dwellers in southern climes associate with wildlife. It darted back and forth across the intervening space in what might seem a meaningless pattern. In its uninterrupted meanderings, it moved as far away as the grass skirt at the pond edges, then back as close as thirty feet from the truck. It was undeterred when three of us—Bob Taylor and Wayne Lankinen, well-known Canadian wildlife photographers, and I—climbed out with cameras. Helen Lankinen, Wayne's wife, remained in the truck on "polar-bear alert," a precaution that I was not yet aware was necessary.

Presently the little animal came almost close enough to the camera tripods to be hand-netted, so close that we saw clearly a half-inch circle of jet black fur, apparently resisting its natural body chemistry, and its coal-black eyes and tiny, twitching button nose. The black features were the only minute deviations from complete winter camouflage. Amazed by the fox's lack of fear at close range, I watched in fascination. To and fro it covered the ground at a fast trot, not stopping except to glance almost casually around; then suddenly, almost as fast as light itself, it would pounce, bite, and lift from drifted snows a small body with a dangling tail.

"Did you *see* that! It grabbed a mouse! And swallowed it!"

Veteran of several years on the tundra, Bob Taylor turned an amused glance toward me. "Yes. Foxes have very acute hearing. They hear the lemmings beneath the snow and pounce on them."

Yes, I thought, *barrenness* is the illusion of limited vision and knowledge. While on the surface of the tundra the fox meandered willy-nilly, beneath the early snows were the tunnels of lemmings, mice, and other rodents among the stunted blueberry bushes and sparse grasses covering the thin age-old loams. Above were the ever-present "karrrroooking" ravens; the occasional silent, white-winged snowy owl, and the sudden, darting peregrines. It was all becoming apparent to me while the scurrying search of the fox took it out of camera range.

We drove on southeastward, ten miles farther along the road. Seaward the hulk of an abandoned steamship lay where a mutinous crew had driven her hard upon the shoals. "There's *one*—over there! Just beyond that second pond! Near the willows," alerted Bob Taylor.

At first glance my eyes, trained to green forest and meadow, failed to see the white-on-white image, but slowly the polar bear form became apparent. It was not truly white on white, but a creamy hue on snow white, a shadowed movement backed by the low winter sun. Then, as the animal saw our movements, a barely perceptible change of path led it a hundred yards downwind, where the sun would catch the fullness of its lush, creamy coat, sharp against the snow. Its pace, seemingly unhurried, was very deceiving; suddenly the big animal was within seventy-five yards. There, just past a hedge of short alder and willow brush, it hesitated and looked to the west. A much larger polar bear was moving from that direction, moving closer to us.

"My gosh! Look at that one!" I exploded.

"That's a good-sized one, Mike. Maybe five hundred pounds. This one," Taylor waved his hand toward the first one, "is aware of it. That's why it's moving off. There is a real hierarchy among the bears. The smaller ones give way to the medium ones, and those in turn yield to the big ones. They usually keep well apart, always wary of an approaching bear."

Beside him, and in front of the vehicle, the fast click, click, click of Wayne Lankinen's motorized camera told of the shots he was taking, all in quick succession. As soon as he filled a roll, he quickly inserted new film into the camera, which was mounted with a huge 600-millimeter lens. Because of his dedicated professionalism he knew that an abundance of good shots ultimately produces a photograph with perfect composition, clarity, and arrangement that will make a startlingly good magazine cover or illustration, or grace an exhibit at a national or international exposition. I watched him as the smaller bear moved around the nearby willows and started out across the ice of the intervening pond. Wayne was so preoccupied with getting the ultimate shot that it became obvious why Helen stayed on the alert, binoculars raised occasionally to her eyes, twisting regularly to all the perimeter of the horizon. Her voice came calmly, clearly, from the truck.

"There is a *third* one coming across the far pond."

Bob and Wayne immediately spotted the newer arrival, then went back to their camera viewfinders. I finally found the newcomer, then studied it through my own 10-power binoculars.

It was a polar bear about the size of the first one, wary in its advance, obviously plotting its course to keep distance between it and the hulking five-hundred-pounder. The first smaller bear had crossed the road and had trekked out to some hedges of willow brush beyond two pond-lakes some four hundred yards distant. There, abruptly, it lay down at the edge of the bushes, from which it would have a clear view to the south-eastern horizon. I was intrigued by the evident thought process. All the bears we had in view at that time had been traveling from the southeast up the shoreline of the inland ocean. The wind, on the other hand, was blowing strongly inland from the shore in exactly the opposite direction, leaving the recumbent bear without the scent from any approach. Its hearing, too, would be hampered by the whistling wind. Sight alone would be its sole means of warning, and its position took full advantage of that single faculty. It was surprising to me that each of the three bears apparently had been quite aware of our presence when we first sighted them, yet we were all using binoculars!

In fact, the larger of the bears, even from a quarter of a mile away, had often turned its head directly toward us, obviously studying the two men while they photographed the smaller bear. The big one's approach over the next five hundred yards had been casually in our direction. Its one deviation had been to look curiously in the direction where, a moment before, the white Arctic fox had left its hunting trail. Perhaps some remnant scent had appealed to its appetite.

The approach of a white bear *is* awesome!

The gait fascinated me because, having seen the species move about only within the cement and stone confines of a zoo, I had no real concept of its true agility or speed. As the big bear crossed the barrens of the tundra his pace had seemed slow, almost flowing. One might characterize it as smooth, but that would not explain the speed of the bear's advance. Within moments the big bear had come the full quarter-mile, at least twice as fast as a hurrying man could do it, yet without any evidence of haste. At first I thought my sense of its quick approach had derived from my intense fascination, which might have affected my consciousness of time. The bear was now on the other side of the two-acre pond directly in front of us, showing uncertainty about continuing in our immediate direction. Bob had folded his tripod, and Wayne was lifting his. The animal was almost too close to use telephoto lenses, which both of them had attached to the camera bodies.

I had climbed back into the vehicle. As Bob stepped up, I voiced my enthusiasm.

"What an amazing animal! They move so gracefully. It doesn't seem possible to describe such motion."

"Their speed is very deceptive, Mike. You see them first in the distance, and suddenly they are right where you are. You have to be careful."

"But their grace! It's difficult to put into words—almost snakelike in its fluidity."

He laughed. "Well! I've heard their movements described to be less like a bear or dog, and more like a pussy cat."

"Pussy cat? Yeah! They slink all right, but—!"

Wayne Lankinen quietly joined the conversation.

"Some say they act more like dogs, but they're no pussy cats, I can tell you!"

We all laughed at his implication. We were watching the larger bear circle at an almost-constant distance from the truck. Between us and the barely visible windswept seas lay intermittent black rock formations, perhaps a hundred feet in elevation, a bulwark that had governed the young bear's path. Wayne drove the truck still farther across the open tundra.

At a point that would place us in the path of any of those bears we had seen, and closer to the whitecaps whipped up by the stormy winds buffeting Hudson Bay, we saw two fair-sized, single bears moving separately on the midhorizon. Then abruptly, only three hundred yards away, we saw a good-sized single bear. Its coat was a surprisingly whiter cream; it seemed almost illuminated from within as the sun, struggling through the overcast, touched the long guard hairs. It was a prime subject for a photographer, nor was it as wary as the three previous bears had been. Wayne drove toward the bear's selected course, and sixty yards from the animal—so as not to turn it away—he stopped the vehicle. The approach of a vehicle drove the animals off their course, but they might approach, even nose against the windows, of a stationary vehicle.

Visiting naturalists both hope for and are apprehensive of such a visit. Unlike a grizzly, a polar bear at the car door or window is usually only mildly offensive. A grizzly will occasionally attempt to get inside, and they actually have battered vehicles so that the car or truck appeared to have been in a street accident. The usual tactic of the polar bear is almost gentle, often a series of nose pushes and occasionally two raised front paws placed against the windows or metal of the vehicle with a series of persistent, buffeting shoves. Usually these investigations cease when the driver pushes the horn button and the bear flinches backward and, occasionally, takes off at a fast run.

Wayne had driven the station-wagon to a position that intersected the bear's path, but the animal moved away to correct that. Twice Wayne and Bob got out of the vehicle to take photographs, but each time the bear moved away, at no time offering them perfect shots. Yet its movements were in a direction that could be followed by taking another of the abandoned army-made road spurs that crisscrossed the landscape.

During our third close approach, the animal moved off in the direction of one of the larger frozen ponds. This sheet of ice was surrounded on all sides with a variety of vegetation, a sharp black filigree of leafless bushes, jutting black rocks, and skirts of yellow-orange dried grasses any of which afforded an excellent natural background for the splendid brilliance of the bear's glistening creamy coat. Wayne drove quickly toward the bear, stopping about a hundred feet from the magnificent animal just as Bob cautioned against "spooking" it. Both he and Wayne pulled their tripods and cameras from the vehicle and quietly moved toward the bear.

Seeming less apprehensive of the vehicle than it had been, the big white animal simply glanced at the men poised behind their tripods as it moved effortlessly through the hedge of willow or scrub alder to the edge of the frozen pond. At the edge of the slick surface it hesitated, then moved right out on the ice. On the far side of the pond was a triangular spur of yellowed swamp grasses backed by a hedge of dark-hued willow brush, a perfect background. Wayne and Bob kept edging up toward the animal, their cameras clicking.

For a moment, the large animal looked back at them, perhaps speculatively, then it sauntered toward a spur of yellowed grasses and, without circling or further reconnaissance, dropped to the ice, with its hind legs just touching the grasses. Apparently satisfied that the two men and the vehicle, which had obviously been dogging its path, did not intend to harm it, it had accepted their proximity without either fear or rancor. It simply lay down on the ice, extended its head over its front paws, and relaxed.

Wayne immediately moved around the hedge of brush in front of him, took several photographs, and edged forward again, this time within seventy feet of the reclining animal. Bob, who had come back to the vehicle to reload his camera, was watching. A moment later, when Wayne took several steps out onto the ice to obtain a clearer view of the animal, Bob spoke a trifle apprehensively, "He's getting a little close. I'm going down there."

"Do you guys carry any guns? Sidearms?" I showed my own concern.

"No, we don't." Taylor shook his head. As he did so he opened his hand to reveal a small explosive device, variously called a "banger," "firecracker," and other names. "These will usually put them off."

He slipped out of the truck, walking very slowly and quietly down the slope to the lake to back up Lankinen. I was nonplussed. There was nothing I could do in the event of attack, a helpless feeling. Bob was nearly to the ice's edge, and Wayne was still moving out farther onto it, actually setting his tripod points into the ice about thirty or forty feet from the prone bear. I watched the sleek white animal's every body movement, particularly the attitude of its head, which was held at a slant across the paws. Its bright obsidian eyes were looking directly in Wayne's direction. The charcoal knob of the nose was working ever so slightly, clearly visible in my binoculars. The click of Lankinen's shutter was audible, and his last approach had caused the bear to focus upon him intently.

"He's too damn close!" I said, without thinking of Helen's feelings, as she sat watching through the front windshield.

"Yes! I think so, too." she nodded. "He gets too engrossed."

"Bob has a banger with him," I offered lamely.

Bob was only fifteen feet behind his friend. Actually, the bear's speed was such that it could have knocked both of them down almost before they could have turned to run. Both men had several years of experience with polar bears, enough to know that fact. My binoculars remained on the bear's head. It was watching Lankinen very carefully. The head lifted, pointing directly at Wayne.

"That bear is nervous! It's going to move!" I stated in a shocked tone.

In that instant the bear rose to its feet in a single movement. It stood erect, three feet across at the front shoulders, facing Lankinen directly. Only then did Wayne lift his tripod and back up with measured strides toward shore. The animal, not more than forty feet away, watched him steadily, then moved two steps out farther on the ice. I breathed a momentary sigh. The polar bear turned and looked back at Lankinen, glanced up toward Bob Taylor, and, also in measured paces, moved slowly out onto the ice at an oblique angle from Wayne.

About ten steps away, it "yawned" and stopped. It then moved steadily across the ice directly in front of the two retreating men. After the yawn the long black tongue slipped in and out of the lips in a licking motion. For a moment I was startled. That yawn and the licking movements of the tongue are consistent with the attitudes of grizzly bears and blacks; they were evidence that the bear was under psychological stress. I don't know why the movements surprised me in the polar bear, since I had witnessed such reactions in both Alaskan brown grizzlies and black bears. The polar bear's behavior was logical, but it had been so regally disdainful of the closeness of men and vehicles that I could not believe from its actions that the animal was perturbed or fearful. Yet, as it crossed the open expanse of the pond in full and startling view, its black tongue was going back and forth out of its jaws like a cat licking up milk.

As Bob and Wayne climbed into the cab, my relief was apparent.

"You guys sure must know your polar bears! If you'd gone that close to one of the grizzlies I was watching up in Alaska last month, you'd have been in danger of real trouble—that bear was showing definite signs of stress."

Bob looked calmly up at me before speaking. "Yes. They lick like that when they are under stress."

Wayne was stoically storing his tripod and putting his camera back into its case. He did not say anything, but I had the feeling that he had calculated the risk against the opportunity to obtain a series of excellent photographs.

Shortly we headed back along the road to Churchill, paralleling the sea. On the shoreline the high green breakers were being abruptly and strangely calmed by what appeared to be a murky syrup. In surprise, I nodded toward the unique phenomenon.

"Yes, it's something different," Bob Taylor replied. "The sea ice crystals here form a slush along the shorelines just before freeze-up. After a couple of days that slush, called 'frazil,' thickens and hardens to form shore ice. Right now the new slush reduces the wave action, as if a blanket had been laid between the beach and the combers. Later, when it solidifies more, it forms the sea ice that the polar bears are now moving in for. It is the signal for them to begin leaving their summer range." He paused, staring out to sea. "It's nearly freeze-up time. Within a few days all the bears here will be gone."

Used to the breakers smashing along southern beaches I could hardly comprehend that such huge combers as these, running ahead of a thirty- to forty-mile wind—clifflike green walls topped by foaming whitecaps when they were only one hundred yards off the beach—could within yards be absorbed by tiny particles of brine.

But there it was happening: Nature's controls against itself.

It was significant on the local calendar, the beginning of the polar-bear migration from the tundra to the sea, their real element. With this freeze-up also comes the constant winter night, seal hunting, and isolation even from their own kind. Their brief enlivening visits through Churchill would soon be over for another season. Yet, as my eyes studied the vast green expanse of stormy Hudson Bay, that time seemed very distant.

Some *first* day!

The Redhead VII

Her daily routine during the first two weeks after emerging from her den was unfamiliar. During earlier years, within a couple of days she had left the denning area to head for the grassy lowlands. There the pungent delicacy of the skunk cabbages would have held her, while the soft muds of the swamp in which they abounded bathed the still tender pads of her feet. Now, with the strident wails of her offspring sounding out at almost the instant she left them, she could not stray far. Even in the early morning light, the cubs had begun bravely to venture from the confines. There was no period when she could safely leave them.

Hunger at the aromas of the budding growth in the swamp became too strong to ignore. Her craving for the yellow lilies was impelling. Early in their second week of emergence she began coaxing the cubs along with her, leading them progressively farther down the grassy slopes and toward the wetlands. Once in the newly greening meadows, they gamboled on the soft grassy mat while she increased her daily grazing there. Her appetite was steadily increasing in response to the growing demand for her milk. Once while she was turning over a rotted log, searching for ants at the edge of the meadow, a startled large-eared wood mouse spurted from under it. Seeking safety it chose a route between her feet. A quick smack of her forepaw flattened it to the hard earth. She picked it up by the tail and delicately sniffed at it.

Attracted by the resounding thump of her paw striking the earth, the cubs saw the object dangling from her lips and trotted jauntily over to investigate. She dangled it where they could sniff at it inquisitively. When their interest waned, she swallowed it and began to lick up the few remaining ants. Above her the noisy remonstrances of a scolding red squirrel went unheeded. Its warning was merely a response to her presence, not alarm at the approach of another creature. She responded to the cubs' quick return to her underbelly by licking them reassuringly.

Within a week she had settled the family on the edge of the swampland. After secreting the cubs in the safety of a small fissure between nearby boulders, she daily waded among the yellow lilies, choosing the more tender of them at will. Once, while she was filling her belly with the lilies she was suddenly alarmed by their squeals.

Her rush startled a young hare from where it had been stopped by its own surprise at seeing the cubs. Driven by her charge, the young animal bounded right over them into the bush. A louder wailing ensued, and she paused patiently to lick her brood.

Daily now the sun's arc was reaching higher over the territory. With the sun's steepening ascent came an abrupt increase in the size and activity of the two cubs. The male was larger and more aggressive than his female littermate, but often found himself outmaneuvered. By mid-July they were climbing nearly to the tops of fifty-foot trees, not only when she put them up the slippery trunks of poplars for their safety but also simply to climb and explore. She knew from her long association with the region just where the borders of the older sow's adjoining territory lay. When she became aware that the large old female had three cubs, she moved her two to the central and northern parts of her own accustomed territory.

Twice, when the young male bear familiar to her from the previous year had intruded into her area, she had lunged at him. During his third encroachment she had found him closing in on the cubs, his nose down, picking up their scent. Her nearly silent rush bowled him over into the bushes, and her teeth gashed his rear flank as he took to his heels. It was the last time she was to find his scent in her territory. Regularly, however, the odor of the big old boar crossed through her boundaries. Each time she encountered his scent, she quickly took her brood as far away as possible from his trail. There they would remain in deep brush cover until there were no further traces of his sounds or scent.

The days of an unseasonally wet summer had passed.

The sun had begun to wane, as the October Indian summer approached, when she first found, to her surprise, the scent of a coyote family hunting in her lands. The sparse berry crop had long since ripened and been consumed to fatten the sow and her cubs. Once again, grasses had become the mainstay of their diets; to this was added a meager mast of nuts. Few newborn grouse had survived that inclement year, and rodents had become scarce.

The scent of the coyotes became abruptly strong at her feet. Woofing angrily, she pawed the ground where a bitch had urinated. Realizing the animal was quite close, she woofed several times in alarm. She quickly sent the two cubs up a nearby tree. Then, without warning, the female of the coyote group suddenly rushed from the brush nipping at her rear. Caught off guard, the sow felt the pinch of sharp canine teeth on her left hind leg.

She was stunned by the sudden attack. Sending the unwilling cubs up the poplars had fully occupied her attention. Now too late to avert attack, she realized that the nearly starving coyotes had silently turned in their tracks when they heard her approach.

While the second coyote growled off to her side to distract her, the third member of the pack ran snapping at her head. Almost instinctively she saw that it was an ill-planned attack, more the result of desperation and hunger than of design. The coyote family had seldom given her kind trouble, except to filch portions of a kill. Also, this particular pack had not visited in her territory before; probably it was just crossing her boundaries in search of food.

Suddenly, she exploded. She lunged at the coyote dog growling menacingly at her side, and simultaneously she swiped at the one in front of her. Her surprising dual reaction caught the one in front off guard, and she knocked the squealing canine into the undergrowth. Its pained, high-pitched scream was so similar to that of a downed rabbit that the male cub loosened his hold on the poplar trunk and came sliding down to land on the ground with a loud thump. Hearing it, the coyotes fled, the injured one limping perceptibly as it ran.

Still aroused, the she-bear roared angrily first after the pack and then at the young cub on the ground, which returned to the tree. As she became calmer, the stiffened hair on her spine began to lie flat. It was with some reluctance that the cubs finally answered her beckonings to descend.

Off in the distance, the sound of three quick reports from a shotgun split the near-silence. It was not an unfamiliar sound to her in the season when the leaves

turned yellow or red and began to spill downward. A protective urge, however, impelled her to take the cubs deeper into the bushes near the ridges, near the den and the meadows where they had spent the early spring. The nightly frosts, too, were telling her that the snows of winter were not long off.

Occasionally during their feedings in the more open meadows, she looked up at the tall ridges toward the sounds and the movements of interlopers. Visible on the open rock bluffs, two of the dreaded man-forms sometimes appeared silently. When viewed, they always folded themselves down, apparently to rest, and when the glint of metal caught the sunlight, she woofed at the cubs and quickly led them deeper into the underbrush.

The voice sounds meant nothing to her.

"She's made it with her two cubs, Dave! It won't be too long before she starts to build a den. I hope she goes back into last winter's one. We can weigh her easily there and give the cubs a good checkup. It's been a tough year for food. But, she *looks* fat!"

The sounds would die away. Ever since the strange collar had been fitted on to her neck, the man-forms had consistently found her location, although they usually watched from a distance. She had grown used to their proximity, but she was still wary of them, and when they were in view, she took cover until she was sure they were no longer near. The cubs had become almost large enough to be her allies, and she was finding them more aware of approaching danger. Occasionally, when she was preoccupied with feeding, they alerted her to danger.

As the nightly cold intensified, she began to tear off leaves and branches, then carry or rake them toward the mouth of their previous winter's den. Puzzled by these unusual actions, the cubs sometimes pulled and scraped with her, vaguely aware of some as-yet-unknown purpose.

CHAPTER 8

How to Live with Polar Bears

"I was eleven years old when I had my first encounter with a polar bear," the bearded young artist stated. "My Dad and I were fishing for ciscoes [white-fish] off the beach a little west of Churchill. The tide was out, and we were waiting for it to come in. I went up in the rocks and lay down in the sun and fell asleep. It was the barking of dogs that awakened me."

He paused, looked over at me, then got up from his work on a sled-dog harness, as yet unfinished, on the sewing machine before him.

"Would you like coffee, Mr. Cramond?"

"Yes, please, Brian. And, it's 'Mike.'"

"Milk and sugar, Mike, then?" He grinned.

"No, it's okay black. Where exactly was this? Near here?"

He poured the coffee into a mug and brought it over to my low-seated easy chair. The speaker was Brian Ladoon, born twenty-nine years earlier in Win-nipeg, Manitoba, where his father, an engineer attached to the Churchill army base, had taken Brian's mother for the birth of their child. Thence-forward, Brian had lived his life in Churchill and on its surrounding tundras and seas. He became a fisherman, a trapper, a sled-dog breeder, and a super-lative painter in oils. During my browsing at the Churchill Trading Post, some of his works had attracted my interest because of their stark, native realism. One typical tundra sunset had reminded me of the master Turner because of its ethereal mists. Now, in his apartment, the walls were lined with his landscapes, some freshly drying.

Ladoon's name had been given to me earlier, during a fact-gathering inter-view with Ken John, district game warden for the Manitoba Department of Natural Resources, Wildlife Branch. I had asked John for a list of local people whose long residence and reliability would assure me of an accurate profile of life in Churchill, particularly their associations with polar bears. John had supplied me with the names of three women and two men. One of the men, John Spence, had survived a mutilating polar-bear attack. Brian Ladoon had lived all his life in the area, knew Churchill, and was familiar with polar bears in the wild. He had not told me that the young man was an artist of rising note; that came as a pleasant bonus.

When he answered my knock at his door, Ladoon extended a rather slender but firm hand. By appearance he would have seemed at home in any modern city. He was of medium height and medium, almost slight, build, with a light, neatly trimmed Van Dyke beard, remarkably blue eyes, and a noticeably level gaze. He was wearing an open shirt and blue jeans, and he smiled sociably. It was after I had explained my reasons for interviewing him that he casually answered my question about the first time he had actually had any close contact with a polar bear.

Artist Brian Ladoon of Churchill, Manitoba.

After he brought me the coffee, I again brought up the subject of his first encounter. He spoke thoughtfully, obviously striving to be accurate.

"Well, when I woke up among the rocks and heard the dogs barking, I looked up and saw a man walking behind them. In between us, about 150 feet away, was a polar bear facing in my direction. It had been moving toward me. I was scared. The dogs went after it, and it turned and ran right into the bay. It was a big bear."

"What then?"

"That was it, my first experience."

"You said you were fishing ciscoes. What for?"

"We sold them for dog feed, got two cents a pound. It wasn't long after that experience that Dad got my brother and me shotguns, 12-gauge."

The firearm was almost a universal local choice. I expressed my thoughts: "That is a good gun for close up on bears. Do you figure it is needed most everywhere you go here?"

He nodded emphatically. "It's a good thing to have a gun anytime you go out in the open here. You may never need it, but polar bears can be anywhere along the coast. You may be busy and not notice them coming. A gun is a last defense."

It was a lead to the question I wanted to ask him. "Have you ever been forced to kill a polar bear?"

"Yes." His eyes were directly on mine.

"Several?"

"A couple."

"Tell me, what was the most dramatic encounter you have experienced?"

He laughed, amused by the question. "They are all dramatic—at the time! It is difficult to say which one is most dramatic." He paused, looking down at the partially sewn dog harness. "Well, there was one out near that ship on the beach, where you were photographing bears—out near Bird Cove. We had been hunting geese and had several of them down on the beach. We were cleaning and plucking them. Our truck was parked by a big rock, and when we saw the bear, it was smelling around the truck. One guy ran to the truck to grab a shotgun. The bear ran around the truck and right at us. Those bears are unbelievably fast. It stopped, then turned, and took off down the bay, taking at least thirteen-foot jumps. It scared the hell out of all of us for a few seconds, because none of us had our guns."

"That wasn't one you had to shoot, then?"

"No. I had to shoot one that was out among my dogs."

The phrase "out among my dogs" was one that I had heard more than once in Churchill. Many people have dog teams in the North. Travel isn't always, as is popularly thought, by snowmobile, aircraft, truck, or car. Sled dogs still play a useful part in the lives of the northern people, and as you pass houses on the outskirts, you see the staked-out teams regularly. The barking of sled dogs can be heard throughout any long night in the town of Churchill, often not too far from the big culvert bear traps at the ends of the main streets.

"You say 'among' your dogs, Brian? Do you mean right *among* your dogs? Don't they kill the dogs!"

He shook his head.

"No, not usually. They are not looking for trouble, just wanting the dogs' food. They just move in quietly. In fact, I had chased a polar bear away just minutes before. I went out again to check the dogs, and all of a sudden that sucker was right there! Behind me! It was so close to me I couldn't believe it, and I hadn't heard a thing. I just turned and shot it. It was a male about 750 to 800 pounds."

A fact of life, no dramatics. Few of us who live in the southern climes would relate such a story so tersely or matter-of-factly. My eyes had been roving about the room, drawn irresistibly to the rows of paintings hung on the walls. Now the obvious authenticity of their rendering was explained. The man who made them also lived them. Above the stair was a freshly painted aurora borealis, startlingly limned against the black night over snow. Its realism fascinated me. Many nights during my life outdoors, I had stared awestruck across northern winter snows at the fluttering play of those northern lights. They were like ghosts dancing among stars set in the blackest of night horizons. I remarked on the paintings, wanting to know more about Brian Ladoon.

"That aurora borealis! It is really something!" I enthused.

"Yes. I like it. It isn't finished, though. Lots of work to do on it yet. Most of these paintings are unfinished. I do them gradually, work on one, then the other, until I'm satisfied."

"Do you sell direct?"

"Oh yeah. But most of those I've finished have been sold. The Trading Post—maybe you've been in there—has a few hung on the walls. They sell them."

"Hell, yes! *Those* were yours! I've been wondering where I had seen your style. I knew it was familiar but couldn't place it. Your work is excellent. Did you go out to art school?"

Brian was smiling as he shook his head.

"No. My father bought me brushes and oils when I was about six or seven years old. I was about thirteen when I first sold one of my oils."

"No real formal study then? Your technique is professional. How did you learn to stretch canvas like that?"

"I just worked at it, read books. It was a helluva job to learn to stretch those canvases right, too."

"Are you going to stay with painting?"

"Oh yes. It's part of my life, my living."

He nodded casually, looking at the harnesses. I was deeply impressed.

"I know paintings, have been around the world to look at the best. You are really very good, and your style is established. You *should* stay with it, Brian! Perhaps, one day, be Canada's top 'northern' artist."

He was looking at me, listening, but not impressed.

"Thank you. I like doing it. Brings in a few bucks."

"What about the dog harnesses?"

"Oh. I'm breeding a line of sled-dogs—the Canadian Eskimo Dog, which is the indigenous dog of the North. There are only about four hundred left in the world. I have about twenty to forty dogs on an average. I bought some Igloolich dogs from away north of here, and have my breeding stocks now to the third generation. By culling out the lesser pups, I have pretty near established the line now—*my line*. I used dogs for trapping for about three years, became interested in a purebred line. The harnesses are always going to pieces. So I make my own!"

"Painter! Harness maker! Dog breeder! Fisherman! Trapper—" I noted, somewhat enviously. "And obviously good at all of them! Tell me, Brian, how did you make out at trapping? Like, a yearly average?"

He thought for a moment.

"Well, over about three years, I averaged about thirty-five foxes, maybe six wolves."

It was typical trapper accounting, describing success on the line.

"What is that in the terms of bucks? Annually!"

He again looked thoughtful for a moment, calculating.

"Oh, about twelve hundred to fifteen hundred dollars—at the prices then."

"Not a hell of a lot, for the tough life required to get them."

"Not really. I made a little money on my meat drying. I had others hunt for me. About ten tons of beluga, wet. And that would dry out to about five tons. I did the meat drying."

"Five tons of meat—dried! How would you keep that?"

"On the rack!"

"Don't the bears and other animals get at it?"

"You've never seen a meat-drying rack?"

"No, not yet."

He got up and removed a file from a cabinet, sorted out some color prints, then brought two of them over to me. The photographs were of a stretch of shoreline with two meat-drying racks on high stilted legs. I remarked that they seemed tall.

"Yeh, up to thirty feet! The meat is safe up there. You just leave it up there once it gets dry. It will keep for two to three years, and will feed a lot of dogs. It is like anything else up here with wildlife, you take it and you use it. You maximize the use of anything you take. Or you are wrong! The government cut off my whaling permit. That makes it tougher to feed dogs. The new policy is to let the native people get their share first. It's a good idea. I'm hoping to get my permit back."

"In the meantime, you paint."

"Yeah, make harnesses. You do what you have to do up here. I don't drink like some guys do—and waste it. I get by okay."

I had to express my admiration.

"You like the life, and you know it well! Most guys couldn't make it up here. They'd starve to death. Tell me, Brian, you said you had killed a couple of polar bears?"

He nodded thoughtfully.

"The native people kill bears for dog meat. When there isn't anything better to eat, they eat them. I'm not crazy about it. I have to coexist with the polar bears, though."

It wasn't impatience, but I felt that such an industrious young man should not be deterred longer from his work.

"The other bear? Did it come after you?"

"Yeah. It had made up its mind. I was working outside and just had a .350 rifle with me. The bear actually sneaked up on me. When I saw it coming, I shot two shots over its head. But I had been cutting up scrap meat, and I guess it had decided it wanted some. It kept on coming. I shot it in the chest at about ten feet. Before that I didn't realize how much power there was in a rifle. It turned the bear right over backwards."

The story was explicit, exacting, bereft of anything but what gets you along in the Far North—the truth.

"Any others?"

He gave me a long, thoughtful look.

"It's illegal to shoot polar bears, Mike. You don't kill them unless you have to. Maybe if your dogs are starving, and you can't get meat. Then a polar bear becomes the means to get by. But you don't take anything up here without a good reason." He was staring down at the unfinished harness before him for a moment. As I looked at his slight build and fine features, I could not help thinking he looked more like a painter you might find deep in any city, in a garret. With his small-boned, useful hands, he seemed an artisan by God's gifts.

"I'll send you a copy of this interview, for you to correct, when it is done—and a copy of the new book when it comes out."

He pointed to the copy of my recent book, *Killer Bears*, where he had laid it after I had shown it to him as evidence of who and what I was.

"I'd like a copy of *that one*! Can I buy it from you?"

It was my turn to smile.

"I can't give you that one. It's a personal one. But I have another one at the hotel—one to give away. I take a couple along on trips like this."

"I'll trade you something for it—we can deal."

"Hell! I said I'd give it to you. No deal!" My eyes were following the rows of his oil paintings. "When you have that aurora borealis finished to your satisfaction—I'd like a price on it."

He was serious for a solemn moment.

"You can buy it now. I'll send it to you when it's finished."

I shook my head. "Brian, I have walls lined with original paintings, those I've bought from artists around the world and some illustrations of my own stories from magazines. When you have *that one* done, we'll talk. I won't sell an unfinished manuscript, even if someone wants it. The price is what it is worth when I've completed it."

He was listening.

"I'd *still* like to buy your book! An *autographed* copy!"

"I'll bring it over this evening. Okay?" I laughed.

Discussing his lifetime as a resident of subarctic Churchill, Manitoba, artist Brian Ladoon said of his association with polar bears, "I have to coexist with them. That is the way it is." And the rest of the longtime residents agreed, each in different ways.

Ken John was the warden in charge for Churchill, a post he had held for three active years. Although general management of the polar bear is directed from head offices in Winnipeg, John headed the Churchill division and the four-man Polar Bear Patrol. During an interview in his local office, I asked him how many polar-bear incidents would occur in and around the small Hudson Bay seaport per year.

"Well, this year we've attended to thirty-four complaints already. I guess over three years, we've handled a hundred bears," he replied.

"What do you consider a complaint?" was my next question.

"Anything that involves a bear present and troublesome. About 95 percent of them are polar bears rooting around in some resident's yard, often after garbage. They become garbage-oriented. Most of the bears just beeline right through town or go around it. On the whole they're very easygoing, nonaggressive."

That described the seven polar bears I had encountered during the past two days. They had impressed me with their tendency to avoid trouble, even keeping their distances from their own kind.

I remarked on this seeming peacefulness. John nodded, and I asked him about his method of handling the bears when he did answer a call.

"We drive up in the truck and honk the horn. About 75 percent of the bears leave immediately. I've seen quite a few, and I have never seen one a vehicle wouldn't move when you drive up to it. But there was one pretty stubborn one, a big male. He seemed to have his mind made up."

"What did you do?"

He frowned at the memory of the incident.

"We also shoot cracker shells at them. Cracker shells are a type of exploding firecracker that goes off with a pretty loud bang. Usually, one is enough to make a bear move. But this bear wasn't moving for anyone. I fired crackers at his feet, and he just looked at us. I hit him right on the side with a couple that exploded against him. He still wouldn't move."

I had wondered about the bangers, crackers, or exploding shells of which people had spoken.

"There is no metal in the shells? They don't hurt the bears?"

"No, the bears aren't hurt by them. The missiles are soft-wrapped. Bears just don't like the sound of them. I guess I used up fifteen or more crackers on this one, and we practically had to push him away with the truck."

Thinking of the grizzly sows' protectiveness toward their cubs, I asked Warden John if the same trait existed in polar bears.

"No, I don't think the sows show nearly the aggressions of a grizzly. We had a culvert trap set out in town here, and a cub-of-the-year got into it. The old lady was moving around outside, trying to figure how to get the cub out. We were a bit worried, so we fired a couple of crackers around her and she took off."

I was surprised.

"She left her cub?"

He nodded, as if it was not unusual. "She moved off about fifty yards when we fired the crackers. Then, as we went in to release the cub, she hung around at about that distance, on the periphery. She didn't make any noise, or any threats, not even while the cub was bawling as we went in to release it."

"No attempt to come back while you were working with the cub?"

"No, she just kept her distance. They lose a lot of cubs on the ice over the winter. The big males kill them."

That is a confirmed habit with all bears, perhaps the main reason why the grizzly mother is so protective of her young. Cannibalism is a trait of most flesh-eating animals. I asked John if he had had any real problems on his own.

"Not really. If you live with them, you are bound to get into an occasional hassle. They are inquisitive, and if they smell food they are single-minded; they go after it. I had one get onto a gas scow in the river, after some barrels of dog food we had there. The tide went out, and the barge was below where it was when the bear got on board. It was dark when I arrived that morning. I had gone down to sleep on the boat. I didn't have any cracker shells, so I threw sticks and stones at it. All it wanted to do was get away. It was a medium male. Finally, it took a big jump up onto the wharf and took off."

The bear's reaction was one I was to find typical.

"Generally, then, they don't show aggression toward a man," I said. As he shook his head, I added, "When I was down with Dr. Charles Jonkel, working with grizzlies, and Dr. Lynn Rogers on black bears, earlier this year, they were experimenting with air horns and squirt repellants to find what might be a deterrent or a repellant. Do you use them?"

He shook his head emphatically.

"We don't use repellant in liquid form. As a matter of fact, the one named Halt is illegal in Canada. All the gasses are banned. Most of the local people just use air horns or crackers. They are legal."

It was a surprise to hear that the product called by the trade name Halt was illegal to use in Canada. Recently a Canadian postman had shown me a container with that name upon it when I had asked him how he handled obstreperous dogs on his route. He told me that he used it or an umbrella. The product was said to be noninjurious to animals, but had the effect of discouraging them when they persisted in coming close. In fact, I had seen one scientist use such a repellant on a black bear only three months before. Within half an hour it was back at the scene of the spraying, showing no sign of distress. It is general knowledge that Canada has a highly protective attitude against any product which may, in civilian use, have any injurious results upon the recipient. But judicious use of any effective, noninjurious repellant against an aggressive animal to prevent injury to humans well may save the animal from death and therefore seems only sane and empathetic.

It occurred to me that it was possible that such deterrents or repellants might be useful in discouraging polar bears. I said as much. Then I asked, "Do you find that the trapping of polar bears is effective?"

"It gets the bears under control for the time being, but it is expensive to transport them away."

It was a universal answer where relocation of bears had been tried, I noted glumly.

"I recently saw a film, made by the National Geographic Society, showing a local native woman who had shot and wounded a bear that was trying to come into her house. Is that fairly common?"

John shook his head.

"It does happen, but it is not common!"

"Have you had to kill any polar bears yourself."

"Yes. I had to kill one. A woman wounded it at her house, and I had to finish it off."

John did not imply that the bear shown in the film was the one he had been forced to finish off.

"While I'm here, I'd like to get some data on the problems and attitudes of women who have lived here for some time. Is there anyone you could suggest?"

He smiled immediately.

"How about my secretary here. She *has* to live with them!" He went to the door and called to the woman who had been at the reception desk when I had asked for him. She came to the door and he suggested she join us.

"Melanie Ratson, this is Mike Cramond. He is writing about bears." Then, turning to me, he added, "Melanie lives just outside of town and has regular visits from bears."

A small, pretty woman, Melanie Ratson was amused at the import of the remark.

"Yes, we get them—all too regularly about this time!"

"Where do you live, and how long have you lived here, Mrs. Ratson?" I asked.

"Oh, we are about eight miles east of here. We live in an A-frame house and have started a rabbit, chicken, and duck farm. We've been in Churchill about five years—at the A-frame about three years."

I couldn't help thinking that Melanie Ratson was dressed as stylishly as any woman you would find in any business office anywhere in North America—no mucklucks, no parka, no checkered woolen flannel shirt. The question I was about to ask seemed ludicrous.

"What kind of weapon do you carry when these bears are around, Melanie?"

She responded as matter-of-factly as if she had been asked how much butter to put in a pound cake or what kind of sewing machine she used.

"Oh, I have a .44 magnum Ruger that I carry."

I couldn't repress a smile. She sure as hell didn't look like a pistol-packin' mama who would be totin' a .44. And in fact, she wasn't. She was simply a Churchill mother who did what was advisable.

"Do you use it?"

"Oh no. We use crackers to scare them off. It is only as a last means. For safety's sake."

"It is an excellent rifle. Ruger has done a good job of reviving the old styles of guns, yet modernizing the mechanisms. I hope you never have to use it on a bear."

She nodded in full agreement.

"Not unless I *have* to! Yes, it is a nice gun, popular. But most people here have never had to kill a bear. Usually our trouble is among the dogs. The bears come in for the dogs' food. In fact, our new lead dog was killed. But we worry more about wolves after the dogs than we do about bears."

The statement brought to mind a sixty-five-year-old memory from when I lived on the Alberta prairies, not much farther south of the sub-Arctic than the town of Churchill. A disheartened letter had come from my mother's brother saying that the wolves had killed and eaten his fine golden collie dog, leaving only scraps of hair in the front yard of his prairie wheat-farm home. Both wolves and cougars (mountain lions) prey on smaller domestic dogs, why not polar bears?

"How often do the polar bears come around?"

Melanie Ratson thought for a moment. "Last year there were seventy-nine times they were around. Almost every day for a while. One of them stayed around for a week. We knew it was the same one because it had a big Number 9 painted in black on its side. It slept about a hundred yards away, in the bushes, until we finally chased it off. Dogs are handy to have around, though."

I asked her about that statement.

"Well, they're handy because you can always tell when bears are around by the dogs' barking. In fact, one of our dogs changes the pitch of her bark as the bears get nearer. You can tell by her higher pitches just how close the bears are. When they are really close, she almost screams. We usually have dogs with us when we are outside."

"How about inside?"

She smiled a trifle ruefully.

"Oh, once or twice we've had one pounding on the back door. And one came right through the yard last year, just sauntered up the driveway. One cracker, right behind it, moved it off. It was a big bear, too."

"What about the children during these times. Do you have any?"

"Yes. We don't let them play outside unattended from April, when the bears come around, until September. In fact, we make sure that they know about bears. And, really, at no time do they go without supervision. Bears can be around at any time of the year."

The words of another Churchill mother came to my mind, and I remarked about her feelings.

"I was talking to Mrs. Kowal at the Polar Hotel. She said that she and her family had never had any bear trouble in the town. That they knew there could always be bears around; that whenever anyone of them is going outside they always look up and down the street, carefully, to make sure there are no bears around—at least any in sight."

Melanie Ratson nodded, "Yes. She's right! We *do*!"

After thanking Ken John, and Melanie Ratson, I went along to ask if Mrs. Lillian Kowal had been able to find the name of a pilot she had spoken about who had had a problem with a polar bear. The distance between the hotel and the Manitoba Natural Resources offices was only about four hundred yards, but it was across a large, open playing-ground park centrally located in the small city. The wind had been blowing consistently at twenty-five to thirty-five miles an hour during the first two days of my visit to Churchill. To thwart the piercing cold gusts it was necessary to pull my buttoned-on parka over my woolen toque. The face string on the parka blocked my vision during my walk, but I was more hopeful than worried about bears. Nevertheless, I crossed the open area quickly.

The blast of heated air in the foyer of the Polar Hotel also brought the smiling face of Mrs. Kowal, the proprietress. I inquired if she had been able to learn the details of the polar-bear incident with the pilot and the helicopter.

She shook her head.

"No, Mr. Cramond, I haven't been able to locate him in person yet, but my husband is trying. His name is Bruce Martin."

In an earlier conversation I had told Mrs. Kowal of a northern grizzly bear that had entered an oil exploration company's aircraft compound, destroyed a helicopter used regularly to scare those animals away from where the men were working on the pipeline. From among a dozen helicopters the bear had chosen the one that regularly chased the bears. She had replied that a similar incident had happened near Churchill.

"I found out that the pilot of the helicopter had to get a new bubble sent up to Churchill to fix his aircraft. He had put his copter down near Field River. It was one used on polar-bear counts. He went over to sleep in another small plane parked nearby. The polar bear attacked his helicopter and smashed the bubble. I'll get the actual details and write to you."

Thanking her, I called another Churchill resident, Diane Erickson. Her brother-in-law, Pat Rakowski, a Winnipeg, Manitoba, Natural Resources employee familiar with the Hudson Bay port, had said she would be able to tell me about some of the bear problems in Churchill. Mrs. Erickson courteously offered to take me out to see her home, where polar bears had indeed been a problem.

Moments after my phone call she picked me up and drove through the small town along a short side road, thence up to the nearby crest of the rockbound headland that overlooks the town. The place was a surprise. When I had first approached it, coming from the airport, the driver had told me that the site was an experimental truck garden designed to produce vegetables in a commercial quantity to supply some of the local needs.

As we got out of the vehicle, Diane Erickson showed me the exterior of the outside greenhouse, saying that bears continually tried to get into it. She also showed me where her husband, Bill, had photographed a polar bear right beside their old farm vehicle parked in the driveway. I noticed that in her hand she had an air horn, the type used on launches and other boats to alert other traffic to their approach, perhaps even more commonly used at stadiums and sports events as a simple noisemaker. She had picked it up from the car seat just as unconsciously as one would retrieve the keys from the ignition.

"Do you find those horns will scare bears away?"

"Oh yes! They do! The bears don't like the sound of it."

Before we entered the house, she turned to the front of the greenhouse-conservatory attached to the southern face of the tall building. Even before she pointed her finger, I saw the broken fiber-glass section. It had the obvious, deep scratches of an attempt to enter. She nodded at the damage.

"That is where one tried to get in. They do, quite often, make some attempt to get in, particularly when they smell food."

She unlocked the door to her home. The entrance was on the basement level with stairs leading to the upper portions of the large building. Beside it was a walkway to the attached conservatory-greenhouse. As she turned to close the inner door, I noted that it had not only a door-handle lock, but also two other husky steel safety latches, below and above the latch. (Most Churchill buildings have an outside door, then a short entranceway, then a second doorway into the inside building—to keep in heat during the seven-month winters.) To my surprise, she latched both locks, and I remarked about it.

"A polar bear can come around any time, Mr. Cramond. If you don't lock up, there is always the chance that will be the time one chooses to visit." She then lifted one of the two wooden cross timbers near the door. As she placed the ends in the receptacles at the sides of the door, I noticed that there were also two such cross-barring arrangements on the door frame. She continued, "And, we put these bars in place at night."

She put the bar down again and invited me upstairs for a welcome cup of tea. As she prepared the tea in the kitchen, I removed my notebook from my leather briefcase, feeling, I thought, very much like a door-to-door salesman in a new town. So much to learn about the country and its people! Mrs. Erickson sat in a chair across from the southern-exposed windows. Looking at her, as I had at Melanie Ratson earlier in the day, I had the same thought. A modern woman. Yet faced with a daily possibility of meeting a polar bear!

I asked her where she had been born.

"I was born right here in Churchill, Mr. Cramond. In 1936. And I've lived here all my life, except for trips. This was a military base at that time, and there were eight thousand people here. There weren't many bears around in those days. We used to pick blueberries up on this hill. We were told by our parents, 'Don't go down to the beach alone!' Occasionally a bear would come along the waterfront."

One of those statements seemed provocative.

"You say that there weren't many bears around *then*?"

Diane Erickson nodded her head, reflecting momentarily.

"No. A military base was here. The bears' denning area is about 150 miles south of here, nearer York Factory. The Eskimos used to kill bears in the denning areas. They don't usually eat polar bear meat, but feed it to their dogs. The younger and older bears might come up here, but the military poached them for bearskins—which were pretty lucrative. There were no bears around here, to speak of, until about 1960 or 1963, when people began to see them around town. They came to the dumps. There were three dumps then, one right on Harbour Road. Bears were often there."

She paused, and I asked a question.

"Was that about when they became a problem?"

"Yes. About that time I was working at the P.O. in town, in 1963. I remember once I looked out of the window on the bay, about the time school was out. I saw what I thought at first was a big white dog. It was a polar bear, right in downtown. It had come at least a thousand feet along the pipeline. A cop went and got his camera. It was just ambling along toward him. Then it stopped and posed for its photograph. The cop took its picture. The kids came out of school to watch. That scared it, and it ran away. It ended up under one of the warehouses. It stayed there for about three days, too frightened to come out!"

There was an expression of compassion on Diane Erickson's pretty face as the memory came back. We talked generally about the polar-bear problem. I asked her about the difficulties that she and her husband faced, actually living within the town limits, but slightly removed from busy thoroughfares.

"Well, Mr. Cramond, one year we had seventeen bears around the house. One November 11 we had five at one time, when Bill was building the porch. There were two sows and three cubs with them. We called town that the bears were on their way."

"You mean you notified the Bear Patrol?"

"Yes. They react pretty quickly to an alert." She paused, reflecting back. "Another time, Bill was working on the porch at the back of the house. He knew there was a bear around. The sow had come up on the veranda around the corner. He saw the cubs but not her. To scare the cubs he sounded the air horn. They left, but the sow still was walking across the porch. Our friend Gail Philbin was visiting. Hearing the 'thunk,' 'thunk' of the bear's paws,

Bill yelled, 'Was that you, Gail?' When she didn't answer, he sounded the air horn again, and the sow took off. You are always listening for certain sounds. It may be a bear."

In the comfortable warmth of the Erickson house it was difficult to think of polar bears outside. Yet the slight remoteness from downtown actually made it an outpost. I asked about the experimental truck-gardening enterprise. Was it successful? Diane Erickson shook her head.

"Not yet. There are always difficulties in a new project like this. But we are doing it according to methods proven successful elsewhere. Would you like to see some of it?"

In the basement she showed me a large conversion apparatus shipped from Norway at great expense. A large fiber-glass container with several compartments, it received all their household refuse and compost material and the waste waters from sink, toilet, and kitchen. The water, drained off through filters, became reusable after storage beneath the basement floor in a deep cement-lined well that also collected all runoff from the roof. The remnant compost was collected in a separate part of the contrivance. She lifted the lid of that unit to expose a very small residue that had no detectable odor, not even that of a regular compost heap such as I have outdoors in my garden. It was a surprise, obviously effective. I said so. She nodded.

"That is several months' gathering. It doesn't produce much usable waste, not as much as we'd hoped. But it is certainly effective."

She led the way into the attached greenhouse on the basement level. It had a southern exposure, but obviously was designed to use furnace and household heating as well as heat from the low-lying sun's meager rays. I noted that, although outside the temperature was about −6 Celsius with a wind factor of some thirty-odd miles speed, it was quite pleasant in the greenhouse. The raised rows of wooden troughs were filled from end to end with various plants from peas to tomatoes, their fruits still abundantly hanging from the vines. The tomatoes, some of them ripened, were mostly in a green to semigreen stage, the leaves and stems yellowing. I noted their abundance. My hostess shook her head rather disappointedly.

"They haven't been a success, Mr. Cramond. We haven't yet been able to control the usual greenhouse rot, mold, and plant parasites. We are trying new controls. I think it is just a matter of time."

My glance went over her shoulder to the patch in the fiber-glass encasement of the greenhouse. There was a mended spot where a polar bear had banged and torn at the outside.

"Then you'll only have the polar bears to contend with!"

Diane Erickson was checking the thermometer reading.

"I suppose so," she nodded, engrossed in her number-one problem, producing a truck garden almost within the Arctic Circle.

The Redhead VIII

Increasingly drowsy, she watched the cubs at play. They now tumbled about each other only halfheartedly. Their bellies were fat, their glistening black coats sleek and ready for winter. Their actions and responses lacked the punch and enthusiasm which had brought them increased muscular strength throughout the longer summer and fall days. They tended to tire of play more easily and fell asleep more readily. Their wails of complaint had become almost a thing of the past. The midday sun daily traveled lower on the southern horizon, and every morning the November frosts made white columns of rime. For over a week the cold remained constant, but the first snow had not fallen. It was as if the weather, after the unseasonably wet summer, was reluctant to deposit the year's final white winter mantle.

Mother and cubs lingered ever closer to the prepared den area. Then for two days the sharpness of the frosts gradually lessened, and a haze began to appear over the face of the sun. Snow, the she bear now knew, would not be long coming. Almost reluctantly the cubs followed her to the meadows, where she fed upon the drier grasses without much enthusiasm. They followed her example as if sensing some need.

One day as they returned to the middle ridge where she had dug a new, larger chamber from the old den, the first flakes were sifting down through the branches overhead. This time she entered the dark haven with some finality. Her cubs followed her in and slept curled close to her belly.

Later she awakened fitfully and saw that the den entrance was snowed in, that the only light was the glimmer from the top of the rock slit. Hunger had left her. The cubs suckled without enthusiasm and only when they found a teat near their mouths. They nestled even closer to the warmth from her belly. The winter slumber had begun for all.

Outside, the winter silence was deepening.

She was never fully aware of when the men came, only that there had been a pricking sensation at her rump. When she awakened, she quickly silenced the bawling of one cub. Still later came the awareness that her coat was wet, as if from fresh snow. She was no longer roundly settled in her nest of branches and leaves, but her cubs were up there on the matted foliage. To place herself again between them and the den entrance she moved sluggishly, then settled once again into the nest. Only sleepy grunts came from the cubs. As she licked at their ears, she felt the coldness of plastic and the faint smell and taste of blood. Around her own neck the mildly annoying collar smelled new and unfamiliar and was more snugly attached.

She was never aware that a heavy snow came that winter. It obliterated all light from the den mouth. The cubs moved only spasmodically, generally when she herself had moved restlessly to a more comfortable setting in the cupped nest.

Much later, the year's increasing trickle of seeping water again awakened her.

In the confined area of the bed the cubs had begun to move more often, and there was now an increasing glimmer of light from the den entrance. There also had been a warming of the den chamber itself.

Once again it was a new birdsong that first penetrated the silence of the den from the trees directly above the opening. Aroused, she moved sluggishly from the nest, then toward the entrance. Suddenly aware that the warmth of her body had been removed from him, the male cub emitted a tentative and plaintive bawl. The other cub stirred, yawned, and also emitted a milder cry.

The fresh, warm air was filtering through the thin snow of the vent hole. She thurst her head strongly through the flimsy wall into the spring sunshine. For a moment she blinked uncertainly. Then, pressing her shoulders solidly into the ice crystals, she pushed hard. The granular wall parted softly, and she thrust herself out into the clarity of an early April day. The breeze carried the strong scent of newly breaking poplar buds and the odors of the lower swamplands.

A new season had come. This time she would not resist the yellow blossoms of the swamp cabbage. The cubs, too, would begin to relish its early-spring flavor and its tonic effects.

Within seconds the cubs came clumsily to her heels. Amid the strange, new brightness and smells, they sat dumbly, staring at nothing. One of them stooped to nibble at the small fringe of new grasses surrounding the cave entrance while his mother looked longingly at the green meadows well below. Then she also began to nibble at the nearby grass shoots.

Three days later she led the cubs into the swamp. All of them had become hungry, and all had defecated the resistant anal plug. As she began to nip off the yellow-green shoots of the skunk cabbage, so did the cubs. At first they seemed overpowered by its strong smell, but they became accustomed to it quickly. Both yearlings caught and swallowed frogs swimming near. The sow slurped up jellied masses of newly spawned eggs as she waded through the dank waters to the muddy pond banks.

As the air became warmer, she rubbed at the itching spots of her nipples. She would now discourage the cubs' occasional nudges.

All three had begun to lose weight daily. She roamed more broadly in her territory, searching for winter-killed carrion. Twice she found the wasted remains of deer where they had starved in deep drifts. Coyotes, crows, ravens, and rodents had taken their share, leaving her hungry for proteins.

It was the third week when she first noticed the trail of fresh deer scent within her domain. Occasionally she tracked it, but always the shy animal seemed to be aware of her, remaining out of her way. At the very edge of the old boar bear's upper ridge territory, she came upon the very fresh scent of the white-tail doe. Steam was still rising from the round, brown balls of excrement expelled abruptly from the frightened animal. The thump, thump of warning hooves was only feet away when she saw the doe clearly. It was quite motionless, half hidden behind a clump of brush alder. She studied the animal silently, motionless herself.

Her impulse took shape abruptly.

The immediacy of her lunge was unexpected. As she sprang, the doe shot off downhill at an angle. A short run later the sow tumbled on the plunging incline, and she gave up the chase. She moved militantly back to where the cubs were now loudly bawling.

As she approached them, they were both standing stiffly erect upon their hind legs. They were staring, as if in fascination at a coiled snake. They were emitting warning woofs.

Still aroused from the short burst after the deer, she quickly plunged at the spot of brush into which both were staring. Her descending forepaw struck the soft, spotted coat of a fawn where it lay, its head pushed deeply between its front legs. It remained rigidly motionless. She swatted instinctively, driving a single gasp of breath from the fawn. She picked up the body in her jaws, carrying it back to the matting of leaves, where the cubs, still on their hind legs, stood fascinated. She dropped the prize, allowing them to nuzzle it inquisitively.

Still uncertain, they jumped and rolled tentatively about it. Later she carried the carcass to a tangle of stumps, there, after a bite into its genital area, she pushed the bleeding remnants under a covering of dry leaves. Later that evening she returned with the cubs, and the three of them devoured most of it.

As the days of June warmed up, her winter coat began to shed, and with it a vague restlessness pervaded her. Daily she became less patient with the maturing cubs and more resentful of their antics. Particularly, the male's growing size and strength disconcerted her. His bites were strong, and his cuffs often hard and shocking. When he began to approach her aggressively she would drive him off. The female cub was more compatible with her littermate than with her mother. The sow still sought and shared foods with her offspring, but when most of the ants in a newly revealed nest were licked up before she could feed, she resented it. Gradually she began to sleep a foot or two away from them and to avoid close contact.

Once again her vague seasonal longings arose, and she was no longer afraid when the old boar's scent was in her territory. The yearling cubs were now almost her own size, the male nearly as high at the shoulder.

The estrous scents developed in her urine. For a week she had been particularly impatient with the cubs. When the male bit playfully at her ear as she dozed, her retaliatory blows drove him ten feet across open grass. Later, when the female cub approached her as if to make amends, she woofed in warning.

Both cubs moved farther away from her, and at night they slept so that logs lay between them and their mother. One morning, as they attempted to follow her along the upper borderline of her territory, she turned and drove them back. Near the ridgetops she searched for a scratched and bitten tree trunk with a definable scent on it. Finding one, she inhaled the fresh odors of the old boar with ardent relish.

When the cubs approached, she ran at them, loudly bellowing and woofing constantly. The following day she drove both yearlings to her lower territorial borders. She then chased the male cub by himself toward the farthest boundary on one corner. As his battered rear end disappeared into the unknown adjacent territory of the older she-bear, the reddish sow turned and resolutely patrolled the upper boundary, urinating regularly on the dry ground. When she later met her female yearling, she did not chase the cub but simply shouldered her roughly out of the way, woofing warnings. The smaller animal trotted disconsolately toward the far corner of the territory where her banished littermate had disappeared.

The big, old boar found the reddish sow the next day. When he left her after the mating ritual, she tracked down another boar and mated again. Still restless, she traveled to the far edge of the older sow's territory, seeking and finding a third willing boar.

A week later she was avidly filling her belly with the ripening berry crop of that year's season. A new seed of life was held in her womb.

CHAPTER 9

What Is in the Future for Polar Bears?

Those of us who sit outside the seven-month winters of the sub-Arctic and Polar regions, our consciences pricked by the knowledge that polar bears are on the endangered species list might leap to the conclusion that the species is in danger of becoming extinct.

That really is not the truth.

By classifying polar bears as an endangered species several countries that formerly allowed progressively more effective hunting, trapping, and killing have halted those modern, often dollar-oriented, and occasionally unsportsmanlike activities. In Canada, because the killing of polar bears for sport or profit has been halted, the bear population is expanding and in good health. Of the estimated twenty-five to fifty thousand polar bears in the circumpolar regions, eight to ten thousand are in Canada. Although killed polar bears that have been examined clinically do contain toxic chemicals such as PCB (polybynlchloride), and although we do not know the long-term effects of such substances, at least for now the polar bear is not threatened with extinction.

Studies continue, however, both in parts of Canada and in the rest of their circumpolar habitat. Part of the reason for going to Churchill, Manitoba, during the bears' migrations back toward their point of departure on the ice was to better understand their circumstances from actual field studies. Both the federal government (the Canadian Wildlife Services) and the provincial government (the Manitoba Department of Natural Resources) are conducting wildlife studies of the animals of the northland. These examinations include polar-bear counting and marking in the areas surrounding Churchill.

During my first day in the company of photographers, I saw the dump, which was a few miles from the city. We parked just ahead of an unoccupied green truck, which was stationed where the occupants had a clear view of the dump face. One of my companions pointed to the darker face of the landfill. "There's the old sow and her cubs."

I stared for some time at the dingily smoking edge of the tangle of city-made rubble, unable to distinguish any animals.

Finally I saw a movement close to a large, square object. It was the sow bear. Although completely in the open, she was almost indistinguishable, smudged by association with the charcoals, offal, and burned residue of the castoff junk. Just beyond her, rooting beside the square object, was a single cub, just as grubby. By contrast, my memory of shiny-coated black bears, sorting trash at a Minnesota dump earlier in the year, seemed pastoral. This scene totally destroyed the dignity of the grand white animals.

These polar bears somehow gave the impression of a forlorn Third World mother and child, grubbing in similar but less rich garbage. I shook my head, unable to accept the sight. At the sound of fresh garbage tumbling down the face, the female had turned around. A large, freshly painted black numeral 8 stood out against the grey of her pelage. Three bears were at the dump, all extremely dirty, pacing and pawing in the village refuse. As we left the area, I was depressed.

When I phoned the Churchill Study Centre two days later, my call was answered by Nicholas Lunn, a student biologist I had been advised to call. He was leaving to do some studies at the dump and would come over to pick me up. When we arrived there, the longer northland shadows were beginning to pocket the depressions in the landscape left by a winter sun that had no reds or yellows of warmth in its light. Lunn drove the truck to the dump face, parking where the green truck had been parked two days earlier. I asked him about his studies.

He was, he said, a graduate student, studying for his master's degree in biology. In 1981 he had been in the Churchill area from October 5 to November 11 studying polar bears. In 1982, the year of my visit, he had arrived on September 24 to continue his work. From July 10 to August 9 he had been studying the behavior of polar bears in the Cape Churchill area, comparing their activities in that denning area, after they came off the ice, to their behavior in the dump area.

I asked him about the dump bears, none of which were now in sight.

"Well, these bears here aren't usually seen anywhere else. They are dump-oriented, perhaps by a mother bringing her cubs-of-the-year. But females that show up here when they have cubs rarely show up in the years they're without cubs."

It was unusual information. I asked him if the bears he had studied in the denning area near Cape Churchill came up through this dump. He shook his head.

"Not to my knowledge. They don't show up in the tabulations of marked bears."

"That is strange, isn't it?"

"No. They don't move far from the denning area until the ice comes. They are all waiting for the sea ice to form; that is their more natural habitat. They're not really at home on the land, although they do range up to fifty miles from the shore in search of food. Their main diet is seals and other sea animals."

This was counter to other widely circulated information I had read. Those reports had stated that polar bears take an annual winter 'ride' on the ice to the southern and eastern shores of Hudson Bay and that when the sea ice melts, they are dumped hundreds of miles from their home. Whole populations are forced by sea currents to take this annual circuit, first by ice-directed travel, then on a return migration up the long coastline to meet the earlier-forming ices of the north. Perhaps Lunn's statements were true of only the local bears.

I asked about the populations he was studying. How many?

"Well, the general population that we see and mark is only a small portion, probably one to two hundred animals, of which an average of one hundred and fifty are between here and Cape Churchill. Very few of the bears from the lower areas would come up here. Perhaps one or two family groups at the dump were from the midsection. Very few males appear here. The oldest male would be about five years of age."

I was listening with some interest, thinking that often a report considered accurate could be quite misleading. I asked Lunn how many bears usually were around the dump.

"The most I've seen at any one time would be twelve, in family groups of one to three, counting a cub with a sow as a family of two and so on. Four sows with cubs could add up to twelve animals."

"It isn't the impression one gets from reading news reports. I had a picture of literally dozens of bears going through here during migration. Do the same groups come back?"

"Our tagging indicates that. The oldest sow we tagged here this year was seventeen years old."

Knowing that scientists use tagged bears extensively to establish their conclusions, I asked, "What information do you get about bears from this tagging?"

"Well, this year we began tagging here on October 6. It was an ear tag. The female at that date weighed 192 pounds; when we reexamined her on November 2, she weighed 219 pounds. Her cubs also showed weight gains: one went from 29 pounds in October to 45 pounds in November check; the other, from 37 pounds to 65."

It was a surprise, that amount of gain on a diet of garbage. I asked about nondump bears. Again Lunn's figures were interesting.

"One record of nondump bears showed that during the same period a female and cub lost 14 percent of their body weights."

"In other words, growth patterns among garbage-feeding bears here are almost identical to those among black bears and grizzlies at garbage dumps in south and west of here."

"It could be. I'm not too familiar with the details of those studies!"

The sun had lowered beyond the cold horizon. In the grey twilight bear observation would have to be under headlights. I said so.

"Yes. They've usually left here around this time."

"Where do they go?"

"Oh, they move off into the surrounding land, rest in the bushes."

It was a logical conclusion.

"During what hours do you watch them?"

"Generally, from just after eight in the morning until they leave. About five hours continuously."

"How do you know where they go at night?"

"On the ones that have collars, we use an aerial." He pointed to a T-shaped antenna lying on the back seat. "We'll go over to the east, and see if we can pick up one."

He drove the truck along a circuit of old army roads that encircled the dump at a distance of half a mile. Almost due east of the dump, well out of sight of it, he stopped the truck in the frozen gravel ruts and got out. In the chill wind off the sea he set the portable base receiver on the engine hood, connected the antenna to it, and turned it on.

"She should be in that direction." He pointed almost due west. "Yes, there's the beep."

I listened but heard nothing and said so. Lunn turned up the volume. The steady "beep-beep" was barely audible to me. It was the first time I had actually seen a locator at work. The direction in which the instrument was pointing indicated that the bear was resting directly between us and the dump. Lunn rotated the instrument, and the sound from the speaker diminished quickly. I asked about that.

"The instrument gives the strongest signal when pointed right at the bear. If you travel in that direction, the animal will be where the signal appears strongest."

"Simple as that!"

"Just that simple. It is an excellent aid to studies."

I had heard a polar bear signal in the night!

The following morning Steve Kearney, Manitoba Natural Resources Department, came over to the hotel. He asked if I would care to go along on a general check of the local polar-bear situation and visit some of the traps. He drove the truck from the hotel to the end of the block, turned left, then after another block turned again into a short lane ending at the waterfront. To my surprise, a large steel culvert-type bear trap sat there on its wheels, the door open. The trap was empty. The fish bait on the trigger had been untouched overnight. I remarked that the night before I'd heard firecracker-like explosions as I returned from one of the hotels nearby, in fact, a block and a half from where we now stood. I asked him if the explosions were automated.

"No. There must have been bears around town. We have a four-man bear patrol here. They use crackers when they spot a bear."

That statement brought an immediate response in my mind. When I had walked down the windswept, deserted main street the previous evening, coming from a slide show on wildlife, the outer door of my hotel had been locked, and the key that had been supplied for entering after 10:30 P.M. would not turn in it. No matter what I did, the lock remained fastened. At first I hadn't thought much about the firecrackers. After all, Hallowe'en had been celebrated only three days before. However, while my insistent banging on the hotel door was going unanswered, I remembered what I'd been told about the use of crackers to scare away local bears. And those explosions seemed no more than half a block away! I looked up and down the short street. It was totally deserted, all storefronts closed and lights out. Kicking the door noisily, I tried the key pushed in tight, loosely inserted, run in and out, and twisted hard. It would not turn. The intermittent popping continued.

"Damn! That *could* mean bears!" was my thought.

I looked around, up and down the street. Not even one shop was lighted; there was not one damn place I could go to get out of the way of a polar bear that might meander up the street. Too fresh in my mind was the grizzly bear and her cub just outside my open cabin window on Admiralty Island, less than a month before. And I had already seen more bears around Churchill than during my entire stay at bear-bound Pack Creek. That thought was disconcerting! The next couple of kicks against the bottom of the door panel almost bent it inward. I yelled loudly, "Anyone in there! Anyone in there?" I could see the empty lobby and part of the registration desk, through the double-glazed and murky outside window. There was no sign of life. The hotel, despite the $45-a-day charge and TV beside the bed, had no one on duty after 10:30 P.M.

My toes really felt the shock of the next two hard kicks. The sound of firecrackers was spasmodic, not far off.

I trotted quickly across the street to the door of the restaurant, also owned by my hotel's proprietor. I knew people had been eating there until after 10:00 P.M. the previous night, because I had visited there with friends. There might be someone still cleaning up inside. That door too was locked.

Banging and kicking on it brought no response. Then a voice came faintly from back across the street.

"Hello there?"

In the slit of the hotel doorway I saw someone's back-lit head. "Hold it! I'm locked out of there!" I yelled. The door closed even as I was midway across. An instant later I got to the hotel steps and kicked hard. The door opened. A man in pants and undershirt was there.

"Where were you?" he asked.

"Trying to raise them at the restaurant across the street. Thanks for letting me in. Do you work here? My key doesn't fit!"

"No. I'm staying here, too. And the keys damn well *don't* fit!"

Later he told me that I was only the first guest he had to let into the hotel that night. Three others had raised hell afterwards. So if you are given a night key in Churchill, and if you don't like raising hell among the exploding crackers while trying to get into your domicile, try the key before you accept it! When I told Steve Kearney about the little affray as we looked at the polar-bear trap, he just grinned.

We visited another trap a couple of blocks down the waterfront. It too was empty, the bait intact. This trap was only yards from a home and other buildings occupied daily. Kearney then drove out of the city in the direction of the airport, where he had departmental business. I asked him what they did with polar bears after they were trapped. I had heard many times that the cost of relocating bears at points distant from where they are captured had become prohibitive, mainly because within hours or days the bears are back to their point of capture.

"Helicopter relocation has become too expensive," he replied. "But we're trying a new system. As we go out to the airport, I'll show you."

Minutes later, he pointed toward a large, squat building on the left-hand side of the road.

"In there the bears are held in individual concrete pens. It will hold up to fifty bears."

"How many are in there now, Steve?"

"Three. It may build up."

"What are the costs of flying them out?"

"About $500 per bear."

"What about the cost of holding them there? And for how long?"

"The feeding costs are minimal. And as soon as the ice comes, a couple of weeks from now, we transport them to the shore. They're only too glad to get out on the ice."

"Don't they come back to feed? Bears do condition quickly."

"We haven't experienced it. They just want to get away," he stated. "Too, we ask people who keep dogs to feed their animals minimally and to keep their stored feed away from the dog area."

"I'm told polar bears don't attack dogs. Is that so?"

"Generally, yes. They're rather dog like themselves. They don't usually attack the dogs, just try for their food. This year there aren't many bears around. There are about six out near Bird Cove. That is the most we have seen this year."

I told him that I had seen and photographed seven bears out there. When I asked him to show me the bear-containment building, he said it was out of bounds to the public. Why? Departmental orders for fear of human contact causing problems. They were making a film record for public display later. *No one*, except from the services, was allowed to enter the experimental station. And no reasonable argument was considered!

I went back to the fact that we had seen seven polar bears out at Bird Cove the first day, and that there seemed to be a line of them moving up from the southeast. I asked him if he had worked with polar bears.

"Oh yes. I worked on them for a couple of years, tagging and counting."

"How many have you tagged or handled?"

"Oh, about a hundred and fifty."

He turned the car off the main road and down toward the windy beach, thence along a side road to a section of shoreline shut off from the open tundra by a ridge of glacially smoothed rock. At the end of the road he checked a V-shaped pocket of sawn timber set among large boulders. It was the site of a wire snare, but it was not set or baited.

"How about snares?" I asked.

"They are effective and not too injurious. The polar bear does not show too much immediate reaction to having its foot caught in a noose. They don't usually struggle too much or injure themselves. They will pull at it for a while, then often lie down."

It was a fact I had observed when watching the National Geographic Society film done in the Churchill area. A trapped bear had not panicked but simply circled, pulling away from the snare. I mentioned that to Kearney.

"Yes, they're almost patient most of the time. We had a big one in a snare on the beach here some time back. It took the 45-gallon oil drum filled with rocks right down the beach and headed for sea. We had some job rescuing that one!"

His was a typical wildlife manager's remark. Rescuing animals from harm was always the most important item on their agenda, even to the extent of risking personal injury. Having often witnessed the sincerity of that concern, I was not surprised to hear it from Kearney.

As we drove back to the airport road, I asked him what he thought was the best drug for darting polar bears.

"We use two drugs: Ketamine, which is a quick knockout, and Rompun, which is a sedative. The bear is completely out while it is being handled."

"What about Sernalyn? It seems to be favored down south."

"It's a good, useful drug, but the bears can see what is going on around them. Have you noticed that their eyes are open?"

I said I had and that it also had to be very carefully measured. He nodded.

By now we were arriving at the airport. Kearney swung the vehicle into a parking area that faced the airport runway. He got out of the cab and entered a small building adjacent to the main building. The area between the two buildings was separated from the parking space by a fence of heavy link wire. Through it, while waiting for Kearney, I watched two men loading a mechanical dolly with cargo. As I stared past them, I could not believe my eyes!

A polar bear was right on the runway. The animal was walking past a medium-sized passenger plane toward the smaller building. It was right out in the area used for passenger debarkation.

A polar bear! Not seventy-five yards off!

The bear was now under the aircraft wing, coming well up the runway between the men loading the dolly and the smaller storage shed. *That*, I had to have on film! I pulled out my camera and ran to the fence. The animal, standing about seventy-five yards off, was looking directly at the smaller building. The workmen obviously were either unaware or unafraid. With the strong link fence between the polar bear and myself, and the distance to the truck and its horn only about thirty feet, I was relatively unafraid. I shoved the lens up to an open square in the fence and focused, taking two exposures. The two men loading the dolly had finished, and their vehicle had moved on silently toward the large airport building. Just then Steve Kearney came out and got in on the other side. I climbed back into the truck and sat down pointing out through the windshield.

"That's a nice big bear! But it looks as though it's been in the dump—by the color of it."

"What bear? Where?"

I pointed again.

"Over there by the aircraft."

"Well, I'll be damned! It shouldn't be there! We'll have to chase him off!"

Immediately, Kearney started the motor. He was backing up before I got my door closed. The vehicle spurted around the smaller of the two sheds, throwing gravel, and I thought, "Yeah! We'll have to chase it off! Who, *me*?" Well, anyway, it would be an experience—perhaps unforgettable! Kearney was powering the vehicle in second gear past the cargo shed, out onto a service road that circled back toward the flying field. My next glimpse of the polar bear showed that it had been turned around, perhaps by the sudden activity of our vehicle. It was headed parallel to the face of the buildings, away from the aircraft.

As the open runway came into view again, the bear was off the airfield, at the edge of it, looking back. The approach of our truck made it move reluctantly away. It would take a few strides, then look back. As the truck came closer, it moved off toward the open tundra. Steve swung the vehicle onto the open plain, then stopped suddenly, in line with the bear's retreat. The animal was about fifty to sixty yards off. Kearney reached in the back seat and came out with a shotgunlike weapon in his hand. In the other hand, he had a bunch of shot shells, one of which he was cramming into the gun breach. I slid quietly out on my side, just as he shouldered the weapon and fired.

The gun's report was about the same as that of a .22-caliber long shell.

From the barrel a single projectile was cartwheeling, it seemed, in the direction of the bear. Almost above the animal there was a flash of bright bluish light, a white puff of smoke, and a loud report. The bear jumped into a faster stride, trotted a few paces, then stopped. It looked back at us as if annoyed but not afraid, as if humans were a nuisance but no real menace. I looked closely at its head. There was no sign of a tag in either of its ears, and there was no numeral on its side. However, by the smudged grey of its coat, it was apparent that the bear had visited the dump. Another shell exploded on the ground beside it. It flinched, then trotted another short distance and looked back; then, as if resolved, began to pace quite slowly away.

As Kearney's gun detonated again, another missile traveled a noticeable winding arc. The trajectory was wide, and it exploded well to the side. The animal simply hastened its walk as Kearney fired two more of the firecrackers.

When I was a youngster we used to be able to buy what we called "electric firecrackers" filled with what we called "silver powder"—as opposed to black—actually an ignitable magnesium compound that exploded with flash like an electric arc and an exceptionally sharp report, very much louder than ordinary firecrackers. Later these fireworks were banned as too dangerous—they could blow off a finger or more. Those crackers now detonating near the bear were, to the eye and ear, identical. No wonder the bear was reluctant to stay.

Now that he was between eighty and a hundred yards away, the crackers were falling far short, but the animal had gotten the idea.

I thought about Game Warden Ken John's words regarding crackers. I could not help wondering what might happen if one had only a single cracker while determined bears were moving in. Did these majestic animals become immune to the violent but harmless noise? I asked Kearney.

"I don't know. I haven't seen one that they won't move."

So that was what "bangers" or crackers looked like, sounded like, and acted like. They do move bears!

It was the fifth day of observation, the height of the polar-bear migration toward the ice, through Churchill. The ferocious white bears, the mankillers of legend, the Eskimos' scourge of the North, had turned out to be a magnificent creamy-white species with an almost aloof glance—a long-necked observer of humanity, a thief of dog food, a common housebreaker, having a deceptively smooth, fast-moving pace. The polar bear is courageous but willing to skirt unnecessary trouble, determined even against violent explosions if it is so minded—a really wonderful animal to watch and record on film!

My visit to Hudson Bay had been with a view to helping in the handling, marking, and field study of polar bears. On the morning of the final day, with my flight scheduled for 1:30 P.M., I had been unable to participate effectively in the fieldwork. When I had asked officials about polar bears being marked in the Churchill vicinity, I was told that only one had been marked at the dump. When I told the man in charge that several of my photographer acquaintances had participated in the departmental marking of bears at Bird Cove and that two had actually been asked to help the marking crew lift such a tranquilized bear, I was told that no local marking was planned for this period. Thus, with a free morning to fill, when I met Wayne Lankinen and Bob Taylor at breakfast, I asked if I could share their costs for the morning trip. Wayne who had hired the vehicle, invited me to go out with them with the same generosity as earlier—no charge.

Helen Lankinen joined the three of us for the trip out to Bird Cove. We drove along the seashore with the gray-green waters in full sight. The beach was a surprise. Where five days earlier the sandy beach was being gently laved with the slushy combers, now there was solid rough ice, brilliant white in the freezing sunlit air. About thirty feet out the shoreline was frozen solid, with some sharper points jutting farther to sea. Freeze-up departure time for the polar bears. Gazing at the ice I reflected that when the sea freezes in Hudson Bay, it shuts down the port but opens up a new world for which ice is the floor. Men no longer venture offshore in boats; dogsleds and snow-mobiles begin to traverse the sea-plain, and polar bears go back to their real domain, now just days away.

I remarked that the freeze-up seemed now at hand. As always, Bob Taylor had been searching the passing tundra and short-branched tree sentinels for the white owl, the snowy ptarmigan, Arctic fox, or polar bear. He glanced at the coast casually.

"Yes! It comes very quickly. Only a few more days, and the bears will take off seal hunting," he acknowledged.

"Does it always come this suddenly—green seas with combers breaking one day—then ice?"

He nodded in confirmation. "Well, Mike, you timed it right. In a week, with this temperature, it will be ice right out into the bay."

He went back to his search of the ponds, plains, and hummocks. We were at the eastern side of Bird Cove, closer to the ridges of glacially smoothed black rocks than during my earlier trip with them. Helen Lankinen, like Bob and Wayne, was scouting the horizon when Wayne, who says very little, spoke emphatically.

"There's one! By the rocks!"

He turned the vehicle off onto a side road that took us directly toward the polar bear's path. Bob cautioned gently as the vehicle drew to within two hundred yards, but Wayne was already braking and throwing the shift out of gear. He reached for his camera almost as the vehicle crunched to a stop. Helen spoke up.

"There is another one! Down in the low spot there. A marked one."

My eyes followed her hand as she indicated the direction.

An otherwise brilliantly white polar bear was slouching across the edge of a frozen lake, a huge numeral 9 painted on its near side.

"Damn!" I thought, "What a shame!"

"You can forget about that one," announced Wayne.

He was setting up his tripod as the bear traveled around us at a distance of about two hundred feet. Abruptly it changed its course moving quickly toward the rocks at the bottom of the snow-capped ridge.

In seconds, Wayne and Bob were back in the vehicle with their equipment. Using a bit of open flatland to get to another road, Wayne quickly short-cut the distance to an angle close to where the bear was traveling. He drove fast enough to intersect with it at close range, and the two photographers were able to get shots of the bear as it passed the black rock formations—a spectacular background. Then the bear had passed the rocks and was headed back the way it had come.

Now a third bear was on its way toward where we had seen Number 9.

As Lankinen drove the truck toward the third bear, it moved toward the sea. The marked one was back in the short bushes, lying down. Now three vehicles were in the area, all, it seemed, occupied in the photographic pursuits that obviously brought a considerable tourist trade to the "Polar Bear City."

Wayne was watching the path taken by the fourth bear that we had seen that morning, and choosing roads that apparently led nowhere, he cut right across the path of the bear. It was moving in our direction, and as we approached it, two other observation vehicles drove in from the west. Off in the distance, where another polar bear could be seen coming toward us from the southeast, was a green vehicle that seemed vaguely familiar. Two men were moving around it, obviously intent on the approaching bear. Taylor and Lankinen were approaching within photographic range of the other bear, which was coming from seaward. One of the other tourist trucks drove up nearby, and a group of photographers got out of it. They were the first group I had seen approach another group of photographers who had "established" a bear and were filming it. They hung back. I got out and watched them. One of them pointed back toward the green-hued vehicle.

"That's that damn research group again! Marking polar bears," he remarked to a nodding of heads.

Now the greenish vehicle was moving slowly in our direction. The approaching polar bear had circumnavigated the pond that had been between it and the marking crew, and now it was approaching at an angle that would take it right across the well-lit backdrop of slightly rising terrain, where photography would be excellent. I watched the bear's majestic approach, thinking how casual it seemed. It stopped and stared at the group, then turned to look down its back trail. The green vehicle was very slowly tracking it, moving purposefully.

"Damn! They're going to nail that one!" someone said, angrily.

About two hundred yards away from our two vehicles, the bear stopped uncertainly on a rising bit of open tundra. To the north of it lay the ridge of rocks where our first photographed bear had gone, perhaps for seclusion from us; to the northwest was the sea; and south and west were two vehicles besides the one pursuing it. The research truck had gotten to within seventy-five yards of the animal, and the crew was out preparing gear.

I thought, "This is what the authorities denied they were doing—or had any intention of doing!"

One of the group had moved toward the bear. The dart gun was up. The bear was standing quite still, unsure of its direction.

Like a racehorse out of a gate, it suddenly sprang forward.

We heard a quick, sharp report.

The charge of the big white bear, directly away from its pursuers, covered about 150 yards. Brian Ladoon's remark came back to me: "They are so unbelievably fast!" The statement was almost inadequate. I have seen many animals, in a race, but not even whippets covered such a distance as fast as the white bear at the prick of the dart. It took one more short burst, then stopped and looked back. It was near a hedge of black brush. It took about half a dozen paces, then almost gently lay down.

The men were back at the green truck, pulling out gear. Wayne Lankinen drove our vehicle the short distance over to theirs and parked near it. Bob Taylor went over to the man remaining there. Two of the crew were already at the downed bear, one of them appearing to thump the chest cavity as a person would handle a victim of heart failure. Bob came back to our vehicle, shaking his head.

My own interest was to get photographs of the full procedure, as I had been doing during several months of work with both black bears and grizzlies. I asked what had happened.

"He says we can't go near the bear for at least half an hour," Taylor informed us. "Those are his instructions, to keep people away."

Inside I was boiling. All three of us, well aware of the procedures of bear marking, were unlikely to be troublesome. What was more, the marking crew knew it! I asked what possible harm could be done by approaching to within fifteen feet, within camera range, of the animal. The crewman was adamant, although he knew of my research and who I was.

Up on the sloping tundra two of the crew were working on the bear with tapes and instruments, one of them occasionally and quickly thrusting up and down on the rib cavity of the downed animal. The third man joined them with a box of gear.

Someone nearby said dejectedly, "I guess they are going to paint another goddamn numeral on its side! Why the hell do they have to do that in this area, when they have hundreds of miles south of here to work on them. We've paid thousands of dollars to get in here, just to take a picture of a free-roving white bear, and we get big painted black numerals and metal-tagged ears. It is stupid!"

It was a statement with which I agreed. I went over and suggested to the crewman, now at the truck, that it would do no harm to allow the two photographers and me to go in close and observe the mechanics of marking the bear. At least, that photo could have a clinical advantage. He shook his head. I argued, but to no effect. He returned to the men working on the bear. Angered, we watched from our heated truck as the crew worked on the downed bear. Finally, one of them came back to their truck. One of our group approached him and then came back nodding his head.

"We can go in, now."

While Wayne and Bob were getting their cameras and equipment, I

Dr. Ian Stirling, of the Canadian Federal Wildlife Service, marking a polar bear near Churchill, Manitoba.

walked across the crusty, granular snow toward the bear. One of the men, possibly the one in charge, was working at the bear's head. Moving around them I took several wide-angle-lens photographs, then moved in close, to within a couple of feet of the animal's head. The exposed eye on that side was taped over with clear cellophane tape; the mouth, blacklined, showed a tiny spot of pink.

Even lying on the snow, the polar bear retained its infinite dignity. The dark-clad, muffled technicians working diligently seemed its servants, attendants, but perhaps—who really knows—its saviors.

BOOK TWO

Maulings and Killings

For my father, Alex, and my mother, Hilda

Introduction to Book Two

Between the years 1977 and 1981 nine separate killings and twenty-four maulings of human beings by black and grizzly bears occurred in areas of North America as widely separated as Montana and Alaska and Ontario and British Columbia. My book *Killer Bears* included a catalogue of authenticated bear-and-man confrontations up to 1980. The recorded total of killings and maulings by the three bear species was 251. In the book I stated that the numbers were low, perhaps only 50 percent of the actual total. This conclusion grew out of my research and travel—three years and forty thousand miles—during which I heard innumerable reports of confrontations.

Within six months of the publication of that book, I received a veritable flood of letters from readers relating tale after tale of bear-and-man conflicts, many of which had not been available for verification during my earlier research. The real confirmation of unreported bear-and-man conflicts came, however, during a subsequent research trip to Anchorage, Alaska. There the Departments of Fish and Game and of Public Safety records showed that during 1981 in Alaska alone 51 bears had been killed by people acting "in defense of life and property." When I asked if 1981 was an unusual year for such attacks, one official said that since 1970 the average had been about 40. He then gave me the departmental figures from 1961 to 1981, which totalled 672. In 1961, 4 were listed as having been "in defense of life and property." In 1970 the number rose to 46, and the annual average for 1961-1971 stood at 17.5. From 1971 to 1981 the high year was 1978, with 58 incidents, and the average yearly count was 49.5.

The increased incidence during the past decade is tied, of course, to the increase in the state population, which more than doubled between 1961 and 1981. These killings are attributable to other causes as well, however.

I asked long-time game-management and field man Lee Miller how many of those killings actually were in defense of life and property. His answer was revealing:

"When it comes down to actual *attacks*, about one in fifty."

"How many were in each category? In defense of life and in defense of property?"

He thought for a moment.

"I'd have to go through a lot of files to find the exact ratio, but I'll guess that the reports say 40 percent were in defense of life and 60 percent in defense of property."

"How are these statistics accumulated? Do you investigate?" I inquired.

He nodded, at the same time picking up several sheets from his desk that had been handed to him after we began our conversation.

"These are three reports just being serviced. We investigate killings very thoroughly, on the spot. We require that a statement be taken from the person or persons, a report filed, and that the skin and skull and, if possible, the carcass be preserved until we can examine them. We process the skins and remains in our laboratory. If there is any indication that the bear posed no threat to a person or property, we press charges."

"In other words, Lee, you don't just accept the word of the person reporting the incident?"

He gave an almost derisive smile.

"That would be the same as a license to kill. We make very sure that the report includes evidence of damage to property or certifiable proof that a life was endangered. At times people think we're persecuting them."

I nodded my head, remembering my recent interview with big-game bowman-guide Ed Wiseman, who had been charged with the killing of a grizzly bear—an endangered species in Colorado—despite the fact that he had killed it with a hand-held arrow and had been severely mauled. Only after months in court was he exonerated.

If the number of man-and-bear confrontations and killings listed in *Killer Bears* is used as a base reference (official reports often are not available from such sources as national, state, and provincial parks), the average number of persons in North America killed annually by bears between 1949 and 1978 is 1.24, and the average number of attacks is 8.6. Between 1979 and 1985, however, nine more killings were widely reported, and fifty serious attacks can be counted in other news sources and in the letters I received from readers. Thus it appears that an escalation has occurred: between 1979 and 1985 the average annual number of killings increased to at least 1.6, and the average number of attacks resulting in serious injury increased to 10 per year. Too, it must be reasserted that those figures show only *news* reports, that governmental bureaus, including offices of parks and wildlife management, as well as investigative agencies, prefer not to reveal their official figures. My personal correspondence indicates that many bear attacks receive only local reporting. Because no source has *all* the statistics available, positive numerical conclusions are impossible.

It is a disastrous revelation that *most* of these tragedies are occurring in parks. Confrontations in the wild seem not to have escalated. These facts *seem* to condemn park management and personnel, but before reaching such a conclusion it is prudent to examine the reported cases of injury and death. That is the purpose of the ensuing chapters.

CHAPTER I

So It Couldn't Happen to You!

"Even when you do what you think is the right thing—Hell!—you don't know what is going to happen with a bear!" said John Chesman of Vancouver, British Columbia, a lifelong outdoorsman who annually plans for months to visit some outlying lake or wilderness area because he likes it out there. Interested in fishing and hunting primarily as relaxation, he gets his limit of trout on a fly, shoots grouse for the camp pot, takes deer or a moose each year for meat, believes in and gives aid to conservation funds and measures. No novice.

He, a few members of the Canuck Hockey Club organization—many of whom are outdoorsmen—and I were talking about bear experiences. They had read *Killer Bears*, and that resulted in a gab session.

John was grinning.

I took him up. "You must have a good reason for that statement, John," I said.

He looked a little sheepish.

"Yes, maybe. There was a bear around our camp up at a North Cariboo lake. When it got too close, I took a shot over its head to chase it off, and it ran right through another outfit's camp."

Laughter broke out all over the room.

John is a careful guy who would take such a possibility into consideration before shooting over a bear.

"John, now, about the details on that—it may be useful in my research."

He smiled, "Sure."

We agreed to get together for a later session when the business of the hockey club wasn't so pressing. Near the end of the season we finally made it.

In his own words:

"Well, it was September, 1980, up at Hen Ingram Lake. A bunch of us had arranged to meet up there for some fishing—darn good trout lake, with some fish up to six pounds.

"The lake is about seventy or eighty miles in from the main highway to Prince George, British Columbia, about thirty from the small village of Horsefly. When you get off the gravel, it is a typical abandoned dirt road. It was put in for some mining development some time ago, and it isn't kept up at all. I rented a camper on a four-wheel drive because it is a rough road, one that an ordinary car can high-center on. There are potholes and ruts up to the axle through much of it, but it ends at Hen Ingram Lake, one of the most beautiful you can get to in the north country—and not too many people do get out there.

"Jack MacDonald (you know him; he's a Canuck scout, one of the originals) went with me, and we got in there about 5:00 P.M. after a real rough trip. I drove the truck up to the lakeside, just off the clearing—a type of turnaround used for the mining trucks at the lake. We cleared out a space for a fire, put the boat in the water, and gathered some firewood from back in the timber. We were in a parklike coniferous forest with a sprinkling of poplars back up on the ridge. You know, the typical north-country background: just a little cleared section at the lake edge, no buildings or prepared camp grounds, just some places that had been cleared out by guys like us who wanted to drive a vehicle in and set up a camp.

"Jack and I weren't in any hurry. Actually, we had come in three days early to set up camp for the other guys, Doug Devitt, Miles Rydeen, and a couple of others. We made ourselves a drink, and Jack took his outside while I set up stuff to get some dinner. He was delighted with the campsite.

"He looked around and said, 'Gee! We don't have anything like this in Ontario! It's sure grand!'"

We both laughed—both of us partial to the British Columbia scenery and outdoors. John looked up at the ceiling, savoring the remembered beauty.

"I started to cook up a meal. Jack said, 'There's a bear!' but I didn't pay much attention. A couple of minutes later I saw Jack going out with his camera. I looked through the window of the camper to see the bear, which was moseying around the little turnaround clearing, about 150 feet away. Jack was moving closer to it for better shots. The bear had also come closer. It was about 150 pounds, a young black bear maybe in its second season, not a big one but big enough.

"MacDonald is seventy-two years of age, and I wasn't that happy about him being near the bear, particularly as *it* wasn't showing any sign of fear. I reached into my duffle and pulled out my old breakdown model Mosberg bolt–action .410 shotgun, which I always carry in my gear when I'm in the woods. I put it together, then put a couple of shotgun slug cartridges into it.

"When I looked out again, Jack was even nearer the bear. And it was keeping an eye on him. I said, 'Hey, Jack! Be careful. This isn't Disneyland, you know! That's a *wild* bear!' He took a bit more serious attitude. He'd been so interested in getting photos that he had lost some of his caution. He moved back a few feet. The bear was now about thirty feet from him, roving curiously back and forth."

John paused, reliving the moment.

I broke in. "That's typical of an uncertain bear."

John nodded his head.

"Yes, I guess so. He wasn't really showing any sign of wanting to take off, not even with the two of us that close. I was standing near the front of the truck with the gun, and in a line with where I could shoot over him without doing any damage. The bullet would go out over the empty lake. I fired off one shot.

"That did it. The bear took off like a streak of greased lightning. While the echoes were still resounding down the lake, we both laughed, thinking that was the end of him. Our supper was cooked, and we went in and sat down to eat.

"A couple of minutes later two guys, whom we hadn't seen before, were standing at the open doorway of the camper.

"One of them said, 'Which one of you sons of bitches shot at that bear?'

"I said, 'I did. I shot over it to scare it off.'

"He said, 'The damn thing ran right into our tent—*right into our tent*! Just as we were takin' a snooze. We yelled like hell, and it turned around and took off. It sure put the wind up us for a minute though!'

"We all laughed and started to talk about it. They stayed around most of the evening, and we had a few drinks. They were from the lower Fraser Valley area—bush-wise guys—and didn't think too much of it.

"But, the next day we were all out fishing up the lake. They were still out in their canoe when I came back into our camp. As I came in, I saw the bear rooting around in their campsite, which was in the timber about 200 yards from our place. I yelled, and it took off carrying a thermos jug—you know, the kind with the handle—in its mouth. It disappeared into the bush. Later I told them what happened, and one of them said, 'Hell, he can *have* the thermos! I'm not going back into the bushes looking for it. He may be in there, and we don't have any guns!'

"They left the lake a couple of days later. Our own party came in, and we fished every day. Got some rainbows up to four pounds."

John showed me the album photos of a catch of the rainbows. When I said that most of them were about four pounds, he said, "Yeah. We had several six-pounders the year before." I made a mental note to look into the facts about Hen Ingram Lake for myself. Another photo of the campsite, taken from the boat, showed the area where the bear had been and the position of the other campsite. Pointing at one photo, he said, "One of our guys was looking for dry firewood a couple of days after the other party left, and he found the thermos bottle right there. It has teeth marks drilled right through it. He keeps it as a souvenir."

So, it was an amusing incident; it wasn't a bear attack. The only thing the bear did was bite right through a metal thermos—and scare hell out of a couple of guys in a tent.

But at just such a campsite, at a lake about a hundred miles south of Hen Ingram, a black bear *did* attack.

Jack Shaw, author of the very successful and authoritative fly-fishing book *Fish the Trout Lakes*, asked me if I had fished Little Blue Lake, a little-known trophy fish lake. When I confessed I had not, he arranged for us to go with another buddy, Jim, the next day.

"Trophy" lakes exist, and Little Blue Lake was one, a lake offering a reasonable chance of taking a five- to eight-pounder—a trophy rainbow.

A couple of years earlier Jack, the best lake rainbow-trout fly-fisherman I've known, retired to "just fishin'." Mind you, he cuts a lot of firewood, and a vegetable garden fills half his homesite acre, and he ties flies—to order—*if* he feels like it. Boats line up beside or behind him when he is on a lake. And, while fishermen ask him questions, he is landing trout after rainbow trout.

Jack's pickup led the way, and it was twenty miles of winding mountain-plateau road. I lost track of our course very early. And *then* we reached the road to the lake! After navigating a short distance over tank terrain, we arrived right at the secluded waters. The setting was so still that the sound of a loon resting a quarter of a mile away on the lake's glasslike surface was like a treble chord struck on a pipe organ in an empty church. It was a remote lake. Only one other truck was parked at the lakeside, its owner already out in a boat well down the lake. Jack, Jim, and I launched our respective small craft and glided expectantly out onto the barely rippled surface. Two rainbows broke water near the launch site. Before Jack and I were set up with our chosen flies, Jim was into a good-size, bright, jumping fish. Then it was Jack's turn, then Jack's turn, then Jack's turn! I got a big, maybe six-pound, darkly colored fish and disgustedly returned it. I was so upset at having to release it that right away I blew an even larger, bright rainbow. About six hours later we came ashore, all of us with the two-fish limit. Jack's four-pounder was our largest.

We were stashing our gear and lifting our boats onto the vehicles when a fourth man came in off the lake. He had about a five-pounder, and he knew Jack. He also fished the lake quite regularly. While I was putting my rods back on the inner camper racks, he was telling my companions about some of his trips earlier in the season, and I heard him laugh a bit self-consciously.

"Yeah, Jack! It was right here that goddam black bear came after me. Right where I'm parked right now. I always park in this spot, if it's open."

Quickly I climbed out of my camper.

"You say a black bear came after you—*here*?" I asked.

He looked at me quizzically, as if I doubted his story. Jack was grinning broadly.

"This is Mike Cramond. Meet Walt Klimach. Mike has a book out on killer bears."

"Oh," said the guy, not too impressed.

He was a local. That is to say, I was a city guy from the outside, not from the Cariboo country. When you're a local, you shut up a little in such a situation. I know that. And, if anyone introduces me as a "writer," the period of uncertainty may last a couple of days, until they see you adjust a cinch, tie a hitch, cast a fly, row a boat. I went right after him, anyway.

"You say the bear attacked you?"

He looked at me for a moment.

"Yeah."

"Here? Right here?"

"Yeah."

"Was it a *big* black bear?"

"Yeah. Big enough."

"What happened?"

"It came after me, and I shot it."

"How about details?"

"What for?"

"I may use it in a book."

"I dunno if I want to be in a book."

Jack Shaw had turned away and was quietly laughing his head off. He knows I'm inclined to be aggressive on a story, an ex-cop with remnants of a get-the-details approach. I suddenly realized that fact myself. I grinned reassuringly.

"Oh, I won't *promise* to put it in a book—*maybe* use it, if it's different."

The guy looked at me for a time.

"Well! As I was sayin', Jack"—he turned to face him directly—"I noticed the goddam bear over there just by those two trees." He was pointing to a spot about seventy-five feet from all of us, in the turnaround, which was enclosed by the surrounding tall timber. "My dog Randy saw it too! The bear was making right for me, and the dog took a run at it. The bear stopped to take a swipe at the dog, and Randy ducked. He ran in again. I made for the truck, where my rifle was on the cab rack. The bear was comin' right at me, swiping occasionally at the dog, which was jumpin' in and out at him.

"It was just by that hump there." He pointed to a rise of earth about twenty-five feet away. "When I got my gun out and threw a couple of shells into it, the bear was still swiping at the dog, but making for me. I put up the gun and fired at its shoulder. The bear went down and made to get up. I clobbered it in the head. It got to about there!" He pointed to a spot about ten feet from him. "I put another shot into him, and he stayed down. I gave him another one in the back of the neck, then rolled him over."

He paused and for some reason looked at me. I suppose I looked curious.

"What in hell made him come?" I asked.

"He stunk like hell. He was wounded! Maybe a week, or a few days, before. Festerin' down one leg with a wound. When I skinned him, he had two bullet holes in him, one in his gut. Maybe .22 caliber holes."

The words had a nauseating familiarity.

"Was he in bad shape?"

"No. Not skinny, not sick, just wounded enough to be mean."

"Any idea who did it?"

He grimaced wryly.

"Oh, maybe some guys came in here fishin', and he bothered their camp. I dunno. Who's to say? Some guys do things like that."

We were all shaking our heads. Some people do do things like that! And some people get killed by bears who have been treated like that by some guys who do things like that!

Some bear incidents, on the other hand, are examples of innocent trust. One of these encounters also came from a Canuck hockey team associate, John Milford, the son of the late Jake Milford, former general manager. His dad had given him a copy of my bear book. John is a young geologist who spends time working in the mountains.

During a break in a hockey game we were watching, he told me what had happened.

"We were up on the Okanagan Range, near Keremeos Creek. You know the area, don't you, Mike."

I nodded, and asked him if he was up where the mountain sheep and goats are, above the timber.

"No, not that high—about 5,000 feet, where there's some grass and timber but it's open in some areas. I had a bunch of geology students from the university. And that bear was some surprise!"

He grinned at the recollection. I asked him what equipment he had with him—anything in the way of a weapon.

"No, I was just carrying a light summer pack and a prospector's hammer. That's all! About noon I had gotten away from the students. They were always asking questions, and I needed a break. When I found an open piece of grass, I decided to lie down and have a rest, maybe get a suntan. I took off my shirt and boots and laid my small backpack beside me. My lunch of peanut butter sandwiches was in it, and it was open.

"I lay back in the sun and fell asleep. When I woke up, I sat up, and as I was putting on my shirt, I heard this noise about as far away from me as that second guy on the phone over there."

He pointed to one of the newsmen from out of town getting off his copy about the first two periods of the game. The distance was less than thirty feet. I said so. Milford continued with a shrug.

"Well, heck! When I heard this noise, I looked around, and there was the she-bear sitting right there licking its bum."

I interjected, "Licking its bum? Not looking at you?"

"No. It didn't pay any attention to me until I made a grab for my boots and started to pull them on in a hurry—then it whuffed a couple of times and stared right at me."

I laughed. "Quit lickin' its bum! Did it come toward you?"

"No. It just whuffed and stared at me. I just grabbed my lunch and walked off, as slowly as I could keep my pace."

"You didn't run? Or move fast?"

"No. I figured to move slowly, not to incite it. It stayed there!"

One of those outdoors situations about which one can't do anything except speculate! I'd had encounters very much like that myself. How close a call are they, really? Who knows? I asked him about previous sightings of the bear. He nodded affirmatively.

"Oh yes, she'd been around there for five days, anyway. She had two cubs, little ones that would reach up to your knee if they stood on their hind legs. In fact, I took pictures of her a couple of times."

"How close?"

"Well, about there, at the end of that news balcony—about fifty yards."

I looked over to the end of the long tier that overlooked the action of the hockey rink and shook my head.

"That's not fifty yards. More like thirty. Too close for a bear—particularly with cubs."

"Yeah. I know that now. I read your book. It's made me more careful."

"How did the sow act when she was with her cubs?"

"Well, she wasn't friendly. She'd whuff at me. I'd leave."

"Why do you think she was that close to you when you were sleeping up the mountain? Did she have her cubs with her?"

"I didn't see any cubs, not up there. I just got to hell out as soon as possible. I don't know what brought her that close. Maybe the smell of peanut butter sandwiches. I don't know. Do you?"

I laughed a bit self-consciously.

"No. I don't. Maybe the peanut butter sandwiches. But she came close enough to get you in three jumps, before you could get up. They're very fast! Maybe she wasn't hungry. But you said she was feeding two cubs in the spring before the berries are out—and they don't do too well just on grass and roots. Who knows?"

Nobody knows!

What about the several bears that have stalked me? Perhaps there were more in deep brush I didn't even see? If I'd found any bear sitting within thirty feet of me in the wilds, I'd have got to hell out of there too, just as quickly as I could without inciting a rush from behind. In fact, I have done so on similar occasions, with my hair standing on the back of my neck—particularly if theirs was also.

It does not matter where bears show up, in a wild campsite or in a well-used highway picnic grounds, they can cause trouble.

Among my many letters the following best illustrates the writer's knowledge, experiences, and reasoning:

Dear Mike,

You very likely get a lot of mail, but I hope you won't mind one short letter.

I am writing to say "thank you" for the commendable job you did in writing the book I have just finished reading, *Killer Bears*.

While I have never had the experience of being attacked by a bear, I am nevertheless well acquainted with black bears. I have lived most of my life near Powell

River [on the coast of British Columbia] and am more or less an outdoors person, having, among other things, been a trapper and a small-game and angling guide. My work has largely been in forest engineering and surveying, though, and I live outside of town ("in the bush").

Over the years I have encountered enough black bears that I can't begin to remember how many there were. Also, I've hunted them for the table and, regretfully, had to shoot a few in protection of property.

At first I was almost indifferent in my attitude toward them, feeling that they would all run from me—which has been my most common experience. My attitude has changed, though, because of the actions of several bears. I now avoid close contact as much as possible. I won't take your time with details, but I have met black bears that will not give the right-of-way on a trail. Also I have found them to be unafraid of loud noises, such as a power saw, and I have twice climbed trees (even though I am well aware of a black bear's ability to climb a good deal faster than I can) when a bear has been aggressive. When a bear starts smashing and biting at the brush and growling, while "popping" its teeth together, and you can see from only about seventy-five feet away that the hair is up on its back, and you are unarmed, you have to do something. While I had enough self-control that I didn't have to change my pants later, I was not brave enough to stand and watch it. I climbed a tree.

What I'm getting at is the point you did such a good job of showing in your book. No two bears are the same. Each one is an individual, and should be respected as such, knowing full well that it might be that one individual that is going to attack for whatever reason, or lack of reason it may have.

Again, thank you for an excellent book. I am recommending it to my friends and acquaintances.

I very seldom ever write letters except the few necessary business letters that one is forced to write. I have been favorably impressed, and I hope you don't mind having to read this because of it.

Yours truly,

GLENN F. ALLEN

Forget the kind words about my treatise on bears. Don't, however, forget what the writer has to say about his own experience with bears. Probably he is more experienced than most of us, having lived many years in the habitat of bears.

Yeah! We'll forget the handwriting and spelling. The first was excellent and easily readable; the following was better than I earn a living with. It is the truth, very plainly stated.

Like that correspondent and this writer, Bill Shaber of Patchogue, New York, is also a hunter and angler by choice. Bill is a fellow outdoors writer who is happy to earn much of his living in the open air. He and his wife, Marion, take every opportunity to drive in their camper to out-of-the-way fishing, hunting, and outdoors relaxation. Once, when they were in Yellowstone Park in a campsite at Madison Junction, a bear became a nuisance.

Let Bill Shaber tell you about it.

Dear Mike,

Your book *Killer Bears* tells it like it is, and I'm sure it is a classic. So much for the compliments.

As you know, I'm a long way from being considered an expert on bears. The way I see it, bears are great animals to look at, but not the kind of animals I want to make friends with.

Having spent most of my life in the great outdoors, I have on occasion come in contact with bears. In fact, I have had several opportunities to harvest the critters on hunting trips, but never the desire. Live and Let Live has been my bear motto.

However, over the years I have become very concerned by the lack of respect and knowledge the camping fraternity has when it comes to bears. I'm sure that the nonhunting campers' lack of respect stems from anthropomorphism, a big word which means attributing human form or qualities to wild animals. These people have been brainwashed through the so-called entertainment media: Walt Disney's "Wild Kingdom" and especially the "Grizzly Adams" show. Because of this brainwashing, many children and adults feel that bears can be treated as part of the family. . . . Taking this one step further, it is also impossible for these people to accept or understand how some humans can hunt, kill, and eat wild animals. For some unknown reason, these very same people have no feelings for the cow that is cut up into steaks or ground up into hamburger. The sheep with its big brown eyes that becomes lamb chops, or the chicken that winds up as chicken in a basket. It may be understandable for children to get upset when they think that Bambi's mother has been harvested, but that doesn't hold true for adults. Adults have the responsibility of explaining the difference between fact and fiction to their children. Bambi and Bambi's mother will never be destroyed: they are fiction.

Mike, I would like to tell you about a series of events that took place back in 1959 and that best illustrate my concern about bears and campers. Distressing as the events were, they could still happen, especially among today's campers, who know little or nothing about bears.

Back in '59 camping for most campers added up to a tent. Recreational vehicles were not yet the vogue, and camping was only for hardy outdoors people. We were campers, and because we lived in the east, a tent camping trip to the west was a challenge which Marion and I had often considered. We decided that this was the year that our daughters Lynn and Judy were old enough to appreciate a camping trip to Yellowstone Park, and also to visit some of the west they had read about in school. After much planning we headed west during the month of August. It was a month that was supposed to add up to great trout fishing in the west, but left much to be desired.

On arriving at the east gate of Yellowstone Park, our first instructions from the ranger at the gate were: "Keep all your food locked up in your car or the bears will get it. Don't feed the bears, and don't get out of the car to watch the bears, also don't stop your car on the road to watch the bears." We had known that there were bears in the park, but we hadn't given them much consideration when we planned this camping safari. Now they suddenly had become one of the most important aspects of it.

We left the gate and headed for a campsite at Madison Junction, bears being the main topic of conversation. We hadn't traveled too far before we hit a traffic jam, the first since we left New York. About four cars up the road, a sow black bear and two cubs were in the center of the road. The campers who had stopped traffic were trying to photograph their two children, together with the bear cubs. They were enticing the cubs with bread and cookies, which meant that they had little or no concern for the safety of their children or themselves. These supposedly responsible parents were doing exactly the opposite of what the ranger had told them, and only a few minutes after he had told them. Luckily one of the cubs got pushy, and the family got back into their car. They were fortunate that no one was hurt, and that they had not caused an accident by stopping their car on the roadway. This was the start of our camping experiences with Yellowstone bears, and campers who believed that bears were their friends. I used the situation to impress my kids with the possible dangers of bears, and as an example of people who believed that rules were made for someone else to follow.

While setting up camp we observed at least three or four bears roaming the area, and one was a sow with two cubs. They all appeared to be at ease with the campers, which, I am sure, gave many of the campers a false sense of security.

It didn't take long to learn that these campground bears were inquisitive and basically beggars. Their only reason for being in the campground was food, and it didn't matter whether it was the steak on your table or the garbage in the garbage cans—they wanted it. Incidentally, the garbage cans were buried in the ground, had heavy lids, and could only be opened by stepping on a foot pedal. This didn't discourage the bears, they just stepped on the pedals and dove into the cans head first.

Our first nose-to-nose encounter with these bears came late one afternoon while we were eating at our picnic table. I had left the ice chest on the edge of the bench, for convenience' sake, and had not considered the bears. Without fanfare a large bear that the campers called "Blondie" walked up and started sniffing the ice chest cover seal, and before I could blink an eye, the bear had taken a swipe at the chest and sent it flying into the brush. Luckily our neighbors had the presence of mind to bang on pots and pans, which scared the bear away. The lesson here was that the ice chest should have been returned to the trunk of the car, not left on the bench.

The bears frequently tried to steal food off the tables while campers were eating. In one case, a camper and his family were eating their evening meal, all sitting on one side of the table, when a large sow ambled up, put her front paws in the center of the table and started enjoying supper. Without thinking or considering the consequences, the man of the family waved his arm at the bear and shouted, "Get the hell out of here!" During that brief instant while he had his arm in the air, the bear reacted and tore his arm open with one fast swipe of its claws. Mike, it could have been his head. This camper's lack of knowledge about bears sent him to the hospital for repairs, ruined his vacation, and shook up his family so bad that they had to rent a cabin until they could leave the park area. It would have been more appropriate for the campers to retreat and let the bear have the food. The only good part about this incident is the fact that it taught other campers a lesson. They were suddenly made aware that they couldn't treat bears like a pet dog.

As I said before, bears roam campgrounds for one purpose only—easy food.

They don't come just because they enjoy watching campers or to have campers watch them. In the same campground I saw tents torn to shreds by bears just because someone left a cookie or bag of potato chips inside their tent. One of my camping neighbors told me he had been fishing, caught a couple of trout, and was on his way back to camp when he noticed a bear following him. He finally decided that the bear was after his fish and getting too close for comfort, so he left the fish for the bear. He was smart. He lived to fish another day.

Mike, this short story will give you some idea as to why I'm concerned about campers and their attitude towards bears, and of course, other wild animals. Our only hope is that someday the entertainment media will mend their ways and inform the public that bears cannot be considered friends or house pets.

The message is especially necessary for those people that live in urban and suburban areas and only get into the outdoors occasionally. Yet as you pointed out in your book, even those people who are considered experts on the ways of bears often become statistics to be written about.

Keep up the good work.

BILL

Oh yes, Bill! Well said.

The star of the bear shows, the grizzly, seems always to lurk in the background when conclusions are drawn. A close study of official statistics, however, shows that the grizzly is the most formidable of the bear species, and that among grizzlies the sow with her cubs is the most dangerous. In my files are many letters that verify these statistics. Consider, for example, the following, dated January 18, 1982:

Dear Mike Cramond:

I would like to introduce myself as Stan Miller, a fourth-year forestry student at the University of Alberta. The reason for this letter is briefly to describe my encounter with a grizzly sow and her two cubs. After reading your book *Killer Bears*, I felt that this information might be useful in your research.

First, I will give you a brief background on the situation. My partner, Bob Golding, and I were working on a contract with the Alberta Forest Service to collect and analyze watershed data for the summer of 1981. We were located sixty miles due south of Grande Prairie, Alberta. At the time of the encounter we were doing a watershed study on Boulder Creek, which involved walking the main channel and its tributaries to locate unstable areas. The encounter occurred shortly after noon on a day in July.

We were walking upstream on the tributary, about twenty feet away from the stream channel. The stream channel had 1.5 chain [100-foot] buffers on each side with cutblocks on both sides. We were looking for a spot to have lunch when my partner first spotted the grizzly sow taking a drink in the stream. Since we were downwind, and the noise of the stream was loud, we were only twenty to twenty-five feet away when we first saw her. She snapped her head around when she first got a glance of us, as we totally surprised her. At this time no cubs were in sight. The sow then moved up onto the opposite stream bank and stood on her haunches to get a look at us. The undergrowth had a fair amount of alder so she had to stand up to see us. At the time the sow did not make any threatening moves or sounds. Our first thoughts were that she was just going to look us over, and then go off on her own way. Stupidly, I tried to get a picture. But, before I could get the camera out of the case my partner yelled that she was charging us. Having no time to do anything defensively, we decided that we would stand up to her (just a reaction to the situation), hoping that our challenge would scare her. A tree was behind us in case she tried to knock us down. We could hear her coming through the alder but were not really able to see her clearly. She came out into an opening, charging directly at us, head down, bellowing, and swerved away from us at approximately ten to fifteen feet away. She then proceeded up the stream about thirty to forty feet and kept going in a semicircle pattern in front of us, up and down the stream slopes in a matter of a few seconds. Backing up about ten feet, she lost sight of us and charged towards us for the second time. Exactly the same thing happened: she swerved at the last second. Every time we could hear her charging we stood still, faced her and prepared for the impact. Proceeding another twenty feet up the slope we could hear her charging us again. Turning around and facing her, she swerved at about twenty feet from us. We decided that with any more charges, the less chance we had of getting out alive. So we hightailed it out of the cutblock as soon as she finished her charge. Upon reaching the cutblock, we noticed two bears about 1.5 chains [100 feet] from us. Trying to keep our senses, we started laughing because we thought the two bears were black bears and were also scared by the grizzly. The reason we thought they were black bears is that they were the size of a full-grown black bear and had a slightly darker coat than the sow, and the high grasses partly obscured our vision. All this time we could hear the sow thrashing around in the stream bottom, bellowing at the top of her lungs and making the most scariest sounds I have ever experienced. We decided this was the time to put distance between us and the sow, so we started running through the cutblock, keeping our eye on the two bears. After we had run for about five to six chains [330–390 feet] into the cutblock we had to catch our breath. Stopping, we watched the other two bears as they were on their haunches looking at us. The two bears were crying at the top of their lungs, and it was then that we realized that they were cubs of the sow. Just as we were about to take off, my partner told me to stop as the sow came out of the buffer area, charging toward us. Having no defense anymore, we just waited for her to come. When she was about one to two chains [66–132 feet] away from us, she suddenly stopped, reared up on her haunches and looked us over again. Seeing that we were not endangering her cubs, she hightailed it back into the buffer area, and her cubs followed right in behind her. That was the last we saw of her and have to thank our heavenly stars for making it out unscratched.

I know this is a brief report and is probably incomplete. If you have any questions please feel free to write or phone me. My address will be listed below along with my phone number. Thanks for your time and consideration.

yours truly,

STAN MILLER

If anything can be called a typical bear-man encounter or confrontation, the preceding incidents can. During my own encounters with bears over sixty years I have experienced similar confrontations without injury to either myself or the bear. My main reaction to such personal stress is to yell loudly at an uncertain bear, one that has seen me close by, appears disconcerted by the sudden encounter, and is acting as if trying to scent me (i.e., raising up on its hind legs, swinging its head about; or half turning away, then looking back). When faced by a bear with its hackles up or woofing, and perhaps popping its teeth—which animal obviously has identified me and shows signs of aggression—I back up slowly or stand my ground, making no quick movements, keeping silent, and always facing the bear. If armed and uncertain what else to do, I fire over the bear (if I have at least four backup shells loaded) and inject another shell immediately. If there is no alternative, I aim directly at the point of entry which will take a bullet into the bear's heart and lungs, break the spine, or enter the skull of the bear. I do *not fire blindly at the massive patch of its hairy body. Anything done under such circumstances (even by experienced outdoors people) is instinctive.* For example, a few people have told me that they found themselves from ten to fifteen feet up a tree with no branches below them. On one occasion, in which I shot a grizzly in midair, I simply cannot remember firing the shot. I was made aware that it happened only because there were witnesses.

Perhaps standing still and facing a bear is the least provocative method of resisting possible attack. However, earlier investigative research into the reasons for bears attacking humans showed that, in dozens of confrontations, such a stalwart stand had no appreciable effect upon the outcome. Further study may be worthwhile.

The Runt I

On the bleak Arctic wastes, the sparse powdery January snows swirled across the hummocks. Occasionally, as the wind dropped, a few flakes settled behind the higher mounds, there forming small drifts that eventually would meld with the hard surfaces on which they rested. Into one such bank of Baffin Island snows the old she-bear dug her annual winter home, the eighteenth such channel and tomb she had dug. Preparing for her fourth litter, she was well aware of events to come, and instinctively she dug upward from the entrance, hollowing out chambers that would entrap the warmth from her body and shut out the sub-zero air. She settled in.

Six weeks passed.

In the ice cave the smallest of the three new lives she had brought forth struggled valiantly toward the warm charcoal-black mound from which he drew all warmth and energy, his lifestream. The struggle to reach the tip of that mound was almost more than the new being could muster from his own tiny resources. Then, repeatedly, just as the warmth finally began to flow into his mouth and throat, stronger siblings shoved the small one aside. Tumbling to the ice floor, he again began the struggle to reach the mound, first straining to turn himself upright. Unsteady on ill-coordinated legs, following the scent of milk, the runt of the litter of new-born polar bears struggled to climb the formidable distance between the ice floor and the warm, black mounds.

First he whimpered, then let out a shrill, urgent wail. Something rough, yet gentle, answered, clumsily lifting him toward higher ground. Milk mixed with saliva was near his nostrils. Avidly, the small jaws opened as the tip of the conical black hummock entered his mouth. He began to suck, as a trickle of warm milk was pressed out by the urgent pummeling of his tiny feet at the base of the mound. Abruptly the milk gave out, when the cub's belly was far from full.

Below him the chuckling sounds of the two other cubs emanated from the belly fur. Whimpering once more, the little one wormed his way along the hairy surface, seeking another mound. Finding it, the cub began sucking again, but once more the milk source dried up before the little belly was half-filled. Yet, even though he was barely sustained, his metabolism induced a powerful drowsiness. Still sucking, he fell asleep and tumbled slackly onto the other cubs. The minor warmth of their bodies was comforting. When the sow's large, gentle, black tongue licked haphazardly at his anus and genitals, bodily functions began, and the cub expelled a tiny quantity of urine and feces.

Reawakening, he found himself almost buried beneath his two heavier littermates. Hunger again became his total motivation. Struggling to lift away the overwhelming burden, he awakened the cubs above him, and they too began to climb hungrily toward the warm, black teats.

The larger cubs planted their hind paws on the runt's body, using it as a step from which to push themselves upward. Above, far beyond, a guttural rumble sounded, somehow encouraging and comforting. The cub finally managed to pull his head from beneath the feet of one of his siblings and began again the struggle upward in the belly fur. Sounds of suckling increased his anxiety. Beneath the well-rounded belly of his female littermate the bulge of a teat was wet with milk. Pushing ahead blindly, he shoved his nose beneath her belly, pushing valiantly toward the milk source. Sucking at the higher teat, however, the female cub held her ground. Below, licking avidly, the runt's tiny pink tongue tasted milk on the damp fur. Abruptly, some enormous inner will burst forth, intensifying the cub's strength. With an upward thrust he lifted the larger cub and fastened his mouth to the vacated teat. The strong unexpected shove broke the female's hold, and the weight of the new milk in her belly made her tumble downward over the intruder into the furred crotch, where she wailed over her defeat.

Fastened to the fresh teat, the smaller animal sucked strenuously, and at last warm fluids began to course into his starved belly. Relentlessly, larger paws began clawing, while a snout stronger than his own pried his small head away from the milk. Once again he fell away.

Strengthened by the small quantity of milk being digested in its stomach, the cub pushed upward silently, this time crawling over his littermates to a higher teat. Again finding meager sustenance at a nearly-empty mound, he released his hold and slid down to another teat, dislodging one of his littermates from it. Below, the purring of cubs with satisfied bellies soon signaled their drowsiness.

The newly freed teat also was nearly empty, but the hungry cub sucked so desperately that the pained mother shook herself, toppling the cub backward. Falling, he struck his head on the hard ice floor.

Partially stunned, defeated, he lay there until some great source of strength lifted him from the cold white hardness to deposit him between the two other cubs next to the enormous forest of long, white, warm hairs.

Once again, still hungry, he fell asleep.

CHAPTER 2

We Are the Luckiest People We Know

In my investigation of bear attacks, trying to discern a pattern in them, I followed a lead to the injuries that Harry and Genevieve Rowed received from two grizzly bears while they were hiking in Jasper National Park, Alberta, Canada. Starting with the superintendent of Parks Canada, I was handed along the executive line to Park Warden Norman G. Woody, a twenty-one-year veteran of government service, at that time in charge of the Parks bear program and research. He was stationed at the park warden's headquarters, in the idyllic woodland and mountain setting near Lake Edith, just east of Jasper. He was a slight man. He offered me some of his freshly brewed coffee, the pungent aroma of which was filling the office. He proudly proclaimed that he had a reputation for the high quality of his particular brew.

While he got cups and poured the excellent beverage, I thought about two more interesting facets of the Rowed incident. First, a man and a woman had been attacked together and abandoned. Second, not one but two grizzly bears had attacked them simultaneously without any provocation. The couple were both fully woods-wise and had been observing all recommended preventive tactics.

Norm Woody had participated in the investigation of the Rowed case. As he appeared to have had wide bear-and-people experience, I asked him if he had encountered many bears during his career.

His answer was nonchalant and explicit.

"Oh, I'd say about four to five hundred of them."

"That is a lot of bears. Any of them give you trouble?"

He sipped his coffee.

"Oh, yes, a few. Most of the time you can bluff them—by facing up to them."

"You believe in Andy Russell's theory?"

He pursed his lips, looking straight at me.

"Not entirely. His son, Dick Russell, works here in bear management. He's a good worker."

I felt it better to be frank.

"I think Andy Russell's opinions particularly those in his book, *Grizzly Country*, are more likely to get people into difficulty with bears than to get them out. He and his sons may have the courage to stand and face an oncoming bear, but most people would break at the last moment—after thus inviting attack. I think such statements encourage people to believe that bears are not really dangerous—encourage them to disregard the probabilities of meeting and having trouble with bears while in the wilds."

He listened in silence and said nothing. I continued.

"This Bambi, Smokey the Bear, Gentle Ben stuff that we see and hear so much of, what do you think of it?"

Woody was still looking at me. I think he knew I was inciting him to comment. Finally, he put down his coffee cup.

"There is no doubt that those things could give people more assurance than they should have with bears. Bears are dangerous. You never know what they will do. We found nothing that might have incited the attack on the Roweds—no nearby kill, no earlier reports of problem bears, no aftermath. We didn't have to destroy the bears."

I saw no purpose in pursuing that vein.

"What about some of your own encounters?"

He looked out of the open doorway and then grinned.

"There was one really big one that I happened to run into on the trail. It was coming right toward me. I stood still, and I faced it. It just ambled right toward me. When I yelled, it didn't stop, didn't growl, didn't even pay any attention. It was a really big one. I yelled and moved toward it. It just came straight on along the trail as if I wasn't there. I moved off the trail a few feet when it just got too close."

"How close?" I inquired.

"Oh, about twenty feet. It just followed straight on down the trail and ambled out of sight. It was sure some surprise. It just ignored me! Most of them will just go on their way if you give way to them, it seems."

I was shaking my head. I replied:

"If you have the guts! A friend of mine, Bill Davidson, tells a tale of borrowing a .375 Magnum rifle with which to go after a grizzly. While Davidson was standing on one end of a blowdown log about one hundred feet long, a big grizzly got up on the opposite end of another blowdown log lying parallel to Davidson's. The grizzly just walked toward him along the other log— there were about four feet between logs—while Bill levered all his shells right through his big rifle and didn't pull the trigger once! The bear walked right past him on the other log and dropped off the other end, after giving him one big sniff just as it passed—no show of aggression, no growling even."

Woody was listening complacently.

"Yeah. It sounds like my own experience."

Something in his preoccupation triggered the next question.

"Before we go on to the Rowed case, have you ever had a bear come after you unprovoked?"

He took a deep breath.

"Yes. I was with my wife on horseback near Cairn Pass. There was a really big grizzly sow with three cubs about 600 yards away, in fairly open country. She was digging roots. I did what I usually do—let her know we were there. I don't think you should surprise them. As soon as she saw us, she started to come."

I wrote "600 yards distant" in my notebook before I interrupted him.

"You said '600 yards.' You mean that?"

He nodded his head.

"Yes—about that. It was a long way off. I just got off my horse, took my rifle out of the scabbard, and told my wife to take the horses and move uphill to get out of the way. I was going to try to turn the sow with the rifle if she kept coming. And she did. I fired two shots to detour her. She went up on her hind legs, then came right on along the trail. I fired one shot into an anthill right in front of her, which threw dirt up in the air. I figured that would turn her. It didn't! She just kept coming. My wife had taken the horses and dog with her, and I was there alone. The sow stood up again, at about fifty feet, then came right at me. I had to kill her with a .270, using a 160-grain bullet right in the head. It stopped her right there."

My own feelings were mixed.

"You figure a .270 caliber is enough? At close range?"

"It always has been!"

"Too damn close for my comfort! Fifty feet! They can come 200 yards, carrying a lot of lead. Do you have any idea why she came?"

"No, she was just one in a hundred, I guess. All I know is that she came *all* the way! Nothing would turn her!"

From what I have heard during my information-gathering, it was not too unusual a circumstance.

"What do you think about marking and tracking bears by electronics?"

"It's given us a lot of information here. I'm all for it. We know where the bears are and what they're doing; we learn a lot about their habits."

"Once you move them, after trapping, don't they always come back?"

"Many of them do. Not all, though."

"Tell me about some of your findings."

"Well, we have a much better idea of their natural range over the year. We found the collar of one of the bears we marked. It went 130 miles north of here. That is a long way."

"You didn't find the bear? Just the collar."

He nodded emphatically.

"It moved off our locating equipment in this area. A farmer up north had complained of predators on his stock. Someone put out poison. We figure the grizzly got it. When we found the collar, it smelled very rotten. I guess the predators cleaned up its carcass—it was over a month after we'd lost track of it."

"How many of the local bears have you worked with?"

"We've collared seventeen grizzlies. Some of them move thirty-five miles in a day. We moved one sixty miles, monitored it for two weeks. It stayed. One we moved seventy miles was back in a couple of weeks."

Woody was more optimistic about moving bears than most of the Parks Canada service people I had talked with. I said so.

"The general opinion seems to be that moving bears isn't doing any good—

that they are back within a couple of weeks or days." I waited for any comment, then went on. "The rule seems to be to kill them after the second return—problem bears, that is."

He nodded.

"If they are persistent and causing trouble, we destroy them."

"Was there any indication that the two bears that attacked the Roweds were marked or problem bears?"

Without delay Woody shook his head.

"No, there was nothing. No current reports, before or after, to connect them with the attack."

"Do you know where I can get hold of Harry Rowed?"

"He has a photographic shop downtown—in Jasper."

We parted after two hours of bear talk. At the photographic shop downtown I was told that Rowed had retired. He just might be at his house on the lake. And where was that? Oh, it was out on the road to the park warden's station, just before the turn leading to the station.

"Well, I'll be damned!" I thought. It would have saved time if I'd been told that. Such reticence is typical of governmental attitudes about direct contacts with bear victims.

Harry Rowed is a photographer and writer, but primarily a photographer. Our careers had several parallels: he also had sold magazines as a younger man, had endured a bear attack, and had written of bear problems.

In fact, almost immediately after he invited me into his living room, he mentioned one of my articles.

"Mike, I remember one piece you wrote in *Outdoor Life* when I was handling it many years ago—a warning about the unpredictability of bears."

It was a pleasant acknowledgment, coming so many years later.

"Yes, Harry. The piece was "Never Trust a Bear"; it was in the November, 1944, issue. You have a good memory. I guess we've both found bears unpredictable—and your wife has, too."

He nodded emphatically.

"Have you read the *Weekend* piece that I did on our grizzly attack?"

The question was a surprise, because until then I hadn't known that Harry Rowed was a writer. In my files he was listed as a professional photographer. As I apologized, he got up and walked into an adjacent room, to return with a copy of the *Evening Telegram's Weekend*. Opened in my lap, the tabloid exposed a two-page layout showing excellent watercolor illustrations to Rowed's article, which was entitled "Grizzlies Bore down on Us Like a Couple of Tanks." For a few minutes we talked about the vagaries of selling items to magazines, tabloids, periodicals, newspapers, and book publishers. As we exchanged our experiences both in the media and afield, we seemed to be assessing each other. When I looked up from the dramatic story in my lap, it was to study Harry Rowed's head—his face, in particular.

"The grizzly didn't get to your *head*, Harry?"

"No. I took off my pack and held it in front of me as a protection. But it bit right through it and a section of my Leica camera—and you know how heavy a metal body they have!"

"Yes, I do. I've carried one. And Mike Markusich, who was attacked by a grizzly north of here, showed me a couple of brass shell casings that had holes made by grizzly teeth—holes that ordinarily would have required a hammer and a cold chisel. Unbelievable power! In fact, grizzlies usually go for the head, biting the face, head, neck, and shoulders. Black bears, though, seem inclined to stun or kill with a blow, or they bite at any extended section of the body."

Rowed was interested.

"Does it seem to be a pattern?"

"Ninety percent of the time or more. But tell me what happened to you."

He looked up at the ceiling.

"Well, my wife, Gen, and I like to get away—have always gone hiking. We enjoy the mountains, the freedom of backpacking on nature trails, almost anywhere in the mountains. We've both done it since before we were married. Later we took our children along. We weren't novices when we were attacked. We knew the chances—or thought we did!"

He smiled somewhat ruefully. I interjected a question.

"Pardon me, Harry. What experience had you actually had with bears—before the attack?"

"Oh, we had some contact with black bears—while the children were growing up here."

"You mean on this property?"

"Yes. My Labrador dog had five of them, actually five of them, up trees at one time around here. The dog had a job keeping them up there. We weren't much worried about black bears. Once while we were building here, a black bear got between us and the kids over there among the trees. It went up a tree."

"No grizzlies?"

He shook his head. He was contemplating Lake Edith shimmering beyond the window.

"No! No grizzlies! Just once we had a grizzly scare, when the kids came running back down the trail near Athabaska River. But no pursuit or attack by those bears—two of them. I didn't even see them. It was also common knowledge that there were sixteen or more grizzlies feeding every evening on the park dump just up from here. I raised a bit of fuss about that. Those bears usually become the problem animals. I don't agree with such practices."

He was looking at me thoughtfully as he finished. I took up the point.

"Parks, and refuse from people in parks, do make problems. They exist everywhere that I have visited, from here to Ontario or Alaska. But my reason for asking you about previous experiences with bears is that almost every person who has been attacked by a bear has had a previous close encounter with a bear or bears."

"You mean that familiarity with bears causes people to be less cautious?"

I nodded.

"Yes. Most encounters and attacks that I have researched follow what you've experienced—a previous close encounter that ended without incident. It is only an ingredient—not a cause."

"That's interesting. You think perhaps the attitude of the person is also an ingredient?"

"Yes, I do. Very much so. I am a hunter. I always carry a gun when I'm in bear country, though not to shoot bears. I don't hunt them—never have—as a game animal. I probably would have been mauled or killed by at least one of those I've encountered if I hadn't had a gun with me. I don't even hike unarmed."

Rowed was looking at me, his eyes serious.

"We think alike—as a result of similar experiences. It sort of spoiled Gen's and my sense of security in the wilds."

His story was one I wanted to hear.

"How did it come about? Warden Woody tells me there was no sign of a kill near the spot. No record of problem bears."

Rowed nodded his agreement.

"Gen and I just decided to go for a hike up the Maligne Lake Trail. We have always found that hiking breaks the tensions, relaxes us. We packed light packs with lunches, and I slung on my camera. I put it on so that it wouldn't interfere when I took off the pack. When a person's pack is dropped, an aggressive bear will usually maul and tear it to get at the food. Gen was carrying a can full of pebbles. It was a pleasant autumn day, and we were wearing light clothing. Neither of us had any thought of danger."

Harry Rowed paused to stare out the window before continuing.

"The trail goes through lodgepole pine up from the Athabaska River. There are lots of bear berries. Gen remarked that it was a good fruit year and the bears should be well fed—going into hibernation.

"We did see some animal signs, mostly deer tracks and elk droppings. There was one small bear scat but no deep claw markings such as a grizzly leaves. Gen did rattle her pebble can a bit more often, however.

"I remember looking up to see Mount Tekarra and thinking that a couple of weeks would add more snow to the light covering on its summit. We were standing where the trail dropped down to a creek, resting a moment, when I heard a loud snorting and then the crashing of a big animal in the nearby underbrush.

"Gen said, 'A moose?'

"At that instant two grizzlies broke out into the clear—rushing right at us! There was no time to climb a tree or do anything defensive. Both bears were bellowing a terrifying 'whuff-whuff.' All I could see was instant death. It was instinct which probably saved me. I had heard 'stand your ground!' I whipped off my pack and held it in front of me, hoping the animal would veer away. In fact, I stepped toward it, hoping I could turn it. It struck me on my left shoulder, bowling me over. It was biting at the pack in front of me.

"Gen was yelling and rattling the can.

"She told me afterwards her one thought was 'How *badly* will we be maimed?' She dodged her bear, saw mine attack me, saw me go down. She moved to help. At that her bear became infuriated and rushed her from behind. Then it moved to the front to disembowel her, typical of most animals of prey. She put up her arms and pushed deep into its chest fur, trying not to do anything that would further enrage the bear. It bit into her stomach.

"I yelled, 'Lie on your stomach! Put your arms over your head.'

"As she did so, the bear sniffed at her and moved off. Then, just like that, the bears left us. We waited a few minutes, afraid that any movement might bring them back. But they didn't return. We then hurried away. Gen was bleeding badly. My own damage was just bruises and a torn and bitten packsack and camera. We hurried back to the car, and within half an hour Gen was in the hospital. She had a six-inch-long gash an inch or so deep in her abdomen. The doctor said the wound had just missed her vital organs, that she was lucky she'd been carrying a small bit of extra weight at her waist. There were other bite punctures. As I said, I had only cracked ribs and bruises, a mutilated camera—which cost about $240 to repair."

Harry Rowed was again looking at the placid lake. Finally he took a deep breath.

"We are the luckiest of any of the people we know who have been attacked by grizzlies."

I nodded.

"You are! All the others I've interviewed have been badly mauled. Several people have been killed. Yes, like my wife and me, you two were lucky!"

In answer to the question whether he had any particular advice to others who are about to enter bear country, Harry Rowed smiled a bit ruefully.

"Just be careful—and hope for the best. Take note of any park signs and any animal signs you see in wild country. Get out if you think you are near bears!"

Moments later, Harry Rowed walked out to my Jeep truck and camper with me. In the shade of some of the trees surrounding his lakeshore home we were talking about our common state of retirement. My eyes caught the movement of a light reddish brown form. It was on the edge of the bush hedge between his and his next-door neighbor's cottage. As I watched the movements of the animal over his shoulder, it came out into the open. It was a doe, moving silently in our direction. I nodded toward the deer.

"Do you have a pet deer?"

Surprised, he shook his head and turned. I moved past him toward the animal. "I'll see if I can talk her over. I think she's looking for food."

Quietly, I moved toward her. She lifted her head and stared directly at me, then moved toward me as I spoke calmly, reassuringly. She came within ten feet of me, her wet nose working to pick up the scent—possibly hoping for bread. Then, as Harry came up beside me, she turned and moved to a nearby wild rosebush. Nonchalantly, she browsed off the bright green young leaves of the shrub. She was not the slightest bit concerned about us. We stood and watched her from a distance of fifteen feet.

"She's skinny," I noted.

"Probably looking for a handout," nodded Rowed.

Not too many years ago we commonly had deer in our own West Vancouver home garden—and once a memorable black bear.

The Runt II

For a month, never quite warm enough, never quite filled, the cub had been over-powered by the rapidly increasing strength of his siblings. As a result, the runt of the litter was learning how to counter his difficulties. When his eyes first had opened to the misty, shadowy whiteness of the den, an awareness of his own separateness had induced an instinctive aggression. During the two months of den life his littermates had doubled in size; his own weight was a third less than theirs, but constantly displacing the other two cubs had developed in him comparatively wiry muscles.

He had also learned to react to the quality of sounds, from the deep, guttural intonations of his mother's beckoning and admonitions to his own high-pitched wailing to distract his siblings and attract a welcome licking from the warm black tongue or even a boost from the great forepaws up to a vacant milk-filled teat. Thus, when the strongest of his pushes, desperately designed to force the head of a littermate from a teat, would not achieve the desired effect, a desperate wail often won a shift of the large, mothering bulk, which dislodged another cub.

At the same time the largest of the litter was learning to take advantage of the shifts that freed a teat. Again and again, with his greater reserve of strength and weight, the large cub easily pushed his small littermate aside. The smaller cub, always last to let go of the milk source, was the one most often shaken free by his mother from a depleted teat. When the mother lay back down in her bed, the fallen cub was still struggling through the belly fur while its littermates were beginning to tumble about or climb on top of each other. The small one soon learned that whenever he joined in these struggles to curl together for rest, he ended up on the bottom, cold from below and nearly smothered from above. Without a belly constantly full of rich milk, he was slower to fall asleep than the satisfied cubs. Only when they were quieted by exhausted muscles and full stomachs would he join in the rounded pile. Too soon he would be rudely awakened when the others, fully revived, rushed again for their mother's belly.

Occasionally, after feeding, he attempted to join his sibling mates in the clumsy tussles that now had evolved from their earlier efforts to gain a topside resting position. Most often, however, he found himself on the bottom, worried by gnawing bites, pinned down by two pairs of paws, or turned on his back while tiny teeth pricked his exposed abdomen.

Usually he withdrew from his boisterous brother and sister, learning to conserve energy in isolation. Before the others he learned to hear and recognize the low moans indicating the mother's willingness to suckle, giving him a chance to be first to a newly filled teat. Nevertheless, the combined efforts of the others generally succeeded in pushing him aside. As a consequence, he learned to find and suckle at the two vacant black mounds, obtaining quickly what might be in them.

At two months, now running around in the confines of the cave, he became vaguely aware of the outside light illuminating the shapes of his littermates. For the first time he actively entered into the tumbling play, and he found that his speed and coordination allowed him to avoid the clumsy, if stronger, movements of his siblings. He also learned that a harsh bite or slap accompanied by lowered tones of growling would achieve what pure brute strength more often did for the other cubs.

The pinkness of their earlier pound-size bodies had become covered with fluffy white hair. With the new covering the chill that had been so constant during his early deprivations had lessened.

The old she-bear began to move from the birthing den, occasionally pacing restlessly to the second and third chambers. Outside, the winds blew less frequently, and daily the light in the white cavern brightened noticeably.

The low-lying February sun remained longer on the straight southern horizon, while occasionally the howl of a winter-starved wolf pierced the thick walls of the den.

The old sow, becoming progressively less patient with the whining and brawling of her young, began to scratch at the ice-blocked entrance. One day her pawing broke through the hard crusts, and her long claws tore into hard-packed snow. She struck at the wall with increased force, crumbling it outward. The fresh scent of clear, cold, air began to touch her nostrils, bringing with it the familiar sharpness of subzero temperatures. Pushing hard with her massive paws, she felt the outside wall of hard snow crumble. She inserted her slender head in the hole that she had made and pushed. Her long neck slid two feet through the shattered snow crust. The fresh air filled her lungs as powdery snow melted dewlike on her nostrils.

The subdued light was still screened by loose ice granules in her eyes, but she fully sensed the new season. She withdrew her head and, with the determination learned during her lifetime of smashing through ringed-seal *aglus* while hunting, she lunged at the obstructing edge of the hole. It gave but little. She began to claw forcefully at the hard packed snow. During the several weeks of confinement, her resources drained by birthing and suckling cubs, her customary strength had diminished. Before the opening was complete, she had tired.

From deep inside the main den the piercing notes of the runt rose above the howls of the others. Dutifully, almost reluctantly, the she-bear turned from the outside entrance to her three cubs.

Clustered together, feeling neglected for the first time in their short lives, the small animals continued yelling mightily. The runt was the loudest of all.

CHAPTER 3

The Mother Instinct

Since humans could first communicate with symbols, she-bears have represented the essence of motherhood. Pit human mother against bear mother in a conflict over broods, and you have a classic confrontation. In the conflict that I will describe, the bear mother began by gripping the human child in her teeth as the child ran in fright from her two cubs, but the human mother won.

In 1979, Sean Clement, the object of the 1977 battle, was standing before me in his family's large home near Wawa, Ontario. Brown-eyed and bright, he was telling of his plan to become a computer technician. Sean's half-brother, Marty, eagerly and proudly assured me that Sean would make it: Sean had been four times an honor-roll student with straight A's in math.

I said to the eight-year-old, who was barely four feet tall and almost too pretty for a boy, "What is your second choice—after computer technician?"

Immediately, he said, "I'd like to be a chef!"

That surprising answer made me smile, and immediately Sean smiled back. As my mind did a swift review of the faces of other bear victims, I thought, "Why do they all have to be so pretty or handsome?" The men's faces, the women's faces, the boys' and the girls' faces all passed before me: the absolutely beautiful face of Susanne Duckitt, eight years old, among a series of small mahogany-framed photos; Mary-Ann Young; Mary Pat Mahoney; Pamela Cramond—yes, my own daughter!—all subjects of bear depredations. Meanwhile, Sean Clement was staring at me cheerfully, ready to answer the next question. I half smiled.

"Sean, how did the bear attack begin?"

He shot a glance over at Sheila Bliesath, who was sitting in a deeply up-holstered living room chair. When she did not respond he blurted out:

"I was going to get a piece of cake"—his glance, slightly guilty, was diverted once again to his mother—"from the table in the dining room. I saw the bear cubs in there, and they scared me. One of them was standing on the propane stove. The other was standing on the meat-cutting board. I think there was some bacon cut for the tourists. I screamed because they scared me. I was just going for a piece of cake."

My glance went to Sheila Bliesath's surprised face. Her words conveyed amazement.

"He never told me that before!" she exclaimed.

I interjected with a laugh. "Not likely! But you probably haven't asked him, and if I know boys, he wouldn't normally reveal that."

She smiled, and Sean's conscience was easier. The unconcealed emotion in his face subsided.

"When I saw the two cubs I just got scared. I ran out of the kitchen, and the mother bear was just there. I tried to run by her—she was about ten feet away—and she grabbed me by my left arm. She started to drag me away."

He stopped and looked over at his mother.

Sheila Bliesath spoke softly of her own memory of the event.

"The bear dragged him about thirty or forty feet. I could see Sean's face, crying and full of terror. She'd drop him, then grab him again."

I was watching Sheila Bliesath's quiet, pretty face as she relived the dramatic situation. Her expression was that of one long accustomed to emotional control, as if she were unwilling to admit the depths of her innermost feelings. As her blue eyes came up from the floor directly to mine, she stopped. I laid my ballpoint alongside my sheet of paper. One reason I was taking notes (which I seldom do) was that earlier in a letter she had decried the unsatisfactory reporting of the events in the news at the time of the incident. Since accuracy of detail should be most important to a newsman in any report, I had assured her that anything I wrote would be subject to her scrutiny and approval.

"Where were you when the bear took hold of Sean?"

For a moment she seemed withdrawn.

"Well—I was with Shirley Fisher, my girlfriend, in the kitchen in another building of the fishing camp, about 150 feet away. There are two buildings in between it and the dining room."

She stopped and looked at me as if she were accusing herself.

"It was up at our fishing camp, as you know. There is a fair amount of room between the buildings. We both heard Sean yell. Shirley immediately got up and went to the door. I wasn't too concerned—Sean used to cry wolf a bit—but Shirley was alarmed. It alerted me. We all ran toward the sounds."

She paused and nodded to Marty and four-year-old René, her young daughter, who were also in the room.

"Marty came with us. Shirley, who was a strong girl, was going to pick up an axe and hit the she-bear on the head. Marty picked up a small round log and threw it at the bear."

She paused. "I was standing there, and I remember thinking, 'Oh my God! No! No! I'll have to go and get the rifle and shells!' Then I remembered Cross, our dog, and called her."

The emotion of the memory was passing openly through Sheila's face, despite her efforts at self-control.

"As soon as I called her, Cross came flying! She went right after the bear's head, and she made her drop him! Sean got up and struggled away. I was looking him over when I looked into the dining room. There were the cubs—little wee cubs. Shirley went to Sean and took him to the other building, and Cross stayed with them. I chased the cubs out of the dining room. It was all so mixed up. I believed that Sean was not too badly injured, as he had walked away with Shirley. When I got back to the dining room door, the mother bear was still there, pacing back and forth. I went to the phone and called the Littles—they're in a nearby camp—and asked her to get a plane, told her that Sean had been injured by a bear and had to get right to a hospital. Then I went back to the door, and the mother bear was still there pacing up and down. I yelled at Marty to go and get our .30-.30 rifle.

Marty, tall and slim, in the bone-forming age of the early teens, spoke up eagerly when she stopped.

"Yeah, I went to the other building for the rifle. . . ."

Sheila interjected, "It was in the other building. The bear was watching me and couldn't see him go out the other way. It seemed like a long time before he came back."

Marty was now smiling, a trifle shamefacedly.

"Yeah! I found the rifle and went to get some shells out of the drawer. The first one I found was a .30'06. I tried it in the barrel of the 30-30—and it got stuck! I had a problem getting it out again. I searched for the other shells and found one, a 30-30, and took it out to Sheila. I asked her if I could shoot the bear if it came after me, and she said, 'Sure, but it's not interested in you!' I handed her the one shell and went back to get another one."

Sheila half smiled.

"Yes, he was bringing them to me one at a time—as he found them. I was standing on the porch now. The bear was about fifty feet away. She was acting as if she was all hopped up—it was pitiful watching her. About ten minutes had gone by, and she wasn't taking off. I decided right then and there she had to be shot. It was very calculated. She had tasted human blood."

She looked a trifle guilty as she said it, as if still regretting the scene. I spoke.

"What did you know about handling guns, Sheila?"

"When I was very young in Michigan, where I was brought up, my parents went out target shooting; but with my stepmother guns were a no-no. It was after I was about twelve, I guess; I handled a rifle first about 1970. I started out with a bolt-action .308, with Cathy Clement. I had shot the rifle but had only shot partridge."

I was looking at her, a solidly built young woman who wouldn't have had any difficulty handling the shock of a rifle if she cared to shoot. She glanced at me thoughtfully for a moment.

"I didn't want to kill the bear, but I knew I had to. She had put the two cubs up a birch tree near the house, and she wasn't going away in a hurry. She was acting almost aggressively. I put the rifle up and aimed and ejected the shell. I said to Marty, 'Did you only bring *one* shell?' "

Marty broke in, "I went to get another shell and came back with it."

Sheila looked at him appreciatively.

"I loaded the gun again and waited for the bear to give me a broadside shot. And I remember thinking, 'It better be good!' I aimed and pulled the trigger, and she went down."

Marty filled in, eagerly.

"The bear was paralyzed in the back legs. All she could do was pull herself toward the corner of the cabin."

Sheila broke in again.

"He brought me another shell, and I ran out and shot her in the head. That killed her, and she lay still. I went to the other cottage, where Shirley was with Sean. She had washed the blood away and was cutting away the hair around his ear, which was badly torn by the bear's bite. I don't know what got into me, because I said to her, 'Don't do that! You're hurting him!' She just quit and looked at me. We bandaged Sean and drove him over to Camp Loch Alsh. The plane, a 180 Cessna float plane, took him to Wawa Hospital, where they sewed him up."

While we were talking, Sean's four-year-old sister, René, came over to my knee, and we made eyes at each other.

"You're René, aren't you?"

As she nodded and shyly looked down, her mother said, "René was there. She was just two years old. She was following Sean into the dining room. She saw everything that happened."

I heaved a sigh.

"She was lucky the bear didn't pick her! Perhaps it was because Sean was nearer the cubs and ran out crying from the dining room. That may have triggered the old lady's reaction."

Sheila said, "I don't know!"

Sean was busy talking to Marty. I looked over at Sheila to find her eyes directly upon me. She spoke deliberately.

"I guess you're wondering why I'm Sheila Bliesath and he is Sean Clement?"

It was my turn to control any show of feelings.

"I don't think it's any of my business, Sheila."

"Well, it may be a bit confusing. And some do make it their business! My name is Sheila Bliesath. I'm not married to Sean and René's father. We live together. They are our children, but they legally take *his* name."

This clarified my thinking about the proper designation of the children. My conclusion had been that earlier she had been married to a man named Bliesath. I said so, and she shook her head. I laughed shortly.

"Who the hell cares!" Then as a genuinely appreciative second thought, I added, "You're lucky—just to have such nice children."

"Yes, I think so too!"

There was a tinge of defiance in Sheila's voice that all the acclamations of free love by the modern woman could not eradicate. Sensing her feelings, I looked down and patted Cross's head.

"What breed is she, Sheila? She looks part wolf."

Sheila's face warmed abruptly while looking at the big dog.

"She is part wolf, they say, but she's also part Husky, part Alsatian too. The wolf shows in her head, and she howls like a wolf at night—and she chases moose."

"And bear!" I added.

Her voice had a proud tone. "She's not afraid of bears."

I nodded emphatically.

"Sean can be glad of that!"

She smiled.

"If it hadn't been for her—he might not have been alive!"

Cross had gone over to Sean, and he was holding her close around the neck. Marty was eyeing the two of them affectionately. It was, thank God, still a complete family. I said that I would like a photo of them for the forthcoming book. Sheila nodded, saying, "We aren't really cleaned up for photos. We're just out of camp." For the interview she had just driven seventy miles, sixty of them on dirt road, from their fishing camp to save me the journey. She had made the excuse that she would have to drive into town later for supplies anyway.

"I look like a tramp, but okay. Where would you like to take it? Outside? Okay! I can get ready in a minute."

She was back in a few moments. I asked her about any conditions that might have brought the bears to the fishing camp at Loch Alsh. Was there a nearby dump? No, not within eleven miles! As it happened, they had taken the bear's carcass out there (minus the head, which the authorities wanted to examine for rabies). But the bear *had* been seen around camp with her cubs. Sheila looked a trifle perturbed when she explained this.

"Tourists like to watch bears. It had been a bad year for berries, and they had been hanging around. We never fed them, and we told the guests not to. The only thing was that Shirley had left out some garbage in a green plastic sack near the dining room back door. The next morning it was torn apart, and Shirley cleaned it up but forgot to put it away. The bears hadn't been bold at all. The tourists liked to watch the cubs. Yes, we knew she had been around, but we thought we were being careful."

I was looking for some common cause, anything that might further my understanding of attacks.

"You say the bear and her cubs had been around for some time? How long?"

"Perhaps a couple of weeks. Usually they stay around dumps in the backwoods. As long as they don't get too bold, people leave them alone."

Marty, who had been listening intently, spoke up.

"Bears are just bears. You don't do anything about them."

His words brought a period of silence among us. I was looking at him, thinking, "Kid, perhaps you don't know how profound and wise that statement is. No, you don't do anything about bears. You do something about *people*! The bears are in place. Give them room." I didn't say that, but his

Sheila Bliesath, with Sean Clements on her left, and Marty Clements next to Sean. Cross and René Clements are in the front row.

alert eyes stayed on me. Like me, he had been brought up a "bush kid," in close proximity to forest, stream, sea, and meadow where animals roamed as they did before white men's interventions.

Sheila brought me out of my reverie.

"Where did you want to take the photo?"

"Over against those trees, I guess, Sheila." I pointed across the street. "The light is good there, and it'll have a more woodsy background."

Across the road the pines and poplars grew on uncultivated land. I arranged Sheila, Sean, Marty, René, and the courageous heroine Cross in a row that would fill the lense—it was a lousy, amateur style of photograph—with Cross in the foreground, lying down and also up licking at faces. I had been an active part-time news photographer for twenty or more years, and I knew better, but somehow this was a family group, one which had gone through a somewhat tragicomic confrontation together: Sean, savaged by a camp bear; Sheila, like any mother, momentarily transfixed before thinking of Cross, the part-wolf dog who attacked the mother bear in defense of her young master; the willing and courageous Marty, who first threw wood at the bear that had attacked his half-brother and then brought one rifle shell at a time; and diminutive René, the tiny, unwitting bystander who had not comprehended the tragedy before her and did not remember it at all. So there they were, in daguerrotype-sterotype: the family that works together survives together!

The photos were in the can, the notes on paper. My work was done. It was time to say godspeed and goodbye. Sheila was patting Cross's head while the dog nuzzled her. The youngsters, parting like chaff from grain, were going back across the street. Sean looked back politely as he left.

I said, "Sean, you take care of yourself! It was nice to meet you. And thanks for the story!"

"You're welcome, sir."

He was following Marty. Sheila and I moved into step in their paths. We stopped on the edge of the lawn at her home, and I put out my hand. Hers came out in answer, hesitantly.

I don't handle farewells too well.

"Thanks, Sheila. I'll be sending you a copy of the story for your approval of it."

She was looking me straight in the eye.

"Thank you, Mike. I'm not worried about the way you'll write it. I may use it myself in a book I write—sometime."

Her words were familiar, a statement I had heard a hundred times.

"Sheila, when and if you decide to write a book, let me see your work. I'll help you."

"Thank you, Mike. Drive carefully!"

There is nothing to beat that old mother instinct.

The Runt III

Increasingly restless at her confinement, beginning to shake off her winter sluggishness, the she-bear lifted herself carefully away from the three sleeping cubs and returned to the broken snow at the den entrance. She thrust her head resolutely into the channel. Overnight snows from a storm had formed a shield of crusted snow that was fragile.

Setting all four feet, she pushed forward resolutely until her nose was clear of the drift.

The Arctic daylight was beginning, the late February sun having risen a few degrees above the southern horizon. As the ice granules that had filled her eyelids melted, she blinked the moisture away. Not fully awake, she stared at the black edge beneath the sun, vaguely aware that the change from somnolent security to active aggression was imminent. If any other animal was nearby, she should hear it or pick up its scent.

Several minutes passed before she sat back upon her haunches. Then, abruptly resolute, she pushed herself through the snowbank. Her gaunt body slithered out of the hole onto the powdery new snow.

Rocking back onto her hind legs, she raised her head, achieving a panoramic view of her surroundings. The nearby ridge of the riverbank, against which the denning snow drifts had collected, curved southward, its contours broken by large chunks of river ice. Her eyes searched, and her black button nose worked carefully, as her ears cocked for telltale sounds. There was an absolute stillness, no movement in air or on land. Then the first new scent came very faintly. The she-bear's nostrils worked carefully, inhaling deeply, but the scent vanished.

She swiveled her head until the low sun came at midhorizon, and then she waited patiently. If the scent came from that direction, any movement, even a distant one would be caught in the low-lying light, its shadows projected over hundreds of yards. The scent came again, this time more strongly. It was a familiar one. To verify it, she blew out a sharp gasp of air and breathed in deeply. Satisfied, she slowly lowered her towering head and sat back upon bulky haunches.

The scent was that of another she-bear and her cubs in a nearby den. This younger bear she knew: its hunting routes intermingled with her own. At this stage the neighbor was not a threat to her or her brood. She sat back on the ice, licking occasionally at the loose snow. Moments later she walked in a small semicircle about the den entrance, sniffing at the snow.

The cold freshness of the air awakened the smaller cub. With it came a strange new brightness, the intensity of which made him blink. With his awakening consciousness came a singular sensation of solitude. The mother was not in the den, and her warmth had gone with her. He emitted a piercing wail.

When the she-bear returned to the hole that she had just opened, she listened to the familiar cub sounds. It was the strident, demanding wail that greeted her, and within seconds of the first wail it was augmented by the lesser shrillnesses of the other cubs. Yet she resisted reentry.

Eventually, aware of her well-filled teats, she reacted. Pawing energetically at the hard snow, she broke away a larger channel, then pushed herself into the familiar dimness. The slight upward incline of the tunnel funneled the panicky wails of the cubs to her. As she came in from the silences of the outside ices, the sounds were knifelike. She shook her head free of snow and brushed past the eager congregation of milling cubs in the passageway, returning resignedly to the far wall of the larger chamber.

There she sat on her haunches, opened her thighs, and allowed her big fore-paws to slide to her sides.

The rush of squalling cubs was all too familiar, the two heavier and taller ones first to reach the two top teats, the smaller one struggling to push beneath them. Minutes later the suckling rush was over. The large cubs piled one upon the other: the small one waited, avoiding the tumble and the mutual face licking. Then, when they had curled up, lounged atop them and slept.

The light was stronger in the cavern, the air fresher. The small cub lay curled alone against the back wall of ice.

Suddenly he was wide awake.

No other life was nearby: no sounds of brawling, no deeper respiration from the huge mother. Frightened, he uncoiled quickly and stood up on his still-uncoordinated legs.

Seemingly abandoned, he stood still, utterly alone for the first time. His abrupt screech came from a convulsive fear deep in his belly. The shrillness of it, echo-ing from the walls, was startling even to himself. For interminable seconds he stood wavering on fear-weakened legs.

Then, faintly, came familiar sounds. His littermates were mewing plaintively in the distance, and he realized that his usual strident wail was not going to be answered. Reluctantly, afraid of the strong light, he forced his clumsy legs to carry him toward the sounds outside. As the tunnel narrowed and suddenly descended, he slid on the ice floor to crumple against the snow sill. The strong light, now right above him hurt his milky-hued eyes. The guttural sounds of his mother impelled him to rise quickly, and he struggled up the ridge of loose, granular snow.

When his nose pushed over the sill, a spear of strong light stabbed into his retinas. He stared at the unfamiliar orb of fire, fascinated, stunned. He then wailed fearfully.

An answering woof from the direction of the sun calmed him. Even so, impelled by fear of desertion, he pushed himself to the top of the ice sill, where the weight of his uncoordinated shoulders tipped him over the hummock. He then slid helplessly outward. The slickness of his wispy fur made him almost friction-free. As he rolled to his side, the speedy slide downward and outward became frightening.

Abruptly he came to a halt against the wall of a large, flat, solidly placed forepaw. A long, black tongue, drawn upward over his neck, shoulder, and face, checked the scream before it reached his throat. Rising shakily to his feet, he stared about. There were no walls. Above, instead of a ceiling, was a glowing blueness finely dotted with small, bright lights. Unfamiliar, scentless air, sharply cold, shot up his tender nostrils.

The effect sharpened his senses. After struggling to his feet, he stood quite still. Snuggled against the rounded haunch of their mother, his littermates mewed and stared apprehensively upward toward her head. Apparently they too were confused by the open expanse.

The she-bear moved effortlessly away from them, swung her neck upward, and cocked her head.

There were muffled sounds of hard snow being scratched a few yards away. Then, abruptly, the smooth curvature of the streamside drift erupted. Small chunks of caked crust slid down the incline and were followed by miniature streams of powdered snow. A whoosh of exhaled steaming breath issued from the freshly broken surface, followed by a second powdery eruption. A large chunk of crust sailed down the bank and settled on the level floor of the river bottom.

The old she-bear watched the miniature eruption placidly. Next, a long, white snout tipped with black, followed by slitted black eyes, shoved upward out of the snow. The snout exhaled loudly to clear the ice granules from its nostrils and shook the snow from its eyes.

One loud, intense woof followed by a series in quick succession froze two of the cubs in place. Fascinated, the small cub watched, heedless of his mother's warning, until a wallop on his shoulder slid him alongside the other two. Without further warning she moved in the direction of their own den, beckoning by sound and head movements.

For the first time sensing a world apart, the small cub defied the threefold domination that had been customary in the den. Still fascinated, he watched the growing eruptions in the snowbank. The other cubs had gone willingly into the darkened entrance. Abruptly he was lifted in a steaming mouth and peremptorily carried into the tunnel. His first, brief moment of freedom was gone.

CHAPTER 4

He Was Chasing Dragonflies

Bob Switzer, nationally renowned host-interviewer of CBUT-TV, looked shocked and depressed as I greeted him in the downtown Vancouver offices of the Canadian Broadcasting System.

"Jeez, Mike, you've heard about the grizzly killing George Doerksen! In the Liard River Park area. Christ!—I sent him up there—we were to do a film on that segment of the parks."

I was slightly befuddled by the almost emotional outburst, unaware of the nature of the situation, just back from a several-week, 11,000-mile caravan trip crisscrossing Canada and the United States researching bear species.

"Who was? Doerksen? You said Doerksen, didn't you? It must have happened while I was away. What do you mean, you sent him up there?"

Bob looked contrite, inconsolable.

"I was scheduled to meet him up there the day after he was reported killed. I was filming out on the Queen Charlotte Islands, doing an Anthony Island Haida-village segment, when the RCMP brought me the word at Sandspit. Jesus Christ! I feel awful about it—awful."

I know Bob Switzer, have known him over many years. He wouldn't purposefully step on a stinkbug to crush it. Fight for the right—yes! But contrive ill for anyone—no! Emotional, yes—capable of empathizing with an interviewed guest in a way that brings real life and magic to television. Apparently he was suffering deep-seated guilt-grief.

I stared at him cold-eyed for a moment, purposefully.

"Hell, Bob—you're wearing sackcloth. You had nothing to do with the attack. I don't give a crap how you relate to it. Grizzlies—and all bears—kill, not in response to any arranged sequence, but simply as a reaction to immediate circumstances. Nobody, perhaps not even God, or whatever powers be, knows what a bear will do under any set of circumstances."

Bob was staring at me unconvinced, but listening. I strove to reassure him with some finality.

"To take credit, as some of our so-called experts do, for knowing what any bear will do—or to feel responsible for initiating the circumstances that led to the killing of a person—is vain conceit—or utter self-pity."

He looked long at me, some relief evident in his broad face.

"You make me feel better, Mike."

"Hell, you've nothing to feel bad about—sad, yes! Bad, no! Was he a good friend?"

He nodded emphatically.

"Yes, over several years. A really great guy."

Switzer and I had fished together over many years and had done an hour TV special, several other interviews, and two programs in regard to my book *Killer Bears* and its research—particularly on killings and maulings by bears and our own experiences with bears in the wilds.

I explained my ignorance of this tragedy.

"I haven't had time to read any of the back issues of the papers—really wouldn't anyway—not even the bear clippigs that Thelma keeps for me while I'm away. She did say that there had been a killing. This Doerksen, who was he?"

Bob still looked rueful.

"He was an entomologist. Specialized in dragonflies. When I was telling him about my "Adventures B.C." series—which I was doing in cooperation with the B.C. Parks branch, I asked him if he would like to cooperate with me on a segment we were going to film in the Liard River area—and he said it would be great, that there was a species of dragonfly in that area that he wanted to study, some little known dragonfly."

"Dragonflies?" I interjected. "Specializing in just dragonflies?" Bob nodded and was slient, contemplating his lost friend. "What a hell of a way to lose your life—chasing dragonflies!"

I don't know what made me say it, except that it did seem too incongruous to accept as a reason for forfeiting one's life.

But that is how George Peter Doerkson, Ph.D., by all accounts a bush-wise wonderful guy—became the subject of the following piece of daily news copy.

CAMPER BELIEVED KILLED BY GRIZZLY BEAR

Fort Nelson—RCMP and provincial wildlife officials continued their search today for a grizzly bear believed to have killed a 41-year-old Tahsis man.

The body of George Peter Doerksen was found Sunday near the Liard River hot springs campsite, about 560 kilometers northwest of Fort St. John.

RCMP believes Doerksen was camping alone when he was killed by the bear. Exact time and cause of death have not yet been determined.

A police spokesman said the campsite was closed Monday and will remain shut until the bear is destroyed. The search involves police, two provincial fish and wildlife officials, a police dog and a dogmaster.

Police said the bear attack was the first since a cyclist was injured three years ago by a bear near here.

During my travels while researching bear-man conflicts and associations, patterns were established in the overlay of my memory that would best have been put in a computer. There seemed to be coming to light a "personality" factor that indicated some human victims as possible candidates for attack or death. This characteristic is only one factor that might lead to clashes between bears and mankind.

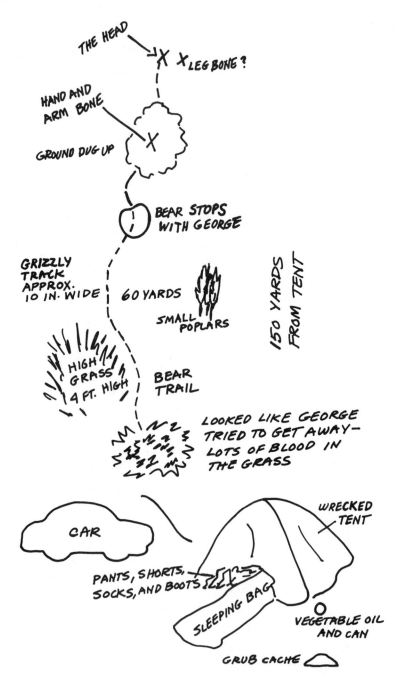

THE HEAD

X X LEG BONE?

HAND AND
ARM BONE

GROUND DUG UP

BEAR STOPS
WITH GEORGE

GRIZZLY
TRACK
APPROX.
10 IN. WIDE

60 YARDS

SMALL
POPLARS

150 YARDS
FROM TENT

HIGH
GRASS
4 FT. HIGH

BEAR
TRAIL

LOOKED LIKE GEORGE
TRIED TO GET AWAY—
LOTS OF BLOOD IN
THE GRASS

CAR

WRECKED
TENT

PANTS, SHORTS,
SOCKS, AND BOOTS

SLEEPING BAG

VEGETABLE OIL
AND CAN

GRUB CACHE

This map reproduces a sketch made of George Doerksen's campsite at the time his remains were discovered. Another map enclosed in Corporal G. A. M. Dodds's letter of January 12, 1984, showed how close Doerksen's camp was to the public lodge and picnic and camping area.

An overlay of many observations made during lengthy studies in the field shows that bears, like all animals (as any farmer-rancher or pet owner will verify), have character traits that could be designated as a "personality." Possibly it is this human desire to "humanize" bears that leads to anthropomorphism and, worse, to the popular image of bears as "good guys."

Perhaps a simple, even simplistic, comparison will bring this multiplicity of bear personalities to the fore. Men vary in their personalities, from gentle saints to vicious killers. A propensity for "planned mayhem" is apparent when bears stalk and invade the "territory" of their victims. Their tracks show clearly that bears often encircle the person they subsequently attack or kill. For example, consider the death of Harvey Cardinal near Fort St. John, British Columbia, January 16, 1984. Harvey Cardinal was an experienced animal tracker, a hunter and trapper. He set out to track and kill a local grizzly bear that had been reported to be out of "hibernation" during January, which was very unusual. Their individual tracks in the snow showed that the bear Cardinal was trailing became aware of its pursuer. It had circled back behind a small knoll, approached Cardinal from behind, and killed him without warning. Cardinal's gloves were still on his hands, and his rifle cocked but unfired. The bear had silently sprung upon him from the rear.

If that had been the act of one man killing another, if human tracks had showed that the attack had occurred from the rear, bereft of any forewarning, without any indication that the victim had attempted to defend himself, the verdict would have been "first-degree murder," even though the man carrying the rifle had openly declared his intent to search for and kill his murderer. Nevertheless, to suggest that a formal trial be initiated is ludicrous; bears, after all, are not human. But those having anthropomorphic beliefs would be the last to see the illogic: The Cardinal bear was "convicted" without trial, hunted, and summarily killed. The word used to describe such an act is "destroy." On the other hand, we also have many accounts of victims of disfiguring attacks who have pleaded for the bear: "Well, you couldn't blame the bear! I was in its territory. It was only responding naturally to my presence." In fact, several victims have pleaded with authorities not to retaliate.

There are arguments for and against such attitudes, but the fact that the attitudes always surface in association with bear-man conflicts does suggest that people most prone to bear assault are people most inclined to overlook the multiplicity even of "character types" among bears—people who think of bears as characteristically nonaggressive "good guys." My study of hundreds of bear attacks strongly suggests that this correlation is statistically verifiable.

It is, however, also an indisputable fact that some bears—to fall back on anthropomorphic terminology—are just like some people: ruthless killers, killers of other species and of their own kind.

Such a bear killed Harvey Cardinal, and such a bear killed George Peter Doerksen.

I did not go to the site of the Doerksen tragedy because truly excellent field investigative reports were available from reliable authorities and from his friends and because the pattern of attack so resembled hundreds of cases that I had filed and categorized during my earlier investigations.

Very simply, George Doerksen (1) was following his professional interest in insects, (2) went into the northern wilds and, experienced from hundreds of such trips, camped in an isolated grizzly habitat, away from the protection of other human beings (there was an established public campsite less than 400 yards away, but his tent was only 200 yards from the well-traveled Alaska Highway), and (3) carried no gun (although he was in country inhabited by grizzlies, no "problem" bears had been seen in the area).

He was killed by a grizzly bear because of that simple set of circumstances.

He was not, in any legal sense, "negligent."

In fact, all official evidence gathered from the site of the killing indicated that Doerksen "kept a clean camp," stored his food in the recommended manner, and did not set out to incite any animal (photographing or studying bears up close is tantamount to inciting attack). He did not invade bear territory in a foolish or reckless manner. He camped in the subwilds pursuing his own special prerogative to enter such territories. Essentially, Doerksen, like most bear victims, was innocent of any provocation.

But he may have been the victim of overconfidence.

After Bob Switzer and I discussed the attack, I let the subject rest in my files until I could investigate it. Then, for source materials, I contacted Bob's friends and associates in the B. C. Parks branch. Utmost cooperation (not always to be had from some parks departments) was immediately extended to me by top authorities, including conference calls for cross-discussion that furthered my research. These calls led to long-distance conversations, then correspondence, with the staff and executives of the Royal Canadian Mounted Police at their Fort Nelson (British Columbia) Detachment, which presides over the policing of the Liard River Parks area.

Discussions with RCMP members at Fort Nelson were open and lucid. Exemplary of their forthrightness is the following letter from Corporal G. A. M. Dodds of that far-north detachment:

> Royal Canadian Mounted Police
> Fort Nelson Detachment
> Box 900
> Fort Nelson, B.C.
> VOC IRO
> "E" Division
> Our No. 833506
>
> 84 JAN 12

Mr. Mike CRAMOND
4875 The Dale,
West Vancouver, B.C.
V7W 1K2

Dear Sir:

RE: George Peter DOERKSEN (BD: 05JULY40)
      Sudden Death—Bear Attack
      Liard Hot Springs—81JUL30—AUG02
      Fort Nelson Detachment Case—81-2366

Further to your request of 83 DEC 12, the following information is supplied.

Mr. DOERKSON held a PhD in Entomology and employed at a sawmill in Tahsis, B.C. He was on a leave of absence to conduct an unsponsored study of Dragonflys in co-operation with the University of Victoria.

Liard Hot Springs Provincial Park is located at Mile 496 along the Alaska Highway some 196 miles north of Fort Nelson. He had been in the area for several weeks and was well known to the Park staff. After he had not been seen for a few days his camp was checked by the park personnel on 81 AUG 02. It was then that it became known of the attack.

DOERKSEN had set up camp about 200 yards from the Alaska Highway in an area that is not frequented by the general public.

Mr. DOERKSEN maintained a daily diary and the last entry was on 81 JUL 29. It is for this reason it is believed the incident occurred late on the 29th of July or early on the 30th.

Enclosed are copies of sketches depicting the campsite which was set up in a open grassy area. There is some indication from the file that he had been bothered by a bear a few nights previous. Some damage was incurred and he apparently had stated that if such an event occurred he was going to shout and holler to scare it away.

It is not known exactly what happened but it appears he was not dragged out of the tent although it was damaged by what appears to be a claw.

A large blood stain was located 15 to 20 feet from the vehicle that was parked by the tent. Leading away from this is the bush area and another further 100 feet DOERKSEN was located. His remains were buried under 4 inches of loose top soil and leaves.

Tracks of paws of 10″ were located in the area. This along with the Pathological examination and comparison of a "Grizzly" skull has lead to the conclusion the bear in question is in fact a grizzly.

Search of the area with dogs and helicopter failed to locate the bear responsible.

There is nothing to substantiate he had taken a photograph of the bear during the attack.

If you are looking for an acquaintance for personal background, I might suggest Mr. Don WAITE of Don WAITE Photography in Maple Ridge, B.C. Mr.

WAITE is well known to myself and had mentioned he knew DOERKSEN and the work he was involved in.

I trust this will be of some assistance to you.

Yours truly,

(Signed)
(G. A. M. DODDS) Cpl.
Fort Nelson Det.

(W.M.B.)S/Sgt,
i/c Ft. Nelson Det.

Doerksen's notes in his daily diary, as quoted in the official files, indicated: "He had been bothered by a bear a few nights previous. Some damage was incurred, and he apparently had stated that if such an event occurred, he was going to shout and holler to scare it away." This statement is indicative of the personality trait characteristic of a person liable to be killed by bears. People sometimes acquire such an attitude when reading stupid, sometimes intentionally misleading statements by self-declared and widely publicized wildlife "experts" who say not only that they have "stood up to bears and made them go away," but that bluffing is essentially an infallible tactic. The fact is, of course, that such a stance can both invite attack and increase the probability of serious injury. This attitude is also the result of conditioning from an early age by images of friendly bears. A prime example is the "Smokey the Bear" forest fire prevention campaign—even by park signs and pamphlets outlining "things to do" to avoid bear attacks. It is unfortunate that almost all wildlife publicity is based on the assumption that bears are not very dangerous when in fact all bears are potentially dangerous.

After sixty-six years with all kinds of wildlife in their own habitats, observing their activities and trying to understand them, I have learned that camping in the wilds is deliberately exposing oneself to attack by bears. As a result, although my wife, our children, and I have camped out in tents in places remote from civilization, at no time did we (or I alone) camp without a dog and/or a loaded rifle or shotgun.

Only once was I ever forced to put the camp gun to use.

In country similar to but much more isolated than Doerksen's Liard River area a grizzly bear chased my springer dog into our tent, then stood outside, apparently contemplating entry. I fired one shot over the bear's head. It fled. If it hadn't, I would have killed it. I would no more go into bear country without a weapon than I would tour a high-crime area of a city in the dead of night unarmed and unaccompanied.

The laws of the land deny outdoor people their principal means of defense against bear attacks. Park regulations prohibit the carrying of firearms, sometimes even by park personnel. Game regulations generally prohibit the carrying of arms in the wilds without a permit.

More recent studies show, however, that the last line of self-defense may not have to be a weapon that inflicts death or serious injury. The modern alternative is as simple as the active ingredient in red pepper or cayenne pepper. Isolated chemically, the ingredient is capsaicin. When that ingredient is applied to eyes, it produces an instant "blinding" effect. When inhaled, it produces lung and throat discomfort. On the other hand, during laboratory tests on humans, such applications have had little or no long-term ill effect. Spraying or otherwise applying capsaicin to the face of an animal does deter the animal immediately. When I saw it used, the bear left the scene. It did return within half an hour, but the application had deterred it immediately.

Laws of the land generally prohibit the use of such extracts and gases, some of which cause painful and possibly permanent injury. No doubt those items known to cause real damage should be carefully regulated. However, the relaxation of laws that prohibit the use of noninjurious elements in self-defense might save lives. In fact, it might be reasonable to require that such a weapon of self-defense be carried in bear country. If Doerksen had carried—and used—a squirt or spray unit he might still be alive.

This alternative "nondefense" is commercially manufactured and available, and the models I have seen could even be attached to a pajama pocket. They are commonly, if secretly, carried in the shirt pocket of many scientists in the field of bear studies.

After five years of researching the facts and factors of bear-and-man incidents, always hoping to find more clues about what causes them and what might prevent them, I gradually became aware of the similarity of personalities of the humans who had been attacked. Hence my inquiry into the personal characteristics of George Peter Doerksen.

After two years I went back to Bob Switzer and again interviewed him about his friend.

Bob was emphatic in his appraisal.

"I knew George Doerksen well—over a period of at least five years and as many on-air interviews. He was what we term in the trade "a good interview." He was responsive, lucid, a likeable personality. We had excellent reactions to his presentations. He knew his subjects very well. He was a dedicated professional with a passion for dragonflies, and he had extremely good photos of insects to display on screen.

I was listening for characteristics.

"Would you describe him as a Green Peace type?"

"No, at least not the publicity-anxious kind. But he had the better characteristics of those protective toward wildlife. Dedicated? Yes. Militant? No!"

"What was he like physically? Bearded, small?"

"He wasn't as tall as I am. About medium height, quite wiry. He dressed casually."

"His general mien?"

His response was immediate.

"He was completely immersed in his subject. In the field he could be so intent on photographing a dragonfly that he wouldn't have noticed a parade going by—completely absorbed—determined to get the ultimate good results."

"In other words, perhaps a grizzly could walk up behind him unnoticed."

After a moment he added thoughtfully.

"Not careless—just completely absorbed."

Bob was looking out the nearby window when I spoke.

"What were your arrangements with him. Any remuneration?"

"Hell, no! George couldn't care less about being paid."

He stopped, a little glum.

"His death still affects you, Bob?"

"Yes. It does! He was such a good guy! I cried when I got the news."

However rudimentary the character sketch, the "good guy" image was indelible.

Right after our final interview, I phoned Don Waite, the man mentioned in my letter from Corporal Dodds. Waite most eagerly agreed to an interview about his friend George Doerksen. Don Waite and I had immediate reasons for rapport. Not only was he a former RCMP officer, but he was a writer, photographer, and most recently a book publisher in the field of outdoors subjects. His most recent publication had been a best-selling book on the photography of birds.

His association with George Doerksen had been through his photography business in Maple Ridge, British Columbia. He had been friends with Doerksen for approximately the same number of years as Switzer had. In fact, Don Waite had supplied Doerksen with the film he was using during his final sortie after dragonflies. I asked him:

"How would you sum up George Doerksen?"

Without hesitation he answered, "I'd say he was one of the nicest and most dedicated guys I ever knew."

"Well versed in the woods?"

"Certainly! His degree was in entomology, a doctorate, and the only way that degree can be gained is by a long time spent in the wilds. He was talking with *National Geographic* about doing an article on his specialty, dragonflies. It's a strange coincidence: I was planning a trip with Richard Canning to photograph sea birds on Triangle Island, off northern Vancouver Island. Shortly beforehand I'd made a trip to Manning Park [British Columbia] to photograph a species of insect—a sedge—and while I was showing them to Canning in a coffee shop, he said, 'My brother was doing a book on insects with the fellow who was killed by a grizzly at Liard River.' My answer was, 'The name wasn't Doerksen, was it? It was? Oh, my God, no! I arranged for some professional-type film for him to take up there.' It was certainly a shock to hear the news so casually—in the coffee shop."

His reactions were almost identical to Bob Switzer's.

"How would you describe him—generally?"

"Well, he was about five-foot-eight, wiry, brown-haired, bearded—you might mistake him for a hippy—not worried about his dress or trying to make an impression. You wouldn't really have assessed him as having a doctorate—in fact, he told me that he was bunking in with a bunch of new immigrant types out where he worked at the mill on Vancouver Island—enjoying it. When the management found out he had a doctorate, they transferred him to a private room of his own. That kind of a guy."

"What about his work—in entomology?"

"I'd say that it was all-consuming with him. The world could be on fire, but George would be so preoccupied with his photography that he wouldn't notice it. His photographs were very good."

"How come he was working in a mill and living in a bunkhouse?"

"Well, I really don't think George cared what he did—as long as he was able to further his studies of insects—particularly dragonflies. He would do anything to get by—and study."

Well, what is there to say? George Peter Doerksen: unselfish, dedicated good guy, who believed that bears are "good guys," too.

The Runt IV

Two weeks had passed since the old female had opened the den and her cubs had moved into the open. She was becoming increasingly gaunt. Three months had passed since she had eaten, and much of her body weight had been transferred to the three cubs. The discovery of the younger she-bear and her single cub in the nearby territory was now threatening, and daily the older bear became more nervous. Shortly after she rid herself of the fecal plug in her lower bowels, she strayed seaward almost a hundred yards.

For several days northerly winds blowing across the estuary of the endless white sea plain had brought with them the inviting scents of other newborns. The she-bear was aware that the ringed seals in their birthing caverns were now suckling their virtually helpless whitecoats. The acrid seal stench, seeping upward through porous snow, wafted across the cold stillness. The scents triggered an insatiable hunger in the she-bear's wasted stomach.

During the past week she had insisted that the cubs accompany her during her ever-greater trips from the den mouth, keeping them ever longer in the rigors of the chill Arctic air.

All was stillness when she emerged for what was to be the final day at the den. The low sunlight offered no warmth, but there was no indication of an impending storm. Growling deeply to bring her cubs near, she turned and strode outward onto the flat ice of the estuary.

The cubs halted in a huddled group, momentarily surprised. The runt hissed in discontent, and the others began also to hiss anxiously. Then, when the she-bear woofed in warning, they swiftly bounded after her. She increased her pace across the open ice.

Two hundred yards farther she stopped. Within seconds all of them were at her front feet, vocalizing. Quite casually she stepped over them. When they bunched up again, she strode off several yards and lifted herself on her hind legs. At that towering height the sounds of her brood were less disturbing. Also, the inshore breeze, elevated by the series of pressure ridges, was stronger. In it was the unmistakable strong scent of a nearby ringed-seal birthing cavern.

Twisting her head from side to side, she ascertained the direction of the odor. Its origin was farther out on the estuary ice, near the point of the bay.

Returning to her cubs, she again urged them to follow. The two larger ones immediately fell into her path. A minute later she heard the piercing wail of the small one, left well behind. Growling at the two cubs nearest her heels, she indicated that they were to remain where they were.

Long strides carried her back to the lone cub. Without any lick of reassurance, she picked him up in her jaws and, carrying him, walked past the others with a purposeful stride. She did not release him. The scent of the seal *aglu* had grown strong enough fully to arouse the pangs in her starved belly, and her actions were deliberate.

About a quarter mile from the den the seal odor became almost overwhelming.

With a gruff warning she unceremoniously dropped the cub in the path of the other two. When she saw them huddled in a tight group, she moved several long paces seaward from them and again rose up on her haunches. For several minutes she tested the wind, locating the direction of one particular scent. Finally she cocked her ear in the direction of a small hummock on the slightly undulating surfaces of shore ice.

Small sounds issued from beneath the mound.

Returning to the cubs, she once more gave them a guttural warning to remain still. When their slight murmurs had subsided, she stalked slowly toward the chosen hummock.

Approaching very deliberately, she halted twice as she rose on her hind legs to scrutinize the small mound. Within fifteen feet of it she stopped, and for several minutes she remained in a catlike crouch. Then, without warning, she was airborne.

Her leap was accurate. When her front feet hit the center of the bulge, her five hundred pounds smashed through the heavy crust. A lightning movement of her paw struck at something beneath her, and in a simultaneous thrust her jaws pierced the broken roof. Her head came up with a quick snap. In her teeth was the body of a white baby seal. The immediate clench of her jaws had broken its spine. From its unmoving body bright ruby blood trickled down its fluffy, impeccably white coat.

Without hesitation she wolfed down the tiny animal. She licked her paws and lapped up the frozen blood on the snow. Then, abruptly, she caught the strong scent just released from an air bubble at the bottom of the den into which she had just broken.

That tentative air bubble, she knew, had been released by the mother seal, which would be returning to the open cavern she had provided for her young. The seal was probably answering the reflections of stronger light now coming through the broken roof. Seals are keenly aware of such changed light conditions; perhaps the adult would venture upward in search of her offspring.

The she-bear waited patiently in a crouched position, ready to plunge into the den if the seal broke water. A minute passed, then another. She relaxed enough to raise her head slightly. That movement was sufficient to alert the mother seal, which had silently pushed its nose above the surface. Quickly it had exhaled, then sucked in breath just as quickly.

Only a ripple showed on the surface but the she-bear knew its meaning. She turned from the smashed *aglu*, well aware that the adult seal would not soon return to the violated sanctuary. She shuffled over to her cubs. Two of them had fallen asleep, but the runt stared up from the center of the pile. He issued a muted whine.

Once again she woofed an admonition. The air held the scent of other birthing caverns, and she was ravenous.

CHAPTER 5

They Were Competing for a Livelihood

Thomas Mutanen's life was a tragedy even before a young polar bear ended it one iced-down midnight in downtown Churchill, Manitoba. On November 29, 1983, Mutanen was killed within a few yards of where, a year earlier and at the same hour, I had been locked out of my hotel while the Polar Bear Patrol was exploding firecrackers to drive the bears from the same midtown street. When the news of Thomas Mutanen's death came over the wires, I wrote to several friends in Churchill and to the Manitoba Department of Natural Resources, Wildlife Branch, to get the background of the sorry event. Especially I wanted to learn about Thomas Mutanen. Was his personality consistent with that of a typical victim?

I expected that local people might know the character of Thomas Mutanen, and I was right. They described him as a sadly forgotten man, squeezed down to the garbage heaps by civilization. In the local parlance, Mutanen was a "breed," of mixed white and Inuit ancestry. About eight years before the bear's attack he had been shot in the leg, during what was described as a "drunken brawl," and had been severely incapacitated. Thereafter he hobbled about using a crutch. He was often seen digging around in garbage cans, and he lived, in part, on deposit money from beer bottles that he found in the cans and on the food that some of the refuse containers held. In addition he received help from the proprietor of the Churchill Hotel, who regularly employed him for odd jobs, until the hotel burned down the week before the polar bear found Mutanen in a back alley. Evidence indicates that Mutanen had recovered some meat and pies from the garbage and that these had attracted the three-year-old bear that attacked him.

In search of a close witness to the tragedy, I wrote Brian Ladoon, a friend of Mutanen, who lived nearby. Ladoon answered by telephone to say that he himself had witnessed the attack, or most of it, and that he was sending me a tape of his description. Following is that account, and although it is couched in the everyday language of the north country, it is not, in any sense, unfeeling.

> Carol was just going to bed. I often talk to her at night just when she is going to sleep—as I do a lot of my work at night. The window was open. We can hear the sounds from the downtown, depending upon which way the wind is blowing. We heard the sounds of a polar bear and people yelling. The time was about 12:00 midnight to 12:15.
>
> We could hear the polar bear hissing. And it sounded like he was behind Nanook and the Seal Apartments, perhaps a bit to the south of Seal Apartments, but somewhere in between.
>
> I said, "There's a polar bear out there!" You know, you could hear him hissing

like a polar bear does and snarling, you know, how polar bears do. And the people continued yelling and screaming at the same time. So I got out on my balcony, where I can see directly down Kelsey Boulevard, and I could pick up the front of the Trading Post store. It's on Kelsey and Bernier streets.

At that point I saw a polar bear dragging a man across the street—right to the corner of the Arctic Inn. He dragged him from the south corner right to the inn, and right between the Arctic Inn and the sewing center. There is a driveway there. The polar bear stopped, and there were two men chasing the polar bear. There were a few others behind them. These two men were coming right up to the bear and throwing snow and stuff right at it. They were trying to get it away from the guy that it had. The bear was up on its hind legs and making bear-type movements. You know, making a hop toward you then backing off to defend its kill.

These guys were coming right up to within three or four feet of the bear. This was happening at about 12:15 to 12:17. I had picked up my .22 rifle, and I had my scope, so I could really see up close what was happening.

I was also tempted to fire, but I didn't. For starts, I didn't want to get into any hassle if something I did went wrong. Also that at 200 yards .222-caliber ammo may not be that good to use.

Regardless of that—that's not the story!—I was watching what happened. Then I went in to get my clothes on. That took maybe about a minute, and I was out on the balcony again. The fellow who shot the bear, Mike Riemer, he ran out of his apartment, which is in the Seal Apartments on the bottom level. He ran right across to the Arctic Inn. I was watching him through my rifle scope. He ran right up to the bear where it was reared up facing him. He shot it once. Then he shot it again. Then he shot again after that. He was within about six feet of the bear when he was shooting it.

It wasn't a very big bear. And I don't think he used a very high-caliber bullet—something in the .22-caliber range—because it was only a small-caliber clip in his gun, like a .222 [a high-velocity, small-game caliber] or a .22 Hornet. I don't know exactly. You can check it.

I saw the bear was dead. With Carol I ran downstairs to see what is happening with the guy. We got there in a couple of minutes, and there were about ten to fifteen people around.

One guy says, "Who is it?" Another guy says, "It's Tom Mutanen."

I looked at the guy, and the scalp is right off the top of his head, torn from his forehead along his temples, and there is a bit of hair hanging loose at the back. At first I didn't recognize him. Then, sure enough, I see it is Thomas Mutanen. Well, it looks like him, anyway. But one eye is knocked out of his head on the left side on his cheek. And right now he is shuddering—expiring, I think you call it.

Carol said to me, "It looks like he is expiring," I think that is the word. "He is on his last breath." When I looked at the guy, I figured that he's finished—well, just because I know that when an animal's got its eye popped out of its head, and is in his condition, it means it's on its last legs. And when a guy is like that, you know you're not going to bring them back. So he was on his way out.

The time now was about 12:22 A.M. or so.

About that time the ambulance came and took him away to the hospital. After that we just went home. It was a bit scary—one of those freaks of nature. The bears had been coming into the streets because we had had mild weather and the freeze-up hadn't come. The polar bears were packed up along the Churchill shore-line, waiting for the ice to form. It being a late freeze-up, you are bound to have more bear encounters than normal. It's a good thing we don't get somebody killed every year. It only happens every seven to ten years.

Brian's last statement about the frequency of bear attacks was like others that I had heard, and it is basically true. The last killing by a polar bear in or near Churchill, Manitoba, had been that of Paulosie Meeko in November, 1968. Polar bear attacks are unusual occurrences.

After listening to the foregoing and reading other communications regard-ing the attack on Thomas Mutanen, I looked back over my assorted polar bear clippings and found the following account in the *Toronto Sun*, dated November 30, 1983:

HORROR ON MANITOBA STREET

MAN KILLED BY POLAR BEAR

CHURCHILL, Man (UPI) A polar bear mauled a man to death on a city street yesterday.

Authorities warned that the annual migration of bear through the northern port is especially severe this year.

Thomas Edward Mutanen, 43, was killed on a city street by what one witness described as a young 300- to 400-pound bear. Passersby tried to divert the bear's attention, but Mutanen died before reaching hospital.

The bear was shot.

The white-coated beasts, which can top 1,500 pounds, have been showing up in increasing numbers this year because of a late freeze on the Hudson Bay.

The bears move inland in June but return in November to the icepacks on the Hudson Bay to hunt seals. Lack of ice on the bay this year, however, has left the bears waiting along the coastline. Some have wandered into Churchill.

An RCMP officer at the scene said, "It was what you would expect from a bear." Sgt. Dick Grattan said he believed it was the first fatal bear attack in town in 17 years.

"At this time, they're really getting quite hungry," said Rick Riewe of the Uni-versity of Manitoba zoology department.

Churchill's location and the lure of food has combined with the lack of ice to lure the bears, Riewe said.

"They built a town in the middle of a migration path," he said. "They provide garbage there, there's incentive for the bears to come back once they've been re-warded by garbage."

A 46-year-old tourist from Milwaukee was mauled by a polar bear last Thurs-day on a wilderness tour east of Churchill.*

The reporter's afterthought, about the forty-six-year-old tourist from Mil-waukee is noteworthy. First, if the report is reliable, there were *two* recent

---

*This news story is reprinted with permission of United Press International, Inc.

attacks. Second, just before the 1982 freeze-up I had been one of those tourists. I had visited the polar bears.

When Wayne Lankinen went out onto the frozen lake to within twenty yards of a large polar bear, to photograph it against leafless yellow brush to show off the magnificence of its silky, creamy white coat, that bear could have taken him in three jumps! And there would have been nothing that the others of us could do. Absolutely nothing. We might have thrown snow at it! It was said in Churchill that local businessmen who transport tourists on field trips to visit the polar bears made a practice of smearing sardine oil on the outsides of their vehicles to attract the bears so that the tourists could get photographs as close as eighteen inches by staying in the vehicle with the windows rolled up. I wonder whether the tourists knew that a polar bear's wallop with a front paw will easily smash through three inches of ice and will break a large seal's neck with even less trouble. The protection afforded by one-quarter to three-eighths of an inch of safety glass would be minimal.

It was also commonplace during my visit to see one to five vehicles standing empty while the visitors, who had used them to drive up close, were moving out across acres of open Arctic terrain toward the bears, to get clearer, "more natural" photographs.

Thomas Mutanen probably smelled strongly of garbage. Probably a half-starved bear—and hungry bears are common when the autumn freeze-up is late—smelled the meat pies or just Mutanen's clothing and immediately was attracted to him.

Scientists who study Churchill's "garbage-dump bears" say that they seldom come through or into town and that most who do are clearly marked and can readily be identified when they show any inclination to remain in the vicinity. That information probably is correct, but at the Churchill airport I saw one obviously dirty from the dump but unmarked. That was after only four days in Churchill.

Mutanen's story does demonstrate clearly that people should not have the smell of food on their body or clothing when they anticipate coming in close contact with any species of bear. On this subject I speak from personal experience: several years ago, when I was in Yellowstone Park, a black bear quickly followed me when my own fingers smelled of bacon. I have no doubt that that bear came after the bacon smell, because to acquire some action film footage, I had been leading it toward me by dropping pieces of bacon along my path while I retreated. It came right up to my vehicle and tore the chromium strip off the car window. I now know that the bear could have reached me in one good jump—a fact I would have denied then because of my athletic ability.

Although my research on Thomas Mutanen's personal traits is inconclusive, it does illustrate the eventual result of baiting bears—of attracting them by design or through carelessness.

The Runt V

Four attacks on the estuary ice *aglus* had provided the she-bear with three new-born ringed seals, and the bulge in her belly was increasing. Abruptly, from some distance, a piercing cry drifted upwind. Her hunting had taken her two hundred yards from the cubs.

At the sound of the small cubs' cry, she trotted swiftly toward them. When she arrived, all three were pyramided, noses to the sky, whining in fear of abandonment. Gusting about them were wisps of dry snow, the harbingers of a storm.

Nuzzling them briefly, she moved toward the far end of the bay, where earlier snows had gathered in deep drifts. Alternately growling, crying, and hissing their anguish, her brood followed her, the runt, as usual, lagging behind.

As soon as the she-bear felt the resonance of deep snow beneath them, she pounced forward and scratched at the icy surface with lancelike foreclaws until she reached the softer substrata. In seconds she was half buried, and her claws were striking the frozen sedges and grasses of the delta. She then tunneled along on the hard ground.

Tiring, she finally pulled herself from the new cavern and found her cubs almost fully covered by freshly thrown snow, subdued both by the cold and by their fear of this new experience. The two larger cubs struggled to answer her beckoning call and obediently entered the new den. With her nose she nudged them down the hole. The smallest of the three, however, lay prone on the windswept snow, all his strength expended, barely breathing.

Quickly she picked him up by the neck and pushed herself with him into the new den. A strong wind was blowing, and she turned to block the entrance with her haunches. She began to lick the runt's face and stomach, breathing warmth to it. The two other cubs, thoroughly chilled and disoriented, huddled against the end of their new chamber.

The runt responded quickly to the warmth. He found a lactating nipple almost immediately, and for once his belly was filled before the other cubs realized that the mother was ready to accept them.

The storm raged for three days outside the quickly sealed den. Cramped for room, the female dug along the hard ground, packing the snow solidly against the walls. Her long claws cut the frozen earth, severing grasses, sedges, mosses, and some low-growing willows. The hungry cubs began to eat these because the famished she-bear was temporarily unable to provide the usual supply of milk.

On the fourth day, as the mother awakened, she listened intently for some time. There was only silence, except for the intermittent crash of ice exploding under pressure, a sound she recognized as signaling the return of freezing temperatures. The cubs, still sleeping in a heap, whined only faintly. Used to the sounds, she lifted herself, woofed a warning to them, then broke through the hardened shell of the den entrance. For a moment she adjusted to the brilliance.

The sun sparkled yellow gold on the disturbed snow, its brassy sheen stretching over the endless miles now revealed beyond the nearby point of land. Abruptly ravenous, she trotted quickly toward the familiar polynya now showing its open waters in the pack ice off the headland. In the channels pressure ice had formed areas where seals regularly birthed in large numbers. In the past she had fed upon that springtime bounty. The prospect drew her like a magnet.

Long strides took her across half a mile of flat ice fields to the jumble of huge, upthrust ice shards. A quick survey revealed no easy access.

Climbing the ten-foot ridge, she stood silent atop the vantage point. Almost immediately the strong scent of freshly born seals came to her nostrils.

The first birthing cavern was no more than thirty feet from the top of the ridge. She carefully slid to the ice below, then listened to the faint but familiar sounds. An adult seal was on the shelf ice in the *aglu* suckling her sole pup. If that female had not heard the sounds of her slide from the pressure ridge, the prize could be both pup and mother.

She studied the hummock patiently. Too quick an approach would not give the seal time to lose its wariness, if it had heard her advance. She was still unsure if she was close enough for the last purposeful lunge. The faint sounds coming from beneath the mound indicated that the snow crust might be thin enough for her to penetrate.

An abrupt silence told her the seal had finished suckling her pup.

Lifting her front feet, twisting slightly upon her tensed haunches, she aimed her upper body directly into the crown of the hummock. Muscles impelled by desperate hunger quickly lifted her. She hurtled through the air in a missilelike trajectory. Forepaws rigidly extended, she broke through the covering of the birthing den. One forepaw met a rubberlike substance, and she immediately hooked her claws through the skin and into blubber. A swift hard blow with her other forepaw drove another set of claws into the squirming adult seal.

Quickly twisting her head, she dislodged the intervening snowcrust. A downward plunge with partially open jaws drove her canines deep into the as-yet-unseen body. Biting hard, she shook her jaws until there was a final gasp of foul air from the seal's lungs, and she knew it would go no further.

Still searching, she thrust a forepaw deep into the den. Her long nails sank into the second occupant, the softer body of the whitecoat. Quickly relinquishing her jawhold on the adult, she crunched into the cub in one motion, lifting it free.

A spasmodic twitch from the adult made her drop the pup on the surface as she plunged her head through the bloodied snow. Jaws clamped into the larger carcass, she gave a mighty heave upward, pulling the whole animal out onto the ice. Aware that the older seal would not now escape, she placed a paw on the smaller one and began avidly to consume it.

When she had finished that meal, she was suddenly overcome by the desperate exertions of the kill. She lay down beside the still body of the ringed seal, assured that, for the time being, there would be no hunger for her and her brood.

After a brief rest the smells of warm blubber so close at hand became too strong to resist. Long nails sliced through the bulging hide, exposing creamy layers of fat. She clawed the preferred blubber free of the flesh and bones, devouring it until almost a hundred pounds of flesh was expanding her belly. Her starvation had ended. She pawed loose snow over most of the carcass, then lay down and licked the offal thoroughly from her paws and face. She rolled herself several times in the snow to remove any frozen traces that otherwise might leave the scent of the kill on her path as she made her way back to her temporary lair and cubs.

As she approached the den mouth, the wisp of a silent white fox with black eyes moved tentatively away from where it had stood nearby. She woofed a warning at it, and it vanished as she entered the small new den. Immediate hissing and growling told her the fox had not harmed her brood. Seconds later all were sharing the new fodder.

The smaller cub awakened first.

Bright daylight ringed the den entrance with a halo of reflecting crystals. The sun was slanted almost directly into the tiny ice palace. The cub allowed himself to slide quietly off the top of his littermates. Something outside attracted him. The large bulk of his mother was missing, but he did not emit his usual plaintive wail.

Slightly steadier legs carried him to the sill of the entrance. There, uncertain of purpose, he stared into the unaccustomed glare. A strange scent wafted inward. There was no identifying sound with it, no form. He pushed his head outward, blinking to improve his vision. All outside was white and calm.

He climbed clumsily across the sill and sat down heavily.

As far as he could see, the white surfaces ran together, then abruptly ended in deep blue.

He was thus staring disconsolately when three small black objects became evident between him and the blue horizon. Two silent beads above a small jet-hued V with a round top. The two brighter black beads winked out. As he stared inquisitively where they had been, the nose moved, and the sharply pointed small head cocked angularly at him.

An involuntary hiss escaped from his startled throat!

The entire body attached to the three coal dots sailed responsively up into the air. Etched against the sky was a puffy, almost pancakelike body attached to a similar length of fluffy, rounded white tail. The fox, a young one itself, had been greatly startled by the intensity of the hiss.

The second hiss was deliberate.

The fox jumped again, less vigorously, easing softly away.

Slowly, the cub backed his feet over the sill and into the safety of the cavern. Against its far wall he snuggled tightly behind the curve of his still-somnolent mates.

Something about the encounter had been reassuring. The other entity had voluntarily retreated.

He slept almost immediately.

CHAPTER 6

Another Idyllic Place of Death

With my foot I pushed open the door of the Jeep pickup-camper, and the sweet scent of summer-warmed conifers wafted into the hot cab. I stepped down onto the thick layer of pine needles strewn on the forest floor and took a deep breath. It was four years since I had stood in disbelief at that same spot, the site of the tragic death of lovely Mary Patricia Mahoney in 1976. I was no more than two feet from my truck and only ten feet from where Mary Patricia Mahoney had been attacked in her tent and killed by a grizzly bear. It had seemed impossible four years earlier, in 1978, when my research had first led me there. On this second trip, in July, 1982, the possibility of a violent death still seemed out of the question in the beautiful grandeur of Montana's Glacier National Park. Yet in the intervening four years, two more people had been killed by grizzlies in this area.

With me, in my recent files, I had copies of the reports required from authorities following bear attacks in the parks. These official documents described the death of Jane Ammerman, Kim Eberly, and Lawrence Gordon. Gordon had been killed in a more remote area of the park, but all three killings had occurred during the 1980 summer camping season. I was on my way to visit the ranger offices that had been required to investigate the killings.

As I alighted from the truck late on that July afternoon, after having driven 400 miles that day, I was glad simply to breathe in the mountain air. Yet, even after my prolonged absence, the location of the Mahoney killing deeply affected me. My objective there was simply to get the facts on the case of Eberly and Gordon, but I could not suppress the deep feeling of compassion that I had for Patricia Mahoney and those to whom she had been lost. In that moment I found the role of detached researcher a difficult part to fill. Drawn by simple reverence for the young lady, I took off my hat and walked once again down the fatal path through the woods. It was impossible, even after the time that had elapsed, to treat her death impersonally. Several other young women had been attacked by park grizzlies during recent years, but she seemed most to epitomize public innocence regarding the limited capabilities of public officials and the nature of bears. She and her group had followed every specific of the camping rules outlined to them that evening by experienced park personnel, yet she had lost her life.

I stared up through the same trees that had cast cool shadows over Mary Pat Mahoney's last struggles, into the same blue summer skies that had shone over her last moments of agony. As always I questioned why such a death had occurred. And today I am still searching and researching for some answer and for a solution to the problem of bear attacks.

Abruptly, on that afternoon in 1982, I found myself at the meeting of the pipeline right-of-way and the footpath. There I stopped for a moment, distracted by my thoughts. Then, turning around, I walked resolutely back along the footpath to the campsite pavement and my vehicle. It was little more than two dozen steps from there to the parks buildings that housed the office of Ranger Terry Pentilla.

This would be my second visit with that efficient young man. The first had been during my research into the Mahoney case, and it had necessarily been short, because at that time information about the case was restricted. In 1982, executives at the central office of the park, in West Glacier, still were tight-lipped about the Mahoney tragedy; I'd had to tap all available information sources in the park just to ascertain just the essential facts. In 1978, Pentilla was unable to reply to many of my questions. In 1982, however, I had the official park reports on the deaths of Gordon, Eberly, and Ammerman, and I had clearance to interview the individuals who had handled the cases. Pentilla was a key ranger in all three cases. I walked down the path to his office.

Inside the small ranger station, two people were waiting to be served. Pentilla was talking to a third person, an exacting inquisitor who probably would lose his footing on a garden path and himself on the way to an outhouse. I kept thinking of how to describe the ranger: "Youngish but mature; very interested in his work, a public servant of exceptional ability, who performs his duties better than most." He apparently enjoyed working with the public, and the public appreciated his help. After the next two visitors had concluded their brief business, Pentilla looked up at me.

"May I help you, sir?"

I could not repress a grin.

"You might. I'm Mike Cramond. We've met be—"

"Oh yes, Mr. Cramond! I recognize you. What can I do for you?"

I looked at my wristwatch.

"If you have time I'd like to interview you at some length. I also realize that it is now 5:30 P.M. and that officially you're off duty."

He grinned. "No, we're never off duty here. I'll be pleased to answer your questions." He nodded to a man behind me. "Another ranger has just come on duty anyway, so we can go into my office—back here."

I followed him. He invited me to have a chair and sat down behind his own desk.

"Are you covering the same subjects as in your recent book, Mr. Cramond?"

I nodded, pleased that he knew about *Killer Bears*.

"Yes, I'm doing another book on bears. A couple of weeks ago I went to the main offices at West Glacier and interviewed Cliff Martinka. While I was there I asked about the Gordon, Ammerman, and Eberly cases. They gave me the official reports."

I reached into my briefcase to pick out the copies of those cases. As I held them up, he nodded, making no request for closer examination, obviously aware of their content.

"What would you like to know from me about the cases?"

"Did you have anything to do with the Gordon case?"

"Yes, I was on that investigation."

One is often embarrassed as a reporter asking public servants particular questions. I felt that some explanation might be in order.

"The reports are pretty clear, but a bit of background, particularly about the setting of each attack, will help me a lot. For instance, would I gain much insight by backpacking into the area where Gordon was killed?"

He stared at me for a moment before answering.

"It depends on what you want to know. You might be a better judge of that yourself. Can you tell me what you need?"

It was a good question. My previous research had shown me that there was no better way to comprehend an incident than actually setting foot on the site.

"Well, I've visited quite a few of the wilderness sites of attacks and killings. So far, every one I've found in its original wild state is a location where I would expect to see wildlife, including grizzly bears. This campsite, for example, which is near a natural meadow and stream. Is that an accurate analysis of the area where Gordon was killed?"

He was thoughtful for a moment.

"Yes, it's typical grizzly country. As you know, most of Glacier National Park is natural wildlife habitat. I know that particular country quite well. In fact, I originally marked the bear that later was destroyed in the belief that it killed Gordon."

The statement came as a bit of a surprise.

"You mean the bear referred to in the reports as 'Number 201'?"

"Yes, that is the bear we destroyed."

Pentilla had shown no surprise or concern at my naming the bear as Number 201, but I was surprised to hear that he had tagged the bear.

In my studies I have considered scientific handling and tagging of animals in relation to subsequent attacks upon humans. In my first investigations only one bear was officially reported as having been handled and tagged, but continuing study has shown additional authenticated cases of marked bears being involved in attacks and killings. There seemed to be no point in pursuing such a clinical projection with Pentilla, but the reasons for tagging Number 201 were a valid subject of inquiry. Phrasing my question more generally, I said, "Laslo Retfalvi, a control biologist who worked in Banff National Park, told me that in that park bears were not simply selected at random for marking. The only bears they handled and marked were nuisance bears, those that had conflicted with human park use. Free-roving bears not having caused complaints were not subjected to marking and study. Do visitor complaints influence marking at Glacier Park?"

"In 1977 we were getting sightings and descriptions of bears, and we stored the information in our computer program, which as you know, we use to supervise public access to specific areas. In the Red Rock Lake sector there were many sightings of grizzlies. Closure of specific areas is a tool to help the public avoid dangerous exposure."

"How did you judge the necessity for closures?"

"Sometimes it's a matter of judgment. For example, when visitors who return from an area say, "I was followed by a bear," we have to judge if such a report meant that the bear was a threat. But we also get reports like those from people who had visited Elizabeth Lake. They said they had been treed by a bear in there. Then there's no question what to do. Following those reports we went in and darted the bear. That animal was Number 201."

"Was the area closed off afterward?"

"Yes, it was."

"The report says Gordon was warned that his travel itinerary included a possibly troublesome bear or bears."

He nodded in agreement. "Yes. It is a pretty comprehensive report on the case."

"Do you think there was anything more that could have been done to prevent the incident?"

He shook his head.

"We kept him fully informed, and he observed the rules. It's just that when people enter wild areas—and they do demand to enter within reason—some conflict with wildlife is reasonably predictable."

"That's a fact." I picked up the file on Jane Ammerman and Kim Eberly. Eberly had been killed by a grizzly; the year before, his brother, Bill Eberly, also had been mauled by a grizzly but had survived. An amazing coincidence! For three years I had tried to locate Bill for an interview. I asked Pentilla if he had any more facts about the surviving brother:

"I have the Jane Ammerman–Kim Eberly file with me. I also have a file on the other Eberly, Bill, who was attacked in 1979. But I can't locate him. He is a biologist; would he be available through the record systems of the park management?"

Pentilla shook his head.

"I don't know where to contact him. He isn't a biologist; he was what is called in employment terminology a Technician, which doesn't involve the same degrees. That may be why the Service hasn't had any recent contact. What can I tell you about the Ammerman and Eberly cases?"

"Well, I'd like to know just where the killings actually happened—so that I can visit the site. I'd also like some idea of the distance between the site and the dump."

Pentilla produced a map and showed me exactly where on the St. Mary River the attack had occurred. I was surprised: the site seemed to be almost in the town of St. Mary, Montana. I said so. He nodded emphatically.

"It happened very close to the main street. You take this road." He pointed to the map. "Just as you come into town it goes out to the KOA camp-grounds. There is a bridge just after you leave the highway; the bodies were discovered a short distance downstream."

It was my turn to shake my head.

"That the Mary Patricia Mahoney case happened right here was unlikely enough!"

"I think you'll be just as surprised, if not more so, by the circumstances of the Eberly-Ammerman killings."

His emphasis surprised me.

"Who shot the grizzly? Were you there?"

"No, it was killed by a young Indian, Bill Powell. He lives on the reserve out on the highway. His father, Rob Powell, is the Glacier County deputy sheriff. The boundary of the local Indian reserve runs in the center of Divide Creek, which put the killings in Indian lands. We had a department trap on the Indian reservation section, but the camp used by the couple was on our side of the creek."

"Do you know anything regarding the occupations of the couple?"

He nodded.

"They both worked in park concessions. And they had recently attended a park orientation session in regard to regulations and precautions to be observed when using the park lands."

I was shaking my head, and Pentilla was looking at me inquisitively.

I spoke my thoughts.

"I haven't recently gone over all my card files, but as I recall, at least a dozen of the people mauled or killed were employed at parks, either by the government or in concessions."

Pentilla showed no surprise at the remark, but he noted that it was an interesting facet of my research. We talked of the cases a little longer, and he told me how to get to the dump and to the home of Deputy Sheriff Rob Powell. I thanked him for his knowledgeable assistance.

As I drove along the mountain road from Many Glacier Park, I was almost unaware of the tremendous grandeur surrounding me. Once on the main highway, I pulled off and read the official report of the board of review for the fourth time:

Board of Review Report
Fatal Grizzly Bear Mauling of Kim Eberly and Jane Ammerman,
July 24, 1980

At the request of Superintendent Iversen, Glacier National Park, a Board of Review was established to consider the bear mauling on July 24, 1980, which resulted in the fatalities of Kim Eberly and Jane Ammerman, both 19 and employees of Glacier Park, Incorporated.

The Board was composed of the following members:

Kenneth R. Ashley, Chairman, Associate Regional Director, Park Operations, National Park Service

Dan Gilham, Sr., Member, Vice-Chairman of the Blackfeet Tribal Council

Dale Harms, Member, Biologist, Endangered Species, U.S. Fish and Wildlife Service

Dr. Steve Herrero, Member, Professor, University of Calgary, Alberta, Canada

Fletcher Newby, Member, Deputy Director of the Montana Department of Fish, Wildlife and Parks.

Curtis Menefee, Attorney, Counsel to the Board, Interior Department Regional Solicitor's Office

The Board convened in public on July 31, 1980, in the lobby at the National Park Service employees dormitory at the district headquarters of the Hudson Bay District near St. Mary, Montana.

The Board members first visited the scene of the maulings and were given a resumé of the investigation by Park Ranger Jerry Ryder. The Board also, at that time, visited the open pit dump hereinafter referred to as Black's dump.

The purpose of the review was to establish the known facts surrounding the incident and to offer any conclusions or recommendations which the Board considered appropriate.

BEAR ACTIVITY IN ST. MARY AREA

Bear sightings during 1980 in the St. Mary valley occurred in a variety of situations including roadsides, residential areas, and backcountry.

Prior to the mauling deaths of Mr. Eberly and Ms. Ammerman, bears caused only one reported incident of property damage in the St. Mary area within Glacier National Park. On July 6, 1980, a medium sized brown adult grizzly with panda markings damaged a tent and sleeping bag and broke into a food cache at a back-country campsite at Red Eagle Lake some nine miles via foot trail from St. Mary. Following this incident at Red Eagle Lake, campsites in the vicinity were closed for three weeks and the Red Eagle Trail was closed for two weeks during June and July because of bear activity.

This season, prior to July 25, 1980, park rangers trapped and translocated only one bear in the St. Mary area. It was a sub-adult black bear weighing approximately 120 to 130 lbs. (now marked with ear tag #70) which was frequenting the Rising Sun Campground. Two culvert traps were set on July 18 but the bear did not enter either of them. Park rangers tranquilized this bear the morning of July 21 and released it 56 miles to the west of St. Mary at Flat Head Ranger Station.

A blond colored grizzly frequented the meadow called Two Dog Flats (three miles west of St. Mary) for about two weeks in early July. Numerous people observed this bear from their cars usually from a distance of about 300 yards. Probably this bear was feeding on strawberries, which were both abundant and ripe. It showed no aggressive behavior toward humans.

Park employees observed bears on at least three occasions in the St. Mary Park Service residential area. On June 24, at 8:45 P.M., a park ranger, while walking a dog, surprised a black colored sub-adult black bear near the maintenance area. On July 7 at 9:00 P.M., children on bicycles observed a dark brown bear with "widely spaced eyes" at the baseball diamond. On July 15 at 11:00 A.M., a blond colored grizzly walked past the garage in the maintenance area, was scared into a tree by dogs, and eventually crossed Divide Creek to the Blackfeet Indian Reservation.

Bears have been observed several times in the vicinity of St. Mary Campground (closed for season). In one instance on June 20, fishermen observed a light brown grizzly and moved into the St. Mary River in order to put some distance between them and the bear. This bear disappeared into the brush nearby. It exhibited no aggressive behavior.

On July 3, park rangers were requested by Lester Johnson, owner and operator of a private campground outside of Glacier National Park, to trap a small black bear that was becoming a nuisance. Permission to set the trap at a dump on lands owned by Hugh Black was obtained from the Blackfeet Tribe and Mrs. Black. When the ranger arrived, a dark brown grizzly was found feeding in the dump. Since a grizzly bear was now involved, further permission was obtained from the Tribe to try to trap this animal. It was also observed in the dump on July 4. Tracks indicated the bear walked around the trap but it did not disturb the bait or trigger the trap during the nights of July 3 and 4. Because the bear appeared shy of the trap and because of the work demands of the July 4 weekend, no further efforts were made and the trap was removed.

Since July 24 there have been three reports of black bears which were killed this year on the Blackfeet Indian Reservation. Mike Smith killed a cinnamon colored sub-adult black bear near his tent home on July 12. Bob Garrow killed another cinnamon colored black bear on July 14 near his home on lower St. Mary Lake. An unknown person killed a black colored adult black bear outside the park, ear tag #73, on July 29, near the Malmstrom Air Force Base Recreation Area which is located on the east side of Lower St. Mary Lake.

FACTS OF THE INCIDENT

Shortly after noon on July 24, Park Ranger Jerry Ryder received a report from Robert Shanahan and Scott Brewster that they had discovered a human body along Divide Creek just above its confluence with the St. Mary River. Ryder notified the Glacier County Sheriff's office, the Blackfeet Tribal Police, and the F.B.I. and secured the scene from the most obvious entry point. They waited until representatives from the aforementioned agencies arrived before moving in to investigate. Mr. Brewster led them to the site.

The body reported proved to be that of Ms. Ammerman. It was located within the boundaries of Glacier National Park along the west bank of Divide Creek, with a sleeping bag. It was approximately 100 yards above the confluence of Divide Creek with the St. Mary River. Another body, that of Mr. Eberly, was located about 60 yards upstream from Ms. Ammerman's body on Blackfeet Reservation land several feet from the east bank of Divide Creek. Both bodies were nude. Across Divide Creek from Eberly's body, in Glacier National Park, was a campsite with typical camping gear scattered about. Some of it was damaged and soaked with blood. Some items, including the tent, two sleeping bags, and some clothing were scattered along the creek as far down as the confluence with the St. Mary River. The clothing showed no signs of damage or blood.

Bloodstains on the ground and on some of the camp gear indicated the attack had initially taken place at the campsite and that the victims either were dragged or, possibly, managed to move to where they were found.

A food supply consisting mainly of items still in sealed containers, except for two apples, was hung 7 to 8 feet off the ground in a willow approximately 50 feet from the campsite. This food was contained in a Glacier National Park plastic sack. These sacks have printed on them complete information concerning proper behavior in bear country. There was no evidence that there had been a fire at the campsite or that any meals had been prepared. There was no garbage or trash in the vicinity that could be associated with the camp.

Subsequent search of the scene revealed some bear scat and what may have been a couple of day beds.

A very good mud print of a bear's paw was found on one of the packs.

Regulations require a permit to camp in Glacier National Park backcountry and anywhere outside an established campground. Mr. Eberly and Ms. Ammerman did not get such a permit, so were in violation of park regulations. One of the purposes of this regulation is to assure a contact between park rangers and prospective campers so that the camper is guided to safer campsites. The location of Mr. Eberly's and Ms. Ammerman's campsite, in what amounts to an isthmus between Upper and Lower St. Mary's Lakes, would indicate it was on the most logical route for bears moving between the park and garbage sources outside the park. The campsite was in heavy brush with restricted visibility. There were few tall trees available in which they could have sought refuge from a bear. A permit would not have been issued by the park rangers for the place they camped.

The tent, which was found snagged on a stake where Divide Creek joins St. Mary's River, had one side torn open. The tent was zipped closed. It was the type with an external frame made up of tubular metal members. These frame members were found at the campsite and were partially assembled with some of them covered with blood. Several of the frame members appeared to have been bent. It is possible that the tent had been erected although there was no evidence that it had been staked down. The warmth of the night (probably in the range of 60° to 65° F) and the fact that the tent was zipped closed indicates that Mr. Eberly and Ms. Ammerman likely were sleeping on the tent fly, ensolite pad, and the sleeping bags outside the tent.

Investigation revealed that Mr. Eberly and Ms. Ammerman left Lake McDonald Lodge the afternoon of July 22 and hitched a ride with Richard Squires to St. Mary's. He dropped them off on U.S. 89 at the junction of the KOA Campground road with U.S. 89. They were seen in the lounge at St. Mary's Lodge that evening as late as 11 P.M. At the time this report is being written there is no information available about their whereabouts or activities from then until their bodies were discovered on July 24. According to records at Lake McDonald Lodge they checked out for Waterton. No evidence of them having visited Waterton has been discovered.

Very early in the morning of July 25 several Blackfeet Tribal members and police, who were patrolling the park/reservation boundary, shot a dark colored grizzly bear crossing the St. Mary's River on reservation land just below the mouth of Divide Creek. The bear was turned over to Park Ranger Ryder. After photographs and measurements were taken, the bear was sent to Bozeman, Montana, for laboratory analysis by Mr. Ken Greer of the Montana Department of Fish, Wildlife and Parks. The bear was a male, then estimated to be 2 to 4 years old, and weighed 258 pounds. Subsequent laboratory tests, including autopsies on the victims and necropsy of the bear by the State Crime Laboratory, as well as by Mr. Greer were conducted. Autopsies of the victims, necropsy of the bear, and laboratory testing of specimens indicate the following:

1. The cause of death for each of the victims was shock and loss of blood.
2. The scat contents of the bear contained cellophane, Styrofoam, and cantaloupe rind, among other things, indicating it was feeding on garbage somewhere.
3. Human hair matching that of the male victim was found on the bear's tongue. Human hair matching that of both victims was found in the bear's digestive tract and in the scat located near the campsite.
4. Evidence of sexual activity between the victims is inconclusive.
5. Ms. Ammerman was not in the menstrual period.
6. Bite marks on the victims' bodies matched the dentition of the bear that was shot.
7. There were no ear tags, lip tattoos, or tag or snare scars on the bear which would indicate that it had been captured or handled previously. The health and condition of the bear was considered normal with no disease or abnormal level of parasites.
8. The age of the bear was approximately 5½ years.

The dump previously referred to as Black's dump is located a half-mile north of the town of St. Mary's on the east side of U.S. 89. It is fee patented land owned by Hugh Black and is within the boundaries of the Blackfeet Reservation but it is not subject to regulation by the Tribe. Although posted with a prominent though crude "Pit Closed" sign, it showed signs of considerable recent use when inspected by the Board. In fact, sometime during the night of July 30, a dead horse was deposited at the dump. The situation at this dump reflects the desperate need for the formation of a cooperative refuse district involving all jurisdictions within Glacier County. This action was urged by the Superintendent of Glacier National Park and the Director of the Montana Department of Health and Environmental Sciences as long ago as 1972. Glacier National Park still holds that position.

A number of large garbage containers located at various pull outs along U.S. 89 also provided possible food sources. According to observations made by park rangers at St. Mary's these containers occasionally overflowed.

In accordance with Glacier National Park's approved Bear Management Plan, information on bears was presented by park rangers at an orientation meeting for Lake McDonald Glacier Park Incorporated employees on June 5. Both Mr. Eberly and Ms. Ammerman were present at that orientation. Ironically, one of the matters discussed was a bear mauling in 1979 in which Kim Eberly's brother Bill Eberly was injured.

CONCLUSIONS AND RECOMMENDATIONS

Conclusion 1

Kim Eberly and Jane Ammerman were fatally mauled on July 24, 1980, at about 4 A.M. by the same bear that Tribal members shot early July 25, 1980. It is also likely that the bear is the same one that was observed at Black's dump on July 3 and 4 which the park rangers attempted to trap. According to the rangers, it appeared to them to be the same bear based on size and color. The fact that the bear had garbage items in its digestive tract is evidence the bear was feeding at some garbage source. During the three or four weeks prior to the mauling only one grizzly of a different color had been observed in the vicinity. And finally, between the mauling and the killing of the grizzly and the date of this report no grizzlies have been observed in the general vicinity of St. Mary's.

Recommendation. Glacier National Park should continue its present bear monitoring system that allows management to identify and respond to potential people/bear problems. The park should continue to seek ways to improve the system's effectiveness in serving as an alert to park management of potential problems that may be accruing both inside and adjacent to the park.

Conclusion 2

The existence and use of the garbage dump may have contributed to the habituation of this grizzly to humans and developed areas and hence to the fatal mauling of Mr. Eberly and Ms. Ammerman. The existence of such a dump in the midst of a significant congregation of residents and visitors where bears are fairly common is a situation entailing a high potential for bear/people incidents resulting either in injury, property damage, or deaths to both people and bears. While the victims were camped in a non-designated area, their camping practice (etiquette) was such that it did not appear to be a major attractant for the bear. Their campsite was located in a logical travel corridor for this bear to reach food sources outside the park, particularly the open dump.

Recommendation. Glacier National Park, as the primary recreational and visitor service agency in the St. Mary vicinity, should take the lead in resolving the local sanitation situation and approach the Blackfeet Tribe, appropriate Department of the State of Montana, Glacier County, and the St. Mary community in an attempt to eliminate sanitation practices that are conducive to attracting black and grizzly bears into close associations with people. Since the Park Service does not have any jurisdictional responsibility, its role can best be as a catalyst to promote such resolution.

Failure to solve the sanitation problem could predispose to future injury. All refuse disposal sites near Glacier National Park should be evaluated for their potential for similar habituation of bears leading to other incidents.

Conclusion 3

Of the five persons fatally mauled by bears in Glacier National Park, four have been employees of Glacier Park, Inc. Orientations are scheduled throughout the park for Glacier Park, Inc. employees during which National Park Service employees present information on how to avoid bear confrontations. This is in accordance with the approved bear management plan. Mr. Eberly and Ms. Ammerman were present at the Lake McDonald orientation on June 5, 1980.

Recommendation. While in this case Mr. Eberly and Ms. Ammerman attended the orientation, it is recognized that it is difficult to schedule enough orientations so that all Glacier Park, Inc. employees are able to be present. It is recommended that, in addition to the orientation programs, each employee be handed a safety orientation packet prepared by Glacier National Park and containing the appropriate bear information. It is further recommended that the employee receipt for the information and that this receipt be turned over to the park for its records. It is further recommended that rosters be kept to record the names of those employees attending the orientation programs.

It is further recommended that key members of the Glacier National Park staff meet annually, as the visitor season gets underway, with the members of the management staff of Glacier Park, Inc. for the purpose of explaining park programs and gaining their support for these programs.

Conclusion 4

Glacier National Park has a well developed bear management information system that is part of the Servicewide computerized Bear Information Management System (BIMS). The system has the capability of incorporating additional reporting from areas adjoining the park.

Recommendation. Glacier National Park should work with the Blackfeet Tribe and the community of St. Mary to encourage reporting of bear sightings, confrontations, or other incidents for incorporation into the System.

Conclusion 5

Despite the fact that both of the mauling victims were Glacier Park, Inc. employees, no one representing the company's management appeared at the Board of Review.

Recommendation. The Park Superintendent should advise the President of Glacier Park, Inc. that he or a ranking management official is not only welcome to attend reviews of Glacier Park, Inc. employee accidents but is expected to attend.

Conclusion 6

Generally, the Board concludes that the approved Glacier National Park bear management plan is adequate.

Addendum

The Board recognizes that the Bureau of Indian Affairs has an important role in establishing and maintaining proper sanitation practices and bear management on the Blackfeet Indian Reservation. The Bureau of Indian Affairs should be included as one of the entities identified in the recommendations made under Conclusions 2 and 4.

In this specific case the plan applied, in that (1) Mr. Eberly and Ms. Ammerman did receive the prescribed information and orientation called for by the plan, (2) the camping situation they chose would not have been permitted had they properly applied for a camping permit in accordance with park regulations, (3) the Bear Management Information System was fully operational so that, had Mr. Eberly and Ms. Ammerman applied for a camping permit, they would have benefitted from up-to-date in-park information. Had they indicated an intent to camp in the St. Mary area in other than one of the designated campgrounds it is likely that they would have been informed that a grizzly bear had been visiting Black's dump. The Board further concludes that, had Mr. Eberly and Ms. Ammerman been responsive to information received during their orientation and adhered to park regulations, they would not have been killed.

Recommendation. The foregoing notwithstanding, the fact remains that Mr. Eberly and Ms. Ammerman were killed in a situation over which they could have had control. The present literature used by the Glacier National Park to acquaint park visitors and employees with bears fully addresses the potential for danger and injury. In our minds injury implies possible fatal results. Perhaps park visitors or employees have not drawn that same implication. Additionally, prior to 1967, no one had been fatally injured in Glacier. With the increased frequency of fatal injuries, including the recent Canadian fatal maulings involving both black and grizzly bears, the Board feels the time has come to clearly state in our literature that the potential for death from bears, even though slight, does exist. It is recommended, therefore, that the Glacier National Park staff review its literature and other means of communication with a view toward stepping up its impact on the park visitor and employee.

The Board commends the Glacier National Park staff, in particular the park rangers of the Hudson Bay District, for the manner in which the incident was handled and investigated. We also commend the Blackfeet Tribal police for their cooperation. Further, it is the view of the Board that the forensic laboratory investigations of the Wildlife Research Laboratory, Montana Department of Fish, Wildlife, and Parks, and the Crime Investigation Laboratory of the Montana Department of Justice, conclusively linking the bear killed on July 25 with the victims, were of the highest professional standards.

The late afternoon sun was moving over toward the western side of the great sheer rock face of the high mountain that dominates the St. Mary landscape and that (I later learned) figured in the legends of the Indians, who would not climb to its summit. Its formidable cliffs and extreme height naturally set it apart, and the thousands of feet of direct drop from the ridge summit are enough to discourage all but the most capable climbers. As I drove into St. Mary, the shadows of the ridge had darkened the cliff faces. Yet in the valley the summer sun shone hot and clear, soaking into the flat earth.

The main highway south, U.S. 89, is aligned with the enormous crags and ridges of the Rocky Mountain chain. The ranchlands through which it passes roll from the gigantic upheavals that ensued when internal stresses cracked the earth surface and forced the broken edges upward above the smooth floor of what was once an ocean. The beauty of the area, and the enormity of the fractured terrain are awesome, even to the frequent visitor. Such splendors are the treasure that the tourists seek. The setting also attracts young people to summer jobs in the parks. The board of review that investigated the Eberly and Ammerman deaths noted that the age of each of those concession workers was nineteen years. Seven other bear victims in my files were under twenty years of age. These deaths and the carnage among young people in highway accidents have one common denominator: synonymous with youth (and what is assumed to be a normal life expectancy) is a subconscious defiance of death.

My somber thoughts were interrupted by the sudden realization that I was entering the village of St. Mary. Just ahead was the turnoff to the KOA campgrounds. I braked and turned onto the stretch of dry gravel road. Within a hundred yards of the turn, the bridge that Pentilla had mentioned crossed the St. Mary River which ultimately enters Hudson Bay. As I drove across the bridge, seeking a place to park, I noted the clear waters flowing silkily to the north. Seeing no convenient parking, I turned around and was surprised to see through the trees the upper roof frames of a nearby building not much farther from the river than the length of a baseball infield. On the south side of the gravel road a short incline, worn by tire tracks, followed the riverbank. I idled the vehicle a few yards along the dirt track, which was lined fairly heavily on both sides with bushes, to a flat, graveled clearing that obviously was subject to flooding from spring runoff.

Once I had parked there, it was only a dozen or more steps to the top of a bank, from which I had an open view of the edge of the river. Below, on my side of the river, sand and gravel led down to a boulder beach.

About fifty yards upstream the sunlit bridge arched over the stream. Downstream the sparkle of running water indicated the entrance of a tributary stream. From that point to the highway bridge was less than one hundred yards.

Surely that was not Divide Creek! Not that close to human habitation and transit!

Hell, I could hear the cars and even nearby music from the village of St. Mary! A none-too-loud yell ought to bring attention from there.

Just as Mary Patricia Mahoney's killing had been unbelievably close to park service installations, so was this location almost on the doorsteps of human beings. Without the narrow skirt of fairly dense bushes the town and Eberly and Ammerman's riverside campsite would have been clearly in view of each other.

Again I looked at the muddy sands below the bank. There were tracks down there, fresh tracks. I glanced upstream and then downstream before descending. In the mud, half a dozen prints of shoes with hard heels mingled with the softer indentations of sneakers. Among them were imprints obviously of animal origin. A bear's footprint is similar to that of a human but is much broader for its length and usually shows dotted indentations where the claws extend from the toes. Even in the loose sands, where the bear's imprint would be indistinct, the difference in width surely would be identifiable. This animal's prints were more doglike.

Closer examination showed only slight nail imprints embedded in the mud. Reasonably sure that no bears had been in this vicinity recently, I went to Divide Creek, a few yards downstream.

The creek flowed out from between the shoreline bushes in a fairly recently eroded bed. The freshness of the bed confirmed information that the center of Divide Creek (the boundary between Indian and government lands) was contestable. This issue had arisen when the two agencies responsible for investigating this attack were attempting to establish their jurisdictions. The recently deceased couple's tent (the presumed location of the attack) was on government lands, but their bodies had been recovered a few yards downstream on Indian lands.

By then I was standing within feet of where a streamside visitor had first discovered the remains of Jane Ammerman. I could clearly hear small sounds and noises coming from the main street of St. Mary. I almost gulped in disbelief.

I walked up the edges of Divide Creek a few yards. The stream flowed through level terrain where the brush varied from waist to head height. Small trees surrounded some open spots away from the bank of the creek. If I wanted to set up a tent away from where people would be using the stream, my choice would have been the site of the Eberly-Ammerman killing. Fresh, clean water would be at hand just outside the tent flap. The larger ponds of the river, no more than a casual stroll away, would be ideal for swimming or bathing. In fact, if I had not known the park boundaries and regulations, I would have assumed that such an idyllic location was freely open for overnight camping.

The shadows of the Rockies were reaching out over the rolling rangeland. A warm, mellow sunlight suffused the clear air and highlighted the mists in the valley. The creek trickled at my feet; just beyond the intervening bushes the sun's rays caught the riffles of St. Mary River, a stone's throw away. The coolness of the surrounding greenery, the trickle of the waters, the soft blue of the heavens, the scoured cleanliness of the creek rocks and small boulders—any visitor, traveler, or passerby would want to sit down, absorb the quiet, and gaze at the faraway rimrocks. Or simply lie with head propped on cupped hands, just to feel the resilient earth beneath and be warmed by the summer day at eventide.

To expect a marauding grizzly bear? No. Never!

As I walked back to the riverbank, I could envision the happy young couple choosing this solitude, so close to the road yet away from other humans. Just as I left the low brush, I heard the splash of a stone in the river. I looked downstream to see a small boy in summer shorts and sneakers standing on the opposite shore. His arm went back, and he threw another stone. Another splash, and he bent down to select yet another missile.

There were no grownups anywhere near him, though I could hear muted voices from the low brush behind him. He was less than fifty yards from where I stood at the site of the double tragedy. It was apparent that he and his parents were unaware that the place they had chosen for family recreation was within seventy-five yards of where grizzlies customarily pursued their travels. My impulse was to yell some sort of warning, however casual. But I did nothing; it seemed likely that such a warning might be considered the nosey intervention of a rather macabre old fool.

To assuage my fears, I walked upstream toward the bridge, keeping a careful eye out for other movement on the river beaches or in the surrounding bushes. At the bridge I looked over at the spot from which I had been told the young Indian Bill Powell had shot at the grizzly. The bear had been well within the range of any accurate shooter, at most fifty yards away.

Returning to the Jeep, I picked up the official reports and made some notes to preserve my memory of how very close to human transit the tragedy had occurred. Minutes later I drove north toward the home of Rob Powell in the Indian reserve.

I wondered if even one of those people on St. Mary's streets was aware, amid the noises of the surrounding traffic, that a small boy scant yards away could even then be screaming with fright.

The Runt VI

The Artic seasons change swiftly off Baffin Island. Ice becomes sea, and land becomes apparent as the scant snows of the Far North dissipate quickly. When the sow hunted now, it was not just for seals and their pups but also for the lemmings, ptarmigans, and foxes on the mosses and low growth or, in the water, for old squaw ducks, eiders, grebes, small diving birds, shorebirds, and occasionally a seal, which she still preferred.

Smaller, easily pinned down by his littermates, the runt had a greater affinity for the mother, the source of nourishment, than did the other cubs. Not as preoccupied as they were with tumbling and tussling, he began to track his mother when she left their overnight denning area, which was now any rise of land that protected them from the wind. When she noticed him at her heels, her warning whuffs and growls were brief and halfhearted. The twenty-third year of her life was weighing heavily upon her, and when the small cub followed her more persistently, she was generally too preoccupied to discourage him.

Thus during most of April he was on the ice with her, at times near the kill of a seal. The day when he had first moved in on a kill marked a turn in his life. His mother's remonstrances at his following her had ended with a final cuff that sent him across the slippery wet ice. Just as she had crossed over the pressure ridges in the land-fast ice, he had begun to trot toward the spot where she had disappeared. There was no sign of his parent, but her scent was still strong in the warming air. Finding a small, upward-slanting fissure, he had climbed up and eventually had reached the top. About two hundred yards away on the ice, his mother was in a strange attitude. Her rump was a high mound and her long neck inclined from that hummock to her nose, which pointed arrowlike at the open water beyond the ice.

Just at the edge of the sea water a black harp seal, whose sausagelike body was stuffed with muscle and blubber, was resting in the sun. He was large enough to be alone yet young enough not to have learned full adult caution.

As the cub watched her, the large white bear glided along the ice with silent pushes of her hind paws. When the seal raised its head in a quick survey of the surrounding territory, the bear stiffened. When the quarry nodded, her slide forward was silent and quick. Half an hour passed quickly as the cub remained quietly fascinated by the sight. Occasionally the strong odor of the seal, a smell he recognized from his mother's breath after a hunt, wafted up to his vantage point.

The cub's own enemy was sleep. His head nodded, and his eyes blinked. His head dropped to his paws. In that instant the seal raised its head and poised its flippers for a spurt for the nearby water.

When the pup's eyes opened fully, it was to witness his mother leaping through the air. Her whole body landed on the seal, her head twisting in a lightning move to sink her teeth into a wildly flying flipper. Two swats of her huge forepaws resounded on the head and shoulders of the seal. A quick bite behind its head, and the body trembled, almost jellylike, before relaxing on the reddening ice floor. A final gasp of air exuded from the lungs, and the old bear let go of the neck.

In a burst of excitement the cub slid down the drift slope of the pressure ridge and across the incline leading to the shore ice. In seconds he was alongside the big carcass, and his parent was scolding him with angry woofs. So great was her own hunger, however, that she almost immediately began to feed and simply ignored him.

While she tore into the body of the animal, small scraps of skin and blubber were tossed to the ice. When a chunk almost as large as his forepaw landed beside him, the cub grasped it in his mouth and was surprised when it slipped greasily down his throat. Anything that he had previously ingested had had a rough passage, such as kelp with granules of sand, sedge, and frozen, browned grasses. This warm flesh had a different effect. He gobbled at other small bits of skin and flesh while the old bear fed ravenously. Finally, satiated, he sat down.

Before she had finished her meal, he had vomited his own into the bluish waters of a nearby pool. Yet he willingly went back to the carcass and picked up more small scraps. These stayed down, in part because shortly therafter he was held firmly in the jaws of his mother, being carried back to their overnight land camp.

Daylight was becoming constant. All three cubs were now habitually on the track of their mother. Her paths led them into the cold waters of the leads that had opened at sea, sometimes for a half hour of swimming in her wake. At other times they crossed long wastes of floating pack ice. They were always moving. Occasionally she took them through long inland passes. Such forays required two or three days of hunger for her, and also for her cubs as her milk supply dwindled. Always the path led to the beach of an estuary where shallow waters united with the sparse vegetation of the lands.

On land the group hunted mice, foxes, even a caribou calf, but it was the sea life that the small male most enjoyed. He learned to course after his mother as she breasted the tall waves and then returned to the ice, which was never far off—an iceberg, pack ice, or a large, individual chunk, upon which they rested after long swims. The ever-present seabirds on the beaches were always good for a chase.

The three cubs were still intermittently suckling when the sun's angle began to decline, yet much of their main diet now consisted of meat. Occasionally added to the flesh of their prey were the still-green sedges and grasses, the sweet blueberries of the tundra floor, and the deeply immersed sea-growing kelps, for which the old lady dived, returning with long fronds streaming from her mouth.

Her girth had enlarged, and her rump had broadened, but her frame was more angular than it had been before the previous denning season.

Fresh winds and light frosts had become fall gales and sudden drops below zero when the signs of walking hibernation began to show in the bears' activities. Hunting was less productive each day. The birds had long since departed from the beaches, and the frazil ice on the beaches was oily. Snow had come at intermittent intervals, and the sow's pattern of foraging had led southward, even across large stretches of open water, to the estuary of the litter's birth.

The runt was now equal in bulk to the female, and he was willing to contest the larger male in a brawl. In competition for position it was now the runt who usually ended on top. A growing leadership was developing in his actions.

CHAPTER 7

He Was Warned

GLACIER PARK RANGERS SHOOT "KILLER GRIZZLY"

WEST GLACIER, Mont. (AP) Glacier Park rangers shot and killed a large female grizzly bear Sunday morning about 10 kilometres from where the mauled body of a Texas man was found earlier in the weekend.

Joe Shellenberger, acting superintendent of the million-acre park in north-central Montana, said the bear carcass was sent to a laboratory at Montana State University in Bozeman.

He said authorities would try to determine if the bear was the one that killed Lawrence Gordon, 33, of Dallas, whose body was found Friday afternoon near the shore of Elizabeth Lake in the rugged northeast corner of the park and about 15 kilometres from the Canadian border.

The grizzly was shot near Helen's Lake in the upper Belly River drainage following a widespread search by rangers from Glacier and Canada's adjoining Waterton National Park, Shellenberger said.

"The bear matches the description of one involved in the treeing of three hikers near Glenn's Lake on Sept. 30," he said.

In my file on the killing of Lawrence Byron Gordon, age thirty-three, late of Dallas, was the above item, which appeared in the *Vancouver* (B.C.) *Sun* on October 6, 1980. It lay on the Jeep seat beside me as I drove out to the Indian reservation home of Deputy Sheriff Rob Powell. In my reading of the U.S. Park Service inquiry into the Gordon tragedy, I had noted that the victim was an aircraft pilot, and that he had carried with him a diary, together with religious material, on his last journey into the wilds.

Attempts to get in touch with Gordon's relatives and heirs had led nowhere. I presumed either that the mails had not been reliable or that they had no interest in my research. Yet I persisted in wondering how an apparently able outdoorsman, who had the capabilities of a pilot, had become the victim of a grizzly bear. Gordon had carefully inquired about the trails that he planned to take, outlining his intentions for park personnel, and he had received warnings that problem bears had recently frequented the area that he planned to visit. He had nonetheless adhered to the plans that he had submitted to the park agencies. His death occurred within the period and area of his projected sojourn. The trouble was that he was in the wilds. He was in country in which at any time a grizzly bear, or bears, may be expected.

Most seasoned wild-lands visitors who know they might encounter bears carry some formidable weapon. When my work has carried me into associations with scientific people in the field, usually someone among the field personnel has had a rifle, a shotgun, or another weapon that would down an aggressive animal. Not one of these people has ever showed me even a remote desire to kill or maim any animal. In my opinion, all of them were perhaps overly protective of the species that they were studying. They carried firearms simply because they did not wish to be hurt themselves. It is possible, too, that in some cases they were required by regulations to carry weapons.

Men of the bush, such as trappers and hunters, carry guns whenever they are in the bush. Trappers carry a small-bore, usually a .22 caliber gun for dispatching a "pelt," but they seldom go without a big-bore gun also. The larger gun is carried to down the game used as camp food or bait, but it is also useful in case of a confrontation with a large predator. Hunters and trappers are among those best prepared to survive attack, yet they know that because of the nature of their work they need protection.

Recently, corporations have begun to recommend that other outdoors professionals, such as surveyors, mining prospectors, and engineers, carry a heavy-caliber weapon as protection from wild-animal attacks.

Then why do hikers and nature observers, including entomologists and botanists, feel that they will be protected from attack if they merely talk loud, carry a can of pebbles, ring a little bell, and adhere to food and camping regulations? Many victims of bear attacks used those provisions—the Roweds, Mary Patricia Mahoney, Fred Scholtes, and at least a dozen others. Now let us consider Lawrence Byron Gordon. The official report on his case reads as follows:

Board of Review Report
Probable Fatal Grizzly Bear Mauling of Lawrence Byron Gordon
September 26 or 27, 1980

At the request of Acting Superintendent Joseph E. Shellenberger, Glacier National Forest, a Board of Review was established to consider the death of Lawrence Byron Gordon which probably resulted from a grizzly bear mauling on September 26 or 27, 1980. Mr. Gordon was 33 years old and a former airplane pilot.

The Board was composed of the following members:

Kenneth R. Ashley, Chairman, Associate Regional Director, Park Operations, National Park Service

Fletcher Newby, Member, Deputy Director of the Montana Department of Fish, Wildlife and Parks

Dale Harms, Member, Biologist, Endangered Species, U.S. Fish and Wildlife Service, Billings

Tony Bull, Member Superintendent, Waterton Lakes National Park, Canada

Winnie Salois, Member, Chief Game Warden, Blackfeet Tribe, East Glacier Park, Montana

Curtis Menefee, Attorney, Counsel to the Board, Interior Department Regional Solicitor's office

The Board convened at 10:00 a.m. on October 22, 1980, at Park Headquarters, West Glacier, Montana.

Lawrence Byron Gordon probably was fatally mauled by a bear on either September 26 or 27, 1980, at a campsite at the lower end of Elizabeth Lake in Glacier National Park. The possibility, though remote, exists that Mr. Gordon died from some other cause and was then consumed by the bear. His remains were discovered on October 3 by Park Rangers Conrod, Benjamin and O'Brian who were investigating a report of a camp in some disarray at that location. The report resulted from an observation made by Jim Kruger and Dan O'Brian from a helicopter late on the evening of October 2. The helicopter was returning to West Glacier following placement and setting of a bear trap at Belly River Ranger Station.

The camp (located at UTM 300.2E × 5418.8N) was in some disarray. A sleeping bag, tent, and foam pad were scattered about along with several other items. Some of the items were torn. There were no signs of a struggle. The only significant amount of blood was found on three pullover shirts near the willow patch in which Mr. Gordon's remains were found. A Seiko self-winding watch with a bloodstain was found. It had run down at 1:30 p.m. September 28. The time shown on this watch, certain notations in religious material in Mr. Gordon's possessions, and his proposed camping itinerary all point to either September 26 or 27 as the date of his death.

The last official visit to Elizabeth Lake by Park Service employees was on September 25. Mr. Gordon had not arrived at that time.

Mr. Gordon was issued a camping permit on September 24. He hitchhiked to Many Glacier and stayed overnight. On September 25 the permit was reissued because of the closure of the Ptarmigan Tunnel where his original route had taken him. This closure resulted from an incident on September 24 in which a grizzly tore into packs of three hikers after they dropped them upon confronting the bear. The revised permit called for him being at Elizabeth Lake the nights of September 25, 26, and 27 coming out of the backcountry on September 28. He was given the usual information, which included information on bears.

On September 30 rangers closed up the Belly River Ranger Station for the season.

During the morning of September 30 three hikers were treed for about three hours by a large grizzly bear with an ear tag in its left ear. This occurred on a trail along the shore of Glenn's Lake. The bear made several unsuccessful attempts to reach the treed hikers but was able to ascend only 15 feet up the tree. The bear tore up the hikers' packs during this episode.

On October 2 park rangers discovered that a bear had broken into the Belly River Ranger Station and the nearby fire guard cabin.

On October 5 park rangers shot and killed a bear near the west end of Helen's Lake (UTM 297.1E × 5412.7N). It was a male grizzly weighing 379 pounds and had an ear tag #201 in the left ear.

The following immediate questions were considered by the Board:

1. Was #201 the bear that killed Gordon?
2. Why was #201 caught and transplanted in 1978?
3. What had #201's activities been between August 8, 1978, the date it was caught, and October 5, 1980, when it was killed?

Deduction, using circumstantial evidence, indicates a strong probability that #201 was the bear that killed Mr. Gordon. The general description of the bear that treed the hikers matches #201. That bear was quite aggressive. Scat samples found in the vicinity of the fatal attack and the Glenn's Lake treeing incident contained human remains. The necropsy conducted by the Montana Fish, Wildlife, and Parks laboratory at Bozeman showed no human remains in the suspected bear's intestinal tract. This may well have been because of the time lapse between the incident and the necropsy. Teeth marks in at least one book found in Mr. Gordon's pack match perfectly the dentition of #201. A grizzly bear was seen at the kitchen window of the Belly River Ranger Station in May, 1980, by Park Rangers Blair and Conrod. The bear had a tag in its left ear but the tag number was not observed. No other ear tagged bears were observed in the Belly River drainage this season.

The question as to why the grizzly bear numbered #201 was captured on August 8, 1978, seems to be that it generally matched the description of a bear reported to have been exhibiting aggressive behavior in the Many Glacier area. The chances are that #201 *was* the bear the park rangers were after but, the park rangers who were involved at the time that we were able to talk to, could not say positively on this point.

A third question, having to do with #201's activities subsequent to its capture also eludes a definitive answer. It was released on August 8, 1978, at the head of Valentine Creek in the Waterton Drainage and observed in apparent good condition as it recovered from the drugging. On August 30, 1978, an ear tagged bear, probably #201 was observed at Red Rock Lake. On September 4, an ear tagged bear, probably #201, was observed on Mt. Wilbur. Both of these sightings were made from a helicopter.

On July 25, 1979, and August 2, 1979, a tagged bear was seen on slopes of Mt. Wilbur.

In 1980 #201 may have been observed in the Many Glacier area.

A tagged bear was observed several times, with one park staff member of the opinion that it was #201 and another staff member of the opinion that it was not #201. In either event, the bear observed was neutral in its activities, showing no aggressive behavior.

CONCLUSION

Mr. Gordon acted responsibly in that he obtained a camping permit and, further, had it revised when he discovered that a portion of his proposed route had been closed because of bear activity. He was receptive to the advice and information imparted to him by three staff members who were involved in issuing his permit. He followed his itinerary. His camp gear appeared clean. The only deviation from good camping practice was that his food cache was too close to what appeared to be his campsite and it had not been secured out of reach of bears. Bear poles were in place near his campsite upon which his food cache could have been secured. He was hiking alone which, in the words of the backcountry pamphlet, "Hiking Alone is Not Encouraged." Mr. Bill Pentilla cautioned Mr. Gordon about hiking alone in the backcountry twice—once when he revised Mr. Gordon's permit and again while he was giving him a ride to the Many Glacier Trailhead.

Although he was not in one of the specifically designated campsites, he was generally in the area prescribed by his permit. Where he did camp others had previously camped, giving it the appearance of being an official site.

In total, it appears that Mr. Gordon acted in such a manner as to reduce to a minimum the likelihood of a confrontation with bears.

CONCLUSION

Those members of the park staff associated with this incident acted properly and responsibly and in accord with the bear management plan. This includes the initial issuance of Mr. Gordon's permit and the subsequent revision that resulted from the Ptarmigan Tunnel closure. It includes the closure of the Ptarmigan Trail because of the grizzly bear tearing up the packs of three hikers at Ptarmigan Lake. It includes the closure of that portion of the Stoney Indian Pass Trail between Stoney Indian Lake and the Cosley Cutoff in response to the grizzly treeing the hikers at Glenn's Lake. It includes the setting of a trap at Belly River Ranger Station in response to the Glenn's Lake incident and also the bear damage to the station. It includes the investigation of the report of the campsite at Elizabeth Lake that turned out to be that of Mr. Gordon. And, finally, it includes a thorough and professional investigation of the entire incident.

The foregoing notwithstanding, this fatality, following close on the heels of the Eberly-Ammerman fatalities, places upon the National Park Service a heavy responsibility to vigorously re-assess the bear management activity. The Board recognizes that the park does re-assess the Bear Management Plan on an annual basis. During the years of 1977, 1978, and 1979 the plan appeared adequate with an apparent stable population of bears co-existing with a heavy human use of the backcountry in a compatible manner. However, 1980 was a different year in Glacier National Park and, apparently, in Alberta as well.

The Board considered a number of questions:

1. Is bear behavior different in Glacier National Park than outside the park? If so, why?
2. Does food stress cause bears to act differently toward people?
3. Were bears subject to food stress in Glacier this year?
4. What criteria should be used in the decision to destroy a bear?
5. Should captured bears be transplanted within Glacier National Park?

DISCUSSION

Bears appear to show less "avoidance behavior" towards people within the park than outside. According to Mr. Newby, it has been "many" years since anyone was killed by a bear in Montana outside Glacier. (Subsequent search of the literature revealed that the last fatal mauling of a human by a bear in Montana, outside Glacier National Park, occurred in 1956.) Bears in Glacier have little reason to perceive man as a threat. This may be an evolving phenomenon involving gradual changes in bear behavior. A host of possible reasons present themselves: more and more hikers resulting in an increased frequency of bears encountering people without receiving a negative experience (aversive conditioning), fewer people using horses, smaller size parties, more backcountry use in early and late season, and possibly fewer management kills now than there were when bear management was decentralized and less formal.

The degree of feeding accomplished by the bears in the three fatalities raises the possibility that these bears were hungry and actually involved in predation. Mr. Dan Palmisciano of the Montana Fish and Game Department laboratory in Bozeman stated that he felt this bear was in about average condition as to body weight and fat content for this time of the year. Whether or not natural foods were available in less than average, average, or better than average quantities at the time of and in the vicinity of the incident was something the Board could not determine satisfactorily. Opinions among members of the park staff varied considerably on this point. There seems to be inadequate knowledge on this subject. The Board feels that it is extremely important that there be some systematic means of evaluating the natural food situation and the degree of nutritional stress the bear population may be under.

The criteria used for deciding on whether to destroy bears is contained in the Bear Management Plan. Using this criteria, 15 grizzly bears have been killed since 1967. Seven of these bears were killed by the National Park Service as a direct result of fatal bear maulings. During that same period a much larger number of grizzly bears were killed on the periphery of Glacier (hunting, accidents, depredation, and illegal kills). Also, during that time, estimates indicate that the grizzly population has remained stable at around 200. The Board feels that the number of grizzly bears killed within the park has probably had an insignificant impact on the population and that some additional number could be taken without harm to the population.

The question of the validity of transplanting captured bears within the park was raised by former Superintendent Iversen and is shared by other park staff members and members of the Board also. The usual reason for capturing a bear is that it is recognized as being a problem. We wonder if it isn't logical to assume that there is a good possibility that the problem is transferred right along with the bear.

We also have a concern that a transplant, regardless of the bear's behavior, may disrupt the home ranges and behavior of bears inhabiting the area of the transplant site. The Board also considered live trapping as a means of capturing bears. The question is, do we get the bear we want? Surely we sometimes do, other times we do not know. The random aspect of live trapping is disturbing. It seems to the Board that once a bear is determined to be a problem bear that a good case can be made for not transplanting the bear back into Glacier National Park.

The following recommendations are made in full recognition that the members of the Board are as hampered from lack of information as members of the Glacier National Park staff and those with whom they consult.

1. It is recommended that the park analyze future bear encounters and all past encounters for which records are available. Such an analysis should include but not be limited to date (time of season); size of party; location; natural food availability; time of day; activity or actions of person(s) at time of the encounter; sex, age, and species of bear; and any other facts that might effect the situation. The purpose of such analysis would be to build a profile or series of

profiles of encounters in order to assist park management in predicting dangerous situations. To make this study more meaningful the work that Dr. Steve Herrero has done on the same subject should be utilized.

2. It is recommended that the park establish a systematic and periodic means of evaluating the natural food situation in representative habitats within the park. The purpose of such a system would be to assist park management in predicting dangerous situations. This assumes that bears tend to be more troublesome when food stress exists, an opinion shared by a number of persons experienced with bear management.

3. It is recommended that the park re-evaluate the capturing and transplanting program with the outlook that, if it is necessary to capture a bear, it is probably troublesome enough to seriously question if it should be transplanted within the park. Preferably, if other agencies are willing to accept the bears this should be pursued. If such transplants are not possible the bear should be destroyed. The Glacier Bear Management Plan allows this latitude.

4. It is recommended that the park re-evaluate what constitutes a problem (dangerous or potentially dangerous) bear. Heretofore, it appears that out and out aggressive behavior was necessary before a bear was adjudged to be a problem. Less troublesome bears have been given a second chance through capturing and transplanting. It appears to the Board that recent experience indicates that we should remove bears from the park (either through transplanting elsewhere or destruction) that have torn up camps, gotten into other than natural food sources, or that have simply become overly familiar with humans.

5. It is recommended that the park give serious consideration to establishing minimum size parties during early and late season. This recommendation stems from a judgment that there is some less likelihood of a bear causing trouble when there are more people and may help preserve, from a young age on, the bear's natural "avoidance behavior" towards people. In midseason even a solo hiker will probably find others camped nearby while early and late the solo hiker is unlikely to find others camped nearby.

6. It is recommended that the park keep up its efforts to encourage neighboring communities to properly handle refuse disposal. Improperly managed refuse collection will continue to provide the potential for human injury or death and relocation or destruction of bears both inside and outside the park.

That report was among the files that I carried with me during my own investigations of the incidents. It lay on the car seat in August, 1981, as I turned off the main highway at the Blackfoot Indian Reservation onto a dry dirt road leading to the ranch of Sheriff Rob Powell. The road led through some excellent pastureland, over a wooden bridge, past the end of a small lake into which a stream flowed, and then to some good-sized farm buildings and the Powell home. The site was one of the best ranch-house locations I have ever visited. The Powell dogs came toward me barking. Using a gruff voice as warning I extended a wary hand for scenting or licking.

A big man wearing a friendly smile, tanned beyond his native hue, came out of the main door of the big ranch house. As I told him who I was and my reasons for visiting, I extended my hand to him. He took it in a strong grip and invited me into the household. Inside the remarkable household Native American art and artifacts blended with mainstream American furnishings. I was made to feel welcome and accepted immediately as a friend. Perhaps it was the effect of the large open room whose furnishings included antlers of elk and deer and well-used tanned animal hides as well as a modern electric fridge and stove in a well-lit kitchen section and a comfortable chesterfield and overstuffed lounging chairs. Rob's wife was a fine-looking woman with broad bones and deep Indian coloring. Rob, who was muscularly native but showed some white features, had the dignity and reticence often inherent in Native Americans. He looked like a man who would be chosen as sheriff. As he introduced me to his wife, she immediately smiled and asked me if I would like a piece of her freshly baked scratch cake.

"I sure would, Mrs. Powell," I replied. "On the road, after 6,000 miles in a camper, you get hungry for good home cooking."

She smiled and went to the kitchen to cut a piece for me. I could feel Rob's eyes casually assessing me. I could not help thinking that I was once a territorial cop—same thing as a sheriff—and was likewise given to assessing strangers. I thought, "He is probably wondering just what I want." I fingered the file in my hands and then opened it at the notes I had recently taken with Jerry Pentilla.

"Your son Bill was the one who killed the grizzly responsible for the Ammerman-Eberly killings."

He nodded quietly. "Yeah. He's away right now. Won't be back until morning. Can I fill you in?"

"Yes, I'm sure you can. You were nearby at the time, according to Jerry Pentilla."

"Yes, we had been keeping lookout for the bear around the area by St. Mary River. They had a trap set up at the dump, which is on reserve property. We had taken a look at it. There wasn't anything there. It was the same evening of the day that they picked up the [victims'] bodies at Divide Creek. We were sitting in the car where we figured a bear might show up. Our sons Bill and John were also driving around on the lookout for the bear. We had been out on the prowl all day, and they were looking for us. They came over, and we talked for a bit."

He stopped for a moment, and I asked a question.

"How old are the boys?"

"Bill is twenty-one, and John is twenty-three."

"What happened after they met with you?"

"Well, they drove back down the KOA road. It was around 11:00 P.M. and dark. They stopped and parked the car near the bridge that crosses the river." He stopped. "You've been there to look at the place?"

"Yes. I took some photographs. I couldn't believe that anyone could possibly be killed by a grizzly *right there*! Hell, there was a young kid throwing stones out into the river, and his parents were just out of sight beyond the bushes, having a picnic, as far as I could guess. It's almost in the center of town."

Rob Powell nodded.

"Yes, it is. I guess that is why they picked the spot to set up a tent—enough bushes to give a little privacy near the creek. I guess nobody would really expect anything like *that* to happen."

"I still can't get over how close it was to the buildings on the main street of St. Mary. What happened after Bill and John parked?"

"They were there just a few minutes when they heard a splashing in the river. They couldn't make out anything, but it had to be an animal. Nobody would likely be swimming there at that time of the night. John reached over and turned on the car lights. The grizzly was just coming out of the river on the opposite bank from where they were parked. The lights stopped it. Bill picked up his rifle and got him in the sights and fired immediately. The bear stumbled as if it had been hit. He was using a 7 mm. caliber Sako sporting rifle. On the second shot the bear went down in a heap. It turned out to be a spine shot. We heard the shooting and came down."

It was a typically spare outdoorsman's story of an animal killing. No dramatics, no wasted words: the facts.

"How big was the bear, Rob?"

"Oh, a fair size. About 300 pounds. It was in good shape, too. It had been a bad year for berries though."

"Do you think the lack of berries had anything to do with the killing?"

"I don't know. The people who study these things seem to be trying to relate attacks to bad berry years."

"Yes, they do. I don't know what to think, either. Only one or two of the 50 or more bears I've researched after they've attacked humans have shown any sign of starvation. In fact, the man-eaters—and this was one—all showed excellent stores of body fat—nothing that would lead one to the conclusion that they were desperate for food, or even that they might have been hungry at the time and found the human an easy kill. Who knows?"

We both sat for a moment, and I again broke the silence.

"The bear that killed Lawrence Gordon, at about the same time, stayed and fed on his remains."

Rob Powell looked up a trifle wryly.

"Yeah, it ate most of him."

"Did you have anything to do with that investigation?"

"Yes. I had to go in there officially. I went into his camp."

I interjected what I was thinking.

"That was a marked bear, Number 201 according to Jerry Pentilla and the official reports."

Powell pursed his lips.

"Yes. The one they *killed* was Number 201."

It was not a criticism nor a denial. I wondered.

"You don't think it was Number 201?"

Powell was silent for a moment, thinking of his answer.

"No, I wouldn't say that—entirely. I'd say there was some doubt about it. The laboratory examination of the carcass didn't verify that the animal had killed Gordon. There were no human remains in its intestines or on its outer body. It was somewhere in the vicinity of the killing. But I wouldn't be sure that it was the one."

He was being fair—not critical, simply skeptical. He must have had a reason. My next question was point-blank, the way I felt Powell would answer.

"You must have a reason for that doubt."

"When I was looking around near the area in which they found Gordon, I saw some big bear tracks. From the size of those tracks, I'd say that the grizzly which made them was between 600 and 800 pounds, a really big bear. The bear they killed was fairly small. To me those tracks cast doubt on the decision about which bear did the killing and eating." He pursed his lips thoughtfully. "And the fact that the lab examination produced no evidence, that also cast some doubt."

It was my turn to nod. I wondered if Pentilla, who had been so frank about marking the bear, was aware of the presence of a larger animal in the vicinity. For almost every statistic on bears that leads to conclusion, there is a factor that brings doubt or confusion.

The bear that killed Lawrence Byron Gordon might have been the one about which he had been warned. But it also might not. Tagging and telemetric studies show that mature grizzlies travel within a sixty-mile range. The larger animal whose tracks Powell had seen near the site of the tragedy might have been the culprit.

The Runt VII

From beneath the black clouds at sea came snow driven by fierce gusts of wind. Frozen particles, brittle as sand, spread like a coverlet over the entire landscape. After the storms settled, there was almost complete silence. Arising one morning from their beds beneath snowdrifts, the small group stood mute in the silence. The zero temperatures had induced a change in their body chemistry; drowsiness was taking hold. The yearling cubs no longer played vigorously, but browsed with their mother on scrapings of frozen grass and sedges.

Three days after the snowstorm the winds blew from the opposite direction, piling loose snow against creek banks, deepening the drifts to more than ten feet. The old she-bear chose a curve of the riverbank where the new drifts were deepest. She began to paw away at the outer layer, reaching into the denser crusts beneath. The very first entryway proved conducive to tunneling. Her big paws quickly shoveled the almost sandlike granules backward, and her brood imitated her, pushing the loose diggings out of the tunnel mouth. Although she had begun to dig late in the short winter daylight, the big bear tired abruptly. She lay down in the incomplete tunnel and went to sleep. Confused by the action, the cubs snuggled against her bulk. They too fell into a sound slumber.

When the torpor left the old bear, the cubs, now almost adult size, began to worry her slackened nipples. Resolutely brushing off her brood, she dug well back into the snowbank until she reached frozen gravels that were not suitable for insulation. She angled off into the packed snow, whose softer texture would better retain what little warmth the den offered. She angled the tunnel upward until her claws broke into loose snow above the outer crust. Then she began to hollow out the sleeping chamber until that area was large enough to contain all four bears. She curled in a ball with her legs across her teats and encouraged the confused and torpid cubs to snuggle against her. She firmly resisted their halfhearted efforts to suckle.

The small male was the last to try to feed. Even though he was not hungry and an ample layer of fat had gathered under his belly and along his back and rear, his hunger had become so habitual that he struggled to fulfil the once-incessant demand. Finally, he sank into a deep sleep with the others.

Sometime later the howling of wolves outside warned the she-bear of possible danger, and she awakened almost completely. She listened carefully to the scratching sounds above, but was not unduly alarmed. Long experience told her that the deep and newly hardened crust would finally defeat the short nails of the big dogs. The eyes of the small male opened when she raised her head. He too heard the howls of the wintering wolves and anxiously looked at his mother to gauge the danger. She responded by curling up even more closely in the group. The warmth she had always given to them she now welcomed as they returned it to her.

Once the sound of long, scraping nails digging away snow nearby told the old sow that the she-bear that had been her annual neighbor was late bringing her cub to the denning area. Her own cubs remained in the slumber of near-hibernation.

During late December the old bear shook herself free of the piled bulk of the cubs. She moved lazily toward the outward end of the tunnel entrance. Something, perhaps the efforts of the other sow, had thinned the plug of drifted snow. A glimmer of light was visible through it. Without real volition she broke through the outer crust and shoved her head into the open.

Ghostly white patterns played across the white land, brightening and shading in their intensity like searchlights playing across a snow-filled stadium. The air was still, and a tightly knit net of stars lay in the black bowl overhead. Many times, when she had been free of cubs, and the sun seemed endlessly gone, she had used those lights to travel and hunt by. She knew that the renewed time of heavy feeding upon seals was yet to come. For now she would no longer hunt the arctic night. Turning, she pushed snow into the opened entrance until a slanted bulwark of it was piled against the wind. Slowly, willingly, she curled up with the cubs, and once more slept.

The next time the small male awakened, he found his mother moving about in the ice cavern, pacing almost aimlessly. Lifting his spare frame slowly, he stood unsteadily upon rubbery legs and watched her. She would turn toward the entrance; then, as if distracted by some vague impulse, she would retrace her short path, there to stand staring at the walls. Gradually he became aware of hunger in his belly. The sow's milk supply, he knew, had almost dried up.

She was alternately panting, then yawning, a sign he knew meant indecision or frustration. He nuzzled the other cubs until they opened their eyes. Their mother, too, approached and pushed at them with her nose. As they got to their feet, she again paced back and forth in the cave. When they approached her teats, she woofed and growled.

Finally she dug away the snows blocking the entrance. Reaching solid ice caused by a thaw and refreeze, she smashed at it, then pulled herself out through the loosely packed covering. The yellow, late-February sun was hanging low on the horizon, and its position reassured her. The cubs, too, pushed out into the cold air and stood uneasily staring at the frozen wastes, but an hour later the group was again fast asleep, curled together in the den.

After a week they were spending increasing periods of time outside the cavern. All of them, one by one, had gone a short distance from the winter quarters to defecate their anal plugs. Hunger was becoming a very real demand. The deep calm of a new weather pattern had settled in.

Ten days after their first breakout, the new trek began. The old lady stiffly climbed the pressure ridges lying off the familiar land point of the outward bay. Her cubs followed her almost passively. The smaller male now followed more closely in her footsteps, and settled alongside her shoulder when she paused to survey the ices lying ahead.

Just off the land point, where the last open-water lead had frozen before their sojourn on the land, she halted and raised her long, scarred snout. In the still air she smelled the odor of a ringed-seal pup. For fully ten minutes she tested the scent for direction, and the small male did the same. The odor was familiar to him. It meant food. Impulsively he strode toward it.

An insistent growl and a woof from the sow stopped him. He vaguely remembered the previous year: if he remained back, proceeding only when the signs and sound of struggle on the ice were evident, there would be no remonstrating or cuffing. His experiences with hard-dealt blows had not been lost.

The two other cubs came up to him, and he woofed at them. When the large male attempted to brawl, he bit him hard on the shoulder. The small female remained where she was, and the three of them waited silently.

The form of their mother, angular from weight loss, was sliding almost awkwardly across an open stretch of ice. Her focal point was a mound of crusted snow. While the cubs watched, her movements became more rigid and intense.

Abruptly her long body sailed skyward, arching directly into the top of the hummock and hitting it squarely, but her spare frame almost bounced, without penetrating the small enbankment. Her great forepaws pounded hard upon the outer surface, throwing snow in all directions. A triangle of crust broke free, and she began to dig furiously with her claws.

The small male could no longer resist reacting. In a split second he was beside her, digging furiously. Although she was aware of him, she did not even growl, and kept burrowing deeper.

Covered with the flying snows of her effort, he dug equally furiously on the side which she had first opened but had abandoned. One of his paws broke through into open space, while the other drew him downward into the foul-smelling cavern. A small, fluffy movement against the rounded ice wall drew his attention, and he immediately bit at it.

The whole roof crashed down upon him, and he felt his mother's powerful claws raking him. He rolled quickly against the den wall, still holding onto the struggling white body. Abruptly, that whole body was torn away from him, disappearing through the fractured roof. Deluged, smothered with loose snow, he pushed upward and outward. There were sounds of other activity above, but no sign of the old bear. For an uncertain moment, he remained still.

In the dim light of the small birthing cavern, he spied a circle of open water. Suddenly it bubbled upward, releasing the spent air from the parent seal's lungs. It was a fact of life with which he would become ever more familiar: the loss of a meal.

Hearing the two other cubs above him, he climbed into the broken section of the roof and thrust his head out of the cavern. The last of the small morsel which had been his first real triumph was disappearing into the gulping maw of his mother. His littermates were gobbling up the blood and pieces of flesh from the surrounding snow.

He emitted great hisses and growls to no avail.

How to Stop a Bear

Among the letters I have received regarding attacks by bears is one from Jim Heine, a game guide of Paonia, Colorado. He wrote: "Dear Mike: I am reading your book *Killer Bears* and thought I would write. I was chewed up by a (black) sow bear, September 5, 1975. The story came out in *Outdoor Life* magazine January, 1979, although it wasn't written quite like it really happened. I don't know if you could actually call her a killer bear, but I feel real fortunate to have been in a tree, bitten five times on both legs, and come away with only 27 stitches." Heine did not say so, but he indicates that like most victims of bear attacks, he had no means of defense when he was treed by the bear.

Perhaps *Killer Bears* is a somewhat-misleading title. Bears of all kinds kill people. They also kill large and small game and others of their own kind. Much more often than they kill human beings, they maul and maim them, the victims surviving as broken and mutilated casualties. Occasionally bears abandon their victims for no apparent reason. Often a kill by a bear, like a human killing, is unintentional. Because bears commonly feed upon their victims, the motive of such a killing may be to satisfy the bear's hunger; but because many more maulings and bitings occur than do killings, it must be presumed in such cases that the bear's intention was to assert its dominance.

To come back to Jim Heine in the tree. Apparently the bear was aggressive enough to climb into the tree with the intention of exacting submission from its intended victim. How could Heine and others in similar circumstances discourage such an attack without actually killing or maiming the bear?

To some that may seem a senseless question. The bear was, after all, attacking a human being. Regardless of the cause, it seems appropriate to use force against force; as soon as possible, somebody should kill the bear so that it will not maim or kill its human victim. If the bear is not killed at the time of the attack, it can be trapped and transported. (However, simply transporting a bear to a different setting has been shown not to solve problems.) Alternatively, an authorized government employee can "destroy" the bear (they do not "kill" bears any more). Or it can be trapped and used for experimentation.

Some people persist in believing that all animals, if treated kindly and with deference, will passively accept the human presence (though, unfortunately, there is very little evidence to substantiate such a belief about bears). In their childhood many people hear variations on the story of the man who removed a thorn from a lion's paw and thus achieved a lasting friendship with the beast. More recent and verifiable are the true experiences of James Capen ("Grizzly") Adams and his marvelously loyal and trusted friend the female bear Lady Washington, who padded over mountain trails and through city streets in his wake. The public is also subjected to the genial Smokey the Bear signs along our highways and on or near government lands. Many also know from childhood the humorous and obviously passive Gentle Ben. Recently a beer advertisement showed another "tame" bear in full movement and color on millions of TV screens. There is little reason to scoff at the gentle souls who, having witnessed all this art, legend, and propaganda for most of their lives, believe it. Among people who have not been brought up with pets or who have spent very little time in the wilds, it is unreasonable to expect even a rudimentary understanding of the laws of the wild. Even seeing a predator kill and devour its prey on the screen does not necessarily instill the conviction that "kill or be killed" is one of the very basic rules of nature.

Most of us believe we have the right to enter wild lands and enjoy them just as much as the natural denizens do. How, then, can we best prepare to meet a potentially dangerous wild animal—a bear, or bears? Presumably we do not wish to be injured. Equally, we do not wish to injure bears that depend on the wild lands for their survival as a species. How do we arm ourselves?

That question has been considered well in our national parks; there we are not allowed to carry guns. Only under license may arms be taken into other wild lands. Neither a knife nor an axe is adequate against an attacking bear. In fact, even guns have let their carriers down at the ultimate instant.

Well, the suburban postman or deliveryman may have the best answer!

Because many people keep dogs, and because postmen and other house-to-house callers must visit homes where dogs are allowed to roam free, several repellents have been developed and marketed for their protection. One such product, known as Halt, is commonly used by meter readers, postmen, and company deliverymen. Inside a container is a chemical that can be squirted to a distance of several feet. When this chemical, capsaicin, strikes the eye, it causes intense pain that generally discourages an aggressor but causes no permanent injury. Gasses such as mace and tear gas have been known to cause permanent damage to recipients—and to users. No doubt, however, as manufacturers are alerted to the public demand, there will be many other new and potent devices discovered and produced that will do no permanent harm.

On-going clinical experiments probably will demonstrate the effectiveness of such repellents in discouraging bear attacks. Even so, repellents will never be a total solution to the problem. Thinking back to the man in the tree—and I have investigated many dozens of such incidents—we can only conjecture how such a victim would have fared had he carried a spray deterrent.

The man in the tree, having the force of gravity added to the stream of the repellent, could in all probability dissuade a climbing bear from coming closer simply because of the temporary rush of tears to the animal's eyes. The subsequent blinding effect would at the very least make its bites less accurate. At any rate, the squirt canister is better by far for the man in the tree than the method that one northern Ontario man used to discourage a climbing bear. When run up a tree by a black bear which climbed after him and bit his foot, that resourceful youth produced a cigarette lighter and, tearing pieces from his shirt, lighted them successively and dropped them burning into the face of the bear. The fourth and fifth burning from the ignited cloth so angered the bear that it twice fell out of the tree. It failed to return for a third try. According to its intended victim, it left the area quickly and in an enraged state, swatting unmercifully at anything it passed. Dropping burning material anywhere in a summer- or fall-parched forest, however, might ignite it like a tinderbox. The human tree climber could be roasted along with the bear and much flora and fauna!

In the Churchill area pressurized canisters with attached air horns are commonly used to repel polar bears. In response to my queries, government bear-control officials told me that an air horn definitely deters most white bears—as does the strident honking of a car horn. Yet, because the bears find the noise disturbing rather than alarming, horns should not be considered a certain protection.

Wildlife managers commonly use what they familiarly call "crackers" to ward off the white bears. Mainly, these are shotshells fired from a shotgun. On the other hand, bear-patrol personnel at Churchill told me that as many as fifteen or sixteen "crackers" exploding about, and actually against the fur of, one determined polar bear were necessary to move that animal away from a city house it was visiting.

I saw one such cracker device in the breast pocket of a wildlife photographer. It was about the size of a penlight or heavy fountain pen. When I asked about it, the photographer told me that it was a small form of cracker that was hand-aimed and held. It was, he noted, illegal under Canadian law but was his "last form of defense" in case of emergency.

There have been studies of the effects of repellents on polar bears, but as with grizzly and black-bear studies, the results are inconclusive. In 1983 two scientists, Dr. Lynn Rogers of the Minnesota Forestry Branch, Ely, Minnesota, and Dr. Charles Jonkel, of the University of Montana, informed me that at least a couple more years would be required before any real conclusions were reached.

The days that I spent observing Dr. Rogers's black-bear studies were interesting and informative. I happened to be a witness as Rogers tested a determined female black bear with a spray repellent. His annual study notes show that six bears were experimentally sprayed, five of them free-roving black bears. The notes describe the effects of the capsaicin solution as follows:

"Upon being sprayed in the eyes, all bears immediately shut their eyes, whirled and quickly retreated at least seven meters, where they rubbed their eyes with their paws. No bear showed any aggression or made any vocalization after being sprayed. Previous tests have shown that capsaicin solution produces no lasting harm to the skin or eyes."

The last sentence is a reference to a 1962 experiment in which a researcher intentionally sprayed capsaicin solution into his right eye. He reported that the eye burned for nearly thirty minutes despite washing and blotting, but the next day the eye had returned to normal. Such dedication is not uncommon among good research people. The information thus received is invaluable in efforts to determine the effects of capsaicin on bears. Dr. Rogers carried no defensive weapon other than the squirt repellent while handling and filming bears.

Also being tested are folding devices that expand to a large size quite quickly and by their apparent bulk repel and deter bears. One such device is the common umbrella. When I queried meter readers, postmen, and delivery men about their favorite defenses against aggressive dogs, one of them showed me a small folding umbrella that he occasionally pops open in front of him. He declared that it had always driven off any dog with which he had a problem during his rounds. He also carried a liquid repellent in a canister in his inner breast pocket, but he had not used it often because doing so would not "be good public relations." He did say, however, that rather than be bitten or injured, he would use it. Generally, though, the opened umbrella was enough.

Large objects suddenly produced between a man and a beast are the subject of some of Dr. Charles Jonkel's studies at the University of Montana. He informed me that he and his associates used a large section of plywood sheeting. At first, the edge of the sheet was presented to the animal. Then, as the bear continued its approach, the plywood sheet was turned so that the flat side was toward the oncoming animal, presenting the visual appearance of much greater bulk. The approaching animal, after suddenly being confronted with what appeared to be a very large, bulky object, immediately turned aside and usually retreated. The effect of bulk as a deterrent is also manifest when bears in the wild are observed to respond very quickly to the approach of a bear that is apparently larger than they are.

Current evidence suggests that in the future liquid or gas repellents will prove the most effective of all repellents. "Crackers" and other explosive devices might start fires and in some situations are illegal. Bulky expanding units may prove unreliable and unwieldy. Air horns definitely are annoying and repellent but they lack the painful effect that might be necessary to deter a bear. As has been noted earlier, the use of a lethal weapon such as a gun is generally quite restricted—and undesirable except as a final measure. Thus a small penlike squirt gun filled with a solution that causes intense pain but has no permanent effect is to be preferred as a weapon of defense. Besides being effective, these canisters are both practical to carry and readily available.

That such items as capsaicin squirt guns are subject to governmental regulation does restrict their availability to the general public. What good reason justifies withholding such repellents from citizens who would use them only to avoid injury? Like sticks, stones, switchblades, and handguns, such weapons can be procured by would-be criminals and used to disable intended victims. Restricting their availability only leaves the law-abiding person defenseless; the criminal will always find a weapon. Instead, illegal use of combative or defensive arms should be subject to very definite and unrelenting punishment. If squirt repellents were perfected and readily available to people who in their recreation or work are subject to animal attacks, much human and animal misery and tragedy would be prevented. Knowing that both the animal and I can be protected from any permanent injuries by use of a repellent, I would argue for that protection and willingly take any consequences.

The Runt VIII

The first invasion of a seal's birthing den had been relatively easy. Two days passed, however, before they could break into another. The thaw that had come during their long sleep had made the ice caps almost impenetrable. Because of the mother's weight loss, her impact was not enough to break them. By the time she dug through the shell-like coverings, the seals would have departed. Her desperate search drew them ever farther out on the ice.

Miles from their home bay, she saw a black cloud hanging low on the horizon. Recognizing it, she traveled fast toward it, followed by her brood. It was a moisture cloud, which in calm weather accompanies the formation of polynyas in the ice during winter months.

Young seals that were not birthing would be using the open water there. She was growing more gaunt and stiff each day and the cubs were almost constantly murmuring with hunger and disappointment. There was no milk left in her teats to sustain them.

The smell of open sea drew her on. The small male almost kept pace. The scent and feel of water made him eager to enter it. Tidal pressure ridges showed ahead. Almost forgetting her cubs, the gaunt old bear lunged upward and over the bulwarks to slide down the opposite side in the hope of finding an open lead.

Suddenly she heard clearly the whoosh of small whales spouting. The scent of their exhalations told her their location, and she mounted the final pressure ridge in near-desperation.

Before her was a pool of shallow, open water closed at the seaward end. The free ice had been forced by wind under the edge of the shore ice, trapping a pod of small white whales. Six of the long-tailed belugas, including two calves, circled in the ice-bottomed pool, desperately seeking an opening to the salt water that was now a hundred yards away.

Without hesitation the big female bear plunged into the pool and swam deliberately toward the closest calf. She had no fear of the large adults: their panic was evident in their frequent spoutings. The calf was swimming slowly toward the group that was forming.

Swimming quickly alongside it, she swatted with all her strength at the unblinking black eye nearest her. The calf quivered from head to fluke, then lay still on the water. As a final sigh escaped from its lungs, the old bear shoved its head onto the shelf of ice and scrambled from the water to grip the snout in her teeth.

Back legs set and slipping frequently, the small male was there pulling with her. The two of them dragged the five-hundred-pound carcass onto the ice. The mother and her cubs ripped into the blubber beneath the rubbery hide.

When her belly hung low, the old she-bear lay across the tail fluke, licking at her bloodied paws. She seemed unaware of the other five threshing, panicked belugas.

Not so the small male. Belly filled to capacity, he sauntered almost cockily along the edge of the entrapment and sat watching the frantic movements of the disoriented pod.

Finally, he decided to try his own luck. As he had witnessed his mother do countless times, he crept silently along the ice until he was in line with most of the whales. Trembling with eagerness, he waited for one of the mammals to swim close enough for a headlong jump. When it was six feet away, he jumped.

His back legs sailed him missilelike out over the water to land squarely upon the back of a large adult beluga. Panicked by the sudden attack, the adult spurted blindly into the group, stampeding them toward the end of the pond where the mother polar bear was feeding on the calf blubber. The cub drove his nails and teeth into the skin of the adult. The whale desperately plunged full tilt into the herd. Unable to change course because of its impact with the others, the beluga slid halfway up the ice shelf. The sow immediately sank her teeth into the bulge behind its neck and with her forepaw fiercely struck its head. The struggles of the large white animal were reduced to death tremors.

Satisfied that the prize he was riding was his own, the small male growled deeply at his approaching littermates. It was several minutes before he would allow them even to lick at the blood congealing on the snow.

That night, bellies filled, the four bears curled together behind a tall triangle of broken pressure ice.

The depth of the growl that awakened them was menacing beyond anything the young cub had heard before. Instinctively, he was on his feet in the instant that his mother also rose. Fifteen feet away, at the carcass of the adult beluga, an enormous male bear's triangular head rose above the intervening ice ridge. The answering growl from his mother was startling. She sprang over the barrier directly at the big male.

Rising with incredible speed to his hind legs, he dodged her attack. As she slid beneath him and stopped against the bulk of the beluga, he smashed down heavily with both front paws on her ribs. Desperately she twisted away, barely missing the bite of his jaws. Unnerved by his vicious strength, she kicked herself backward thirty feet along the sloping ice. Satisfied that she would give him no more trouble, the male turned to feed again on the whale carcass.

Limping badly, the female circled wide, uttering a series of low calls. Then, with her offspring at her side, she began a slow, limping trot that would put distance between them and the marauding male. Her breathing was hoarse in her throat. When eventually she lay down in a shelter of erupted pressure ice, the runt licked at her face. In her nostrils was fresh blood, and her response to his attentions was slight. Still frightened, they huddled against her.

The whimper of the other cubs awakened the runt. The overnight bed was colder than usual. He pressed close to the bulk of his mother, but there was no warmth there. Her body, usually limber, was stiff. He sniffed deeply. The smell of death was in the sheltered hollow. He nudged the sow's head. One eye was open and glazed with ice. The whimpering of his littermates was unnerving, but he too whimpered. In the full daylight, when the mother still showed no signs of moving, they worried briefly at her head, which was unresponsive and solidly frozen to the ice.

They were distracted by the howl of a wolf, which was echoed moments later from another direction. The howls were repeated intermittently. Then they began to converge.

Remembering the sow's apprehension of the big dogs, and knowing that there would be no protection from his mother, the smaller male took the initiative. Aware that wolves seldom entered water in search of prey, he trotted toward the tumble of ice leading seaward. The two other cubs followed silently at his heels.

The lead had been forced on him.

CHAPTER 9

The Kokanees Were Running

"I should have packed my .308 rifle, but it was a park—a very big park with a lot of grizzlies. The government men had quite a few grizzlies tagged in the area. You aren't supposed to pack a rifle in a park area. Maybe it wouldn't have happened to us if we had. The grizzly just came around the bend of the creek and came right at me."

Wilfred Lulu was sitting in the chair opposite me in the bright, modern living room of his ranch-style bungalow in a smart new subdivision in Cache Creek, British Columbia. His tanned, smiling face was full of animation, the features that he had inherited from his Indian ancestors adding to his rugged good looks. He did not appear to have the wired-together disfiguring scar tissue or facial contours so noticeable in many who have survived an attack by a bear. It was heartening to see a man so unscathed by the experience.

"You don't show much sign of a grizzly attack."

"Thanks. I was lucky."

In the corner of the room nearest my chair, leaning decoratively against the wall was a set of elk antlers separated from the skull, a Royal with very large central beams. On a small table by the wall were two glass-mounted photographs of very good-looking horses. The furnishings were in contemporary good taste.

I nodded toward the framed photographs.

"Those look like registered quarter horses?"

"They are. My daughter, Elaine Herbert, has won several barrel races on one of them. The other is a comer. I do a little calf roping. Elaine won second place in the Canadian Indian Rodeo Association and the Northern Indian Association events in 1978. They were good horses. But the one on the left had to be destroyed; he had swamp fever."

"That's too bad! You have been a cowboy then?" I said.

"Oh, yes! Most of my life."

"Where were you born?"

"Right here, fifty-two years ago. I cowboyed for Cornwall Ranch when I was growing up as a kid. And over at Ashcroft Manor Ranch."

"Did you ever run into any of the local grizzlies?"

"Only a couple of times. I've seen grizzly tracks around Cornwall Lookout a couple of times. Near Joe Bedard Lake. My son shot a deer, had to leave it, and a grizzly was eating on it when he got back. Clarence—with Ralph Sandy—ran up to it on a horse and yelled. The grizzly backed off and left. There aren't many grizzlies left in this country."

That is a fact: cattlemen and bears do not get along, and usually the bears are the losers, the grizzly first, then the black bear. Both species do take calves, though not many, and bears occasionally disrupt ranch management.

I acknowledged that and more:

"You never quite know what to expect from a bear. Your own attack is about as typical as one can expect. You can't know what to do: stand your ground, fall on your face, back up, or stand still. If they decide to come, you get it!"

He nodded with a rueful smile. I prompted him.

"What were you doing in that far north country? You're a cowboy."

He smiled, showing a white line of even teeth.

"I also handle big equipment, Mike. The big stuff: cats, scrapers. There's a lot more money in handling big equipment than there is in riding the range for a ranch! I change around. I was working for the Alwin Mining Company. We were proving up the claim for a new mine, gridding the area for core drilling. The young guy with me, Gordon Wood, was an engineering student from Clarkson, Ontario."

I acknowledged the situation:

"More than one mining exploration guy has got it after years without a gun! Our son, Grant, is a mechanical and civil engineer. When he was eighteen or nineteen, like many young bloods he was out in the bush on Vancouver Island doing soil and water samples all through the mountains. He ran into black bears on a couple of occasons. I suggested that he pack a rifle. His answer was, 'Heck, Dad! You've always told me they won't hurt me!' He laughed at my suggestion. He had a short-barreled .303 British commando carbine that I'd given him, but he said it was too heavy to pack all day—with the other gear."

Wilfred nodded with an appreciative frown—which rapidly turned to another rueful grin.

"You never think *you* are going to be the one who gets it!" He paused for a moment as if choosing his words. "Mike, did you ever think about how you were going to die—where you'd meet your Maker?"

It was a surprise question. He waited with an expectant expression in his eyes. I pulled my nose thoughtfully and exhaled as he waited for my answer.

"Well, yes. I have—occasionally. More where I'd like to go than anything. Yes, I guess I've wondered. I hope it's not in bed!"

Lulu's expression changed to agreement.

"Yeah, not in bed!" He was shaking his head. "I've often wondered where. It's funny, when that bear started coming, I thought, 'This is my Maker!'"

Now I was nodding in agreement.

"Yeah. I know what you mean. I've had that sensation a couple of times—too damn close!"

"This one was pretty close—" he nodded reflectively. "This grizzly."

"Tell me about it! When was it?"

"It was the thirtieth of August, 1969. The kokanees were running in the streams, and the bears were feeding on them. You'd see some of the marked bears, with a yellow collar and a miniature radio set on them, carrying electronic beepers. Or a colored ribbon that the scientists who were studying them had put on them after they measured and tagged them."

Mine was a loaded question, one that had to be asked:

"Was the bear that came after you tagged or wearing a collar?"

He shook his head emphatically.

"No, it wasn't a tagged one! I saw it clearly as it came. The stream zigzagged there, and we were walking the beach, between the bank and the water. There were lots of grizzly tracks in the sand. We knew they were in the area—just didn't figure on having to face one, I guess. This one was about thirty feet away when I first saw it. It came right at me! I guess it heard us talking and rattling our tools and equipment—we were carrying survey chain and an axe—and it came at me just like that.

"Did you get a swipe at it with the axe?"

"No. My buddy, Gordon, was carrying that. The bear just came so quickly there was no time to do anything. I put my arm in front of me. That was when I thought, 'This is my Maker!' It bit into the arm, then threw me into the creek. I remembered what my Dad said: 'Play dead.' I believed him. That's what all the old people used to say. They used to face them with bows and arrows. I guess they knew the best things to do. I remembered shoving my head right under water and trying to stay still. He was mouthing my arm. I guess when I came up for breath he got some bites at my head, took a chunk out of the top of it.

"He'd pull me over, I'd roll back. I remember thinking, 'I got that one over!' My buddy was still standing near the bank. He was yelling, but there was nothing he could do. I must have been bleeding pretty badly into the stream. There didn't seem to be anything he could do to help. Then suddenly Gordon took off downstream. The grizzly left me and took off after him. Gordon went up the five-foot bank, and the bear missed him.

"I lifted my head from the creek. The grizzly was hightailing it right down the creek, not on the bank. I thought he was leaving. Then I heard Gordon scream. The bear had him. It had grabbed him in the fleshy part of the leg and was dragging him sideways. He only screamed once, then there was silence. Maybe he fainted with the pain, or played dead. I don't know.

"After a while I raised my head and asked, 'Gordon, how you doing?'

"He said, 'Keep quiet! He may still be around here!'

"We waited a few minutes longer, then stumbled about a quarter of a mile to our truck. We were both pretty bloody from the experience.

"There was a CB in the truck, and we radioed camp headquarters. They sent out a chopper right away. I remember thinking, 'It's 10:30 at night—it was still light in the Yukon—and there wouldn't be a doctor in.' But there were all sorts of people to greet the copter.

"It was a surprise. There was even a newspaper girl there. I remember her saying, 'Isn't this wonderful! To be right on the spot to interview someone who has just been mauled by a grizzly!' She came right into the operating room, before the nurses shooed her out. I never did lose consciousness."

He was looking at his arm.

"You know the only time it really hurt was when the teeth hit my funny bone. That felt like an electric shock had zapped me. That *hurt*!"

"What about Wood? How was he?" I asked.

"When I got to him, he was still lying there, in shock I guess—perhaps a little hysterical. He was bleeding, but not badly bitten. In fact, they sewed up his ass, and he went out a couple of days later to the same spot to get our gear. I was only in hospital a couple of weeks."

My curiosity was still unsatisfied.

"Did they get the bear that mauled you guys?"

Wilfred Lulu's face was immobile for a moment before he broke out in a confidential grin.

"I think so."

I waited as he studied his own thoughts and judged my reactions.

"Mike, it was a park area. I told you they were marking bears in there. You weren't supposed to pack a gun, so no one went out to kill it."

I was watching his face, wondering what was behind that statement. He finally shrugged.

"About a week later there was a hell of a crashing in the storeroom off the camp kitchen. One of the guys looked out, and there was a grizzly tearing the hell out of the place. Some guy said, Okay, you grizzly hunters, if you want one, it's right here on your doorstep!"

Wilfred Lulu looked at me thoughtfully before continuing. I reassured him by saying, "If a grizzly came tearing into my camp, I wouldn't give a damn what the regulations in the park were. If it was smashing up a storeroom—I'd kill it!"

Wilfred said quietly, "I guess someone did!"

My own grin confirmed his thoughts: simply that men will do what they think best at the time, law or no law. Law is pretty poor armor with which to protect flesh and blood from any angry bear. Somewhere reason and resolve must bridge the gap. I said so.

"But, Wilf, what makes you think that it was the same grizzly that attacked you?"

He lifted his arm and undid the cuff of his shirt.

"Well, first of all, the attack happened only about a mile from the camp. The bear that they shot had badly festered jaws. The head was big, and the top teeth were broken off. You look at my arm." He pointed to several scars. "The underside is marked with big holes where the big lower teeth went in. On the upper side there are just small cuts that would come from small teeth—no big ones. Same on one side of my neck."

My surprise at the logic was evident. He held out the marked arm to show me clearly where the perforations were.

I nodded my head.

"That's pretty conclusive evidence, Wilf. You know, that is a funny thing! The bear that attacked Bob McKelvie was reported as having festering, worn teeth. I looked at its skull a couple of days ago. Doug Robertson has it at his home in Kamloops. It had old worn and rotten teeth."

Wilf was interested in the statement.

"Yeah, that could be what makes some of them cranky," he said.

"It could be! Was there any sign of a kill near where you fellows were?"

Again he shook his head emphatically.

"None! The grizzlies were eating Kokanees on the river. The fish were running—spawning. You know, the little red salmon. But come to think of it, Andrew Hanna, a young fellow who was in the hospital at the same time with me was also attacked by a grizzly. He said he was looking at a grizzly kill when the bear hit him. He was lucky! There was a helicopter hovering right there to scare it off."

Here was a surprise: another item to add to my statistics on attacks by bears with dental problems, as opposed to attacks by sows with cubs and by bears protecting their kills. I said so to Wilfred. He nodded, then changed the subject.

"You know horses, Mike?"

"A little. When I was a kid I used to exercise them for a riding stable—most of them quarter horses—and I rode them on the prairies at my grand-father's. As a big-game hunter I had to spend a lot of time on horseback—sore ass and all!"

He laughed, an infectious grin on his face.

"It's a good life—tough. And it doesn't pay very much!"

That had been my own experience, I ruefully acknowledged:

"Yeah. Recently I've ridden a couple of fall roundups at Lac La Hache at preg-testing time. A friend of mine has a ranch up there."

It was time to go. Wilf thrust his hand out enthusiastically.

"Mike, next time you come this way, you come in!"

My own grip was much more than casual.

"Yeah, Wilf. I'll bring you a book."

"I'd sure like that."

The Runt IX

The waters of the polynya strongly attracted the lead cub. Its wide expanses offered security, which seemed nowhere assured on the ice. He plunged into the sea, followed by his siblings. Tiring after an hour of aimless swimming, they climbed weakly onto the shelf of a large piece of drift ice. Wind and tidal current moved them almost fifty miles a day during their three-day sanctuary. When the bumping of its inshore edge in shallow waters aroused them, they moved uncertainly ashore. There, detecting the scent of a ringed-seal carcass, they eagerly trotted upwind.

A new, warm scent mingled with the seal odor. It was the smell of their own kind. Alarmed, they halted. The newer scent, however, was familiar; this was the young sow that twice had denned nearby. With the mingled odors came the scent of her single cub.

Hesitantly, driven by hunger, they were drawn across the shore ice until the remnant of the ringed-seal carcass was in clear view. Only a tiny movement was visible near it. Alerted by their approach, a white puff of fur shot skyward, the arctic fox jumping high to reconnoiter. Growling, it arched, its back in defiance; starved and abruptly reckless, the cubs charged toward the torn carcass.

Avidly, as the unnerved fox scurried away, they gobbled up tidbits; seconds later, their heads were buried deep in the flesh of the ringed seal. A warning woof came from close at hand, a note of aggression in the sound. The young mother and her cub were approaching. Circling downwind, her narrow snout always pointed directly at them, the sow stayed between the intruders and her cub. When she had sized them up, she put her head down and approached, an explosive huffing issuing from her throat. Her cub trailed behind her apprehensively.

Unwillingly the lead male retreated from the carcass, his belly not quite filled. His littermates backed away with him. The large bear rushed forward, feinted, then stopped short. Twice she rushed them, and twice they retreated. She and her own cub began to feed.

As the summer days became warmer, the adult female proved to be a good hunter—better than their own mother toward the end of her days. All four cubs had begun to play together. Soon the sow adopted the entire brood and without complaint allowed them to follow her. Filled daily to his capacity and seldom hungry, the male that had been the runt was outgrowing the others. When the young mother located a fruitful hunting or food-producing area, he was quickly at her side. The myriads of ducks and grebes, the swirling masses of shorebirds, and the flocks of noisy geese, each became prey. Watching his foster mother, the dominant cub quickly learned to swim under a flock of water-borne eiders and grasp them from beneath with a swift lunge of his rising jaws. When the molting geese were grounded, his headlong rushes among them left fluttering and dying long-necked fowl that the three trailing cubs finished off. His eagerness to create such mayhem was encouraged by his growing dominance of the cubs. He killed not only for food but also for the submissive licking he received from the long black tongues of his siblings. After gorging themselves, the bears began their instinctive ritual of cleaning offal from their coats and paws. In this, too, the three now always deferred to the former runt and even sought his initiatives.

When summer was well advanced amid plenty, he had far outgrown the other cubs. The group had easily adapted to the young mother's bent, traveling in an arc that brought them back to the land with its scents and smells of caribou and musk oxen. Berries were abundant among the mosses, the grasses and sedges full and rich with seed. Most of the time the former runt browsed or grazed comfortably with his group.

One day when the young male licked at the face of the larger female, the snap of her teeth just missed his jaw. Surprised, he stood off from her, yawning broadly in confusion.

Detecting a strangely attractive scent emanating from her, he moved to her rear to test it. At that she bit him on the shoulder. The other cubs, made curious by his surprised yelp, moved in. Then the mother ran directly at her own cub, swatting him forcefully. Surprised and fearful, all four cubs backed off. When they lay down to enjoy the warmth of the sun, she did not rest with them. Three days later she had become actively aggressive. One frosty morning she was gone. She did not return.

During the ensuing weeks the abandoned two-year-olds remained together. A slight torpor came over them as their local daily food supplies dwindled. Their leader grazed alternately upon the frost-bitten grasses with their still-active ground squirrels and lemmings. Occasionally out at sea he dove for kelp. Much of the time they rested as a group on the beach, sometimes half-buried in the wind-drifted piles of loose kelp. The air had become more crisp, and a strong sea wind was gusting almost constantly from the north. Large green waves topped with foamy whitecaps beat day after day upon the frozen sands of the beaches.

One day they heard an unfamiliar noise, from the otherwise still air above them. A large bird flew over. Its size was disconcerting, if not menacing. The second time it visited, it seemed to approach more directly, circling. The third day, the noisy bird hovered above them even longer, then gradually it sank to the land.

The lead cub, wary of the invader's size and noise, moved along the beach away from the landing. The other three remained in a group. His warning woof, copied from their parents' calls, lacked sufficient authority. In fact, his own male littermate trotted inquisitively toward the bird.

As the cubs watched, smaller chicks issued from the strange bird and moved beachward. Tall, upright, with the stance of animals not alarmed but inquisitive, they did not appear threatening. They walked erect. The lead cub had witnessed that attitude occasionally in the stance of an alert, inquisitive caribou or in an uncertain member of his own kind. However, these visitors remained erect. Their attitude was disconcerting.

Three of the tall, dark beings approached the lead cub's littermate, now also standing on his back legs to survey and assess the interlopers. At a respectful distance the tall visitors stopped. The sun glanced off a slender, polished object extending from the forepaws of the closest visitor. A bright spear of yellow light suddenly flashed from its outward end, followed by a sharp, hard report even more intense than new ice breaking under pressure. As if bitten without warning, the young male turned and batted at the air. Feeling the sting of something in his haunch, he bit quickly at the area. Too late connecting the pain with the intruders, he ran directly toward his larger littermate. The invading group followed. For the first time the guttural sounds of mankind loudly reached the lead cub's ears.

"There's a bigger one! Right where he's heading! I hope it sticks around—when this one goes down!"

Answering sounds, quiet, short growls, came from the other intruders. He watched them carefully. His other littermates, now shielded by a rocky point, had become alarmed and were trotting fast in the opposite direction along the open beach.

As the leader watched, the normally surefooted, now stricken, young male faltered and stopped in his tracks. With lowered head, he swayed unsteadily then flopped to his belly and stretched out on the sparse snow, legs extended.

The intermittent growls of the intruders took on a higher pitch.

"He's down—okay! We'll get the other one. Jack, give that one the antidote!"

Abruptly the lead cub recognized that the dominant intruder, its stance now menacing and aggressive, was moving toward him. Abandoning his reclining mate, he swiftly trotted away. After he had covered several hundred yards, frequent glances over his shoulders told him that the lone intruder was no longer in pursuit.

On the rise of a rocky headland, safely unseen, he watched the three visitors huddle over the prone body of his littermate. In the distance, also well warned by the vagaries of the aliens, the two other cubs had taken refuge in the broken rocks of the shore ridges. It was almost sundown when the abrupt, thunderous roar of the big bird again broke the silence.

During the ensuing twilight, the leader went downwind, trying to detect the scent of his fallen littermate. When he caught the scent, it carried the smell, not of blood and death but of warm life. Furtively he approached the body, a humped shadow on the leeward side of a snow-filled willow brush clump. The prone young male was breathing heavily. The leader touched his nose to its mouth, then licked at the head with some curiosity; normally the other animal would respond immediately.

Abruptly, his own head went up, listening, wary, sensing the stealthy approach of others. Like ghosts the other young bears came slowly from the evening mists.

Still unnerved by their experience but unsure of the alternatives, all four bedded down for the night behind the willows where the tranquilized cub had been deposited. The brush sheltered them from the gusting winds.

The strange man scent lingered. Undesirable and disturbing, it was an odor that the lead cub would remember and avoid thenceforth.

CHAPTER 10

The Unguarded Moment

She was a tall, gangly-legged doe, and her coat was tattered with the uneven-ness of springtime molt, as she came out of the timber near Cameron Lake in Waterton Lakes National Park, Alberta. I put my hand out and talked to her. Still she approached, her large brown eyes appearing to bulge on each side of her head, accentuating her large mulelike ears. She extended her head fully as she came, almost unhesitating, to where I stood alongside the front bumper of my Jeep.

"How are you, old girl? You look skinny." I noted out loud.

Her shiny nose was within inches of my left hand as I said, "Too bad, old lady, all you get is salt."

Before I had completed that sentence the cold wetness of her muzzle was touching my hand. Her tongue remained in her mouth. She did not lick, just nuzzled and pulled back. Her eyes, brown with a flicker of light on them, were on mine.

I shook my head. "Parks don't allow you to be fed, old girl."

She backed off, moving slowly toward the timber.

She got only the touch of human empathy and the salty residue of per-spiration, but to me she gave an inexplicable feeling of oneness with the world.

Just five minutes earlier, at Little Prairie Picnic Ground, 1.7 miles back along the entrance road, I had photographed the beautiful setting where five-year-old Allison Muser had been bitten, torn, and killed by a grizzly bear.

I had gone on along the road from Little Prairie Picnic Ground to check the entire area surrounding the site of the attack. The extraordinary early June snows on the northern slopes of the vast mountainous cup at the far end of still-frozen Cameron lake had drawn me from my Jeep with camera in hand. As I was returning to the camper, I realized that the ice in my re-frigerator was low. Because I was unlikely to find block ice in Waterton Lakes Village that early in the season, I took a plastic bag from the cup-board, and, using a saucer, stripped back the leaves covering some snow near the vehicle and ladled ice crystals into the bag. When I looked up, I was surprised to see the old doe about twenty feet away in the bush. I had been thinking of bears, and seeing her brownish coat moving between the trees had given me a real start.

I straightened up, gasping, "You old dame, you made me jump!" Then, as she stared back, I added, "How are you? Come on, let's have a look at you."

She remained quite still while I was talking to her. When I turned to walk away, the sounds of her steps on the old snow crust came quite clearly as she followed me. She walked right out onto the blacktop of the parking lot. I pursed my lips and squeaked at her, talking to her softly. She just stood there irresolute. After opening the back door of the camper, I placed the packed snow in the cooler, then looked for a map that I needed. When I came out again, the doe was moving along the skirt of timber, toward the front of the vehicle and parallel to it. My thoughts were "She's been fed before. She's used to looking for a handout. Too bad that parks have to prohibit the feeding of all animals. But the real bastards among humankind, those who are amused by putting pepper in bread, razor blades in Hallowe'en candies, they spoil things for the good ones!"

Similarly, those who feed a deer are committing an act quite different from those who put out camp leavings for a bear. A defensive doe might slash out with her front hooves to protect her fawn. Possible, but highly unlikely.

A grizzly bear from this same wooded area killed a young girl, whose feelings toward it were probably the same wonderment and excitement that was now traveling through my sixty-six-year-old frame following the trusting nuzzle of that doe mule deer.

Less than an hour before, right in the town of Waterton Lakes, two young wild mountain sheep had run at each other and butted heads alongside the first main-street signpost. As I drove slowly past them, they had backed off to butt again. When I was just past them, four more bighorn rams had ambled up the center of the main highway entrance, their enormous, top-heavy serrated brown horns circling in concentric rings at the sides of their heads. The approach of the Jeep only twenty feet behind them had not hurried their unconcerned pace along the street. Nearby, on the lawns of two local cottages, groups of three to five ewes and lambs had walked or fed.

During the previous evening my passage onto the main street had been blocked by ten or twelve bighorn sheep, wandering about, less fearful than domestic sheep or cows. Like the episode with the deer, all this conveyed an air of unreality. When I stopped at the park ranger's house to press the doorbell, a single long-legged ewe was ambling up the opposite sidewalk. I spoke to her casually.

"What in hell are you doing down here? You should be up in those mountains!"

Her ears perked up, and with her yellowish eyes focused on my face, she came straight toward me. I was uneasy; she was a big animal. I looked about for signs of a lamb, just in case she was being protective. There were none. As I walked over to the front seat of the truck for some writing paper, she came right across the street. I thought, "Damn! You can't feed them. Wonder if she thinks this sheet of paper in my hand is food and wants it."

I leaned over the engine hood and wrote a note to the ranger, pretending she was not there. When I turned around, she was standing within six feet of me, and as I moved along the side of the camper toward the house, she followed me like a dog. I talked quietly to her.

"You old dame! I can't feed you. This is a note for the ranger. Now, damn you, don't give me a bad time. If you eat it, I'll just have to write another."

She followed me right up to the ranger's back door, where I tucked the note into the crack of the jamb. When I turned she was about five feet away, and as I spoke to her, her head cocked to one side.

"Now, you leave that damn note alone. Hear me?"

She stood watching me as I walked past her stern and returned to the camper. She was still staring as I got into the cab. Having filmed mountain sheep on their home ranges in the Cassiar Mountains and in the Cariboo Mountains of British Columbia, I knew that the closest they would allow me to come was about 150 yards. Usually they spook at 300 yards, particularly if they have been hunted—even at a mile, if they see humans moving in their direction. This unusual tameness was disconcerting.

My mental response was, "Jeez, Bambi land for real!" It is difficult to believe if you haven't seen it.

The townsfolk did not seem even to notice the animals. On the weekend of July 2, 1977, Paul and Anne Muser of Regina, Saskatchewan, brought their five- and eight-year-old daughters, Allison and Philipa, to visit the wonder-world of Waterton Lakes National Park, where aeons ago the Rocky Mountains were thrust broken-plate fragments 5,000 to 10,000 feet above the surrounding plains. As one looks to the south, west, and north, the grandeur of the park gives new meaning to the words "enormous," "stupendous," and "colossal." In fact, to the uninitiated the vistas seem unreal.

Paul Muser took his family about nine miles up the Cameron Lake road, where he went fishing in Cameron Creek, near the Little Prairie Picnic Ground, which, in spite of its name, is in a vast, winding mountain valley at the bottom of an immense tree-covered rockslide that extends thousands of feet up into the snows of the mountain ranges. The picnic ground nestles by a crystal-clear creek in a deep greensward—the most likely looking piece of grizzly-bear country you could find anywhere!

Most hunters choosing a place to watch for wild animals crossing from range to range would want to sit on the side of that slide, right where it rises above the picnic and outhouse sites—where Paul Muser left his young daughters to play while he wandered along the bush-lined banks of the creek (which flows within twenty feet of the park service buildings).

Because the Musers were immigrants to Canada from South Africa, it is unlikely that they had any idea what a perfect big-game environment they had chosen for picnicking. It is the natural habitat of both grizzlies and black bears—not to mention elk, mountain sheep, hoary marmots, bluejays, hawks, deer, and squirrels. Yet few people besides big-game hunters would consider the valley anything but a beautiful wilderness vista.

The day before, while driving to Waterton Lakes National Park, I had passed through Lethbridge, Alberta. There, at the offices of the *Herald*, I had picked up the file of stories that the newspaper ran at the time of the Muser tragedy. They began on July 2, 1977, with the story of the killing and continued reporting the news as it came:

FIVE-YEAR-OLD DIES AFTER BEAR MAULING

Waterton Lakes National Park wardens are searching today for a black bear that killed a five-year-old Regina girl as she waded in Cameron Creek Friday evening.

The attack occurred at the Little Prairie Picnic Ground, located between the town site and Cameron Lake, at 7:30 p.m., Park Superintendent Jean Pilon said in a telephone interview today.

Allison Muser died en route to a Calgary hospital after her parents had rushed her to Cardston General Hospital.

The girl and her eight-year-old sister were wading in Cameron Creek while their father was fishing a short distance away but out of sight. He came running when the girls screamed and scared the bear away.

Four wardens are looking for the bear, and two more will be joining the search with tracking dogs.

"As this has been the only bear encounter in the area this spring we're pretty sure there is only one bear in the valley," said Pilon.

"From the descriptions we have it is a four-year-old bear, which should make it easy for park wardens to identify," said Pilon.

[Monday, July 4, 1977]

WARDENS SHOOT BEAR, HUNT ANOTHER BLAMED FOR MAULING

By Mike Harrop
Herald Staff Writer

WATERTON—Park wardens have killed one of two black bears involved in the death of a Regina child, but the hunt continues for the bear blamed for the fatal mauling.

Waterton Lakes National Park Superintendent Jean Pilon said an average-sized brown-colored black bear sow was cornered and shot with the aid of a helicopter Sunday evening.

The bear was one of two bruins involved in the slaying of Allison Muser, 5, who died enroute to a Calgary hospital Friday after being attacked by a black bear.

Allison and her sister were sitting on the bank of Cameron Creek while their father fished within hearing distance, Pilon said.

The surviving sister told wardens the girls saw two bears—one black with a brown snout and a smaller brown bear.

The attacking bear was identified as the black one, Pilon said.

Wardens theorize the remaining bear is a boar because the black bear mating season is underway.

Pilon described the attack as a relatively savage, "mean" attack. The bear appears to have intended to eat the girl. No other cause for the incident has been found, he pointed out.

An around-the-clock hunt is underway in the Cameron Valley, where armed wardens are using bear tracking dogs and the helicopter to locate the remaining bruin.

The bear is thought to still be in the immediate area, although they "travel all over the place" during the mating season, Pilon said.

The valley is closed to hikers, and visitors are being told to remain by their automobiles and to fish Cameron Lake from boats only.

Other areas of the park are considered safe for visitors, Pilon said.

However, he cautioned that the entire park is a bear area, and persons should govern themselves accordingly.

The incident was Waterton Park's first bear-caused fatality, although an Illinois girl was killed in a grizzly bear attack last fall, about 35 miles away in Glacier National Park.

The last serious bear incident in Waterton occurred two years ago when a sleeper was mauled by a black bear, after he swatted an animal walking past outside his tent.

[July 5, 1977]

PURSUING WARDENS FEAR BEAR HAS LEFT WATERTON

By Mike Harrop
Herald Staff Writer

The search continues for the bear that killed a Regina child Friday in Waterton Lakes National Park, and wardens now fear the bear may have left the park.

The animal may have moved into Glacier National Park in Montana or into British Columbia, a Parks Canada spokesman said in a telephone interview today from Calgary.

The site where a bear killed Allison Muser, 5, is only a few miles north of the United States border and is even closer to B.C., Eric Bailey said.

Bears travel up to 30 miles per day this time of year, and the animal could have left the search area in Waterton's Cameron Creek drainage.

Glacier Park officials have closed the boundary trail to prevent hikers from stumbling onto the bear, but are not searching.

"We'd have no way of knowing if it was the right bear," Clyde Fauley, resource management specialist, said in a telephone interview from West Glacier, Montana.

"Once he crosses the line we'd treat him like any other bear," Fauley said.

The park destroys problem bears the second time they are trapped, he said.

In Canada, wardens are playing a "waiting game," Bailey said. "They'll find the right one, but it may take a week or two weeks."

Wardens will know when they get the right bear because they're looking for either a very young or a very old animal, Bailey said.

Only a very young animal on his own for the first time or a very old bear in poor condition and unable to forage normally would attempt to eat a human being, Bailey said.

Park wardens are continuing to patrol the region where the incident took place during daylight hours, and traps have been set.

Park visitors are being stopped and told to remain near their cars and boats on roads and lakes in the Cameron Creek vicinity because of the bear.

The hunt was hampered by inaccurate directions given wardens following the incident, Bailey said. It was nearly nightfall by the time articles abandoned by the stricken Saskatchewan family and a blood trail led wardens to the right area.

Bailey could not confirm that one bear has already been killed in the hunt.

Park Superintendent Jean Pilon said Monday a female bear thought to be accompanying the killer bear was slain with the aid of a helicopter Sunday night.

But Bailey's information failed to support the story, and he questioned whether a bear had actually been killed.

Warden Ernie Brennan, the official on duty at the park, had no comment on the apparent discrepancy.

[July 6, 1977]

BEAR PATROL CONTINUES

Hope of finding the bear which killed a five-year-old Regina girl Friday is diminishing, but Waterton Lakes National Park wardens continue to patrol.

Traps will be left in place and patrols will continue for the foreseeable future, Park Superintendent Jean Pilon said today in a telephone interview.

But hope of finding the animal lessens daily. The bear "could be anywhere," he said.

Allison Muser died enroute to a Calgary hospital Friday after the bear's attack. It was frightened away by the screams of her eight-year-old sister.

Working on the sister's description, wardens feel they have not yet found the right bear, thought to be a black bear boar with a brown snout.

Wardens killed a brown-colored black bear Sunday, on the chance the girl's description of the bear was inaccurate, but doubt it was the killer animal, Pilon said.

[July 13, 1977]

WARDENS CERTAIN RIGHT BEAR KILLED

A grizzly killed in Waterton Lakes National Park Tuesday may be the one which killed a Regina girl July 1, a Parks Canada spokesman said today in a telephone interview.

Eric Bailey of Calgary said the bear is an old, undernourished 250-pound grizzly, black in color. It was killed near the picnic ground which Allison Muser was visiting the day she died.

Allison's eight-year-old sister described the bear as "black," Bailey said. The description and a report that the bear was accompanied by a brown one first led wardens to seek a black bear.

A brown-colored black bear was killed in the early stages of the bear hunt, which lasted 1½ weeks.

The Waterton warden service is convinced that the right bear has been killed, and is removing bear traps and baits from the Cameron Lake area where the incident took place.

They felt they were looking for either a young bear or an old one which had lost its hunting skills.

The attack occurred while the girl and her sister were sitting on the bank of Cameron Creek where their father was fishing.

Trails in the Cameron Creek vicinity will remain closed for a week, to prevent hikers from encountering other bears which may have been attracted to the area by scents from trap baits.

[July 21, 1977]

DEAD GIRL'S FAMILY PLEDGES MAULING SUIT

The parents of a five-year-old girl killed by a grizzly July 1 in Waterton Lakes National Park will sue Parks Canada for negligence, her mother said Wednesday.

Allison Muser and her husband Paul of Regina say they intend to sue because they were not informed of the presence of bears on their visit to the park.

Regina lawyer Gary W. Kinnar said he is filing notices of the action with Parks Canada and Waterton Lakes National Park.

The Muser family came to Canada from South Africa four years ago and know little about Canadian wildlife, Muser said from Regina.

"We had no more thought of a bear being there than of there being a lion," she added.

Allison was mauled by a black grizzly while she and her eight-year-old sister played on Cameron Creek.

She died later that night in an ambulance between hospitals in Cardston and Calgary.

[August 10, 1977]

PARK CHIEF TOLD FAMILY PLANS SUIT

The family of a five-year-old girl killed by a bear in Waterton Park last month has notified the park superintendent they will sue, says the lawyer handling the case.

Gary W. Kinnar said Tuesday in an interview from Regina the Paul Muser family must wait 90 days until the suit can be started under terms of the Crown Liability Act.

Allison Muser died July 1, enroute to a Calgary hospital after being attacked earlier in the day by a grizzly.

[November 2, 1977]

BEAR VICTIM'S PARENTS FILE SUIT

Mike Harrop
Herald Staff Writer

A Regina couple Tuesday filed a lawsuit asking compensation for an incident in which their five-year-old daughter was killed by a grizzly bear in Waterton Lakes National Park July 1.

Don Hibbert, deputy clerk of process for the Federal Court of Canada in Regina, said today in a telephone interview that the suit will be sent to Ottawa for action.

In the action Paul and Anne Muser ask for costs and damages without setting an amount.

In another telephone interview Tuesday, their lawyer Gary Kinnar, explained that the suit is broken into two parts.

First, the Musers ask compensation because they say the Crown should compensate bear victims without question, as would a homeowner who keeps a dog which sometimes bites.

They also ask compensation because the park was allegedly negligent. The suit breaks the negligence into seven different sections, Kinnar said.

The Musers contend the park was negligent when it failed to warn them as they entered the park, and when it failed to post adequate signs.

They further allege the park failed to control and manage the park's bear population and failed to provide methods of escaping a bear attack.

Negligence was also involved in the park's alleged failure to supervise the Little Prairie Picnic Ground, where the incident occurred and in the park's failure to enact regulations to control bears in the park, the Musers say.

They also contend negligence was involved when the picnic ground was designated for public access.

After being served with the suit, the Crown has 30 days to file a statement of defence. The matter then goes before a hearing to discover whether grounds are adequate for a court hearing.

If the action passes the test, the trial date is expected to be set.

Jack Holroyd, acting director of Parks Canada's western region in Calgary, said the park service will have no comment until a response is filed.

[January 4, 1978]

GOVERNMENT DENIES FAULT IN GRIZZLY MAULING DEATH

A government lawyer Tuesday denied Waterton Lakes National Park officials were at fault in the July 1 grizzly mauling death of a child near Cameron Lake.

In filing a statement of defence in behalf of Parks Canada, department of justice lawyer Barry Collins of Saskatoon said the child's parents should have known there are bears in Waterton Park, and acted accordingly.

The statement was filed in Saskatoon, and will be forwarded to Federal Court in Regina, where the action is being brought.

Collins denies an allegation of negligence filed by Paul and Anne Muser of Regina, the child's parents.

The couple ask compensation for their daughter's death. She died after being mauled by a grizzly on Cameron Creek.

Without setting an amount they ask to be paid because the park allegedly failed to warn them of bear danger, to control the bear population, to provide a means for escaping a bear attack and to supervise the picnic ground.

If there is no out-of-court settlement of the matter, each side will examine the other under oath.

[September 27, 1978]

REGINA EXAMINATION SET AFTER WATERTON BEAR-MAULING

HERALD PASS BUREAU.

An examination for discovery into the bear-mauling death of a five-year-old Regina girl last year in Waterton Lakes National Park will be held Thursday and Friday, Nov. 2 and 3, in Regina.

The Paul Muser family of Regina is suing the federal government for the death of their daughter Allison July 1, 1977 near Cameron Creek, claiming the parks branch was negligent in not warning visitors of bear dangers.

In a telephone interview from Regina, department of justice lawyer Barry Collins said the examination will allow both parties to cross-examine each other "to sort out the facts."

The examination will allow both sides to determine "which areas they agree or disagree on," he added.

Collins said he would seek to have the proceedings closed to the public, but the Musers' solicitor, Gary Kinnar, said an open examination "would be all right by me."

In a telephone interview from Regina, Kinnar said the publicity would likely aid his client.

"But it would appear the counsel for the Crown would feel public presence would not be conducive to full and frank disclosure," he added. "I can recognize his position."

Kinnar said he expects a 1979 trial date, possibly as early as February. The trial will be held in Regina.

The Musers will likely wait until the trial to present their monetary claim for the death of their daughter, Kinnar said.

[November 3, 1978]

NOV. 16 CONCLUSION SEEN IN BEAR-MAULING EXAMINATION

Herald Pass Bureau

An examination for discovery into the 1977 bear-mauling death of a Regina child in Waterton Lakes National Park will likely conclude Thursday, Nov. 16, a lawyer acting on behalf of the dead girl's parents said Tuesday.

The Paul Muser family of Regina is suing Parks Canada for the death of their daughter, five-year-old Allison, claiming Waterton park officials were negligent in warning of bear dangers while failing to supervise the picnic grounds where the mauling took place.

The examination for discovery is being conducted before an anticipated 1979 federal trial to "narrow down the contentious issues and to help determine the facts," said Muser's lawyer, Gary Kinnar, in a telephone interview from Regina.

The examination will also facilitate a possible out-of-court settlement, he added.

During the first two days of discovery held last Thursday and Friday, the Crown cross-examined Paul Muser, while the family's lawyer questioned former park superintendent Jean Pilon.

One more day of examination, to be held Nov. 16, at which time the mother will be questioned, should conclude the proceedings, Kinnar said.

If the matter goes to trial, a court date will be set during the next several weeks.

The family has not revealed the monetary compensation it will seek.

With that file of clippings, which I had read and reread, I drove to the Waterton Lakes Park administration offices, which are in the middle of Waterton Lakes Village. The head ranger had not been at his home when I had left the note that I feared the mountain sheep might eat, but the gate warden had told me that the chief warden would, however, likely be back at the office at 8:00 A.M. today. I had left word that I would be in to see him. The receptionist said the chief warden would be back at 9:00 A.M. When he finally arrived at about 9:30, after attending to some pressing park business, he invited me to come into his office and said, "I felt it would be better to have my superintendent here during any discussion."

The superintendent entered unsmiling. Immediately he pointed out that the case of *Muser* vs. *Parks Canada* was under litigation. He said that they could not make any statements and that they had not made any statements to anyone.

I replied that I was not seeking statements but the verification of known facts. My purpose was to present those details to the public in my book in the hope that those facts, along with many others, would "scare the hell out of the readers." Thus many more tragic encounters between human beings and bears might perhaps be prevented. The two officials expressed their disapproval of my intent to "scare the hell out of the readers." In the park system, they said, continued employment depends upon inviting the public into the public lands to enjoy and use the domain. I accused the two men of being "sensitive," a charge they denied. Telling them about the book to the best of my ability, I took nearly two hours. In the conversation I asked to see the site of the Muser attack and the surrounding terrain, but they would not disclose the location, saying that that information had legal implications. That, I said, was nonsense; the location had been disclosed in the *Lethbridge Herald* as Little Prairie Picnic Ground on Cameron Lake Road. I added that, if they would not give me the information, I would get it without them. I then presented the Parks Canada map that had been given me at the entrance to the park, which had two sites marked along the road. I asked them which one was Little Prairie Picnic Ground and held out the map. They indicated that the last, unnamed site on the map was known by that name. I observed that such an identification could have no bearing at all in any court case, and that I was a former cop with some experience with law in the courts. I stated again that I was not interested in opinions and that I had none myself. My presentation had to be unbiased, allowing my readers to reach their own conclusions from the actual facts and conditions.

Things went better after about an hour. Some minor corrections in the news items were inferred. The weight of the bear was 212 pounds, not 250. The statements of spokesmen for the Parks had been "taken out of context" when they were quoted as saying that "the attacker was apparently an old bear which hung around the picnic area because it was too old to fend for itself." Park personnel had not had previous knowledge of any bear being around the area. Such news statements were factually incorrect.

The next news item that I chose to bring up was the statement, allegedly from Park Superintendent Jean Pilon, that the bear appeared to have intended to eat the girl. This they hotly denied as untrue. I explained that it was my intent to determine whether there is a tendency among some bears to devour their victims immediately and a tendency among other attacking bears to maul their victims into submission and then leave. I was pursuing this, not because I wanted to give my readers a cheap thrill. Rather, by convincing readers that bears—like sharks—do eat people I hoped, among other things, to deter some of the damn foolishness with which park employees have to contend—such as a woman wishing to spread jam on a child's face or hands so that a bear could lick it off for a photograph. The two officials categorically stated there that there was no indication that the bear intended to devour the child. Her injuries had been from biting and severe mauling.

It was my main contention that the descriptions of the bear were inadequate for my purposes. First it was described as a black bear, then as a black bear in the brown phase; then the 250-pounder (now corrected to 212 pounds) was described as an old, black grizzly. The officials pointed out that Philipa, Allison Muser's sister, had seen the bear standing on its hind legs. Although the pelage on the upper sides of the grizzly that was shot carried the normal lighter-brown to grey hues, its belly and legs were what the child had said: black. The animal, they continued, was not an old bear; its age was established as six years. It showed no signs of illness, injury, or deformity except that it was very scrawny for a grizzly of that age. It was healthy. The month of July, the parks officials pointed out, is a poor period for bears in the Rocky Mountains, there being little of the mature fruited vegetation that fattens them from August until late October.

The report that "the Waterton warden service is convinced that the right bear has been killed" in the July 13 *Herald* was also unsubstantiated. Would they explain it to me?

Yes, they would.

No previous encounters with bears had been reported from the area of the attack. Traps set with honey, deer meat, and other viands known to attract bears were out under surveillance for twelve days following the death of the Muser child. Three bears were killed within a couple of days, and the killed grizzly was in the area of the tragedy. No others had been seen. No further traps were visited; no further sightings were reported. There were no further incidents. It seemed logical to conclude that the guilty bear had been destroyed, but there was no certifiable evidence which bear had done the kill-ing. It was the opinion of the parks investigator that the type and species of the bear should be classified as unknown. On none of the three bears' car-casses was there any evidence that identified it as the killer.

After that session I drove up to the environs of Little Prairie Picnic Grounds. Stopping again at the scene of the tragedy, I walked over several acres of the terrain along the creek. It was a typical western mountain valley floor: dense patches of grassy meadow and willow brush, varying in height from waist deep to over my head. Any wild animal could approach within ten to twenty feet unseen in any portion of it. Paul Muser or any other angler would have had to pick his way between hedges of brush to get to any sweep of water, and in 90 percent of the spots he fished, an animal five to fifteen feet away would be obscured from his vision. Nor was there a place where he could have obtained a clear view of the picnic site. Even the buildings, set deep in a clump of trees, were mostly obscured from view.

It is a one-in-a-million chance that a bear could take a child right under her parents' noses (park statistics show that millions safely visit the environs of bear attacks). Yet, if it were going to happen, Little Prairie Picnic Ground, with its nearby stream and lush verdancy, would be the place.

As I walked throughtfully back to the Jeep, I noted among the green grasses some small blue violets like those that as a prairie-born kid I used to pick and bring to my mother. Mingled with them were the white stars of strawberry blossoms that later produce inexpressibly sweet and aromatic wild berries for which my father used to give me a shiny nickel a cupful. Allison Muser could have delighted in plucking those luscious red jewels during July. Once when I was thus occupied about a hundred miles north of where I was now standing, a grizzly had appeared a few yards away, on a slide like the one near Little Prairie Picnic Ground. Although I was hunting at the time, I had failed to notice the big animal until it was far too close. I had a logical reason to be watching; Allison Muser and her family did not.

Late in the afternoon, when most of the animals were on their pre-sundown move, I returned to the picnic ground for some photographs. Be-fore I got past the first curve, just a quarter-mile up Cameron Road, a moun-tain sheep ewe appeared right on the highway. A couple of hundred yards farther along, a bighorn ram with a full-curl rack came right up to the truck just as soon as I stopped to grab the camera. Before I could refocus the lens, he was too close for a photo. As I was twisting the circle of metal, making adjustments, he actually nudged my elbow where it was protruding from the window. He would not even back off far enough for me to be able to focus the lens. He ducked only when I tried to pat his head between the immense horns.

Later, while I was rephotographing Little Prairie Picnic Ground, a deer walked across the road within twenty feet of me and then between the Parks buildings.

Nearly a mile along the road toward Cameron Lake, I stopped beside a doe on the edge of the timber. She was about thirty feet off the road. I talked to her, and she came right out of the woods and up to where I stood. When I photographed her, she was so inquisitive about the camera that her nostrils and eyes filled the eyepiece. She too reached out delicately to muzzle my hand—presumably searching for bread or other tidbits.

Halfway back to the village, I stopped to photograph two large bighorn rams jousting among four others. While I photographed them, a ewe came up to the camper window and licked the perspiration from my fingers. She continued to do so while I tried to photograph her with the other hand.

Such is the wonderful trust of the wild animals in Waterton Lakes National Park. Those seconds of mutual trust displaced all my theories about contacts between humans and wild animals.

I am not a person who believes he has certain powers over animals. Nonetheless, I often hear remarks such as, "Why! My dog went right to you. Look at him make up to you," or, "That cat never went near anyone else who came into this house!" Even, "Did you feed him something?" My only explanation is that I think animals know when they can trust you—that they know if you like them. And I like animals—all of them."

That opinion leads occasionally to questions such as, "You, a hunter, can say that? How can you kill them when they trust you?" In reply all I can say is, "Not when I'm hunting them, they don't! They stay as far away from me as they do from any other hunter!" The degree of trust exhibited by the Waterton Lakes wild animals exceeded all my previous experience. Yet even there I would not go within 200 yards of a grizzly or black bear unless I carried a high-powered rifle or shotgun. Whatever the courts might decide between the Musers and the Crown, a lovely little girl lost her life there through human trust in wild things.

The Runt X

Within a week the November shore ice had extended a mile to sea. This new plain became the major platform of the winter sea hunt for the wandering males. It gave them a raft to walk on and closed off the great expanse of open water from the seals, who now must keep their breathing holes open. It was those breathing holes for which the bears avidly searched.

The old males, who knew the ice and what it meant, were the first to leave. From somewhere inland they came and sauntered outward from shore. Knowing the aggressive manners of the larger bears, the two-year cubs were always careful to give them a clearance of several yards. The big animals were swift in attack for only a few yards and gave up quickly when outdistanced by the agile younger bears.

Watching the passage to sea of the older, scarred males, the largest cub felt impelled to follow. Keeping a safe distance between himself and one of these adults, he advanced. At that the other cubs followed. The old male growled but continued seaward. He growled again, but hastened outward—through the entire short day. When he did halt, it was to bury his nose in the scant snow shoved up by his paws—apparently to sleep.

Uncertain, yet knowing of no other course, the four cubs settled down at a distance. They, too, shoved their muzzles protectively into the snow or into the fur of their neighbor.

The crunch of teeth awakened all but one of them. The female, which had curled up at the outside of the group, was now held by the neck in the big male's jaws. As he lifted her, the quivering of her body was her final movement. The big animal's jaws had severed her spinal cord. He gave her several savage shakes before dropping her. Fresh blood had soaked into the hairs of his long, black, scarred nose and face.

Springing up, the three males spurted in whichever direction they had been facing. The old bear ran after the leader for less than fifty yards before he turned, woofing aggressively. When the three cubs found each other, the big animal was feeding on their littermate. It was a lesson none of them would forget.

On the following day, they found the remnants of a large bearded seal abandoned on the ice. For two days they fed at it. The scent of the killer male was on the surrounding ice, but there was no sign of his return.

A dark twilight was on the sea now, the only brightness that of a full moon or the aurora borealis. Both were bright enough to hunt by. The lead male had quickly learned to test the air for the breath of an exhaling seal and then to trace the direction. Always it would lead to the seal's open breathing hole. Finally he learned to spot the larger ones and to wait patiently until the seal's nose came to the surface for a full breath. At that moment, a quick grasp with his canines and an assist from his claws driven into reachable flesh would sometimes bring the seal out onto the ice. More often, however, the animal would escape with a quick downward pull. Hungry days would follow.

In the open the winter blizzard came suddenly across the wide sweep of frozen sea, its small gusts bearing fine, hard granules of ice. On this expanse the hummocks so common on land were rare. As he had learned from his mother and the adoptive female, the lead male shoved his head into a small patch of snow, rear end to the wind, and allowed a drift to build against him. Within an hour the denlike covering would be complete, housing the three of them during their winter dormancy.

January brought them out of the ice only twice, once to take a seal and gorge upon it. The daylight of February aroused them more fully. Disturbed by the grinding of the sea ices, the leader finally began to move northward some distance each morning, toward the distant white foothills that he knew lay closer to the polynyas. There they would find those pressure ridges where his mother had fed upon the white-coats. He was followed by the other two males.

At the end of their dormancy, the bears' weights had ranged from 200 pounds for the cub of the adoptive parent to the leaner 250-pound bulk of the former runt. That summer, and the one to follow, brought him increasing bulk, well beyond that of his companions. More often now, they waited for the results of his kills and fed on the abundant remnants. More than once he had charged large bears and driven them from their kills. His two mates had only growled and popped their teeth during his aggression, but they had stood firm.

Even larger males, when faced aggressively by all three, retreated fairly quickly. The leader was learning that his kind had a strong instinct for self-preservation, fighting only in desperation. The constant tumbling and brawling seldom got beyond a slight wound or a heavier-than-usual blow. When their bellies were full in summer, amid the wet pools of melted ice, they often engaged in mock battles. He, the largest, most often won. On occasion, a bear of their age would join them temporarily, but seldom did a larger bear do so. The older bears usually moved singly.

One day in the late fall of his sixth year a smaller bear approached his group. A strong, provocative scent preceded her, and she was trailed at some distance by a much larger bear. For some time the group of three watched her brash approach and took note of the tailing bear. All three were vaguely disturbed by her smell. It was a scent from which, during earlier seasons, they had always been driven, usually by the abrupt appearance of a larger, fiercer old male, or a series of them.

The female stopped upwind of them, urinating on the sparse snow, and the leader moved slowly, pigeon-toed, toward her, watching the large male in the distance. The female moved toward the young male, her long nose extended. Swiftly he moved in beside her. The smell of recent breedings enveloped her.

Suddenly an overpowering instinct assailed him. His testes seemed to bulge and swell and his penis slid partially from its case. Without further hesitation he rushed at her in an attempt to cover her rear. Swiveling quickly, she backed against him to assist his entry.

He barely noticed the roar of the bear that had been following her. His previous attempts to cover a female had been either resisted or had resulted in play, the latter usually interrupted and thwarted by the sudden, militant appearance of a larger bear.

Suddenly the popping of teeth near his left side brought his head away from its position over the female's, and the massive swat of the aggressor struck him on the hip. Long fangs aimed for the side of his neck. As quickly as the mating urge had been aroused, the urge to do battle supplanted it.

He twisted about so quickly that the older bear did not see it in time. The teeth of the dismounted bear slashed into the cheek of the older animal, tearing deeply downward into the neck toward jugular vein.

Ripping free of the slanted bite, the intruder reared on hind legs in an effort to dominate by height. When the young bear arose, his height was nearly that of the adversary. Without hesitation he lunged and swatted hard, driving the old male onto his rump. Instantly he gripped the throat of his adversary; once again a mighty shake and the big bear was free, but blood spurted in a stream onto the snow.

Frenzied now, the younger bear swatted at the challenger, who was retreating in an attempt to recover. Mercilessly, as if attacking a large bull seal, the six-year-old rushed in, paws flailing, teeth slashing. The battle lasted less than two minutes. Blood flowed freely from both of them, but much more from the old bear.

Finally, head bowed, rear hunched up, intimidated, the old bear backed away. Two short rushes made him retreat even farther. When he had retreated thirty feet, the young victor turned. Where the battle had begun the female was allowing his littermate to mount her. With a roar of new-found power he charged and, with his shoulder, bowled the two of them over, sending them sideways across the snow. He watched as his littermate, bellowing in pain, galloped into the distance, the second littermate trotting behind. Nearby, the female cowered, unsure of herself. Within minutes he mounted her.

It was the beginning of his solo existence.

CHAPTER 11

"I Am Not an Aggressive Type—the Bear Was!"

"The second time the bear came toward me it made a semicircle onto the trail to my right. It came right up and sniffed at my thigh as I remained still. It touched me with its nose. I took off my packsack—very carefully—and reaching out, tossed it a couple of feet away on the trail—just as I'd been told to do if a bear threatened to attack. I thought it might take the bear away from me. The bear turned and pounced on it, bit it, and shook it—but didn't paw at it, didn't even make a hole in it. It was just about the bear's body length from me. I made a step away, and with unbelievable quickness the bear turned and sank its teeth into my leg."

There was still an uncomprehending look in Karen Austrom's frank blue eyes as she voiced those words. We were sitting in the glassed-in conservatory off her mother's living room, comfortable in stuffed wicker chairs amid well-tended indoor plants. Karen raised her voice emphatically:

"Bears are unbelievably strong! I'm not a weakling—physically. We used to have a terrier dog we thought was strong. We'd give it pieces of cloth, an old sweater or something, to get a hold of. It would tug and grip it and shake its head, but it didn't give any idea of the strength of a bear. I have wrestled with my brother and could take care of myself, but the quickness and strength of the bear was something else! You just can't comprehend the strength of a bear. I guess I immediately realized there wasn't anything I could do."

She was expressing the same shock that has entered my mind when watching bears. I saw a bear bite right through and break off a two-by-four timber that had been stuffed into its culvert trap. I have seen bears tested for their reactions to druggings. I watched an attempt to turn a bear inside a trap by inserting a stick through an aperture. The wood snapped off as if it had been hit by a bullet or by lightning. I remember well the awesome strength of a twenty-five-pound bear cub struggling to get loose from my arms, seeming to exert the force of a six-foot athlete when held against its will. I understood what Karen was saying.

Karen took a deep breath, and in that second I really saw her for the first time. She had a strongly bone-structured prettiness that struck me as typically Greco-Roman: clearly defined forehead, straight-bridged nose, firm chin. Her large, soft blue eyes determined her feminity. She was the type of girl that makes people think, "Gee, she'd be great fun!" She could have handled the paddle of a canoe or swum across a lake with you. Given you a good game of tennis. A girl men like to hold close while dancing. A girl who would laugh with you. The absence of her arm took none of that away.

Why in hell do bears always seem to pick the best of us!

That very sorry fact had been uppermost in my thoughts when I had first heard of Karen's bear-inflicted injuries, which for some reason I had believed were caused by a grizzly bear. As I was then just out of the day-to-day news business after thirty-five years in the general reporting profession, I was still a "member of the press" to both friends and acquaintances. Thus I received a personal tip: "You might want to talk to this girl. She's just recuperating— and she may have a good story for you." Having also recently completed two years of research for a book intended to better our understanding of why bear attacks occur, I was reluctant to interview any more victims and particularly this one at this time. Most of the bear-attack victims I had interviewed had been given time to recover from their emotional trauma. Even so, in those interviews I shared strong feelings. I was really hesitant to probe what I knew were raw wounds, both to body and psyche. Consequently, I had put off contacting Karen Austrom for a couple of years.

Then one evening, while I was working on this book, a young woman, Elizabeth Murdock, called me and told me that she was a friend of Karen Austrom, a girl attacked by a bear a couple of years before.

"Yes," I replied. "I have her case in my file, but I didn't want to disturb her."

"That is nice of you," was the reply, "but I think Karen might tell you her story. I haven't asked her, but she's my friend, and we read your book about bears and found it very interesting. I like your approach to the subject."

Thanking her, I said, "Yes, I'd very much like to talk with Karen—if she wants to talk to me and won't be disturbed by such a discussion. Will you be seeing her?"

"She's studying in London, Ontario," was the answer. "I'll write and explain what I've done and what you've said." Later Elizabeth Murdock called to say that Karen Austrom had agreed to meet with me. My letter to Karen brought the reply that during the Christmas and New Year vacation from classes she would be in Vancouver.

Her young voice was a pleasant surprise when we arranged to meet at her suburban Vancouver home two days before Christmas. When I could not find the number on the house, she came down the stairs in blue jeans and a sweater.

"Hi. I'm Karen, Mr. Cramond."

Her outgoing personality was immediately apparent. So was the one difference between her and any other girl you would meet. She wore a stainless steel hook where her left hand would have been. And that was noticeable only because I did not know how to put out my own hand to greet her. It was not her disability but my own that left me feeling awkward. She moved easily beyond my confusion as she said, "Come on into the house, Mr. Cramond."

As we sat in the sunroom I suggested that Karen tell me about herself and what led up to the attack.

"It was in July, 1979. I was a second-year biology student, headed for a degree in medicine." She smiled a bit wryly. "But the time in hospital after the attack changed that: I decided to go into therapy. At that time I was looking for a summer job, and Parks, British Columbia Provincial Parks, was employing summer help. I got a job as a 'student naturalist' in Mount Robson Park—in the Rockies, south of Jasper. It's a small park, not really like the big Jasper and Banff parks."

She looked up with her frank blue eyes as if to be assured that this was the information I was looking for. I nodded.

"One of the jobs we had to do was to walk the two-mile trail from Red Pass Parks headquarters up to Berg Lake. It was the time of year when new plants were coming into blossom, and we were to watch for new flowers and such—so we could tell the visitors what they were or what to look for as they hiked up. About half way up the trail there was another lake."

She hesitated, and I took the opportunity to ask a question.

"How much experience did you have in wildlands, Karen? As you were growing up, were you outdoorsy?"

"Yes, I guess so. My dad and mom took us out camping as a family. Dad liked to fish the streams, and we did a fair amount of it each summer. We camped out. I liked the outdoors. One summer we went on a longer wildlife outing trip into the Chilcotin area. About twenty of us were flown in—a coed group, called Eco-Summer, with five leaders and two assistants. It was a high school group, and I was eighteen years of age. The leaders were grads of Victoria and Simon Fraser universities, knowledgeable in the woods. We were twenty-three days covering the ground from Taseko and Fishem lakes, where we had been set down, all the way to Anderson Lake, where we got the train back. It was some trip."

I was surprised to hear of young people taking such a trip. I knew the country from many years of travel. I had crisscrossed it by air and was in the first four-wheel-drive vehicle to make the connecting link between Squamish and Lillooet. We were traveling from the south on a logging road when it just ended in a blank wall of timber. We heard a bulldozer crashing around back in the timber, and we pushed on, on foot. The operator was flabbergasted to see us come from the bush in front of him. They were just cutting their initial path from the connecting road at the northern end and were following red ribbons left by engineers. They had expected to reach our road later that day but didn't know that they were so close. Then, very generously, the crew cut a swath through the remaining one hundred yards, bulldozing trees and logs aside so that we could take the jeep over the path of the 'dozer treads. I had run into a grizzly bear on that trip and had taken a photograph of a two-year-old black bear. It was grizzly country all the way from there to Taseko Lake, where Karen's group had begun their trip. In *Killer Bears* I devoted a couple of chapters to the area. One chapter was entitled "Killer Grizzly Capital of the World" because so many attacks and killings have happened there. I shook my head at the thought that a student group had been taken through such rugged and possibly dangerous terrain.

"Karen, that is real grizzly bear country!"

"Yes, I know that—now! But we didn't even see one bear, of any kind."

I was nodding my head.

"You were lucky, possibly because your group was large enough to be noisy and because it was wild country, where the animals are shy—not imprinted by having a lot of people in their area."

"Yes, I think so. I think park bears are more dangerous, because they become used to people actually feeding them around the campsites—"

"You've seen that sort of thing, Karen?"

"Yes. It happens all the time in the park campsites. You see people taking photos. . . ." She lifted her arm, as if holding a camera to her eye, and made a shutter-release motion with her finger. "It doesn't matter what you give them to read in the way of pamphlets; the warnings don't seem to make any impression!"

She sighed. I nodded my own assent.

"You had to find out the hard way. A bloody shame!" I exclaimed. "And you had been given instructions on how to react in the event of possible bear attack?"

"Oh, yes, we were well briefed. They gave us explicit sessions and instructions and material—all that was then known." She was shaking her head ruefully. "In your book you said there isn't anything you can do that will definitely prevent an attack. That's right. I did what I believed was right—according to all instructions—and the bear ate part of me!"

Her statement was so shockingly matter-of-fact that my mental reaction, "Jesus Christ, no!" was muttered almost audibly. For an instant I flashed back to my interviews with Cynthia Dusel-Bacon, who had lost both arms to a black bear and was saved only by her gasp into a hand-held radio, "Come quick! I'm being eaten by a bear!"

I interjected, "This wasn't a grizzly, Karen?"

"No! It was a black bear."

"Oh, for God's sake, I thought it was a grizzly bear attack! Most Parks attacks are, and I don't have a newspaper clipping on it. It was just presumption on my part."

"There wasn't much in the news about it—it was kept pretty quiet. But it *was* a black bear."

She stopped as if surprised that I was not aware of the details. I mumbled what came to my mind:

"I didn't check up as I should have. Black bears cause almost as many incidents as grizzly bears, yet people don't realize that they are very dangerous."

"Yes, I know—*now*."

"I interrupted you, Karen. Sorry. When did you first see the bear?"

She looked up at the ceiling, then back at me.

"Well, I was about a third of the way back from the lake—Berg Lake—on the trail. . . ."

I stopped her again: "What kind of trail was it?"

"Oh, a little over six feet wide. You could get a vehicle up it—except that there were barriers put into the path so that people wouldn't take their cars up. It was a nature trail, lots of width."

She hesitated, then continued. "I came to a small bend, and downwind of me about 25 feet the bear was just coming up the five-foot bank from the stream. It stopped on the edge of the road as it saw me. I guess we both saw each other at the same time. The stream was in freshet—roaring with the spring runoff. The bear then came into the middle of the road and sniffed at the air, looking right at me. I stayed still. Its head was down, sniffing at the air. I remember thinking 'Oh, *that's a bear! What am I going to do?*' While the bear was sniffing, I took one step back. When I did so, he took three quick steps toward me—and stopped. His head was still down, sniffing. I think he was uncertain. It seemed that I stood there a long time. He left the trail, in sort of a semicircle about ten feet away from me, as I turned my body facing him but without shifting my feet too much. And I thought 'He's going to go away.'"

She stopped momentarily, seeking clearer definition of what happened.

"It was as if he was on the end of a rope—the distance he kept away was that even, circling toward my back. He seemed to be more uncertain as he moved. Then he walked slowly off, about thirty feet, and climbed up a tree, like a shot. It was amazing how fast he went up. A person couldn't outclimb him."

She was silent a moment, remembering. I spoke my question.

"Was it a young bear?"

"Yes. It was a two-year-old."

"Oh boy! The worst of the blacks—uncertain about themselves. The old lady drives them out, and they are looking for territory."

"Yes, I know. Perhaps their aggression is a result of that uncertainty."

That she knew about the nature of two-year-old bears came as a surprise. Perhaps the topic had come up in one of her biology courses—although I have yet to see it in print. On the other hand, my own research has verified the theory to some degree. Two-year-olds—grizzly, black, and polar—are even more likely to kill humans than are bears of any other age, including old bears, which frequently are physically impaired. In particular, killings by two- and three-year-old black bears are increasing.

I said some of this to Karen, who agreed and then continued her story.

"The bear wasn't that big. I thought, 'Now that it's up the tree—that far away—it's time for me to move down the trail.' He was about thirty feet up in an aspen tree, among the branches. The tree was about twelve to fourteen inches at the butt. He was staring over his shoulder, watching me. I thought, 'He's going to leave me alone now.' "

She looked at her lap for a moment.

"I watched him for about what seemed to be three minutes—maybe— then I started down the trail. I guess I got about three steps before he slid down the tree—so fast I couldn't believe it. I stopped, and he came back the thirty feet he'd gone, right onto the trail again."

Karen's face showed no sign of distress as she talked, as if it were all just a matter of fact.

"Then he sniffed and made a semicircle to my right side, then moved up close. While he was sniffing, he touched my right leg. It was then I took off my packsack and tossed—well, sort of dropped—it about four feet away."

"What was in your pack, Karen?" I asked.

"Well, not much. I'd had breakfast when I got up, about 6:30 or 7:00, and I had put in only an apple, an orange, and a hard-boiled egg. There was some rain gear and a sketch pad, to do drawings of plants and flowers I might find newly out along the trail—nothing in the way of sandwiches. But dropping my pack was something I had been advised to do. It's in most booklets: 'Drop your pack to divert the animal's attention.' "

I shook my head, thinking back to my own experience of dropping pieces of bacon while I trotted for the safety of the car and watching the black bear stop to pick them up, giving me just enough time.

I interjected, "It does work, sometimes!"

She nodded.

"He turned and pounced on it, bit at it, and shook it—didn't even put a hole in it. Then, when I moved, he turned and bit my thigh and threw me right to the ground. I landed on my stomach right beside him. He had let go of my thigh, but almost in the same bite he had hold of my elbow. I hadn't screamed before, but when he took hold of my arm, I thought I'd better scream. I guess I screamed for a minute or two. Then he was tearing at my right arm, and I made a conscious decision not to scream any more, as he seemed to become more aggressive when I did. The river was very loud anyway, and it was quite early in the morning and unlikely that anyone would hear me. I remember thinking 'They haven't heard me now.' I was still on my stomach. I could only think, 'What am I going to do now?' He had me down on the trail for about five minutes and was eating my right arm."

The words were shocking to me, though they were familiar from half a dozen interviews with survivors.

"Didn't you fight at all, Karen?"

"No. I'm not aggressive, I guess. I thought of what I'd been told and heard: 'Lie still, and they will think you're dead and cover you up and go away.' "

My head was shaking involuntarily.

"Unfortunately, as you know, that applies more to grizzly bears. Black bears seem to start eating immediately."

Karen nodded emphatically.

"This one did! He pulled me about four or five feet off the trail, behind a bush, and held me down for about five or ten minutes. Time was sort of suspended then—I don't really know how long it was. It was as if I was somewhat detached from my own body. He had my forearm and was tearing away the skin and eating. I turned my head away. I thought 'I'm not going to look again!' He started to drag me further off the trail into the bushes. I curled up in a fetal position, and he just kept dragging me by the arm. About thirty feet from the trail I felt a root sticking out and grabbed at it, thinking, 'If he gets me into the deep bushes they'll never find me.' "

I had heard words similar to Karen's in earlier discussions. She continued.

"When I held onto the root, it stopped him; I guess he figured he had me well enough hidden. He began to feed on my upper arm. There wasn't much conscious pain. I remember a crunching as he bit through my elbow, and a real searing pain—when he must have bitten through a nerve center. Then he was eating at my shoulder."

Karen was speaking in a level tone, almost clinically; I was all knotted up inside. She went on.

"I was just lying there. I hadn't screamed since I was on the trail. Later he started to bite at my lower back—as if he was sampling me—and I remember thinking, 'I can't let him do that!' I extended what was left of my arm toward him to eat, and he bit at it. Then he took a couple of bites at my head. He scarred my forehead."

She lifted her hair back, exposing her right ear.

"He bit through this ear. And there is a scar on my temple on the left side—looks like a wrinkle."

Actually, from five feet away she showed no scarring.

"They don't show from here, Karen," I said. "You don't show scarring at all—not compared with some of the people I've talked to, particularly those attacked by grizzlies. Grizzlies seem to go immediately for a person's head."

She nodded. "I've heard that."

"Thank God it was a black!" I offered rather lamely.

After a moment she continued with the details of the attack.

"I was just lying there after he bit at my head, and he put his paw on top of me and held me down—and belched! I guess he had eaten enough. About this time Fran Benton, my supervisor, came up the trail—as I hadn't returned. She saw my pack on the trail. Then she saw the bear and called out to me. I was very weak, and she had trouble hearing me. She asked if I was hurt, and I said my arm was gone. I was too weak to move. . . ."

Karen paused in recollection.

"Some people had come up the trail behind her. She got some pans from them and rattled them, and the bear left me. But he stayed nearby. I couldn't see him, but I could hear him not far away. Fran could barely hear my answers, and she thought I was further away into the bush. I was too weak from blood loss to speak very clearly. I was lying there about twenty-five to thirty minutes—I don't know exactly how long it was—when a fireman came down the trail with his wife, son, and daughter. Fran had gone back down the trail to get help."

She paused as if clearing up the details.

"The man called out to me. As my voice was very faint, he also thought I was further off the trail, but he came right in. He saw the bear—it was just about fifteen feet away—but he just went ahead. He got his son, a fourteen-year-old boy, to help roll me onto his shoulders, then picked me up."

She stopped for a moment.

"I blacked out for the first time right then, but I came to about a minute later, when he got me to the trail. He was carrying me in a fireman's hold. A couple of other men came down the trail and spelled him off a little, but they didn't carry me far. He carried me most of the way down the trail—about two miles. Fran couldn't drive our vehicle up the trail because the gates were locked, and the superintendent had the keys. They put me in the back of the park's vehicle and waited for the ambulance to get there. I was conscious all the way to the hospital."

That part of Karen's tale is often repeated by victims of bear attacks: the ordeal is seldom mercifully ended with unconsciousness. Shock seems to suspend the terrible pain—and to constrict the arteries, cutting off the flow of blood. Death seldom occurs as a result of hemorrhage if help comes in time.

Karen had related her story almost dispassionately. I have noted the same calm in most survivors I have interviewed. I asked Karen about her air of acceptance.

"I've told the story so many times that, I guess, it comes easy. At first I told and retold it—perhaps because I wanted to but also because people asked me about it. Perhaps it was good for me."

I could not stop a little smile. I was thinking of Ted Watchuk, who had said, "When I was in hospital, I got verbal diarrhea. I wanted to talk about it and told all the details to everyone who came to see me. I guess it helped me to recover from the shock." Other victims had said similar things.

I repeated that statement to her.

She nodded. "Yes, I think it does help. When I was going through rehab they encouraged me to talk."

Karen's mother, a pleasant, motherly woman, came in carrying a couple of cups of coffee, with sugar and cream, on a tray made of clear-finished strips of natural wood. The intricate design required the fitting of a dozen or more pieces of wood on the flat surface. Mahogany and black walnut were interspersed with lighter birch and maple. When I admired the tray, Mrs. Austrom said simply, "Karen made it."

I was surprised. I work with woods and build things, but I have always avoided making such a tray or table top, or even a breadboard, because fitting the woods requires such precision before gluing. I guess Karen noticed my reaction, because she smiled, and said, "Yes, I made it, during rehab. They get you to do things like that to help your dexterity. I'm going into physiotherapy. That's what I'm studying now, since I decided not to go into medicine. I know I'll like it better."

Her apparent unselfish dedication floored me a little. Yet she was simply fitting into a pattern of many other people who have been through the tough parts of life—including victims of bear attacks. Determined to help others just a little—no, a lot!—they are more attuned to life and the hard way between the rocks.

I stopped staring at her tray and looked over at Karen.

"I build boats and have built houses, but using my two hands, I'd have some difficulty doing a tray like that! I'm very surprised!"

Karen smiled offhand.

"Oh, you'd learn," she said. "It isn't that difficult. It just takes more time. You learn to be patient with yourself."

The early setting of the sun, on the day before Christmas Eve, had made the afternoon grow dimmer. Karen had given me a considerable part of her short time at home. I asked if I could get back to her with other questions when the things she had told me had settled in my mind.

"Sure, any time," she said. She would be in Vancouver until January 3. Between Christmas and New Year's would be fine.

The day after Boxing Day, I picked her up and brought her to visit with my wife, Thelma, and me in our home. We showed her the spot where Thelma had to reach for our daughter, Pamela, in front of a black bear that was at the baby's crib; and we told how Thelma had carried Pamela in her arms past the bear as I came out to the verandah with a rifle. Karen as not surprised. She was noncommital when I took her into the den where I am typing this and showed her my row of guns, which line a wide case above the typewriter. I pointed out the .32–20 rifle with which I killed the first black bear that attacked me without warning. She simply nodded without comment. When we returned to the living room, I asked her to share with me some of what she knew about bears—knowledge that she apparently had in abundance.

To my surprise, she said, "My brother, Carl, just missed being attacked by a grizzly bear—after I was attacked."

"He was attacked too?"

"He wasn't mauled. One came after him. He and his partner were doing some timber cruising up in that area between Squamish and Pemberton. I don't know the exact location."

She was referring to an area of British Columbia just sixty miles north of where we sat—the home of my first pet, a grizzly cub.

I interjected, "That *is* grizzly country. I ran into one there. Did it come after him?"

"Yes, it did! It was about fifty yards from him and his partner when it started to come. Carl ran toward twin trees—there were two growing out of one stump. He got up in the V between them and sort of walked up it—you know, his back against one, and his feet pushing up from the other—until he got up about thirty feet, where there were some branches. Then he went to the top of the smaller one. The bear came up and almost got hold of his foot. His buddy had gone up another one about fifty feet away and was hollering. The bear let go of Carl's tree and slid down. It went toward the other tree but didn't try to climb it. Then another bear came along. The two of them stood at the bottom of Carl's tree and pounded it and shook it. But they didn't try to climb up again. It may be that in its first climb the grizzly had knocked off most of the branches beneath itself. Carl was up there about eight hours before they went away. They didn't go after the other man in his tree."

"He was lucky. I'll have to talk to Carl about it later."

We began to converse more generally about bears and bear encounters. She drew me a diagram of the Mount Robson Park stream and mountain path where she had been attacked. She drew it very clearly and pointed out some errors in what I had written—exact to the last detail.

"How long were you in hospital, Karen?" I asked.

"About two months. I was a week and a half in Seton Hospital, at Jasper, Alberta, which is near Mount Robson Park. That was where the ambulance took me. They flew in some very potent antibiotics after the operation, and I never did have any infection."

That was a surprise to me, and good news. I asked her if she knew the names of the drugs, but she had forgotten. It was encouraging nonetheless to hear that there was such potent medicine.

Most of the other victims I had interviewed had suffered severe infection, loss of tissue, and months of drainage. Karen had not.

I asked her what she knew about the bear itself.

"The assistant park superintendent went up to where I was attacked and shot it. It was a two-year-old male in good condition, fat and healthy. It weighed only 150 pounds—and I weighed close to that. It was a surprise that it could be so strong."

"Do you think it was a park bear?"

"I'm almost sure it was. The bears are around the campsites and the dump, which wasn't more than a couple of miles from where I was attacked. I think it was a park bear, not afraid of humans."

I was thinking of my own records regarding attacks, particularly attacks by black bears. A pattern was developing: bears of all species attacked women, girls, and boys more often than they did grown men. Dr. Charles Jonkel and one of his assistants, Carrie Hunt, had discovered that all bears are deterred by bulky objects, even by the sudden opening of an umbrella in front of them. I asked Karen what made her think it was a Parks bear.

"Well, it had a full stomach. Besides parts of me, there were food scraps in it. They autopsied it thoroughly."

Everything Karen said had been confirmed in my own studies. I asked her if she had a message that might help other people. She responded without hesitating. "There is no formula in a bear encounter. My doctor said to me, 'Why didn't you hit it on the nose! You should have been carrying a walking stick!' I couldn't convince him that there was nothing I could have done. I'd say to anyone who is going into the wilds: *'Be well prepared for bears! Know all you can about them!* You have to realize that they aren't like the ones you see on TV, not like Smokey the Bear or Goldilocks's three bears. They are not only going to maul you; *they are going to eat you!'* "

Her words had a nerve-jarring reality to them.

She should know.

The Runt XI

By his twelfth year the former runt of the litter measured eleven feet from nose to tail. At the onset of his land travels he weighed more than a thousand pounds. He was equally at home on the windswept seas and beaches or traversing overland passes to other large islands. It mattered little where he moved, for his path was not crossed eagerly by any other bear, and his dominance was seldom tested.

Since his eighth year the sounds of aircraft passing over the North Pole had become as customary as the restless grindings of colliding ice floes. On the other hand, the buzzing of small aircraft and the popping paddle sounds of the large birds that hovered occasionally were signals to move quickly away. The noisy, slow, hovering ones would land nearby, and the upright occupants would emerge to stalk and stun the less wary members of his kind. Upon rejoining the group, these members would be sluggish; sometimes, too they were blackened in a way that made them conspicuous during a seal hunt.

Two females bearing strapped-on devices had approached him. Something he did not comprehend in these newly attached units irritated him. One female wearing such a device came too near to a seal he was stalking. He pounced on her, tearing at the offending object. When it fell to the ice, the female had been wounded by his teeth and was barely breathing. He had stalked away stiff-legged, yawning and shaking his head angrily.

Twice a great bird had stayed very near him, each time for almost a week. Always when it hovered overhead he ran off, often weaving through the pinnacles and ravines of pressure ice, always avoiding contact.

At one summer's end, when food was scarce, he traveled overland to a river mouth that would provide spawning char. This time he also found two of the big birds, sitting on the delta, their crews moving between them and a gray rectangle erected in the shelter of the riverbank. Something about the activity piqued his curiosity, and he lingered nearby behind a tall mass of glacial boulders.

At the same time he detected the scent of meat and wood smoke. It had been several days since meat had filled his belly, and the scent drew him. Used to stalking, he bided his time. Eventually, he knew, the strangers would become unwary.

When the sun was at its lowest point and a deep twilight had settled over the estuary, he padded silently along the beach to where the scent had been stronger. Now they seemed to come from more than one place.

After dusk the strangers gathered inside the mysterious gray triangle. For an hour he listened to the unusually monotonous cadences of their voices from inside. When they no longer uttered such sounds, he twice circled the tent.

In front, where the smell of burned wood was strongest, he scratched some of the aromatic grease from the sandy soil. Licking his paw, he found the flavor delicious. Lifting his big head, he sniffed carefully for more. The scent was intermingled with the offensive smell of the visitors. Their odors, associated with the chase and with interruptions of more pleasant activity, had become repulsive. Although apparently not deadly, the visitors were repulsive, to be avoided. His impulse to leave was strong.

The lingering scent of the aromatic fats, however, persisted. This time it was coming from the top of the riverbank. Silently he padded up to the bank and with one leap landed on the level, grass-covered delta above. Dimly, in the twilight, he saw what looked like a bubble of ice. A few paces from it another of the huge birds had its narrow wings slightly spread. From the far one came the odor of wind- and sun-cured blubber.

Cautiously he walked toward the ice bubble surrounding the bird's innards. That place held the strong scent. Tall as it was upon spindly legs, it did not dominate him. He rose twice upon his own hind legs as if to bluff it. When after five minutes it did not awaken or change its stance, he walked up to where the legs were planted firmly on the moss.

Standing on his hind feet gave him enough height, and he batted hard at the ice sheathing. The thing rocked but remained inactive. Once again he smashed at the ice covering, this time caving it inward. The thing still did not retaliate.

He stuck his head into the innards, where the meat scents were strongest.

From the area of the tent came an animated chorus of human sounds. Their high-pitched tones told him of their excitement, the excitement that usually preceded their attack. He was unafraid but determined not to let them near him. His lunge took him through the strange ice on the opposite side of the bird. Sharp metal gashed his shoulder. He dropped to the ground on the opposite side.

Three of the creatures were running on their hind legs up the riverbank, waving their forepaws excitedly.

"Goddam! It's a polar bear! Jeez! Look at the size of that bastard! And we don't have a gun!"

For a moment the bear stood his ground. The hesitancy of the smaller animals heartened him. He yawned mightily, staring back at them. None of them made any movement to attack. He rose up on his hind legs to show them his size.

"Good lord! He must be twelve feet tall! Let's get the hell out of here! He might attack! To hell with the 'copter!"

Hearing the higher tenor of that sound, he feinted a rush in their direction. In an instant they scattered, disappearing back over the riverbank.

He trotted away, heading for the pass leading between the nearby hills. Even if they would not attack him, he did not like their smell. Nor was he hungry enough to kill what did not appeal to his appetite. When the moon had gone another full orbit, he was thirty miles farther north, well away from the humans. After crossing the valley, he came down into the bay, which he knew held kelp and, sometimes, a herd of walruses.

The long walk over the mountain had made him hungry. Grasses, sedges, and berries, interspersed with a gulped lemming or ground squirrel, were not enough to sustain his large appetite, nor to add bulk to his layers of fat. The moulted birds of the flatlands and deltas had once again become airborne and thus impossible to chase. The open water gave the seals ample opportunity to escape in the depths. There were no beluga. The noisy gatherings of walruses on the nearby reef and point, however, presented a challenge.

As the sea came into view again, his attention was drawn to the low-lying point and its tiny, tidally separated reef island. In the bay behind the rock peninsula small bull walruses were gathered. Cows and their yearling calves cluttered the water and the shoreline off the point. Almost in the center of the herd was the pyramidal bulk of the dominant bull, which occasionally raised its head to bellow. Its deep tenor was a challenge.

Carefully, so as not to expose his body needlessly, the big bear used the intervening rocks, ridges, low brush, and sand dunes to hide his approach. He had stalked to within fifty feet of where the bull was beached on the point. Then, at the frightened belch of a nearby cow, he reacted involuntarily. As she disappeared into the water, he sprang in two jumps across the small channel to the rock upon which the dominant bull was resting. The bear's flying body hit the bull just at the slanting curve of the shoulder—but barely moved it. It was as if he had hit the rock itself.

The enormous head of the walrus turned with a speed almost equal to his own, and a downward slash of the long yellow tusks slid off the attacker's exposed haunch. A blow of the bear's forepaw, powerful enough to decapitate a large bearded seal, sank as if into a partly frozen mass of kelp.

The walrus's large black flipper lifted the huge bear off his feet, tumbling him into the water. Before he could recover, the bull was in beside him, the ponderous head thrusting with unbelievable speed. The walrus was not cowed; he was aroused! The bear backwatered to avoid the slashing tusks, then resolutely, head to head, attacked again. His canines sank deep into the cheek of the larger animal and held as the walrus quickly rolled over, taking them both under water. Surfacing, the bull shook mightily, and the bear's teeth tore through the tough hide, followed by a spurt of blood.

Instead of turning, as would a seal, the huge bull lunged at his adversary. A heavy tusk hit the bear on the head, and a gush of his own blood blinded him. He dove underwater. Spotting the submerged rounded belly of the other animal, he bit violently into it. Immediately the big belly rolled out of the water, propelled by large flippers. As the bear surfaced, he pounded his fifty-pound paws twice into the ribbing. In the water, however, the walrus was in his own element. He rolled over quickly, pulling the bear underwater again before he could take a deep breath.

He had to let go or drown.

When his head came to the surface, the walrus was ready, and only ten feet away loomed the hulks of others of the herd. Bleeding, and aware of the strength of numbers, the bear swam quickly ashore.

For three full days he lay and licked his wounds, resting in piles of kelp. When the slash on his head finally stopped bleeding, a long black scar began to replace the white hairs. For the first time since he had been the runt of the litter, his combined cunning and strength had come to naught.

He was a wiser bear.

CHAPTER 12

The Downtown Banff Killings

One bear—much too late it was proved to be just *one*—killed one man and maimed four others during a week of summer vacations in the Canadian Rockies. The year was 1980, and the place was the world-famous holiday center of Banff, Alberta. Statistics on park bear killings and maulings show that it was not a happy year. It is still very difficult to get information on this array of attacks. Each year multitudes of summer visitors pass through Banff, leaving the imprints of thousands of credit cards plus many millions of dollars in cash. Any suggestion that one cannot walk around this bright, modern town without risking attack by a grizzly or a black bear threatens the local merchants' livelihood.

That thought passed through my mind many times as I endeavored to pry the facts from the offices of Parks Canada, first in downtown Calgary's high-rise business section, then at the Banff district headquarters, and finally beside the stream where the victims—ordinary park visitors and a transient—had been attacked.

I wanted exact information because with it I could enlighten the public, prepare them for the possibility—it's not a probability, but a million-to-one chance—that they might encounter an aggressive bear—while wandering through the wild lands of North America.

The following list catalogs the results of five visits to a short stretch of Whiskey Creek during a ten-day period in that summer of 1980:

1. Ernest Cohoe   Dead of injuries
2. Brian Kelver   Badly mauled
3. Andres Leuthold   Mauled
4. Robert Muskett   Severely mauled
5. Remy Toblar   Badly mauled

If you happen to be a compulsive angler (that is, if the sight of a clear flowing stream makes you want to get the rod and reel from your car's back seat and cast a bait or fly), you would succumb when you saw Whiskey Creek, which is right in the center of Banff, just off the Trans-Canada Highway. The creek passes under a railroad spur, and although fishing from the willow-shielded banks is pleasant, it is easier from the small railroad trestle where Ernest Cohoe was attacked. It is not difficult to push through the thick brush to where the bear dragged Cohoe, and his agonized cries should have been audible in the nearby centers of human activity. Remember: that particular bear was to get *four more* victims before it was finally killed.

Having recently had full, explicit investigative reports handed to me at the offices of Glacier National Park, and having enjoyed the full cooperation of

the United States authorities in my investigations of the three other park killings of 1980, I expected similar cooperation from Parks Canada authorities.
Each of the United States authorities I talked to had even read *Killer Bears*
and understood my objectives.

In the Parks Canada offices in Calgary, I was given the name of a Parks
executive in Banff and told that he had the information I needed. Within
hours I was at the door of that executive in his Banff offices. When I asked
for the official reports on the five bear attacks in 1980, however, he said he
would not release them. Adamant in my belief that because they were public
documents, they should be released, I presented my identification as a member of the press. That made not one iota of difference. He said again that
under no circumstance would he release such documents or copies of them,
nor would he allow me or anyone else access to the information contained in
them. When I asked if the official reports were in his office, he answered that
they were and that they would not be released. No amount of commonsense
argument would budge him. Finally, though, he did authorize me to interview one Parks official who had been a member of the committees responsible for investigating Ernest Cohoe's death and the ensuing maulings.

As in the United States, a lawsuit often is directed against Parks Canada
management after a bear attack in a national park. The victims or their families accuse Parks officials of being fully or partially responsible for the attacks. In the event of such a suit, all evidence gathered by government inves-
tigators must be disclosed in full to the solicitors of the injured party. Thus
there is no reason to withhold it from the public or the news media. Yet if
Parks Canada anticipates a lawsuit resulting from a bear attack—and Parks
officials seem thus inclined—they are reluctant to release information that
might affect their defense. In most cases they remain unwilling until the lawsuit is settled and the date of possible appeal is past. Although such evidence
is gathered by public servants at public expense, bureaucrats feel that they
may rightfully withhold all evidence unless to do so threatens the safety of
the nation.

There is a complicated way of circumventing that official position: to ask
my local member of Parliament to present to the Legislative Assembly, in
the House of Commons, the questions for which I require an answer. Then,
when the annual budget of the recalcitrant department is under consideration, the member of Parliament asks my questions. Because the budget cannot be passed without satisfactory answers to all pertinent questions, the unhappy bureaucrat has little choice but to reply. As a newsman I have used
this method of obtaining information, but I find it a very demeaning way of
extracting from a public agency information to which any media reporter is
rightly entitled. If I had used this method with the Parks executive who refused me access to the reports on the Banff bear attacks, I would have had to
wait months for disclosure of the documents, and I would have had the expense of returning to Alberta from Vancouver—not to mention the transcon-

tinental haggling by mail. Thus I was relieved when I received permission to interview one of the Parks employees involved in the investigations of the attacks, Area Warden P. Jacobson.

I drove to meet Warden Jacobson at the ancillary local quarters for Parks personnel in Banff. A typically very pleasant Parks field representative, he had been the senior warden in charge at the time of the five attacks. Like most such men, he was straightforward with his answers, and he offered to take me to the scene of the attacks.

The drive from his headquarters to the site of the attacks on Ernest Cohoe and Robert Muskett was a revelation. Until we actually arrived at the site, I had no idea where we were going. Imagine my surprise when we returned directly to the thriving modern townsite.

After parking his vehicle, Jacobson led me to the railroad spur, which was about two hundred yards away, and to the small railroad trestle under which the stream flows. The stream is pondlike there because of beaver dams downstream. We stood on the wooden structure examining the surrounding area. The sounds of the city south of the adjoining main railroad line were clearly audible, and commercial buildings were near at hand. In its proximity to downtown Banff, the site was almost identical to the site near St. Mary, Montana, where Jane Ammerman and Kim Eberly were killed by a grizzly. No more than a handful of people on this continent would identify either site as being grizzly country. It is, most people would concede, within grizzly country, but those same people would disqualify the sites themselves because they are virtually in the midst of residences, hotels, restaurants, shops, and backyards. Both St. Mary River and Whiskey Creek are undeveloped borderlands, slight green-strip buffers between a town and a transcontinental highway.

To adjust mentally to the idea that Whiskey Creek was grizzly country, I had to look up the valley toward the mountaintops and rock slides, which towered over us where we stood in the open on the railroad trestle. Yet the whole of the Rocky Mountain range was once grizzly country, and it still is, though the great bears' populations are sadly diminished. Banff, Alberta, stands in the center of this natural grizzly habitat.

Although the great silvertip bears are less than sociable, they do go wherever they please. Not far away from the railroad trestle was a restaurant garbage-storage unit. This one was enclosed, according to regulations, within a chain-link fence. If the bears find such a source of food accessible, they establish a pattern of dependency on it and, as a result, become territorial. They will defend such territory against any intruder. Very probably this behavior pattern explains Cohoe's sudden death and the maulings of four others.

The habits of the grizzly bear require that it be close to forest and bush, its sanctuary when it is not feeding at its chosen sources. The brush and timber surrounding both the St. Mary and the Banff killing sites provide limitless sanctuary. The sites also afford excellent green grass for fodder. And the streams themselves are essential for the bears. Not only do they provide water in abundance, they are also easily negotiable paths to the mountain slides.

When he was attacked, Cohoe was one hundred feet from a man-made path that grizzlies might reasonably avoid during daylight but did use at night. The reaction of a grizzly to intrusions on its territory by any intruder, even one of its own kind, is to retaliate immediately: to attack and subdue. And that is what the grizzly did!

On August 24, Ernest Cohoe and his son, together with Cohoe's friend Robert Muskett and his son, walked, with the intention of fishing, to the spot on Whiskey Creek to which Jacobson later took me. While Cohoe was just downstream from the culvert bridge, they heard the bear crashing about in the bushes. Sighting Muskett, the bear chased him, knocking him down and biting him. It then went after Cohoe, and upon catching him, it knocked him down, mauling him severely and biting him about the head and face. Having satisfied itself that the intruder was down and incapacitated—and also somewhat aware of the sounds of human activity nearby—it then left Cohoe. He was able to get up and push his way out of the bush, while the two boys ran for help.

As Jacobson and I stood at the edge of the railroad trestle looking downstream, I asked him where Cohoe had been attacked, the exact spot.

He pointed to the end of a small pool about thirty to fifty feet downstream.

"He was down there in the bushes, just near the willows."

The willows were less than the length of a tennis court from us.

"Jesus Christ! I'd walk in there any day of my life—right now—without the slightest thought of meeting a grizzly bear, let alone being attacked!"

Jacobson nodded. "It would seem unlikely," he agreed.

I was staring at the very dense surrounding brush. Anyone who followed a bear into that would have to be within arm's length of the quarry to be able to detect its presence. Any tracking of a bear in such cover would have to be within minutes of its sighting, while the grasses were still depressed. Parks personnel could have used dogs trained to track bears, but such a dog would be hard to recruit on short notice. Although I have tracked wounded bears without a dog in forest and brush, only an extreme emergency could persuade me to enter such an area in search of a bear knowing that it had just killed or fatally mauled one person and injured another. I expressed that thought to Jacobson and then asked, "What did your department do about this attack?"

He answered without hesitation.

"We followed the usual procedure in such cases. We posted the area against entry by the public and set up tracking stations around garbage dumps. We had extra patrols out at night and set out baited traps in the area."

The answer was what I had expected.

"These are the normal steps following a bear attack?"

He nodded assent.

"Yes. There was a special crew of Parks employees assigned to investigate the incident and to prevent any recurrences. The whole area was well covered with notices designed to inform and exclude the public from this whole area."

I shook my head.

"The public doesn't pay much attention to such postings. Obviously, when Toblar and Leuthold came in, and then Kelver, those notices were still posted, and the preventative and emergency measures should still have been in effect. Were they?"

Jacobson's glance was candid. His nod confirmed the words.

"We were still working on the case."

"Yet it happened. All these other people were attacked!"

Jacobson nodded.

I had found him cooperative in every respect. There were particular details that I also wanted to probe, but I felt that in view of the attitude of the senior executives, my asking those questions would only put Jacobson in a difficult position. I asked him if he would show me where the attacks on Toblar and Leuthold had taken place. As we drove around the wooded area to the opposite side, my mind was on the clipping that had appeared in the *Vancouver Sun* on September 2, 1980:

TWO MORE HURT IN BEAR ATTACK

BANFF, Alta. (CP) A tourist from Switzerland was reported in serious condition in hospital after he and a local resident were attacked by a black bear Monday, the latest in a series of bear maulings which have resulted in three deaths in less than three weeks.

Monday's attack was near the area where Ernest Cohoe was mauled by a bear eight days ago. Cohoe, 38, of Calgary died in hospital on Monday. The bear was killed by park wardens.

Banff National Park wardens said Remy Toblar of Switzerland, in his 30's, and Andres Leuthold, 25, a garage attendant in Banff, were attacked when they walked through a bush area to take pictures of beavers.

Leuthold, who was not seriously injured, said after his release from hospital that he played dead when the bear charged.

"I just saw the bear coming running out of the bush. He bit me and then he went for my friend. He left me after I pretended to be dead."

Leuthold said Toblar tried to climb a tree but the bear got him down.

When park wardens arrived in the area, the bear was gone. Toblar was conscious but seriously wounded in the head, abdomen and legs.

On August 14, two oilfield workers were killed by a black bear, in attacks about one hour apart, near the northwestern Alberta community of Zama. That bear was killed the next day.

Some of the facts in the foregoing were on my mind as we rode to the other attack sites. I also had in mind another clipping, dated August 25, 1980, which said, "Parks Canada spokesman Ken Preston says a black bear, not a grizzly, as first believed, was likely responsible for an attack Sunday [August 24] on a Calgary man in Banff National Park. Preston said the bear was large, with brown coloring which might have given it the appearance of a grizzly."

The details in those news reports had long puzzled me. Perhaps Jacobson had an explanation. Referring to the statements, I said, "Park employees eventually shot a *grizzly* bear, identifying it as the attacker of Toblar, Leuthold, and Kelver. How did that identification come about?"

Jacobson's response was immediate.

"Our first real evidence that the bear was a grizzly came from a plaster cast of the animal's tracks at the site of the attack on young Kelver."

My own investigations and experiences suggest that terms such as "brown-hued bear" (the description given by Muskett, Toblar, and Leuthold) imply a grizzly, not a black bear. It was difficult for me to appear unbiased, but I remained quiet.

Jacobson stopped the Parks vehicle beside the main line of the railroad, where downtown buildings backed right up on it. Near those train tracks he led me to where Whiskey Creek flowed from the forested green strip between the highway and the railway tracks. The brush was much less dense here than at the railroad spur. This point, where Leuthold and Toblar had been attacked, was only a couple of hundred yards directly east of where Cohoe and Muskett had been attacked.

Jacobson led me the short distance along the bank of the quietly flowing stream to where the garage attendant and his Swiss friend had met with the bear. He indicated the sites of the attacks. I photographed the area, mainly as proof that nothing in its appearance would tell an uninitiated person that this was grizzly country—even when it was heavily posted with warnings.

What more was there to say? Or more to ask? After all, I was at that moment standing, undisturbed, where Toblar and Leuthold had been attacked by a grizzly bear as they followed the placid little cityside stream. They were trying to photograph the beavers whose dams had widened the stream where Cohoe had been fishing.

Silently, we walked back toward the railroad track and our vehicle. Looking at the back-door entrances of the buildings across the railway tracks, I asked what businesses were there. One that Jacobson pointed to was a restaurant. Nearby, beside the tracks, was the depository for garbage from the restaurant. Refuse cans from the restaurant were deposited inside a chain-link enclosure while awaiting collection.

One of us mentioned that even a fenced-in area can attract bears. All restaurants discard leftover food whose tantalizing odors can waft many miles to the noses of hungry bears.

As we walked back to the car, I happened to see, lying on the ground in full view of forest and railway tracks, a white pillow. Spread down the slight incline from it was a grey "bunkhouse" blanket. Obviously this was a recently used bed.

I walked over to it, noting that the pillow still had the outline of a head impressed into it. The owner, who had abandoned it no more than a couple of hours before, was not in sight. Jacobson had come up with me. As I pointed it out, I exclaimed, "What the hell do you make of *that*! Sleeping out here within a few yards of where five people were attacked by a grizzly bear!"

Jacobson was shaking his head.

"That is strictly against Parks regulations. Anyone entering the park is informed, both orally and by road signs and pamphlets."

"Yet despite all that they sleep right here, out in the open!"

"They do."

Picking up the pillow and folding the blanket under his arm, he carried them to the Parks vehicle and placed them carefully in the cab.

I was still wondering. They looked like government-issue bedding.

"Where do you suppose those items come from—a pillow and a blanket—worth only a buck or two but just left there?"

"Probably stolen," he asserted noncommittally.

I was thinking ahead to the discovery of their removal.

"I doubt that the owner will claim them."

"I guess not. They would be charged immediately if they did."

He drove me back the same way we had come, along the highway. He pulled off the road at an intermediate spot in the green strip and indicated where Brian Kelver, the twenty-year-old, had become the fifth victim of a bear attack in ten days. There, all bloodied, he had been met by Chris Allen, aged nineteen, who also had been hitchhiking along the highway at the time.

I did not see that much was to be gained in walking around the exact site of this attack. The entire area was visible from the main highway.

As a follow-up, the news story in the *Vancouver Province* of September 4, 1980, is presented in full:

DEATH OF A GRIZZLY MAY HAVE ENDED REIGN OF TERROR

BANFF, Alta (CP)—Parks wardens Thursday shot and killed the grizzly bear they think is responsible for three attacks on humans, one of them fatal, less than a kilometre from the town in the last 10 days.

The bear was discovered Thursday morning trapped in a snare set by searchers the night before. It was shot and immediately airlifted out for preliminary examination and measurement.

The carcass of the mature male grizzly was to be transported to Airdrie, near

Calgary, where it will get a detailed examination at a federal department of agriculture laboratory.

The bear was killed the day after an attack on Brian Kelver, 20, of Ontario. Kelver is in stable condition in a Calgary hospital suffering from severe blood loss.

Wardens Thursday used a helicopter equipped with an infra-red device to scan the one-kilometre square section of woodland north of this Rocky Mountain resort town to ensure no other bears were in the area.

Spokesman Ken Preston said the scan turned up no further large predators and a cordon that had encircled the area for the last 72 hours will be lifted. However, the area will be closed for two or three more days while further checks are conducted.

The bear killed Thursday was about two metres long and weighed 340 kilograms.

"We don't want to jump to any conclusions that it is the right bear," said Preston, but added later, "I'd bet my shirt on it."

Kelver reportedly told officials he was trying to cross the forest to the Trans-Canada Highway when the bear struck.

He said he knew the area had been closed because of earlier attacks but wasn't sure where the boundaries were.

Chris Allen, 19, was hitchhiking on the highway when Kelver appeared out of the woods.

"He came up the road saying: 'I was mauled by a bear. I'm hurt. I'm hurt,'" said Allen.

A description given by Bob Muskett of Calgary, a victim of the first attack, led wardens to believe they were looking for a black bear. They shot and killed one last week near the spot where Muskett and his companion, Ernest Cohoe, 38, of Calgary, were attacked while fishing Aug. 24.

The Parks spokesman did not have to give up his shirt, but to my way of thinking, the issue was unresolved. I had in mind the following news item, from the *Vancouver Sun* of September 4:

BANFF GRIZZLY MAULS FOURTH MAN

BANFF, Alta (CP)—Parks wardens say a single grizzly bear mauled its fourth victim Wednesday in Banff National Park, in the general area where three others have been attacked in the last 11 days.

The wardens now believe they were mistaken in killing a black bear August 23, presumed to be the animal that attacked Ernest Cohoe, 38, of Calgary on August 24. Cohoe died in a Calgary hospital last Monday.

It was also on Monday that a bear attacked Remy Toblar, 29, of Switzerland, and Andres Leuthold, 25, of Banff.

Ken Preston, Parks Canada Information officer, said Wednesday night that wardens have intensified the search for the bear, doubling the number of men to 40 from 20.

He said the latest victim, a man of about 20 whose name was not released, was found Wednesday afternoon near the Trans-Canada Highway which runs through the park. The man staggered onto the Norquay Road just northwest of the Banff townsite and was spotted by a hitchhiker. The man's arm was torn and his face a mask of blood. He was admitted to hospital.

Preston said Wednesday's attack occurred in a cordoned-off area just north of the townsite, within 200 metres of the earlier maulings.

"We have followed tracks from the latest attack and it has been established they are the tracks of a grizzly bear," Preston said. He said the bear may be an extremely dark brown grizzly, mistaken for a black bear. "The reports we received about the bear came from people fleeing for their lives and you can't blame them."

Preston said the body of the black bear found by a search party after the first attack has been burned, making it impossible to match the bear's teeth with bite marks on Cohoe's body.

The area of the attack is known as Whiskey Creek, where wardens erected warning signs following the first attack. Preston said the later victims apparently ignored the signs.

He said two people were charged earlier Wednesday with illegally entering the area. Bear traps of the "humane" type, which will hold but not hurt the animal, have been placed in the bushy area.

Meanwhile, park residents living near the area say they are afraid.

"Of course we're worried," said Hans Weissmuller. "I've got two little kids and we're keeping them indoors until this is settled—I'm as nervous as I can get."

I have italicized an interesting passage in this news account. The bite of the grizzly was unavailable to match any tooth marks on the victims. It is unusual to dispose of the skull of any bear associated with an attack on a human being. Such skulls usually are preserved at the time of the animal's demise and sent to laboratories for examination for rabies, even though there has yet to be a case of any such skull showing signs of rabies infection. The stomach contents are autopsied to reveal any evidence of human remains, clothing, or other items associated with the incident. Why then was the body of the black bear burned?

Lying on the seat of my vehicle as I drove through the park on my way home was the following story, which had appeared three days before, in the *Calgary Sun* of July 23, 1982:

MOM, DAD CHASE GRIZZLY OFF
TOT SNATCHED FROM KILLER JAWS

by John Gradon, Staff Writer

Banff National Park's chief warden told yesterday of a frantic mum's "incredible" rescue of her three-year-old son from beneath a fearsome 200-lb. grizzly.

Anna Harrop charged at the bear which had grabbed her son, Brendan.

And as her husband, Tony, pounded at the beast's forehead with a shoe, Mom snatched the toddler from the jaws of death.

She hauled him clear from beneath the bear's body and carried him to safety.

Wonderful Family Effort

Said chief warden Gaby Fortin: "In 10 years as a park warden, I've never heard of such an incredible thing. The little boy is alive today simply because of this wonderful family effort.

"The mother and father went in there without the slightest regard for their own safety. He stood there hitting the bear with a shoe in his hand.

"The bear apparently seemed stunned at what was going on and the mother grabbed Brendan right out from under him."

A few minutes later the boy was laughing at the escapade, he says.

Amazingly, Brendan only needed a few stitches to neck and back wounds.

The incident began Wednesday as the Harrops, from Prince George, B.C., were touring Alberta in their trailer.

In the party were Brendan and his mother and father, his sisters, Deirdre, 13, and Triona, 10, big brother Conor, 7, and two 20-year-old relatives from Ireland.

The party stopped for a picnic at Taylor Creek, about 20 miles west of Banff.

Says Fortin: "The Irish girls and Brendan were standing on a small bridge when the bear—a young male about three years old—appeared from the bush about 10 feet away."

Wasn't Quick Enough

"Naturally they all ran, but little Brendan wasn't quick enough. He was scooped up by the bear. The bear had a grip on his clothing and carried him about 30 yards across the dried-up creek."

Electrician Harrop and his wife led the charge of fury and fear against the snarling bear.

Brendan's brother Kieran, 17, who had decided not to join the family for the Alberta tour, spoke to the Sun from his Prince George home.

He says the family have so far not even phoned him to tell him of the incident. "They would take it in their stride. Dad is a very cool customer but I can imagine my mum screaming and charging at the bear."

Thus bears were continuing to attack visitors to Banff National Park. My wristwatch showed me that it was July 26, 1982. I had been on the road for a month, and during that time I had traveled over 6,000 miles visiting the sites of bear attacks, listening to those who had been attacked or had investigated the incidents, and doing my own investigations. Now, just five miles away at Taylor Creek Campsite, was the newest site of a grizzly bear attack.

In my mind I could hear the words of Tom Ross, superintendent of Banff National Park at that time. While visiting him in his office, I had asked him about this latest bear attack, and I took note of his reply: "Several people came into the area [where the Harrop boy was attacked] right after the attack, and were attempting to feed the bear—despite warnings from others still present who had witnessed the attack on the boy." I was to hear the same from two other people who knew about the attack and its aftermath.

There were some five hundred miles of hot road ahead of me. I was tired, so tired that I missed the turnoff to Taylor Creek and was well beyond before I realized that I had missed it. "To hell with it!" I thought. "If people are so stupid that they will hand-feed a grizzly bear right after it has attacked a small boy, *what can I possibly learn* by standing on the spot and wondering? If you've seen one of those roadside picnic sites, you've seen a thousand of them! So, what difference does it make if a grizzly attacked a small boy at just one of them?

Does the public really want the truth about bears?

BOOK THREE

In Pursuit of Bears

For our son, Grant, and daughter, Pamela

Introduction to Book Three

My introduction to the use of wildlife was early in this century. My father, an Irish immigrant to Canada, was a scion of the "sporting set." My English mother was a horsewoman, the daughter of a master of the hunt (fox and hounds). Both of them influenced my attitudes regarding wild game. My grandfather put me aboard an English saddle at age four (I slid off after the first ten paces), and I was taught to shoot a rifle (at red squirrels in Alberta, Canada) at age five.

Although I have killed seven bears, I am not a bear hunter in the sense of being a deer hunter or a duck hunter—in determined pursuit of the species. I shot four of the bears because I had no choice. My first pet was a grizzly bear cub, and since that small beginning my interest in bears as a family has grown and led me across two continents.

As a youngster, after the turn of the century, I was implanted on the coast of British Columbia in the "bush," the aftermath of earlier and continued hand logging. I shot my first grouse with a slingshot that I had made from red rubber strands cut from an automobile tire inner tube and bound by string to a freshly cut broadleaf maple crotch and a pouch cut from an old shoe tongue. When I brought the downed ruffed grouse home to my mother, she cleaned, stuffed, and roasted it for our evening meal, and my father gave me a dime. Thus I became a mercenary hunter when very young, and I must admit that the thought of a new silver dime enhanced my aim. Subsequently, especially in hard times, our family ate a lot of venison and wildfowl— along with salmon and trout.

At the age of forty-two I became a salaried outdoors columnist-editor for a daily newspaper and thus a paid entrant into the taking and use of game. During my twenty-three years in that position I received ten national and international awards for articles on the conservation of life and wildlife. My personal initiatives brought about the creation of one of the largest waterfowl preserves in the world and perhaps a thousand other wildlife sanctuaries, the building of fish hatcheries, the regulation of commercial fishing, the establishment of several conservation organizations, and the introduction of hunter-safety controls and institutions.

As I write this, my duck decoys lie cleaned and restrung, ready for setting out on the Fraser River salt marshes. My salmon rods and fly rods are in their travel racks in my camper, and in my pocket is a "deer tag," should I wish to take a deer while hunting grouse. Yet, though my viewpoint on hunting comes from personal bias, I will stake my personal achievements for the preservation and conservation of wildlife against those of any other living wildlife protectionist.

The moral question of whether to kill *anything* has been a fundamental problem of philosophy and religion ever since humans began thinking about more than personal subsistence. The ethical question is and will be argued endlessly. One who is opposed to violence against any other form of life must exclude what is necessary to sustain his or her own life. All humans eat foods that are organic, that are or have been part of a living thing: fruits, leaves, roots, stems, seeds, and the like. Living organic forms subjected to cutting, bruising, or breaking respond by repairing the damage. Their purpose is to continue their existence to fruition and the formation of seeds. Any seed, such as a bean or a kernal of corn, wheat, or rice is a "fetus." Thus, if you eat a seed, you "kill"; if you pick a leaf, dig a root, sever a limb, or harvest a fruit, you have committed an act of violence. The vegetarian thus kills life-forms just as surely as does the eater of meat. The degree of killing is the crucial consideration. When the ecological balance is maintained, all species theoretically can survive. Perhaps the final statement should be that no species deserves to be exterminated.

As you read the following chapters, which relate my own experiences and those of friends and acquaintances during a lifetime in "bear country," please remember that understanding of man's associations with wildlife is evolving continuously.

CHAPTER 1

The Skid-Road Bear

West Vancouver, British Columbia, lies at the foot of the Pacific Coast Mountains, and aside from the mile wide strip of suburban village stretching ten miles westward along the seafront, the timber beginning at the shoreline extends almost unbroken from that tidewater inlet right to the subarctic regions. When my father settled us there in 1918, a mere thread of road led only half the distance from the village to our house. Two miles beyond, we lived next to an inoperative salmon cannery, about which were clustered a dozen fishermen's and workers' shacks containing as many immigrant Japanese families. Above us was timber, all the way to the mountaintops. By 1918 that forest had come to be called second growth. The earlier selective loggings had provided lumber, mainly for housing in Vancouver, but also for masts and planking on sailing ships, which still anchored in front of our waterfront property. The forest growth that was left, along with its current regrowth, provided enough timber to sustain handloggers, the only inhabitants above the road except the wild game that had proliferated in the newly opened forest areas.

Wild bracken fern, fireweed, some grasses, much salmonberry and thimbleberry bush intermingled with fiddlehead fern, huckleberries, shiny evergreen salal bushes, and dogwood and alder trees: the forest flora made an ideal habitat for willow (ruffed) grouse, blue grouse, band-tailed pigeons, many black-tailed coastal deer, the occasional cougar, and numerous bears. The coastline led westward before it made an almost right angled turn to become the wet foot of a fjord stretching northward to a narrow valley that reached deeper into the mountains following the Squamish River and its forking branches. In the upper end of the Squamish valley the coastal brown-bear, or grizzly, habitat begins. Four good-sized streams split West Vancouver at regular intervals, providing prolific schools of salmon.

I did not see the first black bear that came to inspect our property, but my father did. He had been rather silent during our breakfast, but when my brother, Pat, and I had done our chores, he spoke quietly. We were, respectively, six and nine.

"Boys! Perhaps you'd better not go up the skid road today."

We both stared at him, surprised and wondering. He was taking his time, choosing his words. Boys ready for play are not patient. Pat, usually the spokesman for freedom, broke out.

"Why, Dad?"

There was not the usual answer, "Because I say so!" or "Because I don't wish it!" Instead our father pursed his lips before continuing.

A black bear in British Columbia's Squamish valley.

"Well, this morning, before you were up, a black bear and her two cubs were in the garden."

"Gee! Where?" we responded in an excited chorus.

"She looked right in our bedroom window."

"Right in!" in subdued awe.

"Yes, she peered in. From a couple of feet back. Then she went down on all fours—as soon as I got out of bed. She took her cubs back up the garden path and across the road—up the skid road toward the old mill."

We both were stunned by the news. Almost daily we used the old skid road, which led up across the seldom-used railway tracks, thence into the rotting compound of the original millsite, and on into the active handlogging claim just above the mill. The grease-blackened skid road also led us to the abandoned but nearly intact shingle-bolt flume that in earlier times had brought the cut cedar from the top of the mountain to the mill, but which we then used as a kind of dry bobsled run. Not once in the six months we had lived there had we seen a bear. The handloggers had warned us about them, but being city kids, we thought they were just trying to scare us off because we were too rambunctious about their small camp and operations.

Our father's words, we knew very well, could be trusted. If he said, "The bear went up the skid road," then it did! I faintly recall a cold feeling in my groin. Our home was a cottage of the type common to the day, without a basement to lift it above ground level, and the window edge over which the bear had peered was no more than four feet from the ground. My own bed was on the lengthy front verandah, which was surrounded by only a half wall, rising about three feet from the ground, and a mosquito netting. The bear, had she been interested in small boys, could have pushed her head through the netting just four feet from where she stood on her hind legs to peer at my recumbent parents.

It was fully two days before we went forgetfully back up the skid road to play on the flume. We did see one rounded, berry-filled purple bear plop on the way. We had seen them before.

Later, during the month of August, when we were up at the millsite digging in the huge piles of sweet-smelling cedar sawdust, the screams of Mrs. Penfold attracted my chum Jimmy McCullough and me to where she stood with her arm protectively about her white-faced son, Percy, who was our age. Two handloggers were offering her placating words in quiet tones.

"Don't worry. We'll find her!" one of them said just as we ran up.

Percy was standing tearfully at his mother's side, biting his lip.

"What happened, Perc?" I asked, gasping for breath.

"S-S-Sis"—he stuttered when he was frightened—"S-S-Sis was near a bear. *We* were!"

"Jeez! Did the bear eat her?" I exclaimed.

There was a soft, despairing moan from his mother. Mrs. Penfold was what in those days was known as a "widow woman," a mother of two young children, living alone in a tiny unused shack near the cabin of the two log-gers, for whom she cooked some meals and thus survived without paying rent. She kept her two children neat and tidy, and neighbors generally were good to her. Like most of us she augmented her daily food supplies with red huckleberries, which grew wild at that time of the year. With a lard pail apiece, Percy and Sis (I didn't ever know her name), who was about five years old, had gone a hundred yards up the skid road to a patch where huckleberries grew thickly.

Percy had gone to a patch a few yards from Sis, then moved into the bushes a few feet to where the red globules flourished in a large clump. Amply watered by seepage at that spot, they were larger and more abundant than at the patch where Sis had begun picking. He had his lard pail almost filled and several times had beckoned to her. There was noise and movement in the bushes, and he believed she was picking berries on the side oppo-site him.

But as he told it when I asked if she had been eaten, "I dunno if she's et—or not. I didn't see her. On'y the bear. I was talkin' to her, and she wasn't sayin' nothin' back. So I figured she was mad, and I yelled loud at her."

He paused round-eyed for a moment, then blurted out, "Of a sudden the bushes in front of me, the one I was pickin' opened up wide, and a bear, standin' on its hin' legs, was lookin' right into my face. Right where I figured Sis was!"

The loggers were listening intently. The taller, slimmer one, the teamster wearing the work-shined leather apron and the pants stiffened by sweat and dirt and permanently bent forward at the knees, wiped a grease- and earth-begrimed hand across the tobacco-stained circle of his mouth and then spit a long orange stream at a log end.

"Did you see her—Sis? Was the bear near her?" he asked.

Percy looked utterly miserable, ashamed and afraid to answer.

"Come on boy! Hurry now! Answer me!"

"I dunno. I just saw the bear, and—I run home—to here!"

The two men were carrying felling axes, razor-sharp on their narrow cut-ting edge, bright from daily use, and shafted with springy, reddish, sweat-polished yew-wood handles. The smaller man tilted a crumpled, sweat-stained hat off his wet brow and spoke calmly.

"Percy, you show us where she is. Don't be afraid!"

The teamster spat emphatically. "We won't let the bear hurt you! Let's go!"

The aproned tobacco-spitter eyed me sternly.

"You other two kids, you stay right here!"

"Yessir," Jimmy and I intoned.

Armed only with felling axes, those two stringy muscled men showed no fear of going after a bear. The tall one, with longer strides, put his hand on Percy's reluctant shoulder, easing him ahead of them up the greased logging trail, talking softly to him. Within twenty seconds they had passed the small horse barn and rounded the first curve of the thickly bush-lined skid road. When they disappeared from view, Jimmy's eyes met mine. A single thought was in both our minds.

I nudged him. "Wanna go?"

"Let's!" was all he needed to say.

Keeping to the grassy edge so as not to snap a twig and be heard in pursuit, we subdued our giggles of anticipation. There is something about Irish kids (Jimmy was one too) that relishes the advent or portent of trouble, and we both got our share. Near the bend, just before the rising skid road straightened out, we passed the horse barn, which was almost covered on three sides with deciduous trees and bushes. The men were just going out of sight around the next bend, about fifty yards ahead, when we passed the first bend. We were whispering conspiratorially when a loud, lengthy noise reverberated from behind us. Startled, we both jumped.

"You hear a bear growl, Mike?" Jimmy asked timorously.

"It was a horse farted in the barn!" I answered derisively, uncertain. A moment later a restless iron-shod hoof clumped to the barn floor, and we both giggled. For a long moment we stared up the trail. Would the men kill the bear with their axes? Had it eaten Sis? We experienced all the visions childish imaginations could devise but little resolution to go farther along the narrow bush-lined trail.

A ring of laughter came suddenly from up the road, echoing through tall, gray green-alder trunks. They must have found her, and now they were coming down the trail. I saw the flash of a jauntily swinging axe blade and pushed Jimmy backward down the trail.

"They'll catch us if we stay here! We'll sure get hell! Run!"

"Aw, gee! How'll we know if they killed the bear?"

"Later, later!" I urged him toward camp, taking the lead.

Down at the clearing, with Sis on his shoulders, the teamster logger greeted the sobbing Mrs. Penfold.

"There wasn't no bear there, ma'am! She wasn't in no danger!"

Sis was smiling, looking wonderingly at her tearful mother, nodding her head in agreement. Her lard pail, half full of berries, was still in her hand.

The teamster looked thoughtfully at all of us.

"We seen signs of bear lately! More'n one day while we been workin' up there. May be better if you kept the kids on the other side of the millsite. There's lots of berries along the flume and by the railroad tracks!"

Still too emotionally choked to speak, Mrs. Penfold thanked him with her sad eyes and walked toward her shack holding Sis by the hand.

Percy looked at Jimmy and me accusingly.

"You guys followed us up there!"

"We only went part of the way!" I argued.

The teamster was eyeing me again.

"I told you kids to stay here! I ought to kick the pants off both of you."

He raised his broad-knuckled fist in a mock gesture. Jimmy was looking right at him innocently.

"Was the bear right there, mister?"

The teamster was disarmed. He grinned good-humoredly.

"There had been a bear there! Perc here saw him. We found the place where he was eatin' on the other side of the bushes, where Perc saw him and where he crapped in the grass. He must've run when Perc yelled. Mebbe saved his sister."

"Gee!" Jimmy and I both gasped together.

Percy was blushing with pride.

"I sure *did* see it! It was right where I could touch it!"

"Then, why'n't it bite you?" Jimmy pursued forthrightly.

Well, none of us will ever know why. Bears are that way sometimes.

The Cannibal I

The sunshine on the high elevations of British Columbia's Cassiar Plateau warmed the clear air of the basinlike valley in its ring of high peaks. Two five-month-old grizzly cubs, tired from their tumbling run-and-swat play ran to their mother and there sucked gluttonously from her two lower teats. The lush vegetation, berries, vines, and bulbs, and the abundant marmot population had made her body round and full, and her milk was plentiful and rich. Quickly satiated, the tired cubs licked the traces of white liquid from each other's faces. Then, where the sow had gouged out a pan of fresh earth seeking white lily tubers, they curled in a ball. Soporific from the effect of filled bellies, warm sun, and sweet-scented soil, they struggled only briefly to use each other as a pillow.

The stronger male cub pushed his head across the neck of the drowsier female. He then regurgitated the excess of warm fluid that his gorged belly would not hold. As the warm sun's rays filtered deeply into his fur, sleep overcame him.

Abruptly he awoke, his ears pierced by the frightened snorts of his mother. Beyond her, from a distance he could not judge, came a strange whirring, chattering sound. It was like nothing he had ever heard. Accompanying the chattering metallic noises were strangely guttural animal sounds.

"Put the camera down, Johnny! The old bitch is up watching us!"

The strange commotion continued. It was drowned out by his mother's agonized warnings. He and his sibling stood stiffly upright in the stance of prairie dogs, staring in the direction their mother faced. The unique animal sounds became suddenly excited.

"Oh Christ! She's got two cubs!"

Abruptly, the hind feet of their mother threw dirt upon her cubs as she plunged in the direction of the sounds. Her agile bulk lunged fiercely away, as she headed protectively at the source of the strange noises. A second later, in the open, she was up on her hind legs, her head moving in an arc, seeking by scent and sight to locate the intruders more exactly.

The ear splitting detonation was as piercing as that of very close lightning but shorter and sharper. It echoed and re-echoed about the valley, paining the male cub's tender ears. He was barely conscious of the whimper of his littermate snuggling against his side. The roaring sounds from his still upright mother stopped suddenly. Within a split second he heard her again rushing through the low bushes toward the source of the menace. Still audible was the whirring of the camera. Once again, just beyond the second narrow skirt of bushes, the head and shoulders of his mother appeared, as she stood upright a second time.

"Jesus! She's gonna come all the way! Shoot her!"

In quick succession there were two more of the sharp crashes. Accompanying the second detonation was the whoosh of air expelled from torn lungs, then the heavy thump of a body.

Above the sounds of dying came the low, unfamiliar grunting tones of the adversaries, and the sound of brush breaking as they moved warily from their cover.

"She's *down*! Hit her again!"

"Damn! I didn't want to kill her! But she was comin' so fast!"

"She'd a got to us!"

The low moans of the cubs' mother were only fifty feet away. He started toward the only source of protection he had ever known. Then came loud, clumsy sounds of approaching animals pushing through the brush, the thumps of their footfalls accompanied by warning tones. Finally, he heard the sudden desperate sigh, the final gasp of life escaping from a dying creature. The sound was not unfamiliar: it resembled the last wheeze of a dying caribou calf or that of a young predatory wolf caught too near their spring den, or the last sounds of the life breath being swatted from a fat marmot dug from under a boulder.

Suddenly, without knowing why, the cub turned and ran in the opposite direction. The sound of his littermate pounding at his heels only urged him on. The noise of the strange animals near his mother receded into the distance. The cubs' headlong rush took them back to the denning area where the sow had raised them following the melting of the snows from the valley. He sought for and found the welcome darkness of the den, where it had been dug in the glacial silt of the creek bank. Within seconds his panting littermate, whimpering, snuggled in beside him. He too began to whimper.

That night was the coldest he had known.

An Indian summer frost made each star sparkle against the black depths of the sky. His sister had whimpered along with him the whole night through. Even that had been a comforting sound. As the hours crept slowly by, he twice went to the mouth of the cavern seeking the warmth of the fat belly that had suckled him. Despairing, he returned each time to the other cub.

A light blueness awakened in the eastern sky, resolving into saffron hues, thence to fiery red, and almost suddenly to the brightness of day. Cold and hungry, he went back to snuggle against the mewing bundle of his littermate. An hour later they both stood up on their hind legs outside the den, bawling their loudest, bellies sunken with hunger.

All that day they slept and bawled. The next night was warmer, and they snuggled close, hungrier, expectant. Hunger was now a pain in their stomachs; their whimperings were almost a whisper. Both of them had been exhausted by their long periods of bawling. They had slept deeply. Now, as they arose, a weakness was in their legs.

Some instinct suggested to the cubs that they return to where their mother had last been with them. The back trail leading across the valley floor had been worn, in places a foot deep, by the annual tread of woodland caribou migrations. All along it was the scent of the she-bear, stronger where the fresh morning dews had dripped from her fur as she daily brushed against bushes. The familiar smells still hung on the surface of the soil, cold but distinct. They led to the small open meadow in which she had last been digging. Hunger was extinguishing the memory of the reason for their flight from the place. More strong was the recollection of the family group.

The male cub stood on his hind legs, bawling loudly. His crying echoed back from the walls of the valley. In the distance a wolf howled. That menacing response cut the bawling short. The yelp, bark, or howl of a wolf had always brought their sow quickly to her feet. When she was on guard, a swift hard blow from her forepaw had taught the growing cubs, early, not to make noises which would reveal their location. Dimly the cub remembered that warning notes had been her last reaction in this place. Too, there had been the strange assortment of foreign noises.

But now there was only blue sky—and silence.

For several moments the two cubs sat side by side in the center of the little open meadow. Only stillness was in the crystal air.

A slight thermal draft came down the nearby creek channel. Faint upon it was the scent of the sow.

Immediately both cubs bawled.

Otherwise the silence remained unbroken.

Instinctively they stopped their bawling, this time without the distant howl of the wolf. When the breeze wafted downstream again, the mother scent, now strangely corrupted, came once more to them. The male cub moved up the breeze toward the disturbing scent. As he passed through a hedge of thick brush, the sow scent became stronger. More aggressively he pushed across a small area of tall grasses into a second low hedge. The scent was growing stronger, more acrid. At the edge of the green shrubbery the sow smell was suddenly quite strong.

In the middle of a trampled-down area of grasses and low shrubs, the yellowish tufts of her shedding undercoat reflected the noonday sun. They had found the prone hulk of the sow. Emitting a loud squeal, he ran to the prostrate form. The large head was lying over a boulder. Two legs on one side were raised almost upright by the gases forming in her abdomen. Her teats, wet with dew, were warmed by the sun on the uppermost side of her body. She looked almost as if she were alive.

His hungry lips and pink tongue thrust hard against the strangely stiffened teat. Almost instantly beside him, his littermate also began to suckle.

CHAPTER 2

The Flume Bears

It was not long after the handloggers went after the black bear, armed with felling axes, in defense of Sis Penfold. With whatever substitutes for brains in Irish, perhaps all, young boys we had contrived a plan. The three of us, totaling about twenty-five years in age, would go about a mile and a half up the old shingle-bolt flume and "hunt" some black bears where the lineman had seen them feeding regularly along the right-of-way for the high-tension line.

This high-voltage transmission line carried power from distant hydroelectric plants to the Howe Sound Copper Mines, which were many miles up the fjord of Howe Sound, and at that time were one of the world's largest copper resources. The two-hundred-foot right-of-way, cut through almost virgin forest, was kept cropped of any trees that might interfere with the transmission line. The clearing allowed a sunny, fertile landscape for the growth of many wild berries: thimble, blackcap, raspberry, gooseberry, salmonberry, blackberry, strawberry, and, in late August, literally hundreds of pounds of ripe huckleberries. Small swampy spots in the glacially filled pockets and undulations of the unique batholithic rock formations provided alternate vegetation, such as skunk cabbages that flourished during spring and early summer. In effect, the right-of-way was an ideal habitat for bear.

Between the power line and the narrow waterfront road a strip of deep forest and regrowth, averaging a mile in width, was a barrier to most human travelers. Along the entire north shore the strip was cut by less than a dozen trails, which were mostly unused, overgrown logging skid roads. The flume once had carried shinglebolts from near the summit of Hollyburn Ridge, 3,000 feet above, the millsite, just above sea level. The main mill buildings had fallen down, and the outbuildings were awry, but the flume was still almost intact.

That shingle-bolt flume was very much a part of the bear hunt we three boys were planning. The V-shaped chute was about four feet across at the top with a carefully fitted V-block about a foot wide placed in the bottom, making it almost watertight. The flume passed through rugged rock formations, the spindly timber legs rising in some places fifty feet above sudden valleys, fissures, and glacial moraines, at times using the granite bluffs as footings for long bridges.

The chute, which was about forty feet off the ground where it crossed the power-line right-of-way, provided a commanding view of that clearing for about half a mile on one side and less than three hundred feet on the other. It was at the juncture of the flume and the power line that my buddy Jimmy McCullough, our Nisei Japanese pal, Seiji Homa, and I planned to hunt a

bear. I think we actually used the expression "kill a bear"! We planned. . . .
well, we thought. . . .

My father kept a .22-caliber repeating, pump-action Winchester rifle in
the back corner of his bedroom closet. Both my brother and I could borrow
it when we had permission. I was well tutored in its use, having accompanied my father on his hunts for grouse or pigeons, and ducks since I was
five. He also had taught me to disassemble, clean, and oil it. Because permission was almost invariably granted but was nevertheless an inconve-
nience, my brother and I both cautiously "borrowed" the rifle whenever we
expected Dad to be away or fully occupied for a few hours. As he had a
small but growing general store, tearoom, gas station, and boat rental, he
generally was too busy to notice all that went on with his two boys.

The rifle was what was called a takedown or breakdown model. On its
receiver was a knurled bolthead with a slot in it to receive a dime or screw-
driver, with which one could unscrew the bolt and release the barrel from the
butt. Thus the gun could be either packed into a short space or, as I discovered, concealed quite well on my person. I would simply take the rifle apart,
shove the barrel down my pant leg, slip the butt end up into my opposite
armpit under my shirt, sweater, or coat, then walk right past my father (not
too close) and off on my journey. It made very little difference that the barrel
down my pant leg made me walk with a stiff limp, as I usually did have a
"gimp" of some kind from climbing and falling out of trees, school sports,
wrestling, judo, fights, and falling off my bike (which had a bent front frame
that caused severe problems).

On the day of the hunt I was just across the road from the store, limping
up the skid road toward our assigned meeting spot for the bear hunt, when
my father's voice rang out from the front of the store.

"Michael!"

"Yes, Dad!" I answered prayerfully. I was undoing the top button of my fly
so I could slip out the gun barrel from the leg of my pant and run. Dad's face
was not really stern, however.

"If you are meeting Jimmy up there, you boys stay out of the dam!"

"Yes, Dad, I know. We will!"

As a customer came to the storefront, he turned away. I was glad he had
not seen the utter relief on my face. His admonition had been deserved: the
small water supply for three houses came from a tiny seepage spring about
which a ten-foot-wide concrete dam had been built. Occasionally, during the
hot summer months, Jimmy and I had skinny-dipped in the cool waters—
until we had been caught.

I heaved a sigh of relief and limped up the trail. Then, about one hundred
feet ahead of me, Seiji and Jimmy poked their heads from the bushes. I hurried to them.

"D'ya get the gun? D'ya get it?" Jimmy asked eagerly.

"I got it. I got it! My dad almost caught me, though!"

"I know. We heard him," acknowledged Jimmy.

"I got shells," grinned Seiji, extending a palm with several shiny copper-jacketed .22 cartridges. "I got six from Nojima!"

We were elated. Six shells would be enough to kill a herd of bears, we thought. I had seen a .22-long bullet go right through six inches of cedar, and Seiji said one had gone through an eight-inch standing alder tree trunk.

We'd kill 'em all right!

Jimmy, who had lived in the city most of his life, was less certain.

"I dunno! Wood ain't *bone*. Bears' heads are made of bones."

I argued that either Seiji or I could hit one right in the heart, and that was the way to kill them—in the heart! We sneaked up the trail leading to the flume end, bypassing the handloggers' shack (their operations had been halted temporarily by shingle-bolt surpluses), and climbed into the flume where it terminated at a recently dried-up pond. Its height at that point was about fifteen feet, but thereafter it varied from six feet to forty feet up near the power line. To be so high made us feel quite sure of ourselves, and our courage, as a threesome, was high. We believed that bears could not climb fast. Even if they could, we could all run faster than most of our school-mates, if they did.

We were exalted with expectation, as we sweated from the climb up the occasionally slippery flume. We were nearing the bears, which we had so often heard fed right along the power line in the open. Just where we came from the shadows of the surrounding timber, a granite outcropping directly under the flume provided a footing without stilts. We paused for a moment of discussion: a bear could jump right onto the flume by climbing that out-crop—but we could run past it before it could climb in.

Just at the border of the open right-of-way we peered over the plank edge toward some dense huckleberry patches. The crushing of rotted wood, or of a branch, drew our attention to a huge black head that was right then pulling whole branches into its pink maw, stripping off berries, leaves, and all. It was a large female black bear, and near her three yearling cubs were divest-ing the bushes in a like manner. Perhaps even adult men would react the way we did.

"Jesus, there's bears down there!" I choked out quietly.

"There's three—" Seiji managed.

"I gotta pee!"

I don't know who said it, but it applied to all of us. We quickly back-tracked almost to where the flume met the granite outcrop. We eyed that vulnerable spot with some trepidation, yet found it safe for relieving our-selves over the side. The ensuing parley on attack was brief. I was to shoot first, as it was my rifle; Seiji second, because he was a good shot and had contributed the shells; and Jimmy last, because he was not as adept or trained with rifles. We only considered the question whether we should shoot at all insofar as we discussed where the bears could get us if we did not get them. Children's courage is often fostered mainly by peer judgment. I had quelled whatever fear (lots of it) was in me. Jimmy was always my dependable ally. Seiji was a kamikaze in that he feared loss of face almost more than death. You simply could not scare him; he would fight anyone, large or small (he later took on the Canadian government and won citizenship for his people). Our team was nearly indomitable.

I peered secretively over the edge of the flume, some forty feet up—and found myself almost directly above the bears. They had moved, or we had miscalculated. My head snapped back like a yoyo on a string. Jimmy witnessed the act.

"Why'd you duck?" he whispered.

"They're right down *below* us! They're comin'!" I replied.

"Holy Heck! Mebbe we'd better run!" said Jimmy.

Seiji remained calm. He peered over the edge with all his Oriental composure. He took so long that I started to pull him back—just as he ducked.

"They're goin' along the trail toward the bluff!"

I leaned over the flume edge to ascertain if he was right (or perhaps just because I was scared, and trying not to show it). Sure enough! The old lady, leading the two cubs, was shuffling toward the bluff. I don't know what happened inside me (later the response would become instinctive), but all of a sudden the rifle was at my shoulder and pointed, I thought, at the top of the shoulder on the big, black female.

Crack! Then a metallic clicking as I injected another shell. *Crack*!

The roars of the bear seemed to fill the whole valley and to shake the trees. And they came directly following my second bullet. The roars should have jellied my legs but seemed instead to fit them with steel springs. I passed Seiji and Jimmy in the first two jumps, going down the flume at whatever speed a half-grown boy can travel when full out.

"Run! They're comin'!" I remember shouting.

None of us stopped during the first quarter mile. Even when we fell, we kept sliding. We sped off the flume and headed toward the shacks of the handloggers. We could take refuge there if the bears came. At the edge of the millpond Jimmy grabbed my shoulder.

"Where's your dad's rifle, Mike?"

I remember my chin quivering with sudden fear. *Where was the gun?* At that moment I could not remember. In the flume? Had I dropped it there? Or over the side? Bears were one thing; my father's ire was another. I looked at Jimmy.

"Will you go back with me?"

"Jesus, not now! Mebbe tomorrow. D'ya kill the bear?"

"I dunno if I even hit it!" I answered dejectedly.

"Sure yelled loud!" said Seiji with some awe. "I'll go up with you, with Jimmy—tomorrow."

In fact, we left the rifle for two full days, during which I sweated blood over whether my father would go to the bedroom closet to take it out. Fortunately, he was kept busy with a new addition to the store counters. When we went back for the rifle, it was lying right in the flume within ten feet of where I had shot it. No bear lay below. None was ever reported dead along the powerline or near it. No cubs were around. (If the female had been killed, the cubs would have stayed for at least two days.) None were reported, and we did not see any. So in our boy minds we concluded that we had done no harm.

Jimmy, who was nearly nine years of age, was the elder stateman among us. He and Seiji were almost a year and a half older than I was. The time of our "bear hunt" was just after the turn of this century; the setting was the backwoods. None of that, however, justifies the act. We were children, thinking as children do, influenced perhaps by biblical quotations about beasts and man's dominion over them. We all went to church or Sunday school, and sometimes listened, in an age when it was your "right" to take, kill, or devour game.

I have never lost my feeling of guilt.

The Cannibal II

Hunger burned in the cubs' bellies as they suckled the once-familiar teats of the sow grizzly. Even the unfamiliar consistency and odor of the soured milk had little effect upon their avid desire to swell what had always been amply filled bellies. Abruptly, however, the teats became dry and unyielding. The male cub pushed his female littermate away from each of the teats. Valiantly she fought to return.

Finally, exhausted and weak, she sat whimpering beside the mother's familiar head, there desperately awaiting the awakening which had always before produced the gentle licking of the mother's warm, pink tongue, followed by a fondling from her solicitous paws. Instead, a blast of gas escaping the inflated intestines erupted from the open mouth. The noise frightened the cub, as did the unfamiliar gurgle coming from the throat. She cowered.

The male also jumped back, startled. He finally realized that there was no more sustaining liquid in any of the teats. He went to the sow's head and batted playfully at her ear. Before, when she had dozed with her belly flat to the ground to rest her scratched and sore mammary glands, his ploy had awakened her.

Yet there was no response. She remained quite still, in the absolute silence of death.

Ever since his mother's early feedings on the winter-killed caribou after their departure from the winter den, he had become used to the sour, acrid scent of carrion. He did not yet recognize the aura of death which hung about the downed sow. In the distance he heard the yapping of an animal that his mother had always treated disdainfully unless it came too near her kill, or was approaching her young too closely. It was a coyote's call, a sound he knew but did not fear. The female cub moved disconsolately nearer her littermate, brushing close against him, still whimpering constantly. He welcomed her warmth. Seeking solace, he snuggled more closely against the fur of the sow's hump, there pushing slightly under its curve. The now unresponsive teats, he knew from experience, would renew their abundance only after an elapsed period. Hungry, both cubs slept.

The sound of swishing wings partially awakened him. Before he could open his eyes, a hard, pointed beak struck at his eyeball. He raised his head just in time, and the strike missed a direct hit.

With a squeal of pain he sprang to his feet. A raven, surprised that not all the animals were dead, jumped backward and upward into flight. The cub's flailing paws just missed it. The big, black bird's wingspread was greater than his own length, yet there was no fear in him. When his mother was feeding upon caribou and mountain-sheep kills, he and his littermate had disportingly chased these large birds. Now, aroused by the sudden attack, he watched as the obsidian feathers, first ruffled by the contracted skin, relaxed back into their sleek, shiny layers. The raven then uttered that familiar *skurrooock* that travels miles over somnolent and silent air. The beady eye, still watchfully turned toward him, was fifteen feet away, atop one of the stunted conifers of the high plateau.

Again the *skurrooock* sounded deeply. A growl emanated from the cub's mouth, its throatiness a desperate imitation of his mother's tone. For moments he remained rigid, with his back humped, threatening. Then once again abruptly aware only of his hunger, he turned and rushed to the teats where they lay exposed to the summer sun. Only a faint trace of sour liquid came to his suckling. At the sound of the activity, his sister, also awakened by the raven, came rushing around the inert body. Moments later totally disappointed, they both sat back and whimpered aloud.

The bark of the coyote broke into their chorus, this time from nearby. Alarmed by its closeness, both of them ran to the shelter offered by the back side of the sow and remained there quietly.

Only a slight rustle of grass gave evidence of the female coyote's approach. Suddenly the animal appeared less than six feet away, poking her head furtively out of the low brush. From her mouth dangled the bodies of two field mice she was carrying to her own den of pups.

Recognizing the dangling animals as the kind of food his mother had been giving him during recent weeks, the starving male broke the barriers of his caution. He rushed headlong at the inquisitive, owl-faced coyote.

So sudden and unexpected was the attack that the coyote, although equal to the cub in size, opened its mouth and swerved away in fright. The two field mice dropped to the ground. In a split second the cub had swept them up in his own jaws and swallowed them whole. He then growled with a new authority.

The female coyote, timid by nature when confronted by the grizzly species, backed away, then turned and slunk from the obviously determined cub. He was heartened by the unexpected turn of the encounter, and the demanding void in his intestines was slightly assuaged. He went over and nuzzled his littermate. Since the loss of his mother's sounds, the female cub's whimpering had taken on an almost reassuring note. Desperately they both returned to the sow's head, awaiting some movement or recognition.

CHAPTER 3

Brownie

The grizzly cub's exact place of origin was unknown to me. But this I do know: He was the first pet to be, however briefly, my own. He became known in our family as Brownie, and I still think of him by that name.

The cub was a grizzly of the silvertip type, and he was given to me by a Mr. McKenzie one afternoon when I was between seven and eight years of age. The said Mr. McKenzie was a conductor on the ill-starred Pacific Great Eastern Railway, which was commonly described as "starting nowhere and going nowhere."

The Pacific Great Eastern began (or ended, whichever way you saw it) at the small village of Squamish, British Columbia, at the extremity of the mountainous Howe Sound fjord. The line ended (or began) at Prince George, then also a village on the frontier. A separate fifteen-mile section of the railway ran from North Vancouver, then an upstart "city" on the northern shores of Vancouver Harbor, through West Vancouver, where we lived, to Horseshoe Bay (also isolated). The grandiose, undercapitalized company went into insolvency before it had accomplished its final coastal linkage, but its avowed intent was to connect (as it did fifty years later) the vast northern interior of British Columbia with Vancouver, already an important seaport, Canada's "pride of the Pacific." The railway ran along a narrow, sometimes precipitous, always isolated right-of-way through prime moose, deer, and black- and grizzly-bear country. It is likely that the cub came to me as the result of a train-track problem. Even today, the carnage wrought by modern trains going through narrow passes and deep winter snows, sometimes banked fifteen to twenty feet high by plows, is excessive on moose trapped between these barriers.

Naturally, when I heard that a cub was at the McKenzies, I visited it. The family had built a new home about a quarter mile down the road. Brownie was given to me on a steel dog chain which had tethered him to a post of the house. He came with Mr. McKenzie's blessing (and, I now suspect, with some relief). Few details of even such an exciting event as being given a grizzly bear cub impressed themselves clearly upon my mind but the important details do. Whatever training Brownie received had been at the hands of another grizzly cub and a patient parent. I recall clearly that he bit, he climbed up legs, he scratched, he hissed and whined, and he gamboled to the end of the tether and well beyond, while dragging me on my seat of my pants or knees and elbows. And, I remember very clearly, he did not stop for any rest.

By the time I got him to the edge of our waterfront property, he almost had me beaten. My face had been scratched (and, alternately, licked); my

Another Squamish valley black bear.

hands were in disrepair; my new hand-me-down tailored pants were torn in two places, one knee showing and bloody; and I was bathed in sweat and quite desperate. At the property edge we were met by my father.

"Michael! What have you got there—now!"

"Dad, help me please! He'll get away!"

My arms were so tired from holding the chain and fighting him off that I was actually desperate.

My father's blue-eyed stare was somewhat amused, unyielding.

"Did you say 'get away,' son?" He wagged his head and clucked his tongue. "I'd be more surprised if *you* can!"

He shrugged and was turning away.

"Aw, please, Dad. Please—"

That seemed to make up his mind, and he turned and strode down the path to the house.

"If he got you this far . . . you'd better let him bring you the rest of the way!"

He walked unconcernedly down the garden path leading to the back door. Although his face was turned away, I somehow felt he was watching the fun through eyes in the back of his head, grinning broadly. Just as he put his hand out to turn the back doorknob, his voice resounded ominously, "Then we'll decide what to do with the *both* of you!"

I heard my mother's voice querying him. The thought entered my head that she would be my ally. Distracted for a moment, my attention left Brownie. It was enough. His sharp teeth sank into my pant leg, right where my leg was in it. I let out a yell and swatted at him. He made the mistake of rising up on his hind legs to bat back at me, and I caught him with a full hard swing of my fist right on the jaw, knocking him sideways to the end of the chain and sprawling on his butt.

He let out a wail that would have done justice to a cat with two tails, both stepped on at once. And it all happened as my mother, my hoped-for ally, came out the back door.

"Michael, *shame* on you! *Shame*! The poor—"

And as she was coming close, Brownie, who sensed sympathy the way a blotter does liquid, went to her outstretched hand, pulling me with him. His long pink-grey tongue slid over her hand, and she drew back with a frightened start.

"Oh! Oh! It's a bear, not a puppy!"

"Yeh! Archie's dad gave him to me. Can I keep him? Can I, Mother?"

The blush beneath her golden hair showed her embarrassment and indecision. It was quite evident that my father had not told her it was a bear that I had just brought home. She was overwhelmed, and I pushed hard.

"He's tame. I'll look after him. Can I?"

Her eyes were taking in my disarray.

"Oh, Michael! Look at your new pants! Honestly, I don't know whatever

I'll do with you!" She turned hesitantly toward the back door, where I saw my father's grinning face just leaving the aperture. Mother looked helpless. "Alex! Alex, please!"

In answer Dad's now-controlled facial expression came into view. He walked over to my mother, patted her shoulder, and put his arm round her, just as she broke into tears. His eyes, however, were sternly upon me.

"Of course, you can't keep him, son!" he said slowly. "But for now give me the chain! You go and find a big nail to drive into the post at the corner of the woodshed. He can have a bed there for the night."

The "for the night" was a bit shaky, a disaster. For a week, ever since hearing of the bear, I'd coveted it. Why couldn't I keep it? I'd brought home wounded grebes, ducks, a cat (wild from the bush with a broken leg), robins, a squirrel, even fish taken from both the ocean and streams, and my mother and dad had always helped me succor them, though most of them had died. This young, obviously healthy bear wouldn't die and cause any distress.

"Aw, Dad, he won't eat very much! I'll look after—"

The cub seemed to sense that his future hung in the balance. He remained quiet, cute-looking, and lovable. My father could not have missed that cute cunning.

"Please, don't argue with me, son!" he responded sharply, but relenting.

It was time to leave the argument to fate. I knew Dad's soft spots, and I used them. If he was stern, you did what he asked or requested. I headed for the nail-and-spike box in the woodshed, where the hammers would also be. Looking up at the six broad feet of my father, Brownie was sitting calmly on his haunches, his tongue lolling a little out of the side of his mouth. He was panting, but calculating. My father held him loosely on the chain. I saw the look on Dad's face, and I took hope. His eyes were not stern; he was somewhat amused by the beguiling cub. Brownie, on the other hand, was figuring his next move, not a good one.

I saw it coming. The cub made for my father's nearer leg, put his front paws around it in a bear hug, and bit.

"You little beggar!" I heard my father exclaim.

The next thing Brownie was five feet in the air, hanging by the scruff of his neck on a strong right arm, which gave him two very affirmative shakes. I scooted for the woodshed but heard the squeal of anguish from Brownie. (As a protective measure he would squeal long before he thought he might get a slap.) My father responded in a somewhat disturbed voice. "Now then, ye spalpeen, you've not been hurt! Stop letting on so!"

He spoke in that soft southern-Irish brogue, so beautifully designed for a lullaby, which seemed to cure all cares. It slowed Brownie to a quiet whimper.

So far, so good! I had found a large spike and the carpenter hammer. My father came over with the cub trailing somewhat reluctantly. He had been tethered to a post before, and he seemed to realize that this would be another

such spot, but my father's strength temporarily subdued him. He stood leaning back on the chain while my father handed it to me, and I drove the spike
into it to hold it.

"Michael, did you say that Mr. McKenzie gave you the bear? Or was it
Archie?"

"Mr. McKenzie did—" And I felt bound to admit, "I told him you would
let me have it, that you said—"

His grey-blue eyes had a sterner look.

". . . that *I said* you could have it?"

It was a bad moment, one in which small boys hope the ground will open
beneath them and swallow them. The most inviolable rule in our family was
honesty. You simply did not lie. And Dad always knew when anyone was
lying.

"Yes, Dad, but . . ."

"Yes, but?"

"Well . . . you didn't say no, Dad!"

"And, you hadn't asked!" He shook his head disgustedly, stared up at the
sky as if seeking heavenly advice. "And you know that is a *lie*—not telling
the truth!"

The prickle in my groin lessened. The distinction between not telling the
truth and a lie was something like the difference between manslaughter and
murder. It seemed I was not guilty of an outright lie, just obfuscation, but
that was serious enough. I countered with all my might.

"Well, Dad, I said you wouldn't mind. That you let me have lots of other
wild pets—"

"Wounded ones—squirrels, ducks, fish—all sick or wounded."

I saw an opening.

"Then, Dad, a tame bear, a well one—not sick or wounded. I will feed
him and care for him!"

"Your mother always ends up with those chores! You go off to school and
forget she has them all day long.

He was weakening. I shut up. As I look back, it seems to me he was at
times a big kid himself, that he might secretly have liked to say he owned a
grizzly bear.

"Bend the nail over the chain—"

"But I won't be able to get him off it!"

"I know that! Now you get in and let your mother mend those pants. And
put some iodine on those cuts and scratches."

"Isn't there any peroxide?" I fired back. Iodine stung like hell and left
yellow stains.

"Michael—!" The note of exasperation in my father's voice, I was aware,
could bring a fast cuff to the head.

But Dad had relented some.

It lasted about a week. My bed was on the veranda in the open air, where I could easily hear Brownie's whimpering, and where I could hear my father's annoyed remarks when the cub wailed at night. When that happened I would take one of my Hudson's Bay blankets and curl up with the cub until he settled down. I even took him a hot water bottle a couple of times. But, probably because he missed his sow and sibling, he still wailed occasionally.

As Brownie and I grew closer, he and my family grew further apart. My brother told me Dad was getting rid of him. In my little world that was earth-shattering news. He had gotten loose in both the store and the house; had spilled flour, butter, sugar, and jam; had torn curtains; and had puked in the corner of the living room when I accidentally let him in. It was more than a generally citified family could weather.

He was gone one day when I came home from school, and there was no explanation except that he had been given a good home a long way off. I did not try to find out where he was because I knew that, as I had done before, I would head out for wherever it was and cause my family to hunt for me, even to getting out the police. So I silently swallowed the hurt. I felt that some-how he was still with me—which is hard to explain.

A couple of years later, perhaps three or four, one of our teachers, a forward-thinking one for her day, decided to take the whole class on a nature-study field trip. She even arranged for a free bus, which took us about six miles away up the Capilano River, which was being logged at the top end at the time. There was a good road up to the picnic site above the river, which was a scenic attraction with its torrential rapids running through deep canyons and some immense trees that still stood hundreds of feet tall in the clear mountain air. At the picnic site an early entrepreneur had established a small business, a tearoom-confectionery. And right near the building he had a large iron-barred cage with a bear in it.

Our teacher took us right off the bus and immediately into the field. She instructed us to spread out on the logged-off and regrowing area in search of any plant we did not recognize. Our mission was to bring the unfamiliar plant back to where she sat, on a log, with a large book in which she pressed our plants between the pages and made notations regarding place of origin and other such data. Seiji Homa, my Nisei bear-hunting chum, came along with me. He found a spirea bush with its feathery blossoming tufts and asked me what it was. My parents were hobby gardeners, and both my brother and I had our own flower gardens planted with our own personal choices of fruit trees beside them, so we were familiar with plant names. I gave Seiji a name for the plant, and as his second-generation English was not quite as good as mine, he did not notice slight nuances in the pronunciation. I told him the plant was a rare one.

He rushed up to the teacher with the piece of flowering brush in his hand, excitedly brandishing it.

"Teacher, Teacher! I got *diarrhea*!"

There were some guffaws from the boys, a slight titter from the girls, and some consternation on the teacher's face. She gained her composure and gave him the right name for the plant. I had seen enough. I knew Seiji's right hand could find an eye with a balled fist, and that it would not be long before he found me and perhaps my eye. And soon the teacher would learn where he had gotten the name of the plant. I headed for the bear cage near the tearoom-confectionery. It would be a good time to have a look at the bear, while Seiji, at least, cooled down.

First I went into the confectionery and bought an O'Henry bar with my dime lunch money. My next maneuver, to outwit Seiji, was to go to the bear cage and sort of blend in with the few couples who were staring into the animal's compound. At the picket fence surrounding it, which was about six feet from the iron bars, I stopped and looked at the big bear lying in the dust at the far end of the cage.

Something about the brownish coat and the head was familiar. It hit me with a rush, and I vaulted over the picket fence gleefully, shouting a greeting.

"Brownie! Hey! Brownie!"

My voice had broken just recently, and I squeaked on occasions of excitement. This was one of those times.

The bear got up and stood uncertain, eyeing me at the edge of the steel bars. Its nose worked, its round reddish eyes blinked. It made a bluffing half rush toward the bars, stopped, then came forward with a series of grunts. Then it made a rush right at me. I vaguely heard concerned sounds from behind me.

"Brownie! You old bum!" I was saying.

My hand patted the rough hair of his massive head, and he squealed. Startled, I withdrew my hand. His big paw came out through the bars hooking claws into my pant leg in a lightninglike movement. He drew my foot between the steel stays like a loose banana. The jar was painful and numbing.

"Brownie! Don't you know me?" I appealed.

The answer was a slavering pinkish-gray tongue licking my fingers where they clutched the cage bars in an effort to withdraw my leg. There were screams from behind me, some moans. I was so delighted that I fed the big grizzly my whole O'Henry bar. He took it gently as I patted his great rough head and talked to him. There was a roar of male anger and consternation from behind me.

"Get out of there! Get away from that bear! He'll kill you!"

The tearoom owner's hand gripped a long-spined pitchfork designed for haying. He was upset and yelling wildly at me. Brownie was doing his best to hook his nails once again into the leg of my pants (a method he had learned as a cub to pull that member toward him), while I was still patting his head.

"He'll take your arm off! Get out of there, kid!" yelled the man with the pitchfork.

"I know him, sir! He's *my* cub. My dad gave him to——"

"Shut up! And get out of there before you get killed!" yelled the man, with the pitchfork held almost in my face.

I turned and patted the bear's head in an effort to convince the angry man.

"See, sir! He knows me!"

It was apparent that the tearoom owner was stupified by what he saw. He put the pitchfork almost at my chest, still yelling for me to get out. While he continued to fume, I reluctantly backed away, then vaulted the fence. I was both hurt and angry.

"You're scared of him!" I said offensively.

"I'll thicken your ear if I hear any more insolence from you!" he replied.

I knew when to shut up. And nearby I saw Seiji eyeing me warningly. I looked back at Brownie's almost soft-eyed stare and heard that soft moaning which bears will give in times of uncertainty. Pouting, I walked away. My teacher sheared off my nature-study marks on account of the misnaming of Seiji's flower, and she threatened to report my undisciplined conduct to the school principal. My anguish was softened only by my reunion with Brownie.

Yes, it happened just like that.

I earnestly advise, however, that no one ever consider doing the same thing. It could be disastrous. All boys smell, some more strongly than others, and I genuinely felt that Brownie knew me, just as, for example, hounds will follow a man's track, and sheep dogs will separate their own flock from a mixed one. I assume that my scent, my voice when it broke, and other characteristics were recognizable to Brownie, even though I had grown a couple of feet (just as he had). The candy in my hand was also a delight to him. Yet I was a headstrong boy taking a very foolish chance. Do not try to emulate my example. You may not be that lucky!

I did not go back to see Brownie again. Too tough to face! Later I heard that he had been released or had gone to a zoo, but that he had not died. Our short times together are probably what has made me write three books on bears, fostering an uncertain empathy.

The Cannibal III

As they slept, all was silent in the still autumn air.

The hoary marmots' warning whistles finally aroused the male cub. Often those piercing whistles, ringing out almost constantly over the vast spaces of the high plateau, had made his mother deviate from her chosen path. When she had done so, the detour usually had culminated where large, glacially deposited boulders protruded from higher ground. Into those hummocks the marmots habitually burrowed double-entrance chambers. There they took advantage of the rock and earth cover at the approach of predators. The grizzly bear was their worst enemy, using its long talons and enormous strength to dig away the earth, occasionally overturning even the boulders that were the roofs and supports for the marmots' deeper tunnels. The cub remembered his mother's prodigious digging.

The nearby whistling became more insistent, an unmistakable signal to the bear cubs of a once-familiar food source. Aroused by his hunger, the cub got up from the curled ball in which he and his littermate were lying. Once again he heard the piercing whistle. The path that he followed was not new to him, and it was made even more familiar by the faint residual scent of his mother. The hollowed pathways through the brush surrounding the meadow led to a slight incline, then upward. Mounds of brown, freshly turned earth remained where the female grizzly had dug them out only a week before. From some of the diggings she had extracted the bulbs that were her main forage. A short distance away, at the top of the slope, lay the tunneling from her other major, fruitless dig into the whistling marmot's den. Twice, perhaps three times, from both approaches she had assaulted these burrows yet had not reached the inner den.

The strident, almost challenging whistle of the burrow's owner rang clearly on the Cassiar Mountain air, inviting the two cubs. As they reached the foot of the hummock, the two small bears stopped, uncertain.

The warning whistle was piercing.

The sentinel at the top, erect as a driven post, compressed the air in his lungs, then allowed it to escape suddenly from his partially opened throat and mouth. The shrill whistle of warning was answered repeatedly from nearby and even from a distant knoll. The beady black eyes of the marmot remained rigidly fixed upon the two cubs, whose shapes told him they were his enemy, grizzlies. He stood straight up on his toes, exhaled one even more piercing whistle, then swiveled about and scurried into his den.

In this manner, on previous occasions, he had always defeated the sow.

Alerted by the quick movement, both cubs trotted hurriedly to the top of the little hill. There they were confronted by a deep cavern recently dug beneath an enormous rocky overhang. The smell of fresh marmot droppings attracted the cubs when they sniffed the drier earth at the entrance. They gobbled up the soft, fresh dung balls scattered during the animal's sudden retreat.

Then they sat on the sun-warmed earth, waiting expectantly for they knew not what.

Reassured by the quiet, the hoary marmot poked his head around the end of its inner tunnel. A bright shaft of sunlight partially blinded him. He was still hungry and preparing for winter hibernation, and his caution was lowered. Hearing no movement outside and no digging nearby, he spurted forward hesitantly until his whole body was struck by sunlight.

The flash of fur, similar in hue to his own, at the entrance to the narrow shaft triggered the male into the abrupt rush that earlier had made the coyote drop her prey. Yet, with another flash of sun on fur, the smaller animal was gone. The cub plunged down the shaft entrance, only to hit the solid earth around a boulder at its end. Beside it was a black hole freshly smelling of marmot, into which only half his head would fit. There the chase ended. The tons of glacially deposited boulders above were the impenetrable wall that had stopped the digging of his mother and other grizzlies.

Turning around with some difficulty, he recognized the surrounding chamber as a place that could serve as a safe den. Almost reluctantly he left it. His littermate, weakened by hunger, had trotted about ten feet farther along the hillock. She now lay in the sun-warmed, dry earth near the alternate entrance to the marmot's burrow. Her head lay across a small mounded ridge on the very edge of the entrance. Her hunger pangs, gnawing at her, kept her awake.

The male cub, hearing a noise behind him, swiveled in time to see the marmot's head poke cautiously out of the cavern. His answering rush was triggered by desperation. He shot downward after the animal, deep into the burrow, but again the dam of stone and earth brought him up short. Confused, this time he waited there in the semidarkness. He growled as deeply as his small chest would permit.

Surprised by the ability of the grizzly to enter so deep into its den, the marmot rushed toward the escape entrance on the other face of the earth and boulder mound. That tactic often left a determined grizzly digging right where it last saw its prey, allowing the marmot had time to escape through the second or third portal and scurry for an adjoining burrow.

The sun, shining directly into the second entrance to the burrow, struck the marmot's face. The animal stopped halfway out of the hole, blinking. In that instant the tiny teeth of the female grizzly sank into the back of its neck. Although the marmot was almost half her size and physically mature, the fear and desperation of the female strengthened her hold. Seconds later, the male cub, hearing the squeal of the marmot outside the tunnel accompanied by the sounds of struggle, turned and ran to the affray. He sank his teeth into the genital area, below the exposed belly of the rodent. Having taken hold, he began to shake the struggling animal.

Still, the female hung onto the neck, her teeth becoming even more deeply embedded. The desperate kicking of the animal's feet into his face aroused the male cub's anger. His jaws clamped even tighter. The pull of the other cub stretched the animal between them. One canine tooth sank deeply enough above the genitalia to rip the flesh, releasing blood and intestinal fluid into his mouth.

The smell of food caused him to react immediately, desperately. He bit more deeply into the crotch.

As the struggles subsided, the weakened female let go, but he held on, viciously determined. Near death, the marmot made a desperate attempt to pull itself toward the hole. The cub braced his back feet and hung on. As the marmot turned to bite him, the female reached for the marmot's suddenly exposed throat, and her grip on the softer area closed hard, cutting off the breath of the small animal. Overwhelmed the marmot stopped struggling.

Each let go in turn, biting again and again at the furry ball. The male's fresh bite was in the area of the stomach. The smell and taste of intestines was left on his lips and nose as he released the hold. Freshly incited, he bit savagely once more in the softer area.

A piece of intestine spilled out of the small tear. This was recognizable food. He pulled strongly upon it. Holding it securely in his mouth, he tried in vain to gobble it whole. The female rushed in, taking a similar hold, and a brief, growling tug-of-war ensued. When the gut broke apart, both of them pulled on the detached ends, bringing forth further lengths of gut. As they swallowed their first real food in days, each growled, woofed, and batted at the other.

Before their struggles to feed were finished, the sun had gone down behind the ring of mountains, leaving a bright frost in the chill air. Abandoning the now-unproductive furry ball, the cubs sought the sanctuary of the entrance hole that their mother had dug earlier in pursuit of the same marmot. There, deep within the earth, they curled together and slept.

That night, catching the scent of nearby carrion, a lone wolf howled incessantly, but in the den the sleeping cubs were not awakened.

CHAPTER 4

Without Warning

In 1939, as a constable stationed at Campbell River with the British Columbia Provincial Police force, I had few forms of recreation other than fishing and hunting. But fish and game were plentiful—a valuable supplement when wages were minimal—ninety dollars per month. Much of the Campbell district had been logged over within the past twenty to fifty years, and a lot of excellent game–producing land bordered the Campbell River itself, extending right to the summits of the lower Coast Mountains. Salmon migrated by the hundreds of thousands into the river and its good-sized tributary, the Quinsam River. The latter branched about half a mile up the delta to follow a narrow valley back into the foothills. Much of the lower deltas of both streams was open, muddy land with a canopy of alder trees. The banks of both rivers rose quite quickly, sloping upward to the hundred-foot-high glacially deposited plain.

The Quinsam River was particularly well known for the numbers of coastal black-tailed deer that inhabited its course throughout most of the year.

One afternoon a townsman dropped in at the police station to ask if I would like to accompany him and his buddy on a short deer hunt. As I had made an early start to work that day (sometime before dawn), I jumped at the chance. About an hour later we were on the Quinsam delta. Besides old shirts and pants, we wore logging boots (considered essential in those days for climbing over and walking along downed timber left from logging).

Each of us carried a rifle, and I was a little surprised at the suggestion of one of my friends. "Okay we'll draw lots for position. Whoever gets the short one takes the bottomland; the next, the sidehill; and the longest, the top," he said as he tightened his fist on the three short twigs.

I was about to resist when I realized that my other companion might take his side. My resistance was mainly to hunting at all with more than one man nearby, and also to the type of hunt on which they obviously had agreed. Such a deer "stalk" requires that the low man walk into an area barking like a dog. This simulated dog pursuit is designed to drive deer from the bottomlands up the fairly open sidehills into the quite-open logged-off lands above. In some places such a hunt is called a drive. Perhaps it has its origins among primitive peoples, but more lately it has been customary in the highlands of Scotland, where beaters and game-preserve wardens walk and beat the brush over the heaths, flushing grouse into the sitting guns of their "owners." I shirked my dignity and said nothing.

Of course, I did not get what I had hoped for, the long straw. I got the short one, which put me on the delta, where I knew the doe deer and fawns would be. An unlikely spot for a buck.

As agreed, after the other men had left, I waited ten minutes to give them time to clamber to their respective starting points. Then I started across the swampy delta. My feet almost immediately sank into muddy black loam that was only partially moss-covered. All through the delta lay the carcasses of salmon, which included everything from skulls with gaping eye sockets to partially eaten, almost fresh carcasses with blood still oozing from them. Intermingled with those carcasses were myriads of foot and paw prints: the spidery tridents of crows; the tiny dots of mink, mice, and rodents; the occasional rounded imprints of otter; lots of cloven hoof prints left by watering deer; and a couple of fairly well outlined imprints of both the front and the back feet of black bears.

Only once did I see the quite-identifiable larger imprint of a buck deer, and I looked long in the direction that it led. It was headed for the hillside, beyond where my partners should by then have been. I began reluctantly to imitate the bark of a dog. The barking was the sign that my passage had begun, an alert to the others, who at that very moment had my envy. It does not become a grown man to bark like a dog, and I was feeling a little foolish. I came across another set of bear tracks in a stretch of mud, then heard a deer jump and crash away just as I was looking down. A quick glance up caught the brown-gray flash of a departing doe. I stared after it for a moment to see if a buck would follow. None did. I lifted my rifle up to look at the breech.

The gun was a very light weight, pump-action Remington .32.20 rifle. It was my favorite coastal deer gun because it was very light and extremely accurate at the short ranges within which deer were usually encountered in the rainy coastal forest. It was not a bear gun, not of a caliber that one would choose for such a pursuit. The cartridge would not have had much shocking power in a bear at close range, but it is enough to kill most game with a well-placed bullet. In the gun itself was a tale.

A logger, specifically a bull cook, from upcoast had sought my advice about the caliber of guns to be used for bears. I had told him not to settle for less than a .30-30 cartridge and preferably to get something in a .303, .30'06, or .300 Savage, and I had asked why he wanted to know. With some reluctance, he told me that he had shot eleven shots at black bears up close but had not killed any of them—and this had occurred at a logging-camp garbage dump where there were usually dozens of bears. I had said, "Why don't you bring the gun in? Perhaps it's worn in the barrel or something. I'll look it over for you." A couple of weeks later his rifle had appeared with a box of shells under our police detachment counter. A note, written by one of our off-duty constables said, "Mike! The guy says this gun is no damn good. He left it for you. Said to keep it."

Later the town's general-store proprietor informed me that the same man had ordered a .300 Savage rifle, saying that I had recommended it for left-handed shooters, had paid cash, and had announced his fullest intentions of shooting some bears. I later took the .32-20 out on the range, to find that it indeed did shoot all over the place. There were two very good reasons why the gun had not killed a bear for him. Someone had cut half an inch off the muzzle with a hacksaw and left the burrs on the lands and grooves. The front sight must have been dropped heavily on a stone, or pinched in the vise when the barrel end was cut off: it slid from side to side in the machined groove. So did the back buckhorn sight. Neither sight yielded to finger pressure; both seemed to be firmly set. But the detonation of a cartridge would jar them from position to position. Any marksman's sights' correction after trying a group in one spot would be defeated.

After fitting the sights tightly, those faults were corrected. With a jeweler's file and light emery paper, I smoothed down the rifling edges. Then, when I targeted the rifle, it shot groups as tightly as any high-quality target .22 rifle—"clover leaved" at 50 yards. Earlier during the fall I had taken a buck with it at almost 150 yards. One shot had been enough.

I pulled back the pump action, noted the brass of the shell in the chamber, and pushed on the safety catch again. The slight sounds of one of my companions moving on the ridge came down to me quite clearly. I continued along the delta, slightly behind him, until the flat narrowed to a few feet in width. At that point a rock outcropping created an impasse. Without wading in the stream, I could not get by it on the lower level. The alternative was to climb the heavily bushed-in glacial moraine toward the midpath of the second hunter. But Pacific Northwest rain-forest growth often combines salal, willow, huckleberry, salmonberry, and strong sword ferns together with low growth of new conifers, mostly hemlock. This brush forms a wall a man can push hard against without making an impression.

Just before the edge of the bluff, and leading up its very steep incline, was a well-worn game trail, what we generally called a "bear trail," a veritable tunnel burrowed by the animals through dense brush. These trails are usually about thirty-six inches high and somewhat narrower. They are large enough for use by a bear and any smaller animal, but they are too low for a deer or a standing man. Bears, common on salmon streams, keep such paths open to their height, while the scurrying passage of many other smaller animals keeps the floors worn and free from regrowth.

This bear trail being my sole access to the bluff, I bent down and peered inside. It did not show much sign of light in the twenty feet that I could see from its entrance. It was well worn. In it I could encounter a bear. Although that probability was not great, I looked around for another approach. The timber was impenetrable. Perhaps an extraordinary dropping of ripe hemlock seed cones into such a newly cleared area causes particularly fast and thick growth of seedlings. Whatever the reason, trees had grown so thick that their limbs were interwoven, forming a hedge that could have been cut only with a sharp blade and some determination. This growth continued up the side of the moraine almost to the top. There was no way around it.

I checked my gun safety, then bent down into the tunnel of undergrowth. Within ten feet I was forced to my hands and knees, a posture I did not like. The worn earth stank and was damp, and in places it showed fish scales—an obvious sign that its multiple users—otters, raccoons, minks, skunks, and bears—dragged or carried salmon carcasses up it. This told me that it would open up soon, as those animals usually feed where there is enough light and open space to see the approach of a competitor or enemy.

About forty feet later, much of which I climbed on my knees at a steep slant, I broke out into a small natural clearing. At that point the rock bluff had little or no soil atop it. An open area about thirty feet long, it was tightly surrounded by second-growth hemlocks and some Douglas firs ranging in height from ten to twenty feet. The exposed rocks had mosses growing where moisture could collect, and its sunny southern exposure was ideal for lounging animals.

The clearing seemed a secure haven for man or beast. At its midpoint a tunnel similar to the one leading up from the delta afforded an alternate entrance or escape. The open space was dotted with salmon remains from bones and heads to a couple of partially eaten, fairly fresh carcasses. The place stank a little, but it was sunny, and after the struggle upward I wanted a smoke.

"Bears have been here. Would raccoons or otters have dragged carcasses up this far?" Those were my thoughts.

After rolling a smoke from my tobacco pouch, I sat down at the near top end of the clearing beside a still-green, branched, fir-sapling stump about a foot high. At that moment I heard Frank, the midman on the ridge, pushing his way through the second growth. He could smell the smoke from my rolled cigarette.

"Where in hell are you, Mike?" he inquired with obvious annoyance. "Jeez, is it ever tough going here! That goddam hemlock!"

"I'm in an open spot on the bluff, having a smoke!"

"How do I get there? It's so damn thick I can't see."

His voice came from a point about fifty feet from me and downhill.

"Go uphill about fifty feet. A bear trail, sort of a tunnel, leads right in here from the topside. You can't get to the bottom one."

About five minutes later he crawled in down the second passage and took my proffered tobacco pouch and cigarette papers. While he rolled a cigarette, he turned his sweaty face from side to side, peering around the enclosure.

"What in hell made you come in here?"

"There's a big bluff, and the only way up from the river comes in here. See any deer?"

"One I couldn't get a shot at. Jeez, it stinks in here! Look at all those salmon carcasses. That's strange!"

I had pulled a tuft of brownish grey wool from the top of the fir-sapling stump beside me and extended it for him to look at.

"What's that?"

By Thursday I was away again on another hunt, and we checked the lair many times, but there was never any further sign of the bear's return and the carcass remained untouched, only to be finished off by nature and the many ways of decomposition. After ten days of successful hunting for other game we returned to Kamloops. After my clients had left, I was told through the "Bridge Club" grapevine that Mr. McKelvie was now home, but he was suffering from lack of sleep and nightmares concerning the attack, as he was reliving his terrible moments. I took it upon myself to phone Mrs. McKelvie and I asked her if it would do any good if I came over and talked with her husband and showed him my bear pictures. Mrs. McKelvie was grateful for my call and asked me if I wouldn't mind coming over and seeing him. And it was in this way that I met Bob McKelvie, the man I had been so close to and did not know, being introduced by a grizzly that had mauled and had all but killed him.

That evening Doug and I talked about our lives since we had last fished together. He had gone into the north country to establish a hunting and fishing lodge for wealthy interests. It changed from its original ownership to another and finally came into his own hands. (Now the well-known steelhead-trout fishing camp known as Suskeena Lodge, it is in grizzly country.) I asked him about recent encounters.

"Oh, yes, we have grizzly bears on the river. We share space with them. We've made quite a deal of film footage in the area. You learn to respect them."

"Do you trust them, Doug?"

He looked at me quizzically.

"Do you think I should?"

I laughed. "I just thought you might have some opinions."

"I do. Man doesn't get into trouble with bears unless he enters their domain. If he does, he takes his chances. No one really knows what any individual bear will do. Some of them run. Some bluff. Some come all the way."

I interjected, "Yes, McKelvie proved that—if proof is needed. Have you had to shoot any in your area?"

He studied my face for some time, then smiled ruefully.

"Yes," he said. Then he paused as if considering the statement. "Yes, we had to kill a sow and a pair of larger cubs that became used to the camp. Sometimes paraded right through. The sow began taking her own way, smashing things. I put it off a long time—a year. Finally, they did too much damage. And there was the safety of the guests! The bears just had to go. I am really sorry about it! There was no other way."

His face held a serious expression of contrition, the inner regret of a man who makes the inevitable reaction to trouble all the while feeling a deep sense of guilt but at the same time recognizing that what he feels is more emotion than common sense.

My feelings were with him. I said so.

"I don't think any one of us—at our age and with our experience—can help but empathize with the living things that we once might have considered our just prey."

"You're right, Mike. Life changes some of your thinking." He paused thoughtfully. "What are you going to do, now you're in the area? Going fishing?"

"I wish I were! From here I'm going out to the West Coast—to Bella Coola, perhaps to Kitimat. But I want to talk to McKelvie—to get his side. Just how it happened to him."

"That's a good idea. I talked with him about it at the time. Haven't seen him in some years."

A week later, after I had returned from my 700-mile trip to the grizzly country of the Chilcoltin and Bella Coola valley, a pleasant voice answered the Kamloops telephone. It was Robert McKelvie. Yes! He would like to talk to me about the experience. No, he didn't mind. How about 8:30 P.M. today? He'd be free. He gave me explicit instructions how to get to his home in North Kamloops.

The McKelvie house was surrounded by tall, verdant trees. It was a nice homey bungalow with a broad driveway, in which a pickup truck competed with a boat trailer and the other gear of an outdoorsman. Bob McKelvie was standing beside the pickup, talking to another man. When his friend left, Bob invited me into his home. His wife, Lennis, a pretty woman whose black hair was touched with grey, came and sat with us in the anteroom to the farm-style kitchen.

Bob McKelvie is a big-chested, tall man. His face shows the effect of a grizzly attack and the mastery of a surgeon experienced in cosmetic operations. Bob is still ruggedly handsome, something he would be the first to deny—because he does not believe it. That became evident during our interview.

He first wished to know what the interview was "all about"—my reasons. I explained that the main purpose of this book is to bring a mature, true image of bear-and-people problems to the public, in order to negate the often misleading statements and opinions in the media, where the facts have been disregarded and even distorted. How did he feel about bears?

He looked up at the ceiling, then directly into my eyes.

"No different than I ever did, really. I'm a hunter; I have never killed bears. There were opportunities too. But I don't feel bitter."

It was not a surprising statement. I said so.

"That is a general feeling among those who have been harmed as you have. None of the people I've interviewed harbors any grudges. They wish it hadn't happened, naturally, but they're not bitter."

He was eyeing me as I filled the gap in the conversation. He spoke slowly when I was finished.

"One woman asked me if I felt bitter, and when I said, 'No, why?' She said, 'Well, having to go around for the rest of your life looking like *that!*'"

His eyes were eloquent in his strong face. I don't know when such a well of righteous anger has been quite so strong in me. My words came involuntarily.

"That woman was a bitch! She wasn't looking at you; she was trying to get something rotten out of herself. The rotten bitch!"

Both he and his wife looked at me a bit stunned. I did not know them well enough that I had the right to explode with such frank words. I sought hard to express the truth.

"Bob, you have scars. I know what scars mean. I was badly marked by smallpox when I was a kid. I was conscious of them—until someone said, 'Mike, scars give a man's face character! Hell, all you have to do is look at any good hockey player's face. The good ones all have scars. There is nothing wrong with your face. You look good!'"

He drew a deep breath and allowed a grin.

"My doctor is proud of the job he did—the doctor here in Kamloops. He takes a hold of this ear"—Bob illustrated by taking hold of his ear and pushing back the hair—and he says, 'This one is mine! I put this one back.' He's proud of the job."

Lennis smiled. "Take your shirt off, Bob," she said. "Show Mike the deep one in your back."

He got to his feet, unbuttoning his open-necked checked shirt. She admonished him not to tear it, and undid one of the cuff buttons: "Oh, Bob, be careful! Let me slip this arm off!"

McKelvie's real bulk was revealed. He is a thick-chested, narrow-waisted man well over six feet and 200 pounds. He turned, as his wife gently pushed him around, to show the six-inch long swath at the back of his left shoulder—the claw and bite marks of a grizzly bear. I was a bit amused by the frankness of the man and his wife and responded to the display with a smile.

"Hell, Bob! You're big enough to have tackled a grizzly without a gun!"

He shook his head ruefully.

"We might think that—until a grizzly takes us on!"

Lennis was helping him on with his shirt again, with almost a motherly solicitude for him. All I could think of was how damn lucky they both were to have that sort of relationship with a grown family. He sat buttoning his shirt. My facts were still to be ascertained. I said so.

"The other evening Doug Robertson told me his side of the story. I'd like to hear yours."

"Well, the newspaper and Doug's story in *Outdoor Life* were pretty accurate. I've been a hunter since I was a kid. In fact, I always planned to go to Alaska for a trip—just for one of those big grizzlies they have up there. I've never shot a bear. There was one came nearly into camp where we were hunting in the Anahim Lake area, where you just came from. We hunt moose in there nearly every year, stay at a ranch. And we saw three bears right alongside the road on a trip up the Alaska Highway."

He paused as if reviewing some of the bears he had seen. I asked him about the tragic trip to Tum-Tum Lake.

"Well, my brothers-in-law, Vern and Maurice Murphy, and I went up to Tum-Tum Lake to look for a moose. It was early in the season, and we figured that it would be good country.

"We had a twelve-foot aluminum boat, and we rowed the six miles to the other end. The mountains in that area come around on all four sides. When we got to the other end of the lake, we had it all figured out. Any moose would be on the river. We rowed, pulled, and slid that boat up the creek for five to seven miles. What we figured on was being able to drift silently downstream and pick up a moose on the way."

He grinned ruefully at the memory and rubbed his chin.

"When we hit the end of the lake again, we heard a bawling sound, like a calf bawling. The three of us got out of the boat and headed in the direction of the sound. We came to a shallow pond in the quite heavy bush. I was wearing rubber boots. Vern and Maurice had on leather boots. I said, 'I'll meet you on the other side.' They went around, and I walked across the swampy area. I came to three poplar trees where there was heavy brush behind. The next thing I knew, the grizzly had jumped on my back! I didn't even get a chance to get my rifle up! I lost it when the bear hit me in the back. I remember putting my hands up behind my head and yelling for help. I was down, and the bear was biting at me. It got one ear, and my nose was torn off."

My eyes were on him as he talked. The doctors who pieced his features together had done some job! There was little evidence of such a crippling disfiguration. My mind went to others, who had lost eyes.

Bob McKelvie was continuing.

"The other two boys didn't know what was going on. They heard some noises that they couldn't figure out. Then they heard my second yells. It only took a couple of minutes. The bear came after me again, when I yelled. And they started coming, firing their rifles. The bear took off as they came up. We never did see it again."

When I asked if he had remained conscious, McKelvie looked thoughtful.

"Yes. I stayed conscious right into the hospital. They rowed all the way down the lake, then drove 105 miles. The police met us and cleared the road. I was in intensive care for twenty-one days. The nurses turned me every twenty minutes. They tell me I lost a lot of blood. They used twenty-seven pints to keep me going. Then I was sent to the Vancouver General Hospital. They did more cosmetic surgery there."

Lennis stood beside him. Gently she lifted the hair at the back of his neck to show me the scars of surgery. Then she pushed aside the thick hairs of temple to reveal another one.

"They did a wonderful job," she said almost proudly. The doctor here was so proud of his own efforts."

"I think he should be!" I responded. There was no visible sign of his facial reconstruction.

Lennis McKelvie went into the kitchen, bringing back a pot of tea and plate of moist-looking, lightly iced cake. I gratefully picked up a proffered slice (three weeks on the road makes one appreciate home cooking and care). The fresh cake was even more delicious than it looked, and I remarked on the flavor and texture.

She smiled. "It's a carrot cake. I'm glad you like it!"

The second piece was even better. Bob grinned hospitably when I apologized for being piggish. He suggested I have some more—as he intended to do. I asked him if the bear experience had changed his hunting pursuits.

"No, I still go out for moose every year. We're fond of moose meat. Last year I got a moose after two days out at the Anahim Lake ranch that I told you about. We went back to get it with a horse and wagon—my wife and two kids and I. A grizzly had already buried it. It looked like a tractor had done it, there was that much earth moved over it. The males do that. And then urinate on it."

That bears urinate on a kill was news to me. I expressed my surprise.

"I'll be damned! I wasn't aware of that, Bob. I know that wolverines salivate all over meat. Make it stink so much that nothing else will touch it—but grizzly bears? I didn't know that. Something like a dog marking out its territory, I guess."

Bob nodded. "Yeah, grizzlies do that."

A short time later the couple walked out to my camper truck with me. We had become friends. They made me promise to come and see them next time through their town. I promised willingly. Something else I was finding about people who have suffered that unique tragedy of the wilds that I was researching: they all seemed somehow to be a little larger than life—tempered by adversity, much better than average humankind.

The Cannibal VIII

The slashes inflicted by the teeth of the grizzly sow healed slowly. One shoulder festered because the second-year cub's starving body could not fight off the infection. For over a week he hid himself during daylight, resting in deep brush where the sun barely filtered through, making sure of an easy flight in at least two directions. His body weight had diminished until he was almost as gaunt as a wolf. His temperament became morose and easily aroused. The uncomfortable heat of the summer was over, and the August skies often brought rain clouds. The berries were not yet ripe, and food sources were few. He fed on the grasses of the meadows, but mainly he ate the tubers that he dug from small, multiflowered patches.

He hungered greatly for meat. That longing led him to return to the valley's end, where he had first known life with his own sow and littermate. This had also been the site of the frightening attack by the young sow, which was still fresh in his memory, and his daily foraging brought him closer to the scene of that attack. Yet as he gradually approached the familiar territory, his keen sense of smell could detect no sign of the adult female. Finally, his wide circuit of the spot told him that the female had left, and he moved once more into the meadow where he had killed her cub.

Once again the scent of carrion drew him onward. His memory pinpointed the exact site of his rout. For an hour he circled in all directions around the spot, attempting to pick up any other scent, particularly that of the young grizzly mother. There was none but that of decomposing tissues.

Eventually he was drawn from cover by the tantalizing odors. After the pickings of the coyote and the ravens, little remained of the cub's carcass, but the yearling crushed the leftover bones and gobbled them down.

As he lay down to rest, the sharp reports of rifle fire crackled and reverberated across the meadowlands. Those re-echoing, explosive sounds came from the ring of mountains where he had first discovered the mountain sheep. For a long time he stared at those distant, black-faced rockslides. Something he could not well recall pulled him there, yet he was deterred by the vague memory of the loss of his littermate. Also, it was where the stinking animal had wounded him and driven them away from the sheep carcasses. It was a full day before his instincts answered the call to return. Self-preservation had become his overwhelming motivation.

With the sun bright overhead and a northerly breeze sweeping down the valley, he took a circuitous route to the edge of the rockslides. There, keeping to the bushy terrain, he would be downwind of the area from which the rifle sounds had earlier resounded. When he was within half a mile of that point, the packtrain of five horses and two riders was also moving northward.

That vaguely familiar sight struck terror into him. Turning swiftly, he ran into the bushes of the meadowlands. For an hour he could smell the acrid horse stench mingled with the smell of men. Then the odors were gone. As he emerged from the bushes, he caught the strong scent of fresh meat and guts. He began moving furtively along the edge of the rockslides. There was no movement on the mountainside.

He found the goat carcasses easily, halfway up the rockslides. There were two of them, heads missing, and most of the meat of the younger one was gone. For a full week he ate gluttonously, leaving the kills only to go to a nearby trickle of water from the melting snows on the peaks above. Each night he slept in a deep fissure under a nearby rock, determined that no other animal would get to the meat.

He was wrong.

It was the wolverine. It came vigorously up the rockslides. Its humping walk moved it quickly in the midday sunlight in a direct line for the carcass of the older mountain goat. When it was less than twenty feet away from him, the bear sprang suddenly from the cranny in which he had lain in wait for it.

He was in midair before the wolverine saw him. His heavier bulk drove the animal over on its back, and he bit savagely at its soft underbelly. In an unbelievably quick reaction, the animal sank sharp teeth into the side of the grizzly's neck. Twisting away, he swatted back with equal agility with both paws. The animal was shaken free. It turned with lightning speed, just missing a hold on the opposite side of the bear's neck. His own retaliatory bite caught it high on the shoulder. Rising on his hind legs to his full height, the grizzly shook with all his might. The wolverine's shoulder muscles tore away, leaving hair and blood in his mouth. The wounded animal backed off, hissing with fear and anger.

Enraged by the scent of fresh blood, the bear's temper burst.

His immediate rush bowled the wolverine over among the rocks. In a split second, despite its torn shoulder, it fled, tumbling down the slide, and disappeared from sight into the scrub brush. Although it took the bear a week to finish every scrap of the goat carcasses, the wolverine did not return.

Aggression, and a cunning approach to any area, had become essential to the bear's survival. Four more times during the late summer and autumn he approached new areas from which rifle sounds had come, in which he smelled the strange scents of men and horses. Always he found large portions of other animals. Twice he found full carcasses of headless caribou; once, dismembered mountain sheep; and later, the skinned-out carcass of the young female grizzly whose cub he had killed. Her remains had been in the far reaches of what he was now asserting to be his own indisputable territory. He had grown to over two hundred pounds, and the success of his second fight with the wolverine had brought him much confidence.

The return of the caribou on their annual trek across the plateau brought him a real bonanza. Twice he separated calves from the herds, then, after killing them, stayed on the kill until he had finished them. By habit he still dug for roots and stripped berries from patches where they were abundant. Natural instincts were balancing his diet.

Frosts began to chill some nights.

The wolves appeared on the plateau a week after the first small herds of caribou had moved through. They had come together with the main deer herd, and they hunted brazenly in the grizzly's territory. His anger at their intrusion became constant. When he heard their yipping on the chase, he ran at a full lumbering gait to intervene. Twice he drove them from their downed carcasses. Unable to consume all the meats, he began to bury them under mounds of soil and branches. Afterward he urinated on top of the mounds.

In one of the grizzly's attempts to usurp a wolf kill, the wild pack did not turn tail but turned on him. They had been tearing at the belly of a large old bull with a heavy-antlered head. When the bear's silent approach surprised them, the largest male in the hunting unit ran directly at the bear's head before feinting aside. Three times the wolf lunged in, sidestepping the blows of the grizzly's forepaws. On the fourth attack each of the two wolves which had remained behind him gripped the grizzly's hind legs close to the hamstrings. Only a quick turn in the direction of the enormous rack of the dead bull's antlers saved the bear. His powerful front shoulder lifted the wolf into the air when he struck it, and the wolf landed on one of the long, sharp prongs of the antlers, which impaled it. The second animal at his back legs had let go as the big lead wolf had lunged in and sunk his teeth into the bear's shoulder. The grizzly raised up on his hind legs, bellowing with rage. That motion lifted the lead wolf off its feet, and the grizzly smashed his forepaw hard into its chest. With the breath knocked from its lungs, the lead wolf dropped to the bloodied earth. The bear bit savagely behind the wolf's head, where his teeth crushed the spinal column as his forepaws held down the wildly kicking grey body. Meanwhile, the wolf impaled on the antlers managed to pull itself free. Coughing up red froth, it ran after the other two members of the retreating pack.

Blood was once again running down the scarred fur of the grizzly's previously torn shoulder. He stood roaring angrily after the pack and bellowing at the blue sky.

CHAPTER 9

This One Came in Person

One sunny day last September, while I was hunting for a good two-point buck at the northernmost tip of British Columbia's Vancouver Island, I sighted a total of four black bears. That is not unusual in such a remote area of the continent, where they are plentiful and safe even near the loggers' workplaces. What is unusual, though, is that one of those black bears intentionally came after me.

At one time I would have been skeptical if I heard this story from another person. It was, perhaps, only my seventh such experience during a lifetime of hunting. The animal was a large, fully grown black bear. Since there was logging within two miles, and the road the bear crossed to get to me was well traveled, it would be unreasonable to suppose that it had not seen a man, or that it was unfamiliar with human habits.

I had left my truck a quarter of a mile back down the road to stalk a flock of band-tailed pigeons during my hunt for a coast blacktail. I had come to a road that cut through a small hill of glacial rubble, and choosing the higher of its two banks, I climbed up the steep gravel incline and sat upon a low stump at its crest. The band-tails had flown into the seed timber adjacent to the hummock. The back side of this ridge ran down into a stretch of tangled green timber surrounding a swampy bit of uplands. Wild pigeons frequented the area because the sun-bleached spire of dead snags rising above the live timber afforded them lookouts and roosting places.

The entire area was like a wild berry farm; salal berries could be plucked readily from bush after bush over thousands of logged acres. However, the tangle of debris from logging and the bulldozing of the road through it had formed an almost-impenetrable bulwark of natural growth at least fifty to a hundred feet wide between the road and the adjacent timber. Salmonberry and other second-growth flora typical of the aftermath of logging grew in front of me, forming a thick screen as close as ten feet from where I was sitting in the open. Normally a man or an animal trying to cross through the area would have avoided that tangle.

As I climbed the thirty-foot embankment, the stones and rubble I had spilled alerted the band-tail pigeons. Most of them flew a hundred yards farther into the center of the swampy spot. Using my binoculars, I studied some of the pigeons sitting atop a nearby snag, admiring the ruby tints of their breasts. Halfheartedly, I considered returning to the truck for my shotgun to try for a couple of birds. While so thinking, I happened to look out over the valley in the direction of the vehicle where it was parked alongside the road. Stretching beyond it were two miles of valley, thousands of acres of stumps and fallen trees dotted by patches of yellowed grass, low, green deciduous bushes, and browning bracken ferns. The vista was almost as open as a rolling prairie.

Even without binoculars, I am usually able to pick up big-game animals quite clearly at distances up to a quarter of a mile, perhaps half a mile. My search at that instant was for a buck deer, but my scrutiny almost immediately revealed the obsidian coat of a black bear. The animal was moving out from behind a hedge of sparse deciduous growth and fallen timber.

It was the fourth bear that I had seen in seven hours. There was no special reason to take note of it except for personal amusement. Many of the hours I have spent in forests have been passed watching the antics of bears. But even though the bear family does fascinate me, I do not like the species to approach me any closer than a hundred yards, even when I am carrying a gun. I have no desire now to kill a bear for any reason.

On a scale of one to ten, this black was a perfect ten. The coal-black coat on his strong foreshoulders rippled all the way down to his foot pads, which were like cowboy chaps, or the excellent feathering on a show dog's legs. His belly was rotund (obviously full of wild berries) and swung gracefully with his movements. The animal was about three to four hundred yards away, ambling unconcernedly along the slope parallel to the road. I looked ahead of it, where a gully with a stream in it crossed the road. I guessed that the bruin was probably bent on a drink. It was shortly past noon, and it was hot.

For some reason, almost as a reflex action, I whistled shrilly. I have done it a hundred times. The reactions from bears to a whistle are varied. At a distance of over two hundred yards they quite often do not respond to the first whistle, but they often do to a second shrill blast: it usually stops them. Then they often turn their heads inquisitively in the direction of the sound and stare. If they do not see a movement, they move on as if nothing has happened. At a third or fourth whistle, accompanied by some identifying movement or their recognition of a vehicle, they may do one of several things: run away, move into cover and peer through the foliage, or simply continue on their way. Very rarely, they may move in the direction of the strange human sound.

This magnificent black put his head down and moved forward. He stopped on the second whistle and then stared for at least a minute in my direction. I do not recall moving during that time. He again put his head down and continued along his chosen path along the face of the hill. I got up, moved to a nearby stump, and began to look for the pigeons once more. In my peripheral vision I perceived the movements of the bear. Something about them made me turn once more to stare at him.

He had changed his path. He was using the same maneuver used by hunters who know they have been spotted by game: moving at an angle away from my position, off the parallel, but with an increasing curve that ultimately would bring him in my direction. I looked ahead of him and noted a patch of timber, part of the forest that formed the thickets around the marsh behind me. He had, indeed, turned at a forty-five-degree angle, which would take him into the screen of that growth and out of my sight. That, too, is normal for a mature bear and other wild animals when they are caught in an open, vulnerable position in the presence of a probable predator.

A clicking sound, the noisy, warning wingbeat of a nearby band-tailed pigeon distracted my gaze. I had been fifty yards closer to the main flock than I suspected. Five of the birds burst into flight from the obscured lower portion of the cedars, and as I watched, they flew right across the valley. When they were almost a mile away, they landed on one of the weather-whitened trunks of a burned-out ridge.

When I glanced back at the slope below me, I was not surprised to see that the black bear had disappeared. I searched casually for his characteristic black coat, but there was no sign of him. I turned and looked up along the narrow road, which, after passing through the end of the swamp, stretched for almost half a mile in a straight line. I was confident that the hill beyond that area would bring me a buck in the late autumn afternoon, when the deer usually come out of the higher timber to forage.

At that very instant my peripheral vision barely caught the movement of the bear's quick rush. He had lunged from behind a clump of bushes lying only a hundred feet down the road, then spurted across the dirt road into the thick brush on the opposite side. It was a fast, silent rush for no apparent reason.

What really surprised me, however, was that in a very short period, the bear had completed half of a full circle back in my direction. He had returned on that course to a point which was at least 250 yards closer to my location! That, indeed, was very abnormal for a bear!

Instinctively, I kept quiet. A couple of minutes later, almost where the pigeons had taken flight, there was the sound of a small twig breaking. It was nothing that the ordinary human ear might notice, but it was very distinct to one attuned by years of hunting. Then there was a second, closer sound of movement.

Immediately I whispered, "Why, you old sonuvabitch! You're moving this way!"

With almost complete surprise and disbelief, I listened intently, trying to silence the sounds of my own heightened breathing. Sure enough, I heard a slight rustling sound from the depths of the logging debris, not more than twenty yards away! Keeping a very close watch, I caught the telltale sway of a tall sapling top almost exactly above the location of the sound.

I had to think fast. The distance between me and the thick growth from which the bear might rush was less than fifteen feet. If I waited until I could see the animal, it would be at point-blank range. Thirty years before I had been charged by a bear that close, and my first bullet into it had spattered the animal's blood on my shirt and pants. Once was enough.

Quickly I glanced across the road to the opposite gravel bank. The logging roadway was only fifteen feet wide, the entire bulldozed cut about thirty feet across, and the opposite hummock less than twenty feet high. If I went over there, the bear, even if he ran at a gallop, would have to cross that open roadbed, then climb the open face of the bulldozed gravel and hardpan, just as I now intended to do so.

I slid on my rear down the thirty-foot embankment, then dropped to the dusty road, which I hit with a thump that shook my molars. My knees buckled, and my rifle butt thumped into the sand, but I pulled myself up and sprinted across the road, all in one quick reaction. It took only three adrenaline-fired lunges and jumps to get to the top of that opposite bank. I turned to face the other side.

My heart was pounding audibly in my ears, and I had heard none of my own sounds of transit. Those sounds had been partially muffled, by my landing in the sandy shoulder of the dirt road. The thirty-foot drop between it and the slanted approach on the other side had also acted as a sound curtain.

Just as I flicked off the safety on my rifle, which weas already loaded in the chamber, the big bear's coal-black head showed on the other bank, right beside the stump upon which I had been sitting just seconds before! I lifted the rifle and aligned the telescope sight with its head. In the sight the animal appeared so close that the whole glass was filled with the head and one shoulder.

"You sonuvabitch," I said out loud. "You make just one move this way, and there'll be blood all over that road!"

It looked straight at me, wavered a bit and, moving its head from side to side, backed up a step. It then leaned forward, silently lifting its head to inhale the fresh scent of man which was on the stump. Then, almost like a seal in ice, it backed down into the bushes and disappeared.

For a moment I was relieved, then angry. Just what in hell was that maneuver all about? That bear was definitely after me! No question about it. Stay put! There was absolutely no approach that the bear could take to my present position without being clearly visible for fifty feet before it could find brush cover. I sat there for fully five minutes.

Then, on impulse, I lifted the rifle and sent a 75-cent 7mm Magnum bullet roaring into the stump where I had been. While the echoes were still dying in the hills, I heard the bear crashing through the bushes surrounding the small swamp. This time he was going away.

Minutes later, walking up the road, I came to the spot where the bear had crossed it. The tracks were quite clear. By actual pacing from the foot of the bank where I had been sitting, I figured it was less than a hundred feet. The big animal had come up a small creek channel totally obscured from my view on the summit, then had walked stealthily and soundlessly on sand. Where it reached the road edge as it crossed in my direction, the sand had been deeply disturbed and swept backward by a fast, extremely strong thrust.

On the sandbank that led into the bushes on the opposite side of the road, the paw marks were once again the perfectly rounded imprints of quiet movement. Obviously, it was not only in my imagination that the bear had sped furtively across the road and cut purposefully toward where I had been sitting.

I can present no absolute reason for the stalk, but such the bears' paw prints in the sand proved it to be. Fortunately, no attack had actually occurred. Nothing, however, can alter the fact that this ordinary, mature black bear, having had only slight provocation, changed the direction of its travel and came three hundred yards out of its way in a circle, most of its path completely obscured from view, *right up to the stump upon which I had been sitting—just seconds after I had vacated that seat!*

The Cannibal IX

During the grizzly's second lonely year the leavings of the big-game hunters who regularly intruded in the valley, and the plunder from the wolves' kills on the migrating woodland caribou, added bulk to his growing stature and prepared him for the winter. Once again, in mid-November, he dug into the den in which he and his littermate had slept. This time his well-rounded body had doubled in size and filled the end chamber.

In the spring, because the snowfall had been light, he pushed out early from the dimly lit cave. The open ground was still partly snow-covered. As he searched for fresh grasses, his strides, longer now, took him quickly across the tableland to the dropping edge of the Cassiar Plateau. From there he descended into the valley of the Dease River to find that at the lower level the greenery was well advanced. He also found a new and abundant delicacy: the carcasses of packhorses abandoned to forage for themselves and killed by cold and starvation on the meager grasses in the narrow deltas of the valley.

Because this low elevation had warmed quickly, he stayed through spring. His meanderings led him to a cleared area where a strange square wooden structure on level ground beside the stream harbored enticing new smells. Seeing clearly through an opening, he attempted to push inward, only to be halted by a solid icelike substance. He smashed at the stuff with a tentative paw. Startled for a moment by the strange tinkling sound it made as it shattered, he stood quite still and alert.

No further strange sounds were forthcoming.

Moments later he pushed through the opening. Inside he was greeted by man smells, faint but irritating. More subtle fragrances incited him. Bashing down a small log door, he found a remnant of smoked bacon hanging from a hook. He knocked it to the plank floor, then gulped it down. Moldy bread spilled from a nearby box, and with it a yellow, salty fat that he much enjoyed. As he crushed some hard metal canisters, one by one, they yielded strange juices. He licked the dripping contents from each and from the floor. Still wary of the place, he slept outside in the deep brush overnight, before returning in the morning to finish off all the remaining edible goods.

When the food was gone, he left the cabin and headed back for the carrion horses still left in the wild pasture.

As he fed on the last of the remaining carcasses, another animal similar to his own kind approached. Its black coat caught his eye, shimmering in the sunlight as it moved. It was a male bear as large as himself, but its smell and contour told him it was not one of his own kind. Fearless, he rushed at it. Even more quickly the black bear turned and ran. It was faster, and just as it reached the edge of the trees, instead of continuing to flee, it clambered up a tree with surprising speed.

For over an hour the grizzly stood at the bottom of the tree, venting his frustration by woofing, growling, and yawning. The black bear remained aloft. Determined, the grizzly sat on his haunches awaiting its descent.

The sound of human voices distracted him. He also heard the clumsy branch-breaking tread of two horses. He remained irresolute at the foot of the trees as the high-pitched sounds of the humans reached higher notes.

"Jesus, Jack, the horses are all dead! They didn't make it!"

In silence the shocked men surveyed the skeletal remains in the grassy clearing. Then, abruptly, one of them uttered a sharp exclamation.

"For Christ's sake! There's the bastard that killed them! Up that tree! Gimme my rifle!"

The grizzly stood quietly, stunned by the sudden intrusion. He was partly hidden in the bushes. His front shoulder and head were in full view but obviously unnoticed.

The crash of the rifle came unexpectedly, sharp and earsplitting. The form of the black bear above him emitted a loud whoosh of air as it tumbled down directly at him. To avoid it, he lunged out into the open.

"There's a big grizzly too! Quick! Get him, Jack!"

The grizzly turned and plunged into the deep brush faster than he had ever moved. With huge bounds he ran as if the claws of a ten-foot predator were flailing him, heedless of the sounds accompanying his flight.

"Did you see that grizzly's front shoulder! It's all white!"

Indeed, there was white hair covering the scars from the wounds that the wolverine and the she-bear had left on his right shoulder. The patch would mark him for the rest of his life. His footsteps carried him quickly up the slope to the valley of the plateau. It would be a long time before he again left the high country.

During the following five summers he successfully lived off that familiar mountain-ringed valley. After two spring thaws had passed, other male grizzlies entered the region, but he drove them ferociously from his territory. During his fifth year he found and mated with a sow, but later he aggressively drove her too from the end of the valley. The next year, when she came back with two cubs, he killed her and the two small animals, burying them under a common heap of brush and glacial soil.

It was upon his approach to that mound, which was beginning to send tempting odors of decomposition to him, that he saw the man form. For several minutes the bear watched while the small glistening object in the human's forepaws clicked, its metal and glass parts reflecting the rays of the sun. Aware that death almost inevitably followed the appearance of men in the valley because some hidden power killed for them from a distance, he stayed hidden in the deeper hedges of the scrub alder.

Eventually the tall man mounted a horse and moved away from the grizzly's cache. Then the bear moved possessively into the small meadow and gorged upon the ripened meats. Three days later, without knowing why, he left for the patches of berries that were ripening along the edges of the rockslides.

For over a week he fed upon the small crop of sweet fruit, mixing the mast with the white tubers of lilies. Twice he dug for marmots, but he was rewarded only once, when he cornered a fat denizen and dragged its carcass from the den.

Men accompanied by strings of packhorses now appeared so often on the plateau that they were almost commonplace. At times, when they stayed still, flashes of sunlight glinted from their heads. He had the feeling that he too was being observed, but never, if he saw, smelled, or heard them first, did he allow them to get within a quarter of a mile of him. Only at night, while they made strange noises near their bonfires, would he slink close to their horses. Once, when his strong scent caused a flurry among the hobbled pack string, a stab of brilliant light caught him unexpectedly. Blinded by the glare, he growled a warning, touching off a responding chorus from the men at the bonfire.

"It's White Shoulder! Right among the horses! Gimme a gun! Hurry! Jesus, is he ever big!"

When the stab of light momentarily turned away from him, he plunged into the nearby hedge of alder scrub. Once out of sight, he silently slunk off up the valley. For the rest of the season he avoided any area of the plateau in which men and horses stayed overnight. Sometimes when he was in the open, he saw spurts of earth rising up near him while strange squealing or buzzing sounds ricocheted off nearby rocks. Always these strange phenomena occurred just before sharp, thunderous reports came from the men. He now recognized that those sounds killed.

In his eleventh season on the plateau some buzzing, flying things began to invade the valley. He could not know that the greenish rock outcropping uncovered near his sow's ancient diggings for marmots was asbestos. Soon the visits of the noisy flying machines came more regularly. Occasionally, after they had left a site, he would sit on the landing spot and find there the scent of men.

Finally, one late fall, he casually approached one of his half-buried caribou kills. Many men had been in the valley, and he was growing less wary of them. Yet here was one almost at his kill!

His charge downed the puny being instantly. He bit and shook, bit and shook, while the weak animal pushed away but did not put up much of a fight. Then, suddenly, he realized that it carried the smell of man, the most dreaded animal in the plateau.

An unreasoning fear assailed him. He left the slightly moving thing and ran for the bushes, quickly making his way from the scene. The valley now had too many of the noisy flying objects and too much of the man scent. The wild game were steadily being depleted. For three years now the caribou had come only in sparse numbers, and the once-plentiful mountain sheep and white goats had become more rare. The bear needed more abundant sources of flesh to sustain and fatten him for the long winters to come. In the valley the competiton had brought diminishing returns. It was time to find a new territory.

His powerful long legs impelled him toward the distant ranges.

Epilogue

Bear Hunting: The Rites and Rights

The hunting of wildlife was an integral part of indigenous North American cultures long before European immigration. Archaeological finds in North America show that about nine to ten thousand years ago early nomadic societies hunted the wolly mammoth. These hunters used quite large hunting points, including spearheads several inches long and comparable arrowheads. With the coming of the Ice Age, and as a result of climatic changes, many of the larger animals became extinct. Consequently, later sites (from about five thousand years ago) contain very few bones of large animals. Presumably because the hunters subsisted on smaller game, such as birds and rodents, their tools diminished in size.

The more recent North American Indians of the northern and temperate zones subsisted mainly by hunting wild animals and gathering plants, which served as food, clothing, and housing. The mid-to-southern populations hunted wild animals to supplement the crops they cultivated; the Aztecs and other Mesoamerican groups cultivated both field crops and fish. In none of these civilizations did domestication of animals figure strongly; thus, a "hunter" class became essential to supply the fowl, fish, and flesh needs of the community.

Generally the harvests suited the small Indian populations. The bison, however, was so abundant that some Plains tribes made it their practice to hunt the animals by driving herds of them over cliffs, killing hundreds and even thousands before taking what meat they desired from the carnage at the base of the precipice. Wolves, coyotes, pumas, and other predators, including grizzly and black bears, also fed on these bonanzas.

Hunting was a prestigious occupation, since the hunter provided the meat essential to survival. Indians killed bears for food and clothing and because the animals figured strongly in their religious practices. In many Indian cultures bears were considered relatives of mankind. They were treated with respect, and hunters actually conversed with them in rituals before killing them. The Indian hunter would ask the bear to die peacefully and offer itself as a respected sacrifice for human use (compare the prayers occasionally offered by trophy hunters for similar forfeitures).

European populations expanded progressively after about 1000 B.C., and their social organization allowed an affluent few to accumulate great wealth, which they used to employ explorers and adventurers in an effort to locate new areas and means for multiplying that wealth. As a result, the Europeans, particularly the British, established colonies in the Americas. In North America they found, among other wealth, game animals in abundance: waterfowl, turkey, grouse, deer, bison—and bear. Because these immigrants had virtually no domesticated stock to draw from, they had to draw upon the wildlife. Early European hunters, like the Indians, sought bears (at first the native black bears of the eastern seaboard) as sources of meat, fat, tallow, and hides. Every exploratory venture inland needed professional hunters. In short, the hunter was an essential member of early Colonial society.

The former abundance of bears, and game of all kinds, can be fairly well ascertained by studying the field notes of the Lewis and Clark expedition up the Missouri River between 1804 and 1806. Because there were no other sources of food, Lewis and his men had continually to supply the expedition with meat from the wild. Throughout the daily journals dozens of animals are reported killed (although generally only enough were killed each day for that day's use). If the reader stops to consider that these men were traveling in a narrow line across a vast country, the number of game animals they did not see must have been many thousands the number they did see. All game was plentiful when the Europeans entered the Americas.

With the introduction of European culture came its elite, the sporting set, including those who used the hunt as a status symbol. It was their successors, people such as Theodore Roosevelt, who, by pressuring the government, began to shape the rules and practices of North American hunting. No bill of rights was accorded the wildlife itself. The main governor was the abundance of wildlife or its scarcity. (Of course, there are exceptions: accused of being a cattle killer, the grizzly has been hunted ruthlessly since the introduction of domestic cattle. It is rapidly being exterminated from almost all but its northernmost habitats.) North American hunting operates in essentially the same fashion today. Consequently, the regulations for hunting bears vary with the species. Only one of the North American bears, the black bear, remains generally open to the hunter, and in the historical record the black bear was always the most widespread and abundant species. As of this writing the grizzly bear is protected throughout the mainland United States, with the exception of short seasons in Montana. In Alaska the brown phase is still open to limited hunting. In Canada there are open seasons on grizzlies in Alberta, British Columbia, the Northwest Territories, and the Yukon, but these are very restricted and subject to annual revision.

Other than the "village" permits still available to Indians and Eskimos in the North American Arctic, the polar bear is firmly protected from hunting. The village permits allow native people to take non-Indians into the field to hunt, but the restrictions virtually exclude the average hunter and most trophy hunters from taking polar bears. Some form of annual "regulatory" kill of the white bear is under consideration, because field studies indicate that some of these animals could be cropped without endangering the stability of the breeding stock. Both polar bears and grizzlies are listed as endangered species, however; and hunting regulations for both are likely to remain stringent.

Experience has taught us that only where a species is so abundant that it is endangering its own habitat, or where the population obviously exceeds the necessary brood stock, should any form of hunting be allowed. Thus today's hunter it needed, and tomorrow's will be, only as a means of control.

Index

Aberdeen, Wash.: 79
Adams, James Capen ("Grizzly"): 258, 382
Adams State College, Alamosa, Colo.: 390
Admiralty Islands: 65, 68–70, 84, 103, 114, 155
Aggasis, John: 407
Alamosa Community Hospital: 390, 394
Alaska: brown-bear identification in, 11, 91, 107; territory, 12, 55, 64–67, 72, 85, 428; Fish and Wildlife Service, 13, 65, 169; Highway, 210–11; see also place-names
Alberta, Canada: 142, 428; Forest Service, 181
Aldrich foot snare: 110
Allen, Chris: 310–11
Allen, Glenn F.: 178
Alwin Mining Company: 267
Ammerman, Jane: 225–26, 228, 248, 306
Anchorage, Alaska: 169
Anderson Lake, B.C.: 292
Anthony Island, B.C.: 206
Appalachian Shield: 26, 41, 87
Arctic territory: 55, 142, 146, 428; tundra, 121; fox, 122
Ashcroft Manor, B.C.: 266
Ashley, Kenneth: 229, 245
Asiatic bear: 5
Aspeslet, Malcolm: 390
Athabaska River, Alberta: 190–91
Austrom, Karen: 290–300; brother, Carl, 298–99
Aztec Indians: 427

Baffin Land: 240
Bailey, Eric: 278, 279
Banff (Alberta) National Park: 227, 292, 304, 307, 310, 311, 313
"Banger" (exploding device): 126, 139, 159
Barrenlands, Northwest Territories: 355
Beaconhill Park, B.C.: 10
Bear patrol: 145
Bear species: black, identification of, 3, 5, 9; glacier (blue), 9; Kermodei, 10
Beier, Vern: 69, 70, 72, 73, 88–93, 95, 103, 106–17
Bella Coola, B.C.: 412
Belly River Station, Alberta: 246–48

Beluga whale: 137
Benton, Fran: 296
Berg Lake, B.C.: 292–93
Billings, Miss.: 79
Bird Cove, Manitoba: 135, 156, 159
Bissel, Steve: 395
Black, Mr. and Mrs. Hugh: 231, 233
Black Foot Indians: 232, 234–36, 250; Montana reservation of, 230, 231
Bliesath, Shiela: 196–202
Blue bear: 9
Blue Lake, B.C.: 173
Boulder Creek, Alberta: 181
Bradenberg, Al: 390
Brainard, Scott: 110
Brewster, Scott: 231
British Columbia: province of, 5, 6, 10, 12, 51, 67, 317, 428; Provincial Police, 6, 347, 371; Parks branch, 210; University of, 359; Fish and Game Department, 371, 383; see also place-names
Brown bear, identification of: 12
Bull, Tony: 245

Cache Creek, B.C.: 267
Cairn Pass, Alberta: 187
Calgary, Alberta: 279, 280, 299, 304, 305; Sun newspaper, 312
California, state of: 12
Cameron Lake, Alberta: 274, 276, 281, 282, 286; Creek, 280, 281
Campbell River, B.C.: 347, 372
Camp Loch Alsh: 199
Canadian Esquimo dog: 136
Canadian Wildlife Service: 451
Cannibalism: 37, 140
Canuck Hockey Club: 171
Cape Churchill, Manitoba: 152, 153
Capsaicin drug: 261
Capilano River, B.C.: 341
Capillo, Louis: 256–59
Cardinal, Harvey: 209, 210
Cardiology, of bears: 49, 50
Cardston, Alberta: 280
Cariboo, B.C.: 171, 276
Cascade Mountains, B.C.: 7, 24
Cassiar district, 10; mountains, 276, 361
Channel Flying Services,

Alaska: 71, 72, 96
Chesman, John: 171
Chilcotin, B.C.: 292, 412
Churchill, Manitoba: 121, 127–28, 133, 141, 143, 145, 151, 155, 218, 220, 259
Cisco, fish: 134
Clarkson, Ontario: 276
Clearwater, B.C.: 403, 407, 408, 410
Clement family: Marty, René, 196–202; Sean, 196–202; Cathy, 198
Cohoe, Ernest: 304–313
Collaring of bears: 53, 95; and locator antenna, 154, 188
Collins, Barry: 281, 282
Colorado, state of: 16, 170; Rockies, 382
Conry, Paul: 114, 115
Cornwall Rach, B.C.: 266
"Crackers" (firecracker repellants): 154, 158, 259, 260
Craighead, Frank C., Jr.: 12, 80; John, 12
Cramond family: daughter, Pam, 196, 298, 374; son, Grant, 267, 374; wife, Thelma, 298, 371, 373, 374
Crestone, Col.: 389, 394

Davidson, Bill: 187
Dease Lake, B.C.: 10
Dease River, B.C.: 381
Denning, of bears: 8; of polar bears, 152
Dewar, Jim: 371, 383
Divide Creek, Mont.: 230–31, 237–38
Dodds, G. A. M.: 210, 212, 214
Doerksen, George: 206–15
Dream River, Alaska: 107
Drilling, rifle shotgun: 374
Duckitt, Susanne: 196
Dumps, garbage: 29, 30, 151–53, 221, 233
Dusel-Bacon, Cynthia: 293

Eberly, Bill: 228
Eberly, Kim: 225–26, 228, 248, 306
Edith Lake, Alberta: 186, 190
Elizabeth Lake, Mont.: 244, 246
Ely, Minn.: 16–17, 259
Erickson, Diane: 143–46
Eskimo Dog, Canadian: 136
Eskimo people: 428
European brown bear: 11

Fauley, Clyde: 278
Field and Stream magazine: 356, 372
Firecracker exploding device: 126, 139, 154, 158, 159
Fishem Lake, B.C.: 292
Fisher, Shirley: 197
Flynn, Rod: 114, 115
Fort Nelson, B.C.: 207, 210
Fortin, Gaby: 312, 313
Fort St. John, B.C.: 207
Fowler River, Alaska: 69
Fox, Arctic: 122, 124, 160
Frazil (sea ice): 127

Gallaway, "Ace": 390
Garrow, Bob: 231
Gilham, Dan: 230
Glacier, Montana: National Park, 115, 225–27, 249, 278, 304; county, 229; West, 226, 246, 278
Glacier bear (blue): 9
Glenn's Lake (Mont.): 246–48
Golding, Bob: 181
Gordon, Byron Lawrence: 225, 244, 253
Gradon, John: 312
Grand Prairie, Alberta: 181
Grattan, Dick: 220
Green River, Alaska: 69
Greens Creek, Alaska: 114, 115, 116
Greer, Ken: 232
Gribbel Island, B.C.: 10
Grizzly-bear identification: 10–12

Halt repellant: 140, 258
Hanna, Andrew: 270
Harms, Dale: 230, 245
Harrop, Mike: 277, 278
Harrop, Tony, and family: 312–13
Hawk River, Alaska: 69, 110; inlet, 114
Heine, Jim: 257
Helen's Lake, Mont.: 246
Hen Ingram Lake: 171, 173
Herbert, Elaine: 266
Herrero, Dr. Steve: 230
Hibbert, Don: 281
Hibernation of bears: 6
Himalayan bear: 5
Holroyd, Jack: 281
Homa Seiji: 329, 330–32, 341–43
Horseshoe Bay, B.C.: 336
Houlistan, Carrole: 49, 50, 52, 56, 57
Howe Sound, B.C.: 329, 336; Copper Mine, 329, 336
Hudson Bay: 123, 128, 138, 152, 159, 160, 220
Humpback salmon: 111

Hunt, Carrie: 299
"Hunting and Fishing Club of the Air": 373

Igloolich dogs: 136

Jacobsen, P.: 306, 307, 309, 310
Jasper, B.C.: 186; National Park, 186, 189, 299
Joe Bedard Lake, B.C.: 266
John, Ken: 133, 138, 159
Johnson, Lester: 221
Johnson, Loyal: 110
Johnston, Bruce: 107, 109
Jonkel, Dr. Charles: 140, 259, 260, 299
Juneau, Alaska: 64–66, 70, 72, 88

Kamloops, B.C.: 402, 404, 406, 410, 411, 413; Royal Hospital, 402, 404; *Daily Sentinel*, 410
Kearney, Steve: 154–56, 158
Keenan, L. E.: 396
Kelver, Brian: 304, 309–11
Kennedy, Frank: 405, 408
Keremeos Creek, B.C.: 176
Kermodei bear: 2, 5, 10
Ketamine (drug): 157
Keta salmon: 110
Killer Bears (Cramond): 15, 16, 138, 169, 170, 181, 207, 226, 252, 292
Kinnar, Gary W.: 280, 282
Kintz, Dave: 382, 392
Klimach, Walt: 174
Kodiak bear: 11, 12
Kokanee fish: 268, 270
Kowal, Lillian: 142, 143
Kruger, Jim: 246
Kuhn, Bob: 356–59

Ladoon, Brian: 133–35, 162, 218
Laird River, B.C.: 210; Park, 206, 210; Hot Springs, 211, 212, 214
Lake Creek, Alaska: 107
Lake McDonald, Mont.: 232
Lankinen, Wayne and Helen: 122–25, 159–62, 220
Lattin, Jim: 386
Lee Brothers, hounds of: 383
Lemmings: 122
Lethbridge (Alberta) *Herald*: 276–83
Leuthold, Andres: 304, 308
Lewis, Joe: 396
Lewis and Clark expedition: 428
Lillington, Jack ("Pintail"): 3
Lillooet, B.C.: 292
Little Prairie Picnic Ground,

Waterton Lakes National Park, Alberta: 274, 281, 283, 285
London, Ontario: 291
Lulu, Wilfred: 266–70

McCullough, James: 321, 329–32
MacDonald, Bob: 407
MacDonald, Jack: 171–72
Mace (repellant): 34
McKelvie, Robert: 270, 390, 402–15; wife, Lennis, 412–15
McKenzie family: 336, 340
Mackill, Jack: 357
Madison Junction, Yellowstone Park: 178
Mahoney, Mary Patricia: 196, 225, 229, 237, 245
Malaysian Peace Corps: 114
Manitoba, Canada: Department of National Resources, 133, 143, 154; University of, 220
Manning Park, B.C.: 214
Many Glacier Park, Mont.: 229, 246, 247
Maple Ridge, B.C.: 211, 214
Markusich, Mike: 190, 390
Marion, Jeff: 49
Martin, Bruce: 143
Martinka, Clifford: 226
Meeko, Paulosie: 220
Menefee, Curtis: 230, 245
Mexico: 12
Milford, Jack: 176
Miller, Lee: 169
Miller, Stan: 181, 182
Minnesota, state of: 9, 51, 58, 151
Montana, state of: 169; Fish and Game Department, 249; University of, 260
Mount Robson Park, B.C.: 299
Murdock, Elizabeth: 291
Murphy, Vern and Maurice: 402
Muser, Allison: 274–86; sister, Phillipa, 276, 284; father, Paul, 276, 282
Muskett, Robert: 304–13

National Geographic Society: 141, 157, 214
Navajo Creek, Colo.: 395
Nelson, Rick: 386
Newby, Fletcher: 230, 245
New Mexico, state of: 385
Niederee, Mike: 386–98; father, Dr. W. C., 386
North Vancouver, B.C.: 336
Nuss, Dale: 70, 78

O'Brian, Dan: 246
O'Connor, Jack: 372
Okanagan Range, B.C.: 176

Orchard, Dick: 110
Oregon, state of: 67
Outdoor Life magazine: 189, 252, 356, 371, 372, 402, 404, 413
Owl, snowy: 122

Pacific Coastal Range: 12, 24, 51
Pacific Great Eastern Railway: 336
Pack Creek, Alaska: 65, 66, 68, 70, 72–74, 80, 88, 111, 155
Palmisciano, Dan: 249
Paonia, Colo.: 257
Parks, Canada: 186, 188, 281, 283, 305, 309
Pemberton, B.C.: 298
Penfold, Percy, and mother and sister: 321–23, 328
Pentilla, Terry: 226, 227, 247, 252, 253
Philbin, Gail: 145
Pile Driver, Alaska: river, 110, 115; cove, 110
Pilon, Jean: 277, 279, 282, 284
Platoro, Colo.: 394, 395, 398
Polar bears: 122, 123, 126, 127, 133, 134; patrol against, 138
Powell, Rob: 229, 244, 250; sons, Bill and John, 251, 252
Premolar tooth removed: 50, 93
Preston, Ken: 309, 311, 312
Price, Stan: 64–105; wife, Esther, 77, 79, 88, 104, 107; first wife, Edna, 81
Prince George, B.C.: 171
Princess Charlotte (steamship): 64
Princess Royal Island, B.C.: 10
Province (Vancouver newspaper): 372
Ptarmigan Tunnel, Mont.: 246, 248
Pueblo, Colo.: 383

Queen Charlotte Islands, B.C.: 206
Quinsam River, B.C.: 347

Rakowski, Pat: 143, 144
Randal, S.A. ("Jack"): 394
Ratson, Melanie: 141
Red Rock Lake, Mont.: 228
Regina, Sask.: 279–82
Reimer, Mike: 219
Remington rifle: 348
Repellants: use of, 34, 38, 140, 213, 258, 260; mace, 34
Retfalvi, Laslo: 227
Riewe, Dick: 220
Rising Sun Campground, Mont.: 230

Ritcey, Ralph: 410
Robertson, Doug: 270, 402, 404, 413
Rocky Mountains: 24, 236, 276, 284, 306, 356, 361
Rogers, Dr. Lynn: 9, 15–60, 70, 91, 140, 259, 260; wife, Donna, 16
Rompun (drug): 157
Ross rifle: 375
Rouse, Bob: 394
Rowed, Harry and Genevieve: 186–93, 245
Royal Canadian Mounted Police: 207, 210, 214, 220
Royal Island Hospital, Kamloops, B.C.: 404
Ruger rifle: 141, 142
Russell, Andy and Dick: 186
Ryder, Jerry: 230
St. John, B.C.: 209
St. Mary, Mont.: 228, 230, 236, 306, 307; river, 228, 237, 238; lake, 232
Salois, Winnie: 245
Sandspit, Queen Charlotte Island, B.C.: 206
Sandy, Ralph: 266
San Juan Mountains, Colo.: 385
Saskatoon, Sask.: 281
Satellites, in tracking bears: 55
Schoen, John: 65–69, 71, 73, 103
Seattle, Wash.: 65
Seredick, Ray: 403, 407, 408, 410
Sernalyn (drug): 90, 157
Shaber, Bill and Marion, 178–81
Shanahan, Robert: 231
Shaw, Jack: 173–75
Shellenberger, Joseph: 244, 245
Sholtes, Fred: 245
Siamese Mauser rifle: 114
Siberian brown bear: 11
Silvertip grizzly, identification of: 11
Smith, Mike: 231
Soderstrom, Neil: 15
Spirit bears: 10
Sports Afield magazine: 354
Springfield rifle: 108
Squamish, B.C.: 292, 298, 336
Squires, Richard: 232
Stiles, Henry: 398
Stoney Indian Lake, Mont.: 248
Striegler, Thomas L.: 396, 397
Stump Lake, B.C.: 402
Sturdy, Fred: 390
Switzer, Robert: 206, 210, 213, 214

Taseko Lake, B.C.: 292

Tattoo, of bears: 53, 91
Taylor, Robert: 123–26, 159–62
Taylor Creek, Alberta: 313
Tia Maria Ranch, Colo.: 386
Toblar, Remy: 304, 308
Tranquilizing of bears: 20
Transmitters, use of: 55
Trapping bears: 19, 188; trap types, 19, 69, 139, 154, 290
Tum Tum Lake, B.C.: 405, 406

Unuk River, Alaska: 107
Ursus genus of bears: *americanus*, 9; *americanus emmonii*, 9; *americanus Kermodei*, 10; *arctos horribilis*, 11; *arctos middendorffi*, 11

Valentine Creek, Mont.: 247
Vancouver, B.C.: 78, 121, 171, 291, 298; Island, 215, 418; General Hospital, 414
Victoria, B.C.: 10

Waite, Don: 211, 214
Warner, Susan: 69–96, 103–107
Washington, state of: 67, 79
Watchuk, Ted: 90, 297
Waterton, Alberta: National Park, 232, 272, 274, 277, 283, 286; drainage, 247; Village, 274; Lakes, 275
Wawa, Ontario: 196; hospital of, 199
Weatherby rifle: 111
West Vancouver, B.C.: 193, 319, 333, 374
Wheeler Creek, Alaska: 110
Whiskey Creek, Alberta: 304, 309
White, Steward Edward: 96
Wilkerson, Ernie: 395
Wilton, Wis.: 107
Winchester rifle: 111, 351, 407
Winnepeg, Manitoba: 133, 138, 143
Wiseman, Ed: 170, 382–98; and family, 389–91
Wood, Gordon: 267, 268, 269
Woody, Norman G.: 186, 191

Yellowstone Park: 5, 24, 70, 80, 178, 179, 221
York Factory, Manitoba: 145
Young, Mary-Ann: 196
Yukon Territory: 268

Zinc Creek, Alaska: 115, 116